Essentials of Marketing Research

Joseph F. Hair, Jr.
Kennesaw State University

Mary F. Wolfinbarger
California State University–Long Beach

David J. Ortinau
University of South Florida

Robert P. Bush
Louisiana State University at Alexandria

McGraw-Hill
Higher Education

Boston   Burr Ridge, IL   Dubuque, IA   New York   San Francisco   St. Louis
Bangkok   Bogotá   Caracas   Kuala Lumpur   Lisbon   London   Madrid   Mexico City
Milan   Montreal   New Delhi   Santiago   Seoul   Singapore   Sydney   Taipei   Toronto

Mc
Graw
Hill
**McGraw-Hill
Higher Education**

ESSENTIALS OF MARKETING RESEARCH

Published by McGraw-Hill/Irwin, a business unit of The McGraw-Hill Companies, Inc., 1221 Avenue of the Americas, New York, NY, 10020. Copyright © 2008 by The McGraw-Hill Companies, Inc. All rights reserved. No part of this publication may be reproduced or distributed in any form or by any means, or stored in a database or retrieval system, without the prior written consent of The McGraw-Hill Companies, Inc., including, but not limited to, in any network or other electronic storage or transmission, or broadcast for distance learning.

Some ancillaries, including electronic and print components, may not be available to customers outside the United States.

This book is printed on acid-free paper.

1 2 3 4 5 6 7 8 9 0 QPD/QPD 0 9 8 7

ISBN   978-0-07-338102-2
MHID   0-07-338102-0

Editorial director: *John E. Biernat*
Publisher: *Paul Ducham*
Executive editor: *Doug Hughes*
Developmental editor I: *Anna M. Chan*
Associate marketing manager: *Dean Karampelas*
Project manager: *Dana M. Pauley*
Senior production supervisor: *Carol A. Bielski*
Senior designer: *Kami Carter*
Lead media project manager: *Brian Nacik*
Cover design: *Pam Verros/pvdesign*
Interior design: *Mary Kazak*
Typeface: *10/12 Times New Roman*
Compositor: *Aptara, Inc.*
Printer: *Quebecor World Dubuque Inc.*

Library of Congress Cataloging-in-Publication Data

Essentials of marketing research / Joseph F. Hair, Jr. . . . [et al.]. —1st ed.
    p. cm.
   Includes index.
   ISBN-13: 978-0-07-338102-2 (alk. paper)
   ISBN-10: 0-07-338102-0 (alk. paper)
   1. Marketing research. I. Hair, Joseph F.
HF5415.2.E894 2008
   658.8'3—dc22

                                   2007009178

To my wife Dale, and our son Joe III and his wife Kerrie.

—Joseph F. Hair, Kennesaw, GA

To my father and mother, William and Carol Finley

—Mary Wolfinbarger, Long Beach, CA

This book is dedicated to my wife, Donny, and to my two boys, Robert Jr. and Michael.

—Robert P. Bush, Sr., Alexandria, LA

This book is dedicated to all my nieces and nephews, who will be society's future leaders, and to all my past, present, and future students for enriching my life experiences as an educator and mentor on a daily basis.

—David J. Ortinau, Tampa, FL

Joe Hair is Professor of Marketing at Kennesaw State University.

He formerly held the Copeland Endowed Chair of Entrepreneurship at Louisiana State University. He has published over 40 books, including market leaders *Multivariate Data Analysis,* 6th edition, Prentice Hall, 2006, which has been cited more than 6,500 times; *Marketing Research,* 3rd edition, McGraw-Hill/Irwin, 2006; *Principles of Marketing,* 9th edition, Thomson Learning, 2008, used at over 500 universities globally; and *Essentials of Business Research Methods,* 2nd edition, Wiley, 2008. In addition to publishing numerous refereed manuscripts in academic journals such as *Journal of Marketing Research, Journal of Academy of Marketing Science, Journal of Business/Chicago, Journal of Advertising Research,* and *Journal of Retailing,* he has presented executive education and management training programs for numerous companies, has been retained as consultant and expert witness for a wide variety of firms, and is frequently an invited speaker on marketing challenges and strategies. He is a Distinguished Fellow of the Academy of Marketing Science, the Society for Marketing Advances, and Southwestern Marketing Association, and has served as President of the Academy of Marketing Sciences, the Society for Marketing Advances, the Southern Marketing Association, the Association for Healthcare Research, the Southwestern Marketing Association, and the American Institute for Decision Sciences, Southeast Section. He was recognized by the Academy of Marketing Science with its Outstanding Marketing Teaching Excellence Award, and the Louisiana State University Entrepreneurship Institute under his leadership was recognized nationally by *Entrepreneurship Magazine* as one of the top 12 programs in the United States.

Mary Wolfinbarger earned a B.S. in English from Vanderbilt University and a Masters in Business and Public Administration and a Ph.D. in Marketing at the University of California, Irvine.

Her specialties include Internet marketing, online consumer behavior, and internal marketing. She has been teaching at California State University, Long Beach, since 1990. Dr. Wolfinbarger possesses expertise in both qualitative and quantitative research methodologies. She received grants from the Center for Research on Information Technology in Organizations (CRITO) which enabled her to co-author several articles about consumer behavior on the Internet. Dr. Wolfinbarger's interest in e-commerce and technology extends to the classroom; she developed and taught the first Internet Marketing course at CSULB in 1999. She also has written articles on the impact of technology and e-commerce on the classroom and on the business school curriculum. Professor Wolfinbarger has collaborated on research about internal marketing, receiving two Marketing Science Institute grants and conducting studies at several Fortune 500 companies. She has published articles in *Journal of Marketing, Journal of Retailing, California Management Review, Journal of the Academy of Marketing, Journal of Business Research,* and *Earthquake Spectra.*

Robert P. Bush is Professor of Marketing and holds the Alumni and Friends Endowed Chair of Business at Louisiana State University at Alexandria.

Dr. Bush has published numerous articles in such journals as *Journal of Retailing, Journal of Advertising, Journal of Marketing Education, Journal of Consumer Marketing, Journal of Customer Relationship Marketing,* and others.

David J. Ortinau earned his Ph.D. in Marketing from the Louisiana State University.

He began his teaching career at Illinois State University and after completing his Ph.D. degree moved to the University of South Florida, Tampa, where he continues to be recognized for both outstanding research and excellence in teaching at the undergraduate, graduate, and Ph.D. levels. His research interests range from research methodologies and scale measurement development, attitude formation, and perceptual differences in retailing and services marketing environments to interactive electronic marketing technologies and their impact on information research problems. He consults for a variety of corporations and small businesses, with specialties in customer satisfaction, customer service quality, service value, retail loyalty, and imagery. Dr. Ortinau has presented numerous papers at national and international academic meetings and continues to be a regular contributor to and referee for such prestigious publications as the *Journal of the Academy of Marketing Science (JAMS), Journal of Retailing (JR), Journal of Business Research (JBR), Journal of Marketing Education (JME), Journal of Services Marketing (JSM), Journal of Health Care Marketing (JHCM),* and others. Professor Ortinau has served as a member of the editorial review board for the *Journal of the Academy of Marketing Science (JAMS)* from 1988 through 2006 and continues to serve on the review board as well as the occasional associate editor in Marketing for the *Journal of Business Research (JBR).* In addition, he was co-editor of *Marketing: Moving Toward the 21st Century* (SMA Press, 1996). He remains an active leader in the Marketing discipline. He has held many leadership positions in the Society for Marketing Advances (SMA), and served as co-chair of the 1998 SMA Doctoral Consortium in New Orleans and the 1999 SMA Doctoral Consortium in Atlanta. Dr. Ortinau is a past President of SMA and was recognized as the 2001 SMA Fellow and nominated for the 2007 AMS Fellow. He is currently serving as the President of the SMA Foundation and recently served as the 2004 Academy of Marketing Science Conference Program co-chair and the 2007 SMA Retailing Symposium co-chair.

Since we wrote the first edition of *Marketing Research,* the world has become global, highly competitive, and increasingly influenced by information technology, particularly the Internet. With its steadily growing market share, *Marketing Research* has become a premier source for new and essential marketing research knowledge. Many of you, our customers, have told us that you find it difficult to cover all 18 chapters. Some of you like to do applied research projects while others emphasize case studies or exercises at the end of the chapters. Students and professors alike are concerned about the price of textbooks. *Essentials of Marketing Research* was written to meet the needs of you, our customers. The text is concise and value-priced, yet it delivers the important, basic knowledge found in the big book. It also includes all of the popular features of *Marketing Research,* 3rd edition, in a highly readable and streamlined format.

To provide both teachers and students an exciting, up-to-date text and a complete supplement package, we have listened to your feedback and incorporated it into this first edition of *Essentials of Marketing Research.* We summarize below what you will find when you examine, and we hope adopt, this book.

There are several innovative features of our new book. First, it is the only text that includes a separate chapter on qualitative data analysis. Other texts discuss qualitative data collection, such as focus groups and in-depth interviews, but then say little about what to do with this kind of data. In contrast, we dedicate an entire chapter to the topic, referencing the seminal work in this area by Miles and Huberman, and enabling professors to provide a more balanced approach in their classes. In addition, we explain important tasks like coding qualitative data and identifying themes and patterns.

Second, other texts include little coverage of the task of conducting a literature review to find background information on the research problem. Our text has a chapter that includes substantial material on this topic, including guidelines on how to conduct a literature review and the sources to search. Since students these days rely so heavily on the Internet, the emphasis is on using Google, Yahoo, and other search engines to execute the background research.

Third, more so than other texts, we emphasize the role of secondary data, particularly as part of a company's CRM (Customer Relationship Management) efforts. Increasingly, companies turn to their internal data warehouses that contain already collected secondary information both from within the firm and from external sources such as syndicated studies and data enhancement vendors. Enterprise software systems such as SAP and Siebel that have achieved significant market penetration in recent years, as well as many CRM systems, enable companies to quickly access this information and use it to improve decision making. The other texts have only limited coverage of this important development.

Fourth, as part of the "applied" emphasis of our text, we present two pedagogical features. One is boxed material in some chapters titled "A Closer Look at Research" that summarizes an applied research example and poses questions for discussion. A second, at the end of every chapter, is *Marketing Research in Action,* an exercise that enables students to apply what was covered in the chapter to a real-world situation.

Fifth, our text has an excellent continuing case that runs throughout the book enabling the professor to illustrate applied concepts using a realistic example. Our continuing case, concerning the Santa Fe Grill Mexican Restaurant, is an example students can relate to not only because most have eaten in a Mexican restaurant but because the setting is about two college student entrepreneurs who start their own business—a goal of many students these days. We include specific mini-case studies using this example in every chapter. Since it is a continuing case, the professor does not have to familiarize students with a new case every chapter. Instead, students can build upon what has been covered earlier. When the case is used in later chapters on quantitative data analysis, a data set is provided that actually works as it should when students use it. For example, there are statistically significant differences between male and female customers, and lifestyle attitudes influence satisfaction with the restaurant. Thus, students can truly see how marketing research information can be used to improve decision making.

Sixth, in addition to the Santa Fe Grill case, there are five other data sets in SPSS format. The data sets can be used to assign research projects or as additional exercises throughout the book. These databases cover a wide variety of topics that all students can identify with and offer an excellent approach to enhance teaching of concepts:

Deli Depot is an expanded version of the Deli Depot case included in previous editions. An overview of this case is provided as part of the *Marketing Research in Action* at the end of Chapter 11. The sample size is 200.

Remington's Steak House is introduced as the *Marketing Research in Action* in Chapter 12. Remington's Steak House competes with Outback and Longhorn. The focus of the case is analyzing data to identify restaurant images and prepare perceptual maps to facilitate strategy development. The sample size is 200.

QualKote is a business-to-business application of marketing research based on an employee survey. It is introduced as the *Marketing Research in Action* in Chapter 13. The case examines the implementation of a quality improvement program and its impact on customer satisfaction. The sample size is 57.

Consumer Electronics is based on the rapid growth of the DVD market and focuses on the concept of innovators and early adopters. The case overview and variables as well as some data analysis examples are provided in the *Marketing Research in Action* for Chapter 14. The sample size is 200.

Backyard Burgers is based on a nationwide survey of customers. The database is rich with potential data analysis comparisons and covers topics with which students can easily identify. The sample size is 300.

Seventh, the text's coverage of quantitative data analysis is more extensive and much easier to understand than other books. Specific step-by-step instructions are included on how to use SPSS to execute data analysis for all statistical techniques. This enables instructors to spend much less time teaching students how to use the software the first time. It also saves time later by providing a handy reference for students when they forget how to use the software, which they often do. For instructors who want to cover more advanced statistical techniques, our book is the only one that includes this topic.

Eighth, online marketing research techniques are rapidly changing the face of marketing, and the authors have experience with and a strong interest in these techniques. For the most part the material in other texts often is an "add on" that does not fully integrate online research considerations and their impact. Our text was written in the last year when many of these trends are now evident and information is available to document them.

Pedagogy

Many marketing research texts are readable. But a more important question is "Can students comprehend what they are reading?" This book offers a wealth of pedagogical features, all aimed at answering the question positively. Below is a list of the major elements:

Learning Objectives. Each chapter begins with clear learning objectives that students can use to assess their expectations for the chapter in view of the nature and importance of the chapter material.

Real-World Chapter Openers. Each chapter opens with an interesting, relevant example of a real-world business situation that illustrates the focus and significance of the chapter materials.

Key Terms and Concepts. These are bold-faced in the text and defined in the page margins. They also are listed at the end of the chapters along with page numbers to make reviewing easier, and they are included in the Glossary at the end of the book.

A Closer Look at Research. These illustrative boxes, found in some chapters, are intended to expose students to real-world marketing research issues.

Ethics. Ethical issues are treated in the first chapter and throughout the book to provide students with a basic understanding of this type of challenge in marketing research.

Chapter Summaries. Detailed chapter summaries are organized by the learning objectives presented at the beginning of the chapter. This approach to organizing summaries helps students to remember the key facts, concepts, and issues. The summaries also serve as an excellent study guide to prepare for in-class exercises or exams.

Questions for Review and Discussion. The Review and Discussion Questions are carefully designed to enhance the self-learning process and to encourage application of the concepts learned in the chapter to real business decision-making situations. There are two or three questions in each chapter directly related to the Internet and designed to provide students with opportunities to enhance their electronic data gathering and interpretative skills.

Marketing Research in Action. Short cases located at the end of the chapters provide students with additional insights into how key concepts in each chapter can be applied to real-world situations. These cases serve as in-class discussion tools or applied case exercises. The continuing case—the Santa Fe Grill—uses a single research situation to illustrate various aspects of the marketing research process.

Santa Fe Grill. The Santa Fe Grill continuing case is a specially designed business scenario embedded throughout the book for the purpose of questioning and illustrating chapter topics. The case is introduced in Chapter 1, and in each subsequent chapter it builds upon the concepts previously learned. More than 30 class-tested examples are included as well as an SPSS and Excel formatted database covering a customer survey.

Supplements

The book provides an extensive and rich ancillary package. Below is a brief description of each element in the package.

Instructor's Resources. Specially prepared Instructor's Manual, electronic Test Bank, and PowerPoint slide presentations provide an easy transition for instructors teaching with the book the first time. For those who have used previous editions, there are many new support materials to build upon the notes and teaching enhancement materials available previously. A wealth of extra student projects and real-life examples are available as additional classroom resources.

Videos. The video program contains several hours of material on marketing research from the McGraw-Hill/Irwin video library.

Web Site. Students can use their Internet skills to log on to the book's dedicated Web site (www.mhhe.com.hairessential1e) to access additional information about marketing research and evaluate their understanding of chapter material by taking the sample quizzes. Students can also prepare their marketing research projects with our online support system. Additional resources are offered for each chapter—look for prompts in the book that will guide you to the Web site for more useful information on various topics.

Data Sets.   Six data sets in SPSS format are available at the book's Web site (www.mhhe.com.hairessentials1e). The data sets can be used to assign research projects or with exercises throughout the book. The concepts covered in each of the data sets were summarized earlier in this Preface.

SPSS Student Version.   Through an arrangement with SPSS, we offer the option of purchasing the textbook packaged with a CD-ROM containing an SPSS Student Version for Windows. This powerful software tool enables students to analyze up to 50 variables and 1,500 observations. It contains all data sets and can be used in conjunction with data analysis procedures included in the text.

Acknowledgments

The authors took the lead in preparing this shorter book, but many other people must be given credit for their significant contributions in bringing our vision to reality. We thank our colleagues in academia and industry for their helpful insights over many years on numerous research topics.

We would also like to thank our editors and advisers at McGraw-Hill/Irwin. Thanks go to Paul Ducham, our Publisher; Doug Hughes, our Executive editor; Anna Chan, our Developmental editor; and Dean Karampelas, our Associate Marketing Manager. We are also grateful to our professional production team: Dana Pauley, Project Manager; Kami Carter, Design Manager; Carol Bielski, Senior Production Supervisor; and Brian Nacik, Lead Media Project Manager.

Joseph F. Hair, Jr.
Mary F. Wolfinbarger
David J. Ortinau
Robert P. Bush

Brief Contents

Contents

Part 1

The Role and Value of Marketing Research Information

Marketing Research for Decision Making

1. Describe the impact marketing research has on marketing decision making.
2. Demonstrate how marketing research fits into the marketing planning process.
3. Provide examples of marketing research studies.
4. Understand the scope and focus of the marketing research industry.
5. Explain the ethical dimensions associated with marketing research.
6. Discuss emerging trends and new skills associated with marketing research.

Marketing Research and Decision Making

The Jeep Division of DaimlerChrysler (AG) relies on brand recognition that is synonymous with a "spirit of freedom, adventure, mastery and authenticity." For example, the Director of Jeep Marketing characterizes Jeep Wrangler owners as rugged and adventurous individuals embracing Jeep's brand attributes of a "go anywhere, do anything" lifestyle. While this image was initially successful, recent sales figures indicate the Jeep brand is losing ground in market share to other SUV brands.

One of the greatest challenges for the Jeep Division is keeping up with ever-changing needs, desires, and diversity of its core customer base and expanding the Jeep brand to new markets. Jeep management understands that traditional focus groups and surveys are not enough to really understand this market. Some of Jeep's new marketing strategies focus on individual consumers in order to create a relationship between the Jeep brand and the buyer. Current marketing research activities rely more on information technology and data gathering through "event" sponsorships such as off-road driving clinics, fly fishing contests, hiking and mountain-biking competitions. Special events, while expensive, allow marketing researchers and engineers to generate face-to-face dialogue with thousands of customers to learn more about Jeep core and potential customers and the relationship they have with their vehicles. Jeep engineers are able to record important tangible benefits, product ideas, and improvement suggestions from the customer encounters while marketing researchers get feedback on model changes, lifestyles, and satisfaction.

This new approach recently led to two new brand recognition strategies: the "Ask Dr. Z" ad campaign and the "Jeep Stick in the Mud" challenge to give consumers a chance to personify the new 2007 four-door Jeep Wrangler Unlimited. The new Jeep is portrayed as being a one-of-a-kind, four-door open-air design that expands the Jeep experience to new dimensions. Room for five adult passengers and the most cargo space ever offered is combined with class-leading off-road capability and everyday practicality. The "Ask Dr. Z" ad campaign features DaimlerChrysler Chairman Dieter Zetsche as the Jeep Campaign spokesperson and communicates the benefits of the best of American and German engineering and design: specifically, the innovative design features, quality, reliability, performance, and fuel economy attributes of the Jeep vehicles. In the first six weeks of the campaign, more than 600,000 visitors logged on to the Web site (**www.AskDrZ.com**) and asked more than 4.2 million questions. George Murphy, Chrysler's global marketing chief, reveals that the campaign drove the Jeep brand Web site traffic up consistently by 15 percent over June and Web leads have increased by 27 percent. In addition, IAG Research, an independent third-party service that measures advertising effectiveness, reports that the campaign is significantly outperforming almost every IAG automotive norm: over 80 percent of in-market consumers find Dieter credible and believable and over 70 percent indicated that they understand Chrysler Group vehicles, including the Jeep brand, combine the best American and German engineering and design.

Value of Marketing Research Information

The Jeep example illustrates just one way marketing research operates to solve business problems as well as to clarify emerging trends. Developing a sound research process based on customer feedback enables any size business to make confident, cost-effective decisions, whether identifying new product opportunities or designing new approaches for communicating with customers.

Marketing research The function that links an organization to its market through the gathering of information.

The American Marketing Association defines **marketing research** as the function that links an organization to its market through the gathering of information. This information facilitates the identification and definition of market-driven opportunities and problems, as well as the development and evaluation of marketing actions. Finally, it enables the monitoring of marketing performance and improved understanding of marketing as a business process.[1] The Jeep Division uses marketing research information to identify new product opportunities, develop advertising strategies, and implement new data-gathering methods to better understand customers. These approaches are known as relationship building and customer relationship management. Both approaches are discussed later in the chapter.

Marketing research is a systematic process. Tasks in this process include designing methods for collecting information, managing the information collection process, analyzing and interpreting results, and communicating findings to decision makers. This chapter provides an overview of marketing research as well as a fundamental understanding of its relationship to marketing. We first explain why firms use marketing research and give some examples of how marketing research can help companies make sound marketing decisions. Next we discuss who should use marketing research, and when.

The chapter also provides a general description of the activities companies use to collect marketing research information. We present an overview of the marketing research industry in order to clarify the relationship between the providers and the users of marketing information. The chapter closes with a description of the role of ethics in marketing research. It also includes an Appendix on careers in marketing research.

Relationship Marketing and the Marketing Research Process

Marketing The process of planning and executing the pricing, promotion, and distribution of products, services, and ideas in order to create exchanges that satisfy both the firm and its customers.

The fundamental purpose of **marketing** is to enable firms to plan and execute the pricing, promotion, and distribution of products, services, and ideas in order to create exchanges that satisfy both the firm and its customers. Creating this exchange is the responsibility of the firm's marketing manager. Marketing managers focus on getting the right goods and services (1) to the right people, (2) at the right place and time, (3) with the right price, and (4) through the use of the right blend of promotional techniques. By doing their job marketing managers enhance the likelihood of a successful marketing effort. But this does not eliminate the element of uncertainty. Uncertainty emerges to a great extent from unpredictable consumers and competitors. In order to reduce uncertainty, marketing managers must have accurate, relevant, and timely information. Marketing research generates that information.

Relationship marketing The name of a strategy that entails forging long-term relationships with customers.

Successful businesses follow a business strategy known as **relationship marketing.** Companies pursuing relationship marketing build long-term relationships with customers by offering value for the price. The company is rewarded with repeat purchases, increased sales, and higher market share and profits. Dell Computers, for example, engages in relationship marketing. Dell sees its customers as individuals with unique needs and desires. Its marketing research program is directed toward measuring customer needs and then developing a marketing program around these metrics to build long-term relationships with customers.

The success of any relationship marketing program depends on knowledge of the market, effective training programs, and employee empowerment and teamwork:

- **Knowledge of the market.** For an organization to build relationships with customers, it must know relevant information about those customers. This implies that the company must understand customer needs and desires and use that information to deliver satisfaction to the customer. Nowhere is this more important than in the marketing research responsibilities of the company.
- **Effective training programs.** Building excellence in relationships begins with the employee. In the eyes of many consumers, the employee is the company. Therefore, it is critical, not only in a marketing research capacity, but throughout the entire company, that the actions and behaviors of employees be market oriented. Many organizations such as McDonald's, Walt Disney, and American Express have corporate universities designed to train employees in customer relations. Furthermore, these universities train how to gather data from customers. For example, emphasizing informal customer comments, discussing competing products, and encouraging customers to use comment cards are some ways in which American Express trains its employees in data-gathering practices.
- **Employee empowerment and teamwork.** Many successful companies encourage their employees to be more proactive in solving customer problems. On-the-spot problem solving is known as *empowerment.* But organizations are now developing cross-functional teams dedicated to developing and delivering customer solutions. Teamwork designed to accomplish common goals is frequently used at the Jeep Division of DaimlerChrysler. This is evident in the opening example, where Jeep marketing research and engineering personnel work together to better understand the requirements of their customers.

Empowerment and teamwork facilitate relationship building among customers. These two dimensions, along with training and knowledge of the market, are catalysts for the marketing strategy commonly known as customer relationship management.

Relationship Marketing and Customer Relationship Management

Customer relationship management The process used for implementing a relationship marketing strategy.

Customer relationship management, or CRM, is the process used to implement a relationship marketing strategy. CRM gathers market-driven data to learn more about customers' needs and behaviors for the purpose of delivering added value and satisfaction to the customer. The data, in conjunction with information technology, is then used to develop stronger relationships with customers. CRM is based on a number of fundamental concepts focusing on the marketplace and the consumer. Specifically, these concepts address the following:

> **Customer/market knowledge** is the starting point of any CRM process. The role of marketing research is to collect and gather information from multiple sources about the customer. Key data to be captured include demographics, psychographics, buying and service history, preferences, complaints, and other communications the customer has with the company.
>
> **Data integration** involves setting up a data warehouse to integrate information from multiple sources into a single shared depository of data. The data are used to understand and predict customer behavior and service histories are made available to all functional areas of the company so that anyone who interacts with the customer will have a history of the customer.
>
> **Information technology** has facilitated the expansion of marketing research activities. One role of marketing research is to facilitate data integration using technology-driven techniques. These techniques perform functions such as data mining and statistical analysis.
>
> **Customer profiles** are created and used to improve marketing decisions. Data is collected, integrated into data warehouses, and used to develop customer profiles. Profiles are then made available to all functional areas of the company.

Information sharing ensures that all functional areas of the business have the information they need to improve decision making. Increasingly information is shared through the effective use of executive dashboards. An *executive dashboard* that displays key metrics in real time is often available on an intranet for a select group of managers who are the main decision makers in the company. The purpose of dashboards is to give managers a snapshot of the current status of their business, including recent positive and negative trends, so they can react quickly. This on-screen display of metrics is similar to the driver's console in a car. Just as the automobile's dashboard provides all the critical information needed to operate the vehicle at a glance, a business intelligence dashboard serves a similar purpose whether managers are using it to make strategic decisions, run the daily operations of a team, or perform tasks that involve only their area of responsibility. Dashboards typically display metrics defined by the organization, such as products sold by region or defects per thousand shipped. These metrics are key performance indicators (KPIs), and a typical dashboard brings several KPIs together across critical aspects of the business. Dashboards are a key component of information sharing and increase the likelihood of successful customer relationship management programs.

CRM concepts are embodied in a variety of outcomes based on the decision-making and planning objectives of the company, for example, introducing new products, growing new market segments, and evaluating advertising campaigns. The overriding goal is to provide the necessary data and technology to monitor customer changes while building and maintaining long-term customer relationships.

Marketing Planning and Decision Making

Marketing managers make many marketing decisions. These decisions vary dramatically in both focus and complexity. Regardless of the complexity of a given decision, managers must have accurate information to make the right decisions. It is therefore not surprising that a sound marketing research process is the foundation of market planning.

Exhibit 1.1 lists some of the research-related tasks necessary for marketing decision making. While the list is by no means exhaustive, it does illustrate the relationship between market planning and marketing research. The following sections describe these relationships in more detail.

Exhibit 1.1	Marketing Decision Making and Related Marketing Research Tasks

Marketing Planning Process	Marketing Research Task
Marketing Situation Analysis	**Situation Research Efforts**
Market analysis	Opportunity assessment
Market segmentation	Benefit and lifestyle studies
	Descriptive studies
Competition analysis	Importance-performance analysis
Marketing Strategy Design	**Program-Driven Research Efforts**
Target marketing	Target market analysis
Positioning	Perceptual mapping
New-product planning	Concept and product testing
	Test marketing
Marketing Program Development	**Program Development Research**
Product portfolio decisions	Customer satisfaction studies
	Service quality studies
Distribution decisions	Cycle time research
	Retailing research
	Logistic assessment
Pricing decisions	Demand analysis
	Sales forecasting
Integrated marketing communications	Promotional effectiveness studies
	Attitudinal research
	Sales tracking

Marketing Situation Analysis

The purpose of a **situation analysis** is to monitor marketing programs and determine whether changes are necessary. A situation analysis includes three decision areas: market analysis, market segmentation, and competition analysis. When conducting a situation analysis, marketing research should:

1. Locate and identify new market opportunities for a company (opportunity assessment).
2. Identify groups of customers in a product/market who possess similar needs, characteristics, and preferences (benefit and lifestyle studies, descriptive studies).
3. Identify existing and potential competitors' strengths and weaknesses (importance-performance analysis).

Market Analysis

The research task related to market analysis is **opportunity assessment.** It involves collecting market information to forecast changes. Companies gather information relevant to macroenvironmental trends (political and regulatory, economic and social, and cultural and technological) and assess how those trends will influence the product market.

The role of marketing research is to gather information on macroenvironmental variables and then interpret the information in terms of strategic consequences to the firm. Marketing researchers use three common approaches in the collection of macroenvironmental information:

1. *Content analysis,* in which researchers analyze various trade publications, newspaper articles, academic literature, or databases for information about trends in a given industry.
2. *In-depth interviews,* in which researchers conduct formal, structured interviews with experts in a given field.
3. *Formal rating procedures,* in which researchers use structured questionnaires to gather information about environmental occurrences.

These procedures will be discussed further in Chapters 5, 8, and 9.

Market Segmentation

A major component of market segmentation research is **benefit and lifestyle studies** which examine similarities and differences in consumers' needs. Researchers use these studies to identify segments within the market for a particular company's products. The objective is to collect information about customer characteristics, product benefits, and brand preferences. This data, along with information on age, family size, income, and lifestyle is then compared to purchase patterns of particular products (cars, food, electronics, financial services) to develop market segmentation profiles.

Competitive Analysis

Competitive analysis involves **importance-performance analysis,** an approach for evaluating competitors' strategies, strengths, limitations, and future plans. Importance-performance analysis asks consumers to identify key attributes that drive their purchase behavior and to rank those attributes. These attributes might include price, product performance, product quality, accuracy of shipping and delivery, or convenience of store location.

Following the importance rankings, researchers identify and evaluate competing firms. When a competitor's product has highly ranked attributes, analysts view them as strengths. When the product has lower-ranked attributes, these attributes are weaknesses. When competing firms are analyzed together, a company can see where its competitors are concentrating their marketing efforts and where they are falling below customer expectations.

Marketing Strategy Design

Information collected during a situation analysis is used to design a marketing strategy. At this stage of the planning process, companies identify target markets, develop positioning strategies for products and brands, test new products, and assess market potential.

Target Marketing

Target market analysis
Information for identifying those people (or companies) that an organization wishes to serve.

Target market analysis provides useful information for identifying people (or companies) an organization wants to serve. In addition, it helps management determine the most efficient way of serving the targeted group. Target market analysis attempts to provide information on the following issues:

- New-product opportunities.
- Demographics, including attitudinal or behavioral characteristics.
- User profiles, usage patterns, and attitudes.
- The effectiveness of a firm's current marketing program.

Positioning

Positioning A process in which a company seeks to establish a meaning or general definition of its product offering that is consistent with customers' needs and preferences.

Positioning, or *perceptual mapping,* is a process in which a company seeks to establish perceptions of its product offering that are consistent with customers' needs and preferences. Companies accomplish this task by combining elements of the marketing mix in a manner that meets or exceeds the expectations of targeted customers.

The task of the marketing researcher is to provide an overview of the relationship between competitive product offerings based on a sample of respondents familiar with the product category being investigated. Consumers are asked to indicate how they view the similarities and dissimilarities among relevant product attributes for competing brands or, more directly, to indicate which brands are similar to each other.

The information is then used to construct perceptual maps that transform the positioning data into a picture or graph that shows how brands are viewed relative to one another. Perceptual mapping reflects the criteria consumers use to evaluate brands, typically representing major product features important to consumers along an x- and y-axis.

New-Product Planning

Concept and product testing Information for decisions on product improvements and new product introduction.

Test marketing Information for decisions on product improvements and new-product introductions.

Research tasks related to new-product planning are **concept and product testing** and **test marketing,** which provide information for decisions on product improvements and new-product introductions. Product testing attempts to answer two fundamental questions: "How does a product perform for the customer?" and "How can a product be improved to exceed customer expectations?" In product tests, ideas are reshaped and redefined to identify those that not only meet but exceed market expectations.

Marketing Program Development

The information requirements for marketing program development involve all the components of the marketing mix: product, distribution, price, and promotion. Managers combine these components to form the total marketing effort for each market targeted. While at first this may appear to be an easy task, the success of the marketing program relies heavily on synergy. It is critical that the marketing mix not only contain the right elements but do so in the right amount, at the right time, and in the proper sequence. Ensuring that this synergy occurs is the responsibility of market researchers.

Product Portfolio Analysis

The total product line typically is the focal point of product portfolio analysis. Market researchers design studies that help product managers make decisions about reducing costs, altering marketing mixes, and changing or deleting product lines. Examples include customer satisfaction studies and service quality studies.

Customer satisfaction studies This studies assess the strengths and weaknesses that customers perceive in a firm's marketing mix.

Customer satisfaction studies assess the strengths and weaknesses customers perceive in a firm's marketing mix. Customer satisfaction studies often examine customer attitudes to see if they are linked to purchase intentions, brand switching, perceptions of company image, and brand loyalty.[2] Attitude information enables management to make decisions regarding product or brand repositioning, new-product introductions, new market segments, and the deletion of ineffective products. Chapters 8 and 9 discuss the design of attitudinal research studies.

Distribution Decisions

Distribution decisions involve distributors and retailers that link producers with end users. The distribution channel used by a producer can influence a buyer's perception of the brand. For example, Rolex watches are distributed through a limited number of retailers that project a prestigious image consistent with the Rolex brand name.

Retailing research Studies on topics such as trade area analysis, store image/perception, in-store traffic patterns, and location analysis.

Retailing research includes studies on a variety of topics. Because retailers often are independent businesses, many of the studies we discuss are applicable to the retail environment. Yet, the information needs of retailers are unique. Market research studies peculiar to retailers include trade area analysis, store image/perception studies, in-store traffic patterns, and location analysis.

Retailers collect a great deal of scanner data, which is produced at the point of customer purchase. Every time a transaction is recorded using an optical scanner, the scanner notes the type of product, its manufacturer and vendor, and its size and price. Marketing research then categorizes the data and combines it with other relevant information to form a database. Retailers can then determine the television programs their customers watch, the kinds of neighborhoods where they live, and the types of stores they prefer to patronize. This information helps retailers determine the kind of merchandise to stock and what factors may influence purchase decisions.

Online retailers collect a great deal of information about online customer behavior. The information includes when a Web site is visited, which pages are viewed and for how long, the products examined and ultimately purchased, as well as how the visitor got to the Web site. Online retailers can use the data to improve Web-site performance and customer conversion rates (the percentage who go online who actually make a purchase). The data can be combined with offline retailer data in order to better understand how online visits contribute to in-store purchases.

Pricing Decisions

Pricing decisions involve pricing new products, establishing price levels in test-market situations, and modifying prices for existing products. Marketing research provides answers to questions such as the following:

1. How large is the demand potential within the target market?
2. How sensitive is demand to changes in price levels?
3. What nonprice factors are important to customers?
4. What are sales forecasts at various price levels?

Integrated Marketing Communications

Promotional decisions, many times viewed as integrated marketing communications, are important influences on any company's sales. Billions of dollars are spent yearly on various promotional activities. Given the heavy level of expenditures on promotional activities, it is essential that companies know how to obtain optimum returns from their promotional budgets. This is particularly important as a result of the rapid movement of businesses into online advertising.

Marketing research that examines the performance of a promotional program must consider the entire program. Using the appropriate methodology, estimating adequate sample sizes, and developing the proper scaling techniques are just three key areas of promotional research. Each of these areas is used when considering the three most common research tasks of integrated marketing communications: advertising effectiveness studies, attitudinal research, and sales tracking.

The Marketing Research Industry

The marketing research industry has experienced unparalleled growth in recent years. According to an *Advertising Age* study, revenues of U.S. research companies have grown substantially in recent years.[3] The growth in revenues of international research firms has been even more dramatic. Marketing research firms have attributed these revenue increases to postsale customer satisfaction studies (one-third of research company revenues), retail-driven product scanning systems (also one-third of all revenues), database development for long-term brand management, and international research studies.

Changing Skills for a Changing Industry

Marketing research employees represent a vast diversity of cultures, technology, and personalities. As marketing research firms expand their geographic scope to Europe, Asia, and the Pacific Rim, the requirements for successfully executing marketing research projects will change dramatically. Many fundamental skill requirements will remain in place, but new and innovative practices will require a unique skill base that is more comprehensive than ever before.

In a survey of 100 marketing research executives, fundamental business skills were rated high for potential employees. Communication skills (verbal and written), interpersonal skills (ability to work with others), and statistical skills were the leading attributes required for jobs in marketing research.[4] More specifically, the top five skills executives hope to find in candidates for marketing research positions are (1) the ability to understand and interpret secondary data, (2) presentation skills, (3) foreign-language competency,

(4) negotiation skills, and (5) computer proficiency.[5] Results of this survey indicate there has been a shift from analytical to execution skill requirements in the marketing research industry. In the future, analyzing existing databases, multicultural interaction, and negotiation are likely to be important characteristics of marketing researchers. Marketing research jobs are discussed further in a careers Appendix at the end of this chapter.

Ethics in Marketing Research Practices

There are many opportunities for both ethical and unethical behaviors to occur in the research process. The major sources of ethical dilemmas in marketing research are the interactions among the three key groups: (1) the research information user (the decision maker, sponsoring client, management team, or practitioner); (2) the research information provider (the researcher, research organization or company, project supervisor, researcher's staff representative or employees); and (3) the selected respondents (respondents or objects of investigation).

Unethical Activities by the Client/Research User

Decisions and practices of the customer or decision maker present opportunities for unethical behavior. One such behavior is when the decision maker requests a detailed research proposal from several competing research providers with no intention of selecting a firm to conduct the research. In this situation, companies solicit the proposals for the purpose of learning how to conduct the necessary marketing research themselves. Decision makers can obtain first drafts of questionnaires, sampling frames and sampling procedures, and knowledge on data collection procedures. Then, unethically, they can use the information to either perform the research project themselves or bargain for a better price among interested research companies.

Unfortunately, another common behavior among unethical decision makers is promising a prospective research provider a long-term relationship or additional projects in order to obtain a very low price on the initial research project. Then, after the researcher completes the initial project, the decision maker forgets about the long-term promises.

Unethical Activities by the Research Provider or Research Company

There are numerous opportunities for the customer to be unethical, but there are also several sources of unethical activities that can originate with the research company. First, a policy of unethical pricing practices is a source of conflict. For example, after quoting a set overall price for a proposed research project, the researcher may tell the decision maker that variable-cost items such as travel expenses, monetary response incentives, or fees charged for computer time are extra, over and above the quoted price. Such "soft" costs can be easily used to manipulate the total project cost.

Second, the researcher or the organization may engage in respondent abuse. Research companies may state that interviews are very short when in reality they last up to one hour. Other situations of known respondent abuse include selling the respondents' names and demographic data to other companies without their approval, using infrared dye on questionnaires to trace selective respondents for the purpose of making a sales call, or using hidden tape recorders in a personal interviewing situation without the respondent's permission.

An unethical practice found all too often in marketing research is the selling of unnecessary or unwarranted research services. While it is perfectly acceptable to sell follow-up research that can aid the decision maker's company, selling unnecessary services is completely unethical. There are several other researcher-related unethical practices within the execution of the research design such as (1) falsifying data, (2) duplicating actual response data, and (3) consciously manipulating data collection or analysis to misrepresent findings.

A practice of data falsification known to many researchers and field interviewers is called curbstoning (or rocking-chair) interviewing. This occurs when the researcher's trained interviewers or observers, rather than conducting interviews or observing respondents' actions as directed in the study, will complete the interviews themselves or make up "observed" respondents' behaviors. Other falsification practices include having friends and relatives fill out surveys, not using the designated sample of sample respondents but rather anyone who is conveniently available to complete the survey, or not following up on the established call-back procedures indicated in the research procedure.

Another variation of data falsification is duplication of responses or the creation of "phantom" respondents. This is a process whereby a researcher or field personnel (e.g., interviewer, field observer, or data entry personnel) will take an actual respondent's data and duplicate it to represent a second set of responses. To minimize the likelihood of data falsification, research companies typically randomly verify 10 to 15 percent of the interviews.

Unethical Activities by the Respondent

The primary unethical practice of respondents or subjects in any research endeavor is providing dishonest answers. The general expectation is that when a subject has freely consented to participate, she or he will provide truthful responses.

There are other areas fraught with possible ethical dilemmas within a researcher–respondent relationship. These include (1) the respondent's right to privacy; (2) the need to disguise the true purpose of the research; and (3) the respondent's right to be informed about certain aspects of the research process, including the sponsorship of the research.

Marketing Research Codes of Ethics

Marketing researchers must be proactive in their efforts to ensure an ethical environment, and the first step in being proactive is to develop a code of ethics. Many marketing research companies have established internal company codes of ethics derived from the ethical codes formulated by larger institutions that govern today's marketing research industry. The Code of Ethics for the American Marketing Association can be viewed at **www.marketingpower.com.** ESOMAR, the world organization for enabling better research into markets, consumers, and societies, also publishes a marketing code of ethics on their Web site (**www.esomar.org**). The Marketing Research Society summarizes the central principles in ESOMAR's code as follows:[6]

1.   Market researchers will conform to all relevant national and international laws.
2.   Market researchers will behave ethically and will not do anything which might damage the reputation of market research.
3.   Market researchers will take special care when carrying out research among children and other vulnerable groups of the population.
4.   Respondents' cooperation is voluntary and must be based on adequate, and not misleading, information about the general purpose and nature of the project when their agreement to participate is being obtained and all such statements must be honored.
5.   The rights of respondents as private individuals will be respected by market researchers and they will not be harmed or disadvantaged as the result of cooperating in a market research project.

6. Market researchers will never allow personal data they collect in a market research project to be used for any purpose other than market research.
7. Market researchers will ensure that projects and activities are designed, carried out, reported, and documented accurately, transparently, objectively, and to the appropriate level of quality.
8. Market researchers will conform to the accepted principles of fair competition.

Emerging Trends

The general consensus in the marketing research industry is that five major trends are becoming evident: (1) increased emphasis on secondary data collection methods; (2) movement toward technology-based data management (database technology, customer relationship management); (3) expanded use of digital technology for information acquisition and retrieval; (4) a broader international client base; and (5) movement beyond data analysis toward an information management environment.

The organization of this book is consistent with these trends. Part 1 (Chapters 1 and 2) explores marketing research information and technology from the client's perspective, including how to evaluate marketing research projects. Part 2 (Chapters 3–6) provides an overview of the emerging role of secondary data and Internet search engines, with emphasis on technology-driven approaches for the design and development of research projects. This part also discusses traditional marketing research project design issues as well as collection of qualitative and quantitative data. Practical examples that illustrate how data is used in industry facilitate the discussion. Part 3 (Chapters 7–9) covers sampling, attitude measurement, and questionnaire design. Part 4 (Chapters 10–14) prepares the reader for management, analysis, and interpretation of research data, both qualitative and quantitative. A chapter on the analysis of qualitative data explains the basic approach to carrying out this type of analysis. Computer applications of statistical packages give readers a hands-on guide to analyzing quantitative data. This part concludes by showing how to effectively present marketing research findings.

Each chapter concludes with an illustrated example called *Marketing Research in Action*. The goal of these action illustrations is to facilitate the understanding of chapter topics and to provide the reader with a "how-to" approach for marketing research methods.

Continuing Case Study: The Santa Fe Grill Mexican Restaurant

To illustrate marketing research principles and concepts in this text, we have prepared a case study that will be used throughout all the chapters in the book. The case study is about the Santa Fe Grill Mexican Restaurant, which was started 18 months ago by two former business students at the University of Nebraska, Lincoln. They had been roommates in college and both had an entrepreneurial desire. After graduating they wanted to start a business instead of working for someone else. The students had worked in restaurants while attending college, both as waiters and one as an assistant manager, and felt they had the knowledge and experience necessary to start their own business.

The focus on a single case study of a typical business research problem will enable you to more easily understand the benefits and pitfalls of using research to improve business decision making. The *Marketing Research in Action* exercise for this chapter provides more details about this continuing case study.

MARKETING RESEARCH IN ACTION
Continuing Case Study: The Santa Fe Grill

During their senior year in college the owners prepared a business plan in their entrepreneurship class for a new Mexican restaurant concept. They initially intended to start the restaurant in Lincoln, Nebraska. But a demographic analysis of that market revealed that Lincoln did not match their target demographics.

After researching the demographic and competitive profile of several markets, they decided that Dallas, Texas, would be the best place to start their business. In examining the markets, they were looking for a town that would best fit their target market of baby-boomers and young families. The population in Dallas consists of almost 4.5 million people, of which about 50 percent are between the ages of 35 and 64. This showed them there were a lot of baby-boomers and others in their target market in the Dallas area. They also found that 53 percent of the population earn between $45,000 and $85,000 a year, which indicated the market would have enough income to eat out regularly. Finally, 54 percent of the population was married and many of them had children at home, which was consistent with their target of families.

The new restaurant concept was based upon the freshest ingredients, complemented by a festive atmosphere, friendly service, and cutting-edge advertising and marketing strategies. The key would be to prepare and serve the freshest "made-from-scratch" Mexican foods possible. Everything would be prepared fresh every single day. In addition to their freshness concept, they wanted to have a fun, festive atmosphere and fast, friendly service. The atmosphere would be open, brightly lit, and bustling with activity. Their target market would be mostly baby-boomers and families. Their marketing programs would be ahead of the pack, with the advertising designed to provide an appealing, slightly off-center, unrefined positioning in the market.

The Santa Fe Grill was successful, but not as quickly as the owners anticipated. To improve restaurant operations, the owners needed to better understand what aspects of the restaurant drove customer satisfaction and where they could improve. Some of the questions they came up with included: Are our customers satisfied with the restaurant? Are there problems with the food, the atmosphere, or some other aspect of restaurant operations (e.g., employees or service)? Is the target market correctly defined or do we need to focus on a different niche? What are the common characteristics of satisfied customers? Answering these and other similar questions would help the owners to focus their marketing efforts, improve operations, and be in a position to expand their restaurant concept to other markets.

Hands-On Exercise

1. Based on your understanding of Chapter 1, and specifically using Exhibit 1.1, what type(s) of research program(s) should the owners of Santa Fe Grill consider?
2. Is a research project actually needed? If yes, what kind of project? What areas should the research focus on?

Summary

Describe the impact marketing research has on marketing decision making.

Marketing research is responsible for providing managers with accurate, relevant, and timely information so that they can make marketing decisions with a high degree of confidence. Within the context of strategic planning, marketing research is responsible for the tasks, methods, and procedures a firm will use to implement and direct its strategic plan.

Demonstrate how marketing research fits into the marketing planning process.

Marketing research facilitates the CRM process through the generation of customer/market knowledge, data integration, information technology, the creation of customer profiles, and information sharing. Information related to product performance, distribution efficiency, pricing policies, and promotional efforts is crucial for developing the strategic plan. The primary responsibility of any marketing research endeavor is to design a project that yields the most accurate information possible in aiding the development of a marketing plan.

Provide examples of marketing research studies.

The major categories of marketing research tasks include but are not limited to (1) marketing situation analysis (opportunity assessment, benefit and lifestyle studies, descriptive studies, and importance-performance analysis); (2) market strategy design (target market analysis, positioning or perceptual mapping, concept and product testing, and test marketing); and (3) marketing program

development (customer satisfaction studies, retailing research, demand analysis, sales forecasting, promotional effectiveness studies, product analysis, and environmental forecasting).

Explain the ethical dimensions associated with marketing research.

Ethical dilemmas in marketing research are likely to occur among the research information user, the research information provider, and the selected respondents. Specific unethical practices among research providers include unethical pricing practices, failure to meet obligations to respondents, respondent abuse, and selling unnecessary services. Unethical behavior by clients includes requesting research proposals with no intent to follow through and unethical practices to secure low-cost research services. The falsification of data and duplication of actual responses are unethical practices associated with the research firm.

Discuss emerging trends and new skills associated with marketing research.

Just as the dynamic business environment causes firms to modify and change practices, so does this environment dictate change to the marketing research industry. Specifically, technological changes will affect how marketing research will be conducted in the future. Necessary skills required to adapt to these changes include (1) the ability to understand and interpret secondary data, (2) presentation skills, (3) foreign-language competency, (4) negotiation skills, and (5) computer proficiency.

Key Terms and Concepts

◨ Review Questions

1. Provide three examples of how marketing research helps marketing personnel make sound managerial decisions.
2. What improvements in market planning can be attributed to the results obtained from customer satisfaction studies?
3. Discuss the importance of target market analysis. How does it affect the development of market planning for a particular company?
4. As the marketing research industry expands, what skills will future executives need to possess? How do these skills differ from those currently needed to function successfully in the marketing research field?
5. Identify and explain four potential unethical practices within the marketing research process and their contribution to "deceptive research results."

◨ Discussion Questions

1. **EXPERIENCE THE INTERNET.** Go online to one of your favorite search engines (Yahoo, Google, etc.) and enter the following search term: *marketing research*. From the results, access a directory of marketing research firms. Select a particular firm and comment on the types of marketing research studies it performs.
2. **EXPERIENCE THE INTERNET.** Using the Yahoo search engine, specifically the Get Local section, select the closest major city in your area and search for the number of marketing research firms there. Select a research firm, e-mail that company, and ask to have any job descriptions for positions in that company e-mailed back to you. Once you obtain the descriptions, discuss the particular qualities needed to perform each job.
3. You have been hired by McDonald's to lead a mystery shopper team. The goal of your research is to improve the service quality at the McDonald's restaurant in your area. What attributes of service quality will you attempt to measure? What customer or employee behaviors will you closely monitor?
4. Contact a local business and interview the owner/manager about the types of marketing research performed for that business. Determine whether the business has its own marketing research department, or if it hires an outside agency. Also, determine whether the company takes a one-shot approach to particular problems or is systematic over a long period of time.
5. **EXPERIENCE THE INTERNET.** As the Internet continues to grow as a medium for conducting various types of marketing research studies, there is growing concern about ethical issues. Identify and discuss three ethical issues pertinent to research conducted using the Internet.

   Now go to the Internet and validate your ethical concerns. Using any search engine go to the Internet Fraud home page, at **www.fraud.org/ifw.htm**. Click on the other links and browse the information. What unethical practices are plaguing the Net?

◣ Careers in Marketing Research with a Look at Federal Express

Career opportunities in marketing research vary by industry, company, and size of company. Different positions exist in consumer products companies, industrial goods companies, internal marketing research departments, and professional marketing research firms. Marketing research tasks range from the very simple, such as tabulation of questionnaires, to the very complex, such as sophisticated data analysis. Exhibit A.1 lists some common job titles and the functions as well as compensation ranges for marketing research positions.

Exhibit A.1 Marketing Research Career Outline

Position*	Duties	Compensation Range (Annual, in Thousands)
Account executive research director	Responsible for entire research program of the company. Works as go-between for the company and client. Employs personnel and supervises research department. Presents research findings to company and/or clients.	$60 to $90
Information technician statistician	Acts as expert consultant on application of statistical techniques for specific research problems. Many times responsible for research design and data analysis.	$40 to $70
Research analyst	Plans research project and executes project assignments. Works with analyst in preparing questionnaire. Makes analysis, prepares report, schedules project events, and sets budget.	$35 to $65
Assistant research analyst	Works under research analyst supervision. Assists in development of questionnaire, pretest, preliminary analysis.	$30 to $45
Project coordinator Project director Field manager Fieldwork director	Hires, trains, and supervises field interviewers. Provides work schedules and is responsible for data accuracy.	$25 to $35
Librarian	Builds and maintains a library of primary and secondary data sources to meet the requirements of the research department.	$35 to $45
Clerical and tabulation assistant	Handles and processes statistical data. Supervises day-to-day office work.	$22 to $35

*Positions are general categories and not all companies have all of the positions.

Most successful marketing research people are intelligent and creative; they also possess problem-solving, critical thinking, communication, and negotiation skills. Marketing researchers must be able to function under strict time constraints and feel comfortable with working with large volumes of data. Federal Express, for example, normally seeks individuals with strong analytical and computer skills to fill its research positions. Candidates should have an undergraduate degree in business, marketing, or information systems. Having an MBA will usually give an applicant a competitive advantage.

As is the case with many companies, an entry-level position in marketing research at Federal Express is the assistant research analyst. While learning details of the company and the industry, these individuals receive on-the-job training from a research analyst. The normal career path includes advancement to information technician and then research director and/or account executive.

Marketing research at Federal Express is somewhat unusual in that it is housed in the information technology division. This is evidence that, while the research function is integrated throughout the company, it has taken on a high-tech orientation. Marketing research at FedEx operates in three general areas:

1. *Database development and enhancement.* This function is to establish relationships with current FedEx customers and use this information for the planning of new products.
2. *Cycle time research.* Providing more information for the efficient shipping of packages, tracking of shipments, automatic replenishment of customers' inventories, and enhanced electronic data interchange.
3. *Market intelligence system.* Primarily a logistical database and research effort to provide increased customer service to catalog retailers, direct marketing firms, and electronic commerce organizations.

The entire research function is led by a vice president of research and information technology, to whom four functional units report directly. These four units are responsible for the marketing decision support system operation, sales tracking, new business development, and special project administration.

If you are interested in pursuing a career in marketing research, a good way to start is to obtain the following career guide published by the Marketing Research Association:

Career Guide: Your Future in Marketing Research
Marketing Research Association
2189 Silas Deane Highway, Suite 5
Rocky Hill, CT 06067
MRAH@aol.com

You should also review the *Marketing and Sales Career Directory,* available at your university library or by writing:

Marketing and Sales Career Directory
Gale Research Inc.
835 Penobscot Building
Detroit, MI 48226-4094

Exercise

1. Go to the home Web page for Federal Express (**www.fedex.com**) and identify the requirements that FedEx is seeking in marketing research personnel. Write a brief description of these requirements and report your finding to the class.
2. If you were seeking a marketing research position at FedEx, how would you prepare yourself through training and education for such a position? Put together a one-year plan for yourself identifying the college courses, special activities, interests, and related work experience you would engage in to obtain a marketing research position at FedEx.

The Marketing Research Process and Proposals

Chapter 2

1. Describe the major environmental factors influencing marketing research.
2. Discuss the research process and explain the various steps.
3. Distinguish between exploratory, descriptive, and causal research designs.
4. Identify and explain the major components of a research proposal.

Solving Marketing Problems Using a Systematic Process

Bill Shulby is President of Carolina Consulting Company, a marketing strategy consulting firm based in Raleigh-Durham, North Carolina. He recently worked with the owners of a regional telecommunications firm located in Texas on improving service quality processes. Toward the end of their meeting, one of the owners, Dan Carter, asked him about customer satisfaction and perceptions of the company's image as they related to service quality and customer retention. During the discussion, Carter stated that he was not sure how the company's telecommunications services were viewed by current or potential customers. He said, "Just last week, the customer service department received eleven calls from different customers complaining about everything from incorrect bills to taking too long to get DSL installed. Clearly, none of these customers were happy about our service." Then he asked Shulby, "What can I do to find out how satisfied our customers are overall and what can be done to improve our image?"

Shulby explained that conducting a marketing research study would answer Carter's questions. Dan Carter responded that the company had not done research in the past so he did not know what to expect from such a study. Shulby then gave several examples of studies the Carolina Consulting Company had conducted for other clients and explained how the information had been used, making sure not to disclose any confidential information. Carter then asked, "How much would it cost me to do this study and how long would it take to complete?" Shulby explained he would like to ask a few more questions so he could better understand the issues, and he then would prepare a research proposal summarizing the approach to be used, the deliverables from the study, the cost, and the time frame for completion. The proposal would be ready in about a week and they would meet to go over it in detail.

Value of the Research Process

Business owners and managers often identify problems they need help to resolve. In such situations additional information typically is needed to make a decision or solve a problem. One solution is a marketing research study based on a scientific research process. This chapter provides an overview of the research process as well as a preview of some of the core topics in the text.

Changing View of the Marketing Research Process

Organizations, both for-profit and not-for-profit, are increasingly confronted with new and complex challenges and opportunities that are the result of changing legal, political, cultural, technological and competitive issues. Perhaps the most influential factor is the **Internet.** The rapid technological advances and its growing use by people worldwide are making the Internet a driving force in many current and future developments in marketing research. Traditional research philosophies are being challenged as never before. For example, there is a growing emphasis on secondary data collection, analysis, and interpretation as a basis of making business decisions. **Secondary data** is information previously collected for some other problem or issue. In contrast, **primary data** is information collected for a current research problem or opportunity.

A by-product of the technology advances is the ongoing collection of data that is placed in a data warehouse and is available as secondary data to help understand business problems and to improve decisions. Many large businesses (for example, Dell Computers, Bank of America, Marriott Hotels, Coca-Cola, IBM, McDonald's, and Wal-Mart) are linking purchase data collected in-store and online with customer profiles already in company databases, thus enhancing their ability to understand shopping behavior and better meet customer needs. But even medium- and small-sized companies are building databases of customer information to serve current customers more effectively and to attract new customers.

A second challenge is increased use of **gatekeeper technology** (for example, caller ID and automated screening and answering devices) as a means of protecting one's privacy against intrusive marketing practices such as telemarketers and illegal scam artists. Similarly, many Internet users either block the placement of cookies or periodically erase them in order to keep marketers from tracking their behavior. Marketing researchers' ability to collect consumer data using traditional methods like mail and telephone surveys has been severely limited by the combination of gatekeeper devices and recent Federal and state data privacy legislation. For example, marketing researchers must contact almost four times more people today to complete a single interview than was true five years ago. Similarly, online marketers and researchers must provide opt-in/opt-out opportunities when soliciting business or collecting information. Advances in gatekeeper technologies will continue to challenge marketers to be more creative in developing new ways to reach respondents.

The third challenge facing marketing decision makers is widespread expansion into global markets. Global expansion introduces marketing decision makers to new sets of cultural issues that force researchers to focus not only on data collection tasks, but also on data interpretation and information management activities. For example, one of the largest full-

---

Internet A network of computers and technology linking computers into an information superhighway.

Secondary data Historical data structures of variables previously collected and assembled for some research problem or opportunity situation other than the current situation.

Primary data Information collected for a current research problem or opportunity.

Gatekeeper technology Advanced telecommunication technologies that allow a person to screen incoming contact messages from other people or organizations.

service global marketing information firms, NFO (National Family Opinion) Worldwide, Inc., located in Greenwich, Connecticut, with subsidiaries in North America, Europe, Australia, Asia, and the Middle East, has adapted many of its measurement and brand tracking services to accommodate specific cultural and language differences encountered in global markets.

Fourth, marketing research is being repositioned in businesses to play a more important role in strategy development. Marketing research is being used increasingly to identify new business opportunities and to develop new product, service, and delivery ideas. Marketing research is also being viewed not only as a mechanism to more efficiently execute CRM (Customer Relationship Management) strategies, but also as a critical component in developing competitive intelligence. For example, Sony uses its Playstation Web site (**www. playstation.com**) to collect information about PlayStation gaming users and to build closer relationships. The PlayStation Web site is designed to create a community of users who can join PlayStation Underground where they will "feel like they belong to a subculture of intense gamers." To achieve this objective the Web site offers online shopping, opportunities to try new games, customer support, and information on news, events, and promotions. Interactive features include online gaming and message boards, as well as other relationship-building aspects.

Collectively, these key influences are forcing managers and researchers to view marketing research as an information management function. The term information research reflects the evolving changes occurring in the market research industry affecting organizational decision makers. Indeed, a more appropriate name for the traditional marketing research process is the information research process. The **information research process** is a systematic approach to collecting, analyzing, interpreting, and transforming data into decision-making information. While many of the specific tasks involved in marketing research remain the same, understanding the process of transforming data into usable information from a broader information processing framework expands the applicability of the research process in solving organizational problems and creating opportunities.

Information research process The systematic task steps in the gathering, analyzing, interpreting, and transforming of data into decision-making information.

Determining the Need for Information Research

Before we introduce and discuss the phases and specific steps of the information research process, it is important that you understand when research is needed and when it is not. More than ever, researchers must interact closely with managers to recognize business problems and opportunities.

Decision makers and researchers frequently are trained differently in their approach to identifying and solving business problems, questions, and opportunities, as illustrated in the nearby A Closer Look at Research box. Until decision makers and marketing researchers become closer in their thinking, the initial recognition of the existence of a problem or opportunity should be the primary responsibility of the decision maker, not the researcher. A good rule of thumb is to ask, "Can the decision-making problem (or question) be resolved based on past experience and managerial judgment?" If the response is "No," research should be considered and perhaps implemented.

Decision makers often initiate the research process because they recognize problem and opportunity situations that require more information before good plans of action can be developed. Once the research process is initiated, in most cases decision makers will need assistance in defining the problem, collecting and analyzing the data, and interpreting the data.

A Closer Look at Research   IN THE FIELD

Management Decision Makers . . .

Tend to be decision-oriented, intuitive thinkers who want information to confirm their decisions. They want additional information now or "yesterday," as well as results about future market component behavior ("What will sales be next year?"), while maintaining a frugal stance with regard to the cost of additional information. Decision makers tend to be results oriented, do not like surprises, and tend to reject the information when they are surprised. Their dominant concern is market performance ("Aren't we number one yet?"); they want information that allows certainty ("Is it or isn't it?") and advocate being proactive but often allow problems to force them into reactive decision-making modes.

Marketing Researchers . . .

Tend to be scientific, technical, analytical thinkers who love to explore new phenomena; accept prolonged investigations to ensure completeness; focus on information about past behaviors ("Our trend has been . . ."); and are not cost conscious with additional information ("You get what you pay for"). Researchers are results oriented but love surprises; they tend to enjoy abstractions ("Our exponential gain . . .") and the probability of occurrences ("May be," "Tends to suggest that . . ."); and they advocate the proactive need for continuous inquiries into market component changes, but feel most of the time that they are restricted to doing reactive ("quick and dirty") investigations due to management's lack of vision and planning.

There are four situations in which the decision to undertake a marketing research project may not be necessary.[1] These are listed and discussed in Exhibit 2.1.

The main initial responsibility of today's decision makers is to determine if research should be used to collect the needed information. The initial question the decision maker must ask is: *Can the problem and/or opportunity be resolved using existing information and managerial judgment?* The focus is on deciding what type of information (secondary or primary) is required to answer the research question(s). In most cases, decision makers should undertake the information research process any time they have a question or problem or believe there is an opportunity, but do not have the right information or are unwilling to rely on the information at hand to resolve the problem. In reality, conducting secondary and primary research studies costs time, effort, and money. After deciding

Exhibit 2.1   Situations When Marketing Research Might Not Be Needed

Situation Factors and Comments

Information already available   When the decision maker has substantial knowledge about markets, products and services, and the competition, enough information may exist to make an informed decision without doing marketing research. Improvements in information processing technology mean more information is available ensuring the right information gets to the right decision makers in a timely fashion.

Insufficient time frames   When the discovery of a problem situation leaves inadequate time to execute the necessary research activities, a decision maker may have to use informed judgment. Competitive actions/reactions sometimes emerge so fast that marketing research studies are not a feasible option.

Inadequate resources   When there are significant limitations in money, manpower, and/or facilities, then marketing research typically is not feasible.

Costs outweigh the value   When the benefits to be gained by conducting the research are not significantly greater than the costs, then marketing research is not feasible.

managerial judgment will not solve the identified problem, the next question to be answered concerns the nature of the decision: *Does the problem/opportunity situation have strategic or tactical importance?* Strategic decisions generally have longer time horizons and are more complex in nature than tactical decisions. Most strategic decisions are critical to the company's profit objectives, but tactical decisions can be important as well. For example, Outback Steakhouse recently made a tactical decision to update its menu both in appearance and food offerings. Researching the opinions of customers proved helpful in determining new food items to be included and items that should offered as occasional "chef's specials." Thus, if the problem has strategic or significant tactical importance, then a research expert should be consulted.

Another key managerial question deals with the availability of existing information. With the assistance of the research expert, decision makers face the next question: *Is adequate information available within the company's internal record systems to resolve the problem?* In the past, if the necessary marketing information was not available in the firm's internal record system, then a customized marketing research project was undertaken to obtain the information.

With input from the research expert, decision makers must assess the "time constraints" associated with the problem/opportunity: *Is there enough time to conduct the necessary research before the final managerial decision must be made?* Decision makers often need information in real time. But in many cases, systematic research that delivers high-quality information can take months. If the decision maker needs the information immediately, there may not be enough time to complete the research process. Another fundamental question focuses on the availability of marketing resources such as money, staff, skills, and facilities. Many small businesses lack the funds necessary to consider doing formal research.

A cost-benefit assessment should be made of value of the research compared to the cost: *Do the benefits of having the additional information outweigh the costs of gathering the information?* This type of question remains a challenge for today's decision makers. While the cost of doing marketing research varies from project to project, generally it can be estimated accurately. Yet, determining the true value of the expected information remains difficult. Other questions to consider before starting a research project include:

- What is the perceived importance and complexity of the problem?
- Is the problem realistically researchable? Can the critical variables in the proposed research be adequately designed and measured?
- Will conducting the needed research give valuable information to the firm's competitors?
- Will the research findings be implemented?
- Will the research design and data represent reality?
- Will the research results and findings be used as legal evidence?
- Is the proposed research politically motivated?

Overview of the Research Process

The research process consists of four distinct but related phases: (1) determine the research problem, (2) select the appropriate research design, (3) execute the research design, and (4) communicate the research results. (See Exhibit 2.2.) The phases of the process must be completed properly to obtain accurate information for decision making. But each phase can be viewed as a separate process that consists of several steps.

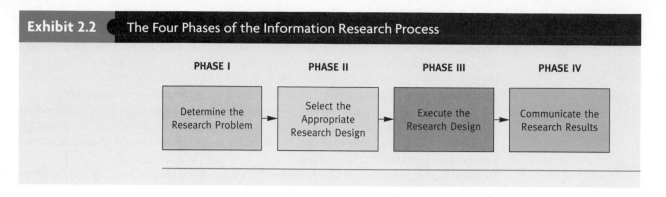

Exhibit 2.2 The Four Phases of the Information Research Process

PHASE I	PHASE II	PHASE III	PHASE IV
Determine the Research Problem	Select the Appropriate Research Design	Execute the Research Design	Communicate the Research Results

Scientific method Formalized research procedures that can be characterized as logical, objective, systematic, reliable and valid.

Knowledge Information that has meaning.

The four phases are guided by the **scientific method.** This means the research procedures should be logical, objective, systematic, reliable, and valid.

Transforming Data into Knowledge

The primary goal of the research process is to provide decision makers with knowledge that will enable them to resolve problems or pursue opportunities. Data becomes **knowledge** when someone, either the researcher or the decision maker, interprets the data and attaches meaning. To illustrate this process, consider the Excelsior Hotel. Corporate executives were assessing ways to reduce costs and improve profits. The VP of finance suggested cutting back on the "quality of the towels and bedding" in the rooms. Before making a final decision, the president asked the marketing research department to interview business customers.

Exhibit 2.3 summarizes the key results. A total of 880 people were asked to indicate the degree of importance they placed on seven criteria when selecting a hotel. Respondents

EXhibit 2.3 Summary of Differences in Selected Hotel-Choice Criteria: Comparison of First-Time and Repeat Business Customers

Hotel Selection Criteria	Total (n = 880) Mean[a] Value	First-Time Customers (n = 440) Mea Value	Repeat Customers (n = 440) Mean Value
Cleanliness of the room	5.6	5.7	5.5[b]
Good-quality bedding and towels	5.6	5.5	5.6
Preferred guest card options	5.5	5.4	5.7[b]
Friendly/courteous staff and employees	5.1	4.8	5.4[b]
Free VIP services	5.0	4.3	5.3[b]
Conveniently located for business	5.0	5.2	4.9[b]
In-room movie entertainment	3.6	3.3	4.5[b]

[a]Importance scale: a six-point scale ranging from 6 (extremely important) to 1 (not at all important).
[b]Mean difference in importance between the two customer groups is significant at p < .05.

used a six-point importance scale ranging from "Extremely important = 6" to "Not at all important = 1." The average importance of each criterion was calculated for both first-time and repeat customers and statistically significant differences were identified. These results do not confirm, however, whether "quality towels and bedding" should be cut back to reduce operating costs.

When shown the results, the president asked this question: "I see a lot of numbers, but what are they really telling me?" The director of marketing research quickly responded by explaining: "Among our first-time and repeat business customers, the 'quality of the hotel's towels and bedding' is considered one of the three most important selection criteria impacting their choice of a hotel to stay at when an overnight stay is required. In addition, they feel 'cleanliness of the room and offering preferred guest card options' are of comparable importance to the quality of towels and bedding. But first-time patrons place significantly higher importance on cleanliness of the room than do repeat patrons (5.7 vs. 5.5). Moreover, repeat customers place significantly more importance on the availability of our preferred guest card options than do business patrons 5.7 vs. 5.4." Based on these considerations, the executives decided they should not cut back on the quality of towels or bedding as a way to reduce expenses and improve profitability.

Interrelatedness of the Steps and the Research Process

When decision makers need assistance, they should meet with marketing researchers to begin the research process. Exhibit 2.4 shows the steps included in each phase of the research process. Although in many instances researchers follow the four phases in order, individual steps may be shifted or omitted. The complexity of the problem, the urgency for solving the problem, the cost of alternative approaches, and the clarification of information needs will directly impact how many of the steps are taken and in what order. For example, secondary data or "off-the-shelf" research studies may be found that could eliminate the need to

---

Exhibit 2.4   Phases and Steps in the Information Research Process

Phase I: Determine the Research Problem
  Step 1: Identify and clarify information needs
  Step 2: Define the research problem and questions
  Step 3: Specify research objectives and confirm the information value

Phase II: Select the Research Design
  Step 4: Determine the research design and data sources
  Step 5: Develop the sampling design and sample size
  Step 6: Examine measurement issues and scales
  Step 7: Design and pretest the questionnaire

Phase III: Execute the Research Design
  Step 8: Collect and prepare data
  Step 9: Analyze data
  Step 10: Interpret data to create knowledge

Phase IV: Communicate the Research Results
  Step 11: Prepare and present final report

collect primary data. Similarly, pretesting the questionnaire (step 7) might reveal weaknesses in some of the scales being considered (step 6), resulting in further refinement of the scales or even selection of a new research design (back to step 4).

▌◖▌ Phase I: Determine the Research Problem

The process of determining the research problem involves three interrelated activities: (1) identify and clarify information needs; (2) define the research problem and questions; and (3) specify research objectives and confirm the information value. These activities bring researchers and decision makers together based on management's recognition of the need for information to improve decision making.

Step 1: Identify and Clarify Information Needs

Generally, decision makers prepare a statement of what they believe is the problem before the researcher becomes involved. Then researchers assist decision makers to make sure the problem or opportunity has been correctly defined and the information requirements are known.

For researchers to understand the problem, they use a problem definition process. There is no one best process. But any process undertaken should include the following activities: (1) agree on the decision maker's purpose for the research, (2) understand the complete problem, (3) identify measurable symptoms, (4) select the unit of analysis, and (5) determine the relevant variables. Correctly defining the problem is an important first step in determining if research is necessary. A poorly defined problem can produce research results that are of little value.

Purpose of the Research Request Problem definition begins by determining the research purpose. Decision makers must decide whether the services of a researcher are needed. Then, the researcher begins to define the problem by asking the decision maker why the research is needed. Through questioning, researchers begin to learn what the decision maker believes the problem is. Having a general idea of why research is needed focuses attention on the circumstances surrounding the problem. Using the iceberg principle, displayed in Exhibit 2.5, helps researchers to distinguish between the symptoms and the causes

The iceberg principle holds that decision makers are aware of only 10 percent of the true problem. Frequently the perceived problem is actually a symptom that is some type of measurable market performance factor, while 90 percent of the problem is not visible to decision makers. For example, the problem may be defined as "loss of market share" when in fact the problem is ineffective advertising or a poorly trained sales force. The real problems are below the waterline of observation. If the submerged portions of the problem are omitted from the problem definition and later from the research design, then decisions based on the research may be incorrect.

Situation analysis A tool that focuses on the informal gathering of background information to familiarize the researcher with the overall complexity of the decision area.

Understand the Complete Problem Situation The decision maker and the researcher must both understand the complete problem. This is easy to say but quite often difficult to execute. To gain an understanding, researchers and decision makers should do a situation analysis of the problem. A **situation analysis** gathers and synthesizes background information to familiarize the researcher with the overall complexity of the problem. A situation analysis attempts to identify the events and factors that have led to the situation, as well as any expected future consequences. Awareness of the complete problem situation provides

Exhibit 2.5	**The Iceberg Principle**

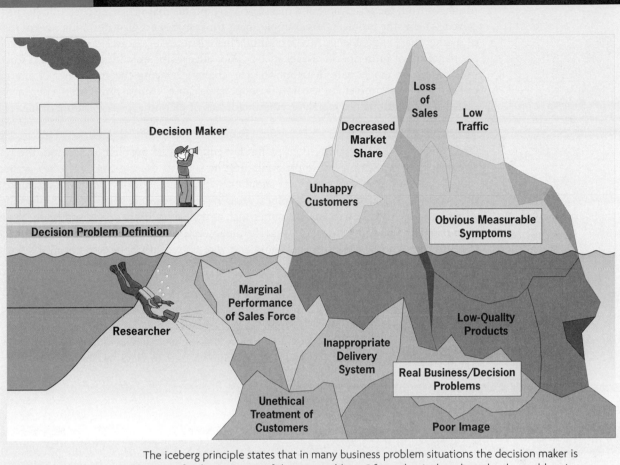

The iceberg principle states that in many business problem situations the decision maker is aware of only 10 percent of the true problem. Often what is thought to be the problem is nothing more than an observable outcome or symptom (i. e., some type of measurable market performance factor), while 90 percent of the problem is neither visible to nor clearly understood by decision makers. For example, the problem may be defined as "loss of market share" when in fact the problem is ineffective advertising or a poorly trained sales force. The real problems are submerged below the waterline of observation. If the submerged portions of the problem are omitted from the problem definition and later from the research design, then decisions based on the research may be less than optimal.

better perspectives on the decision maker's needs, the complexity of the problem, and the factors involved.

A situation analysis enhances communication between the researcher and the decision maker. The researcher must understand the client's business, including factors such as the industry, competition, product lines, markets, and in some cases production facilities. To do so, the researcher cannot rely solely on information provided by the client because many decision makers either do not know or will not disclose the information needed. Only when the researcher views the client's business objectively can the true problem be clarified.

Identify and Separate Out Symptoms Once the researcher understands the overall problem situation, he or she must work with the decision maker to separate the possible root problems from the observable and measurable symptoms that may have been initially perceived as being the problem. For example, many times managers view declining sales or loss of market share as problems. After examining these issues, the researcher may see that they are the result of more specific issues such as poor advertising execution, lack of sales force motivation, or inadequate distribution. The challenge facing the researcher is one of clarifying the real problem by separating out possible causes from symptoms. Is a decline in sales truly the problem or merely a symptom of lack of planning, poor location, or ineffective sales management?

Determine the Unit of Analysis As a fundamental part of problem definition, the researcher must determine the appropriate unit of analysis for the study. The researcher must be able to specify whether data should be collected about individuals, households, organizations, departments, geographical areas, or some combination. The unit of analysis will provide direction in later activities such as scale development and sampling. In an automobile satisfaction study, for example, the researcher must decide whether to collect data from individuals or from a husband and wife representing the household in which the vehicle is driven.

Determine the Relevant Variables The researcher and decision maker jointly determine the variables that need to be studied. The types of information needed (facts, predictions, relationships) must be identified. Exhibit 2.6 lists examples of variables that are often investigated in marketing. Variables are often measured using several related questions on a survey and may be called constructs. In some situations we refer to these variables as constructs. We discuss constructs in Chapter 8.

Exhibit 2.6	Examples of Variables/Constructs Investigated in Marketing

Variables/Constructs	Description
Brand Awareness	Percentage of respondents having heard of a designated brand; awareness could be either unaided or aided.
Brand Attitudes	The number of respondents and their intensity of feeling positive or negative toward a specific brand.
Satisfaction	How people evaluate their postpurchase consumption experience with a particular product, service, or company.
Purchase Intention	The number of people planning to buy a specified object (e.g., product or service) within a designated time period.
Importance of Factors	To what extent do specific factors influence a person's purchase choice.
Demographics	The age, gender, occupation, income level, and other characteristics of individuals providing the information.

Step 2: Define the Research Problem and Questions

Next, the researcher must redefine the problem as a research question. For the most part, this is the responsibility of the researcher. To provide background information on other firms that may have faced similar problems, the researcher conducts a review of the literature. Literature reviews are described in more detail in Chapter 3.

Breaking down the problem into research questions is one of the most important steps in the marketing research process because how the research problem is defined influences all of the remaining research steps. The researcher's task is to restate the initial variables associated with the problem in the form of key questions: how, what, where, when, or why. For example, management of Lowe's Home Improvement, Inc., was concerned about the overall image of Lowe's retail operations as well as its image among customers within the Atlanta metropolitan market. The initial research question was "Do our marketing strategies need to be modified to increase satisfaction among our current and future customers?" After Lowe's management met with consultants at Corporate Communications and Marketing, Inc., to clarify the firm's information needs, the consultants translated the initial problem into the specific questions displayed in Exhibit 2.7. With assistance of management, the consultants then identified the attributes in each research question. For example, specific "store/operation aspects" that can affect satisfaction included convenient operating hours, friendly/courteous staff, and wide assortment of products and services.

After redefining the problem into research questions and identifying the information requirements, the researcher must determine the types of data (secondary or primary) that will best answer each research problem. Although final decisions on types of data is part of Step 4 (Determine the Research Design and Data Sources), the researcher begins the process in Step 2. The researcher asks the question, "Can the specific research question be addressed with data that already exist or does the question require new data?" To answer this question, researchers consider other issues such as data availability, data quality, and budget and time constraints.

Finally, in Step 2 the researcher determines whether the information being requested is necessary. This step must be completed before going on to Step 3.

Exhibit 2.7	Initial and Redefined Research Questions for Lowe's Home Improvement, Inc.

Initial research question
Do our marketing strategies need to be modified to increase satisfaction among our current and future customer segments?

Redefined research questions
- What store/operation aspects do people believe are important in selecting a retail hardware/lumber outlet?
- How do customers evaluate Lowe's retail outlets on store/operation aspects?
- What are the perceived strengths and weaknesses of Lowe's retail operations?
- How do customers and noncustomers compare Lowe's to other retail hardware/lumber outlets within the Atlanta metropolitan area?
- What is the demographic/psychographic profile of the people who patronize Lowe's retail outlets in the Atlanta market?

Step 3: Specify Research Objectives and Confirm the Information Value

The research objectives should be based on the definition of the research problem in Step 2. Formally stated research objectives provide guidelines for determining other steps that must be taken. The assumption is if the objectives are achieved, the decision maker will have the information needed to solve the problem.

Before moving to Phase II of the research process, the decision maker and the researcher must evaluate the expected value of the information. This is not an easy task because a number of factors come into play. "Best guess" answers have to be made to the following types of questions:

"Can the information be collected at all?"
"Can the information tell the decision maker something not already known?"
"Will the information provide significant insights?"
"What benefits will be delivered by this information?"

In most cases, research should be conducted only when the expected value of the information to be obtained exceeds the cost.

◾ Phase II: Select the Research Design

The main focus of Phase II is to select the most appropriate research design to achieve the research objectives. The steps in this phase are outlined below.

Step 4: Determine the Research Design and Data Sources

The research design serves as an overall plan of the methods used to collect and analyze the data. Determining the most appropriate research design is a function of the research objectives and information requirements. The researcher must consider the types of data, the data collection method (for example, survey, observation, in-depth interview), sampling method, schedule, and budget. There are three broad categories of research designs: exploratory, descriptive, and causal. An individual research project may sometimes require a combination of exploratory, descriptive, and/or causal techniques in order to meet research objectives.

Exploratory research has one of two objectives: (1) generating insights that will help define the problem situation confronting the researcher or (2) deepening the understanding of consumer motivations, attitudes, and behavior that are not easy to access using other research methods. Examples of exploratory research methods include literature reviews of already available information; qualitative approaches such as focus groups and in-depth interviews; or pilot studies. Literature reviews will be described in Chapter 3 and exploratory research in Chapter 5.

Descriptive research involves collecting numeric data to answer research questions. Descriptive information provides answers to who, what, when, where, and how questions. In marketing, examples of descriptive information include consumer attitudes, intentions, preferences, purchase behaviors, evaluations of current marketing mix strategies, and demographics.

Descriptive studies may provide information about competitors, target markets, and environmental factors. For example, many chain restaurants conduct annual studies that describe customers' perceptions of their restaurant as well as primary competitors. These studies, referred to as either image assessment surveys or customer satisfaction surveys,

Exploratory research
Research that focuses on collecting either secondary or primary data and using an unstructured format or informal procedures to interpret them.

Descriptive research
Research that uses a set of scientific methods and procedures to collect data that describe the existing characteristics of a defined target population or market structure.

describe how customers rate different restaurants' customer service, convenience of location, food quality, and atmosphere. Some qualitative research is said to be descriptive, in the sense of providing rich or "thick" narrative description of phenomena. However, the term "descriptive research" usually means numeric rather than textual data. Descriptive designs are discussed in Chapter 6.

Causal research collects data that enables decision makers to determine cause-and-effect relationships between two or more variables. Causal research is most appropriate when the research objectives include the need to understand which variables (for example, advertising, number of salespersons, price) cause a dependent variable (for example, sales, customer satisfaction).

Understanding cause-effect relationships among market performance factors enables the decision maker to make "If—then" statements about the variables. For example, as a result of using causal research methods, the owner of a men's clothing store in Chicago can predict that, "If I increase my advertising budget by 15 percent, then overall sales volume should increase by 20 percent." Causal research designs provide an opportunity to assess and explain causality among market factors. But they often can be complex, expensive, and time-consuming. Causal research designs are discussed in Chapter 6.

Secondary and Primary Data Sources   The sources of data needed to address research problems can be classified as either secondary or primary. The sources used depend on two fundamental issues: (1) whether the data already exist, and (2) the extent to which the researcher or decision maker knows the reason(s) why the data were collected. Sources of secondary data include a company's data warehouse, public libraries and universities, Internet Web sites, or commercial data purchased from firms specializing in providing secondary information. Chapter 4 covers secondary data and sources.

Primary data are collected directly from first-hand sources to address the current information research problem. The nature and collection of primary data is covered in Chapters 5 through 9.

Step 5: Develop the Sampling Design and Sample Size

When conducting primary research consideration must be given to the sampling design. If secondary research is conducted, the researcher must still determine that the population represented by the secondary data is relevant to the current research problem. Relevancy of secondary data is covered in Chapter 4.

If predictions are to be made about market phenomena, the sample must be representative. Typically, marketing decision makers are most interested in identifying and resolving problems associated with their target markets. Therefore, researchers need to identify the relevant **target population**. In collecting data, researchers can choose between collecting data from a census or sample. In a **census,** the researcher attempts to question or observe all the members of a defined target population. For small populations a census may be the best approach.

A second approach, used when the target population is large, involves selection of a **sample** from the defined target population. Researchers must use a representative sample of the population if they wish to generalize the findings. To achieve this objective, researchers develop a sampling plan as part of the overall research design. A sampling plan serves as the blueprint for defining the appropriate target population, identifying the possible respondents, establishing the procedures for selecting the sample, and determining the appropriate sample size. Sampling plans can be classified into two general types: probability and nonprobability. In probability sampling, each member of the defined target population has a known chance of being selected. Also, probability sampling gives the

---

Causal research Research designed to collect information that will allow the researcher to model cause-and-effect relationships between two or more market (or decision) variables.

Target population A specified group of people or objects for which questions can be asked or observations made to obtain information.

Census A procedure in which the researcher attempts to question or observe all the members of a defined target population.

Sample A randomly selected subgroup of people or objects from the overall membership pool of a defined target population.

researcher the opportunity to assess sampling error. In contrast, nonprobability sampling plans cannot measure sampling error and limit the generalizability of the research findings. Qualitative research designs often use small samples, so sample members are usually hand-selected.

Sample size affects data quality and generalizability. Researchers must therefore determine how many people to include or how many objects to investigate. We discuss sampling in more detail in Chapter 7.

Step 6: Examine Measurement Issues and Scales

Step 6 is also an important step in the research process for descriptive and causal designs. It involves identifying the concepts to study and measuring the variables related to the problem. Researchers must be able to answer questions such as: How should a variable such as customer satisfaction or service quality be defined and measured? Should researchers use single- or multi-item measures to quantify variables? In Chapter 8 we discuss measurement and scaling.

Although most of the activities involved in Step 6 are related to primary research, understanding these activities is important in secondary research as well. For example, when using data mining with database variables, researchers must understand the measurement approach used in creating the database as well as any measurement biases. Otherwise, secondary data may be misinterpreted.

Step 7: Design and Pretest the Questionnaire

Designing good questionnaires is difficult. Researchers must select the correct type of questions, consider the sequence and format, and pretest the questionnaire. Pretesting obtains information from people representative of those who will be questioned in the actual survey. In a pretest respondents are asked to complete the questionnaire and comment on issues such as clarity of instructions and questions, sequence of the topics and questions, and anything that is potentially difficult or confusing. Chapter 9 covers questionnaire design.

Phase III: Execute the Research Design

The main objectives of the execution phase are to finalize all necessary data collection forms, gather and prepare the data, and analyze and interpret the data to understand the problem or opportunity. As in the first two phases, researchers must be cautious to ensure potential biases or errors are either eliminated or at least minimized.

Step 8: Collect and Prepare Data

There are two approaches to gathering data. One is to have interviewers ask questions about variables and market phenomena or to use self-completion questionnaires. The other is to observe individuals or market phenomena. Self-administered surveys, personal interviews, computer simulations, telephone interviews, and focus groups are just some of the tools researchers use to collect data.

A major advantage of questioning over observation is questioning enables researchers to collect a wider array of data. Questioning approaches can collect information about attitudes, intentions, motivations, and past behavior, which are usually invisible in observational research. In short, questioning approaches can be used to answer not just *how* a person is behaving, but *why*.

Once primary data are collected, researchers must perform several activities before data analysis. Researchers usually assign a numerical descriptor (code) to all response categories so that data can be entered into the computer. The data then must be examined for coding or data-entry errors. Chapter 11 discusses data preparation.

Step 9: Analyze Data

In Step 9, the researcher analyzes the data. Analysis procedures vary widely in sophistication and complexity, from simple frequency distributions (percentages) to summary statistics (mean, median, and mode) and multivariate data analysis. Different procedures enable the researcher to statistically test hypotheses for significant differences or correlations among several variables, evaluate data quality, and test models of cause-effect relationships. Chapters 10 through 13 provide an overview of data analysis techniques.

Step 10: Interpret Data to Create Knowledge

Knowledge is created for decision makers in Step 10. Knowledge, as we have said, is information that has meaning—information combined with judgment and interpretation to facilitate accurate decisions. Interpretation is more than a narrative description of the results. It involves integrating several aspects of the findings into conclusions that can be used to answer the research questions.

Phase IV: Communicate the Results

The last phase of the information research process focuses on reporting the research findings to management. The overall objective often is to prepare a report that is useful to a non-research-oriented person.

Step 11: Prepare and Present the Final Report

Step 11 is preparing and presenting the final research report to management. The importance of this step cannot be overstated. There are some sections that should be included in any research report: executive summary, introduction, problem definition and objectives, methodology, results and findings, and limitations of study. In some cases, the researcher not only submits a written report but also makes an oral presentation of the major findings. Chapter 14 describes how to write and present research reports.

Develop a Research Proposal

By understanding the four phases of the research process, a researcher can develop a research proposal that communicates the research framework to the decision maker. A **research proposal** is a specific document that serves as a written contract between the

Research proposal A specific document that serves as a written contract between the decision maker and the researcher.

decision maker and the researcher. It lists the activities that will be undertaken to develop the needed information, the research deliverables, how long it will take, and what it will cost.

The research proposal is not the same as a final research report. But some of the sections are similar. There is no best way to write a research proposal. Exhibit 2.8 shows the sections that should be included in most research proposals. The exhibit presents only a general outline, but an actual proposal can be found in the *Marketing Research in Action* at the end of this chapter.

Exhibit 2.8 General Outline of a Research Proposal

TITLE OF THE RESEARCH PROPOSAL

I. Purpose of the Proposed Research Project
Includes a description of the problem and research objectives.

II. Type of Study
Discusses the type of research design (exploratory, descriptive, or causal), and secondary versus primary data requirements, with justification of choice.

III. Definition of the Target Population and Sample Size
Describes the overall target population to be studied and determination of the appropriate sample size, including a justification of the size.

IV. Sample Design and Data Collection Method
Describes the sampling technique used, the method of collecting data (for example, observation or survey), incentive plans, and justifications.

V. Specific Research Instruments
Discusses the method used to collect the needed data, including the various types of scales.

VI. Potential Managerial Benefits of the Proposed Study
Discusses the expected values of the information to management and how the initial problem might be resolved, including the study's limitations.

VII. Proposed Cost for the Total Project
Itemizes the expected costs for completing the research, including a total cost figure and anticipated time frames.

VIII. Profile of the Research Company Capabilities
Briefly describes the researchers and their qualifications as well as a general overview of the company.

IX. Optional Dummy Tables of the Projected Results
Gives examples of how the data might be presented in the final report.

MARKETING RESEARCH IN ACTION
What Does an Information Research Proposal Look Like?

Excelsior Hotel Preferred Guest Card Research Proposal

The purpose of the proposed research project is to collect attitudinal, behavioral, motivational, and general demographic information to address several key questions posed by management of Benito Advertising and Johnson Properties, Inc., concerning the Excelsior Hotel Preferred Guest Card, a recently implemented marketing strategy. Key questions are as follows:

1. Is the Preferred Guest Card being used by cardholders?
2. How do cardholders evaluate the privileges associated with the card?
3. What are the perceived benefits and weaknesses of the card, and why?
4. Is the Preferred Guest Card an important factor in selecting a hotel?
5. How often and when do cardholders use their Preferred Guest Card?
6. Of those who have used the card, what privileges have been used and how often?
7. What improvements should be made regarding the card or the extended privileges?
8. How did cardholders obtain the card?
9. Should the Preferred Guest Card membership be complimentary or should cardholders pay an annual fee?
10. If there should be an annual fee, how much should it be? What would a cardholder be willing to pay?
11. What is the demographic profile of the people who have the Excelsior Hotel Preferred Guest Card?

To collect data to answer these questions, the research will be a structured, nondisguised design that includes both exploratory and descriptive research. The study will be descriptive because many questions focus on identifying perceived awareness, attitudes, and usage patterns of Excelsior Hotel Preferred Guest Card holders as well as demographic profiles. It will be exploratory because it is looking for possible improvements to the card and its privileges, the pricing structure, and the perceived benefits and weaknesses of the current card's features.

The target population consists of adults known to be current cardholders of the Excelsior Hotel Preferred Guest Card Program. This population frame is approximately 17,000 individuals across the United States. Statistically a conservative sample size would be 387. But realistically a sample of approximately 1,500 should be used to enable examination of sample subgroups. The size is based on the likely response rate for the sampling method and questionnaire design, a predetermined sampling error of ± 5% and a confidence level of 95%, administrative costs and trade-offs, and the desire for a prespecified minimum number of completed surveys.

Probability sampling will be used to draw the sample from the central cardholder database. Using a mail survey, cardholders randomly selected as prospective respondents will be mailed a personalized self-administered questionnaire. Attached to the questionnaire will be a cover letter explaining the study as well as incentives for respondent participation.

Given the nature of the study, the perceived type of cardholder, the trade-offs regarding costs and time considerations, and the use incentives to encourage respondent participation, a mail survey is more appropriate than other methods.

The questionnaire will be self-administered. That is, respondents will fill out the survey in the privacy of their home and without the presence of an interviewer. All survey questions will be pretested using a convenience sample to assess clarity of instructions, questions, and administrative time dimensions. Response scales for the questions will conform to questionnaire design guidelines and industry judgment.

Given the nature of the proposed project, the findings will enable Excelsior Hotel's management to answer questions regarding the Preferred Guest Card as well as other marketing strategy issues. Specifically, the study will help management:

- Better understand the types of people using the Preferred Guest Card and the extent of usage.
- Identify issues that suggest evaluating (and possibly modifying) current marketing strategies or tactics for the card and its privileges.
- Develop insights concerning the promotion and distribution of the card to additional segments.

Additionally, the proposed research project will initiate a customer database and information system so management can better understand customers' hotel service needs and wants. Customer-oriented databases will be useful in developing promotional strategies as well as pricing and service approaches.

Proposed Project Costs

Questionnaire/cover letter design and reproduction costs	$ 3,800
Development, typing, pretest, reproduction (1,500), envelopes (3,000)	
Sample design	2,750
Administration/data collection costs	4,800
Questionnaire packet assembly	
Postage and P.O. box	
Address labels	
Coding and pre–data analysis costs	4,000
Coding and setting of final codes	
Data entry	
Computer programming	
Data analysis and interpretation costs	7,500
Written report and presentation costs	4,500
Total maximum proposed project cost*	$ 27,350

*Costing policy: Some items may cost more or less than what is stated on the proposal. Cost reductions, if any, will be passed on to the client. Additionally, there is a ± 10% cost margin for data collection and analysis activities depending on client changes of the original analysis requirements.

Research for this proposed project will be conducted by the Marketing Resource Group (MRG), a full-service marketing research firm located in Tampa, Florida, that has conducted studies for many Fortune 1000 companies. The principal researcher and project coordinator will be Mr. Alex Smith, Senior Project Director at MRG. Mr. Smith holds a PhD in Marketing from Louisiana State University, an MBA from Illinois State University, and a BS from Southern Illinois University. With 25 years of marketing research experience, he has designed and coordinated numerous projects in the consumer packaged-goods products, hotel/resort, retail banking, automobile, and insurance industries. He specializes in projects that focus on customer satisfaction, service/product quality, market segmentation, and general consumer attitudes and behavior patterns as well as interactive electronic marketing technologies. In addition, he has published numerous articles on theoretical and pragmatic research topics.

Hands-On Exercise

1. If this proposal is accepted, will it achieve the objectives of management?
2. Is the target population being interviewed the appropriate one?
3. Are there other questions that should be asked in the project?

Summary

Describe the major environmental factors influencing marketing research.

Several key environmental factors have significant impact on changing the tasks, responsibilities, and efforts associated with marketing research practices. Marketing research has risen from a supporting role within organizations to being integral in strategic planning. The Internet and e-commerce, gatekeeper technologies and data privacy legislation, and new global market structure expansions are all forcing researchers to balance their use of secondary and primary data to assist decision makers in solving decision problems and taking advantage of opportunities. Researchers need to improve their ability to use technology-driven tools and databases. There are also greater needs for faster data acquisition and retrieval, analysis, and interpretation of cross-functional data and information among decision-making teams within global market environments.

Discuss the research process and explain the various steps.

The information research process has four major phases, identified as (1) determine of the research problem, (2) select the appropriate research design, (3) execute the research design, and (4) communicate the results. To achieve the overall objectives of each phase, researchers must be able to successfully execute eleven interrelated task steps: (1) identify and clarify information needs, (2) define the research problem and questions, (3) specify research objectives and confirm the information value, (4) determine the research design and data sources, (5) develop the sampling design and sample size, (6) examine measurement issues and scales, (7) design and pretest questionnaires, (8) collect and prepare data, (9) analyze data, (10) interpret data to create knowledge, and (11) prepare and present the final report.

Distinguish between exploratory, descriptive, and causal research designs.

The main objective of exploratory research designs is to create information that the researcher or decision maker can use to (1) gain a clear understanding of the problem; (2) define or redefine the initial problem, separating the symptoms from the causes; (3) confirm the problem and objectives; or (4) identify the information requirements Exploratory research designs are often intended to provide preliminary insight for follow-up quantitative research. However, sometimes qualitative exploratory methods are used as standalone techniques because the topic under investigation requires in-depth understanding of a complex web of consumer culture, psychological motivations, and behavior. For some research topics, quantitative research may be too superficial or it may elicit responses from consumers that are rationalizations rather than true reasons for purchase decisions and behavior.

Descriptive research designs produce numeric data to describe existing characteristics (for example, attitudes, intentions, preferences, purchase behaviors, evaluations of current marketing mix strategies) of a defined target population. The researcher looks for answers to how, who, what, when, and where questions. Information from descriptive designs allows decision makers to draw inferences about their customers, competitors, target markets, environmental factors, or other phenomena.

Finally, causal research designs are most useful when the research objectives include the need to understand why market phenomena happen. The focus of causal research is to collect data that enables the decision maker or researcher to model cause-and-effect relationships between two or more variables.

Identify and explain the major components of a research proposal.

Once the researcher understands the different phases and task steps of the information research process, he or she can develop a research proposal. The proposal serves as a contract between the researcher and decision maker. There are nine sections suggested for inclusion: (1) purpose of the proposed research project; (2) type of study; (3) definition of the target population and sample size; (4) sample design, technique, and data collection method; (5) research instruments; (6) potential managerial benefits of the proposed study; (7) proposed cost structure for the project; (8) profile of the researcher and company; and (9) dummy tables of the projected results.

 ## Key Terms and Concepts

Causal research 33

Census 33

Descriptive research 32

Exploratory research 32

Gatekeeper technology 22

Information research process 23

Internet 22

Knowledge 26

Primary data 22

Research proposal 36

Sample 33

Scientific method 26

Secondary data 22

Situation analysis 28

Target population 33

Review Questions

1. Identify the significant changes taking place in today's business environment that are forcing management decision makers to rethink their views of marketing research. Also discuss the potential impact that these changes might have on marketing research activities.
2. In the business world of the 21st century, will it be possible to make critical marketing decisions without marketing research? Why or why not?
3. How are management decision makers and information researchers alike? How are they different? How might the differences be reduced between these two types of professionals?

4. Comment on the following statements:
   a. The primary responsibility for determining whether marketing research activities are necessary is that of the marketing research specialist.
   b. The information research process serves as a blueprint for reducing risks in making marketing decisions.
   c. Selecting the most appropriate research design is the most critical task in the research process.
5. Design a research proposal that can be used to address the following decision problem: "Should the Marriott Hotel in Pittsburgh, Pennsylvania, reduce the quality of its towels and bedding in order to improve the profitability of the hotel's operations?"

Discussion Questions

1. For each of the four phases of the information research process, identify the corresponding steps and develop a set of questions that a researcher should attempt to answer.

2. What are the differences between exploratory, descriptive, and causal research designs? Which design type would be most appropriate to address the following question: "How satisfied or dissatisfied are customers with the automobile repair service offerings of the dealership from which they purchased their new 2007 BMW?"

3. When should a researcher use a probability sampling method rather than a nonprobability method?

4. **EXPERIENCE THE INTERNET.** Go to the Gallup Poll Organization's home page at www.gallup.com. Select the "Take poll" option and review the results by selecting the "Findings" option. After reviewing the information, outline the different phases and task steps of the information research process that might have been used in the Gallup Internet Poll.

Part 2

Designing the Marketing Research Project

Literature Reviews and Hypotheses

Chapter 3

Learning Objectives   After reading this chapter, you will be able to:

1. Explain why researchers conduct literature reviews.
2. Describe how to conduct a literature review.
3. Discuss conceptualization and its role in model development.
4. Understand the difference between independent and dependent variables.
5. Describe hypothesis testing.

Google and eBay Form New "Click-To-Call" Alliance

After extensive secondary research and literature review concerning online customers' attitudes, preferences, and search and purchase behaviors, researchers at Google and eBay, the two prominent Internet players, met to form a "Click-To-Call" alliance. The alliance calls for Google to begin selling text advertising exclusively for eBay outside the United States and help buyers instantly call an online seller to do business, according to Google. Advanced "click-to-call" technology will enable eBay customers to call eBay merchants or Google advertisers by simply clicking a link on a Web page. Ebay's CEO believes the alliance will provide a whole new way for buyers and sellers to connect online and create a significant revenue stream for eBay and Google. Both organizations concluded the available research information strongly supports the opportunity to provide a new online service that lets Web surfers place telephone calls through their computers or handheld devices when they click on a link in an Internet ad.

Value of Literature Reviews and Hypotheses

Literature review A comprehensive examination of available information that is related to your research topic.

A **literature review** is a comprehensive examination of available information that is related to your research topic. When conducting a literature review, researchers locate information relevant to the research problems and issues at hand. Literature reviews have the following objectives: provide background information for the current study; clarify thinking about the research problem and questions you are studying; reveal whether information already exists that addresses the issue of interest; help to define important constructs of interest to the study; and suggest sampling and other methodological approaches that have been successful in studying similar topics.

Reviewing available literature helps researchers stay abreast of the latest thinking that is related to their topic of interest. In most industries, there are some widely known and cited studies. For example, the Internet Advertising Bureau (IAB) is an industry organization whose members are a Who's Who of online publishers and advertisers. The IAB has conducted a number of high profile studies that are well-known to industry members and available on their Web site. The studies report what works and doesn't work in online advertising. Analysts conducting research in the area of online advertising who are not familiar with major published studies, such as those conducted by the IAB, would likely have difficulty establishing their expertise with clients, many of whom are aware of these studies.

Literature reviews provide information that enables researchers to better understand a research problem or opportunity. Often researchers develop ideas from the literature that lead to hypotheses. Whether hypotheses are developed or not, literature reviews at minimum provide background information for beginning the research process.

Reasons for Conducting a Literature Review

An important reason for doing a literature review is that it can help clarify and define the research problem and research questions. For example, suppose an online advertiser wants to study how consumer engagement with online advertising affects attitude toward the brand, Web site visits, and actual purchase behavior. A literature review would uncover other published studies on the topic of consumer engagement, as well as the different ways to define and measure consumer engagement. For example, consumer engagement can be defined as any interaction with an ad, which may include every interactive action from a simple accidental mouseover of an ad, to participating in a question and answer quiz within an ad, to clicking the ad to visit the Web site. Or consumer engagement might be defined in a way that excludes passive interaction such as an accidental mouseover and includes only active involvement with an ad. Through a review of the literature together with conversations with the client, researchers can decide how to conceptualize consumer engagement in a way that is relevant to the research problem at hand.

A literature review can also suggest research hypotheses to investigate. For example, a literature review may show that frequent Internet shoppers are more likely to be engaged with online advertising; that engagement increases positive attitudes toward the brand; that younger people are more likely to become engaged with an online ad; or that high involvement product categories, such as cars, are more likely to result in consumer engagement than are low involvement categories, such as paper towels. Most of the studies, considered alone, will not be definitive, and may not provide answers to specific research questions. But they are likely to provide some issues and relationships to investigate.

Importantly, literature reviews can identify scales to measure variables and research methodologies that have been used successfully to study similar topics. For instance, if a researcher wants to measure the usability of a Web site, a literature review will locate published studies that suggest checklists of important features of usable sites. Reviewing previous studies will save researchers time and effort because new scales will not need to be developed from scratch. Similarly, researchers can review successful published studies to see what methodologies (focus groups, surveys, or experiments) have been used to research a particular topic. For example, from reviewing published work, researchers interested in Web site usability would quickly find that observation and moderated interaction are preferred to study this particular topic and that experiments utilizing different versions of the Web site (which is called A/B testing) can be useful as well if implemented with care. Focus groups and surveys are not preferred methods because participants' memories are not good enough to give usability experts the specific information they need to improve a Web site and because what users think they might like is different from what they actually like.[1]

Conducting the Review

Literature reviews may include a search of both popular and scholarly sources. With the advent of the Internet, writing a literature review has become both easier and harder. It is easier in the sense that a wide variety of material is instantly available. Thus, finding relevant published studies has become easier than ever. But wading through the results to find the studies that are actually of interest can be overwhelming. Thus, it is important to narrow your topic so that you can focus your efforts before conducting a search for relevant information.

Popular Sources

Many popular sources are available both in the library and on the Internet. Examples of popular sources include *The Wall Street Journal, BusinessWeek, Forbes, Harvard Business Review, Business 2.0,* and so on. Most popular articles are written for newspapers and periodicals by journalists or freelance writers. Popular sources are often more current than scholarly sources and are written using less technical language. However, the findings and ideas expressed in popular sources often involve secondhand reporting of information. Moreover, while scholarly findings are reviewed by peers prior to publication, findings reported in journalistic publications receive much less scrutiny.[2]

Many business students are already familiar with the business articles and resources offered by ABI/Inform or Lexus/Nexus. These databases can be searched through online library gateways at most colleges and universities. The databases cover many publications that are "walled off" and thus not available through major search engines. For example, both *The New York Times* and *The Wall Street Journal* provide excellent business news. However, search engines currently do not access the archives of these and other prominent newspapers. While the archives of these and other publications are often available through the newspapers' Web site, the articles are usually offered on a pay-per-view basis. Most libraries pay for access to many newspaper and business publications through arrangements with ABI/Inform and Lexus/Nexus.

A great deal of information is available on the Internet without subscription to library databases. Search engines continually catalog this information and return the most relevant and most popular Web sites for particular search terms. Google, Yahoo! and MSN are all good at locating published studies. Before performing an online search, it is useful to brainstorm several relevant keywords to use in search engines. For example, if you are interested in word-of-mouth marketing, several terms might make useful search terms: *buzz marketing, underground marketing,* and *stealth marketing.*

Some popular sources are publications staffed by writers who are marketing practitioners and analysts. For instance, the contributors at **www.Clickz.com** who write articles about a wide variety of online marketing issues are specialists in the areas they cover. Therefore, the opinions and analyses they offer are timely and informed by experience. Nevertheless, their opinions, while reflective of their experience and in-depth knowledge, have not been investigated with the same level of care as those available in scholarly publications.

One more possible source is marketing blogs. Many marketing writers and analysts have their own blogs. These sources must be chosen very carefully, because anyone can write and post a blog. Only a blog that is written by a respected expert is worthy of mention in your literature review. MarketingSherpa.com has an annual list of the best marketing blogs. Some of them may be relevant to your topic (see Exhibit 3.1). Good blogs that are written by high profile practitioners and analysts are often provocative and up-to-date. They suggest perspectives that are worthy of consideration in the design and execution of your study. Blog writers may also provide insightful commentary on and critical analysis of published studies and practices that are currently being discussed by experts in the field. However, even blogs written by the most respected analysts express viewpoints that are speculative and unproven. When writing your literature review you will want to be clear in noting that these blogs are often more opinion than fact.

All popular sources you find on the Web need to be carefully evaluated. Check the "About Us" portion of the Web site to see who is publishing the articles or studies to see if the source of the material is reputable. Another issue to consider is that marketing studies found on Web sites sometimes promote the business interest of the publisher. For instance, studies published by the Internet Advertising Bureau have to be carefully scrutinized for methodological bias because the IAB is a trade organization that represents businesses that will benefit when Internet advertising grows. Ideally, you are looking for the highest quality information by experts in the field. The more sources are cited or mentioned, the more likely studies or blogs are to be credible.[3]

Scholarly Research

You may want to search your library for scholarly articles that are relevant to your research topic. But an online search for the same information is easier and more consistent with the way you are used to searching. Google has a specialized search engine dedicated to scholarly articles called Google Scholar. Using Google's home page search function rather than Google Scholar will identify some scholarly articles, but will include many other kinds of results that make scholarly articles difficult to identify. You can find Google Scholar by following the "more" link from their home page. If you go to Google Scholar, and type "online shopping," for instance, Google Scholar (**www.Scholar.Google.com**) will list published studies that address online shopping. Google Scholar counts how many times a study is referenced by another document on the Web and lists that number in the search results (the result says "cited by" and lists the number of Web site citations). The number of citation counts on the Web is one measure of the importance of the article to the field.

Some of the studies listed by Google Scholar will be available online from any location. You may have access to others only when you are at school or through a library gateway. Most colleges and universities pay fees for access to scholarly published papers. If you are on campus while you are accessing these sources, many journal publishers read the IP address of the computer you are using and grant access based on your location. In particular, articles in JSTOR, which hosts many of the top marketing journals, may be accessible through any computer linked to your campus network. However, some journals require you to go through the library gateway to obtain access whether you are on or off campus.

Both popular and scholarly sources can be tracked using Web-based bookmarking tools such as Del.icio.us.com and Linksnarf.com that will help you organize your sources. Using

Exhibit 3.1	MarketingSherpa.com's Best Marketing Blogs

Best Marketing Blogs

Best Blog on General Marketing Topics
Seth Godin's Blog, by Seth Godin
http://sethgodin.typepad.com/

Best B-to-B Marketing Blog
B2B Lead Generation Blog,
by Brian Carroll
**http://blog.startwithalead.
com/weblog/**

Best Blog on Email Marketing
Chris Baggott's Email Marketing Best
Practices, by Chris Baggott
**http://exacttarget.typepad.
com/chrisbaggott/**

Best Blog on Search Marketing
Search Engine Roundtable, by
Bloggers include: Barry Schwartz,
Benjamin Pfeiffer, Chris Boggs, Kim
Krause, Shawn Hogan, Ignacio
Hernandez, Morgan Carey & Dan Thies
http://www.seroundtable.com/

Best Blog on Advertising
Adrants, by Steve Hall
http://www.adrants.com/

Best Blog on Marketing to a Specific
Consumer Demographic
Andy Wibbels, the Original Blogging
Evangelist, by Andy Wibbels
http://andywibbels.com/

Best blog on Affiliate Marketing
ReveNews, by Larry Adams et al.
http://www.revenews.com/

Best Blog on the Topic of PR
Active Voice, by Matt "PodBoy"
**http://podboy.typepad.com/
techvoice/**

Best Blog on Small Business Marketing
Duct Tape Marketing, by John Jantsch
**http://www.ducttapemarketing.
com/weblog.php**

Honorable Mentions: Five More Blogs That Deserve Your Attention

Adland, by (Nom de Guerres): Ask
Dabitch, Clayton Claymore,
Caffeinegoddess and Robblink
http://commercial-archive.com/

Future Now: A Day in the Life of a
Persuasion Architect, by Howard
Kaplan, Anthony C. Garcia Jr., Dave
Young & Jim Novo
http://persuasion.typepad.com/

StartupNation, by Joel Welsh, Jonathan
Hudson, Joan Isabella & Sloan Brothers
http://www.startupnation.com/blog/

The WebMarketCentral Blog,
by Tom Pick
**http://webmarketcentral.
blogspot.com/**

Ypulse, by Anastasia Goodstein
http://www.ypulse.com/

Source: MarketingSherpa.com, "MarketingSherpa's Top 10 Best Blogs and Best Podcast of 2006: Readers' Choice Award Results," June 27, 2006, accessed August 16, 2006.

these bookmarking tools, you can keep track of the links for research projects, take notes about each of the sites, and "tag" the links with your choice of search terms to make future retrieval of the source easy. Bookmarking tools also allow exchanges with a social network, so they can be very helpful in sharing sources with multiple members of the research team.

Divergent perspectives and findings need to be included in your literature review. It is likely the findings of some studies will be inconsistent with each other. These differences may include estimates of descriptive data, for example, the percentage of people who buy from catalog marketers, the amount of dollars spent on advertising, or online retail sales numbers. Reports may also disagree as to the nature of theoretical relationships between variables. You need to dig into the details of the methodology that is used to define variables and collect data. For example, differences in estimates of online retail spending are caused by several factors. Three major causes of discrepancies in online retail estimates are (1) the inclusion (or not) of travel spending, which is a major category of online spending; (2) methodological differences—for instance, some reports make estimates based on surveying retailers while others survey customers; and (3) there is always some degree of sampling error. It is not enough to say that reports differ in their findings. You want to make intelligent judgments about the causes of the differences.

◾ Developing a Conceptual Model

Conceptualization Development of a model that shows variables and hypothesized or proposed relationships between variables.

In addition to providing background for your research problem, literature reviews can also help you **conceptualize** a model that summarizes the relationships you hope to predict. If you are performing purely exploratory research, you will not need to develop a model before conducting your research. Once you have turned your research objectives into research questions, the information needs can be listed and the data collection instrument can be designed. However, if one or more of your research questions require you to investigate relationships between variables, then you need to conceptualize these relationships. The conceptualization process is aided by developing a picture of your model that shows the predicted causal relationship between variables.

Variables, Constructs, and Relationships

Variable An observable item that is used as a measure on a questionnaire.

Construct An unobservable concept that is measured by a group of related variables.

To conceptualize and test a model, you must have three elements: variables, constructs, and relationships. A **variable** is an observable item that is used as a measure on a questionnaire. Variables have concrete properties and are measured directly. Examples of variables include gender, marital status, company name, number of employees, how frequently a particular brand is purchased, and so on. In contrast, a **construct** is an unobservable, abstract concept that is measured indirectly by a group of related variables. Some examples of commonly measured constructs in marketing are service quality, value, customer satisfaction, and brand attitude. Constructs that represent characteristics of respondents may also be measured, for example, innovativeness, opinion leadership, and deal proneness. In Exhibit 3.2, we show a group of items that can be used to measure the construct "market maven," defined as an individual who has a lot of information about products and who actively shares that information.

Relationships Associations between two or more variables.

Independent variable The variable or construct that predicts or explains the outcome variable of interest.

Dependent variable The variable or construct researchers are seeking to explain.

Relationships are associations between two or more variables. When modeling causal relationships, variables or constructs in relationships can be either independent or dependent variables. An **independent variable** is the variable or construct that predicts or explains the outcome variable of interest. A **dependent variable** is the variable or construct researchers are seeking to explain. For example, if technology optimism and household income predict Internet adoption by seniors, then technology optimism and household income are independent variables, and Internet adoption is the dependent variable.

Your literature review will help you identify, define, and measure constructs. Nevertheless, after conducting a literature review and consulting secondary research (see Chapter 4) an analyst may feel there is not enough information to design a full-scale study. There may be several sources of uncertainty: the definition of important constructs; the identification of variables or items that will measure the construct; and the identification of constructs that may have an important role in affecting an outcome or dependent variable of interest.

Exhibit 3.2	Measuring the Marketing Maven Construct

1. I like introducing new brands and products to my friends.
2. I like helping people by providing them with information about many kinds of products.
3. People ask me for information about products, places to shop, or sales.
4. If someone asked where to get the best buy on several types of products, I could tell him or her where to shop.
5. My friends think of me as a good source of information when it comes to new products or sales.
6. Think about a person who has information about a variety of products and likes to share this information with others. This person knows about new products, sales, stores, and so on, but does not necessarily feel he or she is an expert on one particular product. How well would you say that this description fits you?

Source: Lawrence F. Feick and Linda L. Price, "The Marketing Maven: A Diffuser of Marketplace Information," *Journal of Marketing* 51 (1987), pp. 83–97.

For example, an early study of online retailing had as its objective the identification and modeling of constructs that would affect online customer satisfaction and repurchase behavior. A literature review revealed there were existing studies and measures of customer satisfaction and quality in services and in "bricks and mortar" retailing settings. While these published studies are useful in conceptualizing satisfaction with online retailing, researchers realized the online retailing environment likely had unique aspects that might affect consumer ratings of satisfaction. Thus, researchers used qualitative methods (Chapter 5) and pilot testing before designing a full-scale study.

In planning the online retailing study, the qualitative methods were utilized in an exploratory fashion. In focus group interviews, online customers were asked what attributes are important to them when shopping online. The focus groups were followed by a pilot study in which respondents rated the importance of a number of attributes when shopping online. By conducting exploratory research and a pilot study, researchers identified four major constructs of importance to online shoppers: Web site design and functioning, fulfillment (accurate on-time delivery), customer service, and privacy/security.[1] Based on the exploratory research, researchers also developed items (questions) for a questionnaire to measure the four factors. It is important to note that the focus groups and pilot survey were necessary only because the context of online retailing satisfaction was not yet well researched at the time the study was conducted. Otherwise, a literature review might have been adequate to prepare for the study.

Relationships and Hypotheses

Once researchers have identified and defined variables and constructs, they can begin thinking about how variables may be related to each other. The literature review and secondary research often suggest variables to include in the investigation. For example, if researchers want to predict who will adopt a new technological innovation, there is a great deal of research and theory on this topic. The research suggests, for example, that more educated, higher income individuals who are open to learning are more likely to adopt new technologies. The hypotheses could be summarized as follows:

- Individuals with more education are more likely to adopt a new technological innovation.
- Individuals who are more open to learning are more likely to adopt a new technological innovation.
- Individuals who have more income are more likely to adopt a new technological innovation.
- Individuals who have higher technology discomfort are less likely to adopt a new technological innovation.

Positive relationship An association between two variables in which they increase or decrease together.

Negative relationship An association between two variables in which one increases while they other decreases.

The first three hypotheses suggest positive relationships. A **positive relationship** between two variables is when the two variables increase or decrease together. But negative relationships can be hypothesized as well. **Negative relationships** suggest that as one variable increases, the other one decreases. For example, the last hypothesis in the list above suggests that individuals exhibiting higher technology discomfort are less likely to adopt a new technological innovation.

In addition to the literature review, experience with a research context can help decision makers and researchers develop hypotheses. An organization may accumulate a great deal of experience over time with a particular research context which is useful to conceptualizing relationships for future studies. For example, restaurant owners know a lot about their customers as do managers of retail clothing stores. They learn this over time by observing customers' behavior and listening to the questions they ask.

As we mentioned above, to more effectively communicate relationships and variables researchers follow a process called *conceptualization*. Conceptualization involves: (1) identifying the variables for your research, (2) specifying hypotheses and relationships, and (3) preparing a diagram (conceptual model) that visually represents the relationships you will study. The end result of conceptualization is a visual display of the hypothesized relationships using a box and arrows diagram. This diagram is called a *conceptual model*. The model suggested by the four hypotheses we developed about new technology adoption is shown in Exhibit 3.3.

If a literature review and available secondary data are insufficient to suggest strong candidates for explaining dependent variables of interest, then exploratory research will be necessary (see Chapter 5). Exploratory investigations enable analysts to sit down with respondents and find out what they are thinking and incorporate what they learn into further research. The research then takes place in stages. In the first stage, researchers use exploratory research to identify variables, constructs, and relationships that can then be followed up in another study. For example, researchers wanted to determine how a firm's own employees responded to advertising that was directed at consumers. They reviewed the literature and found some anecdotal evidence about advertising campaigns that promised more than employees could deliver. However, they decided the available literature was too limited to suggest enough ideas to explain how employees might respond to advertising. As a result, the researchers undertook exploratory research at four companies. They conducted focus groups where they showed employees current organizational ads and asked employees what they thought when they saw the ads. Based on the focus groups, researchers developed three propositions or hypotheses to test. Employees will respond to ads more positively when:

- Ads are perceived to accurately represent the organization and its employees.
- Ads show values that are congruent with employees' personal values.
- Ads are believed to be effective with the company's customers in creating sales.[5]

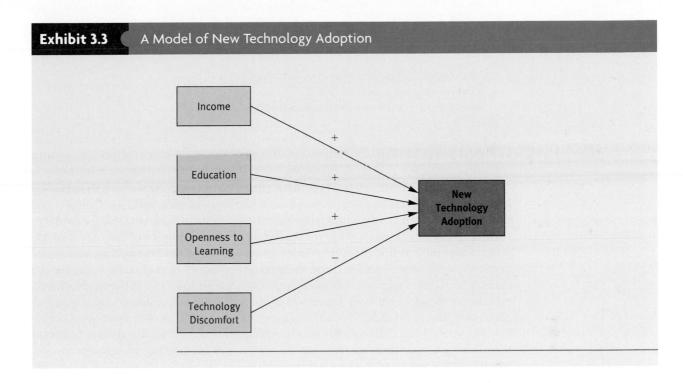

Exhibit 3.3   A Model of New Technology Adoption

Continuing Case: Santa Fe Grill: Developing Research Questions and Hypotheses

The owners have concluded that they need to know more about their customers and target market. To obtain a better understanding of each of these issues they logged on to the Yahoo.com and Google.com search engines. They also spent some time examining trade literature. From this review of the literature, some "Best Practices" guidelines were found on how restaurants should be run. Below is a summary of what was found:

- If you do not have enough customers, first examine the quality of your food, the items on your menu, and the service.
- Examine and compare your lunch and dinner customers and menu for differences.
- Your wait staff should be consistent with the image of your restaurant. How your employees act and behave is very important. They must be well groomed, knowledgeable, polite, and speak clearly and confidently.
- Menu items should represent a good value for the money.
- Service should be efficient, timely, polished, and cordial.
- The cleanliness and appearance of your restaurant strongly influences the success of your business.
- Follow the marketing creed of "Underpromise and overdeliver!"
- Empower your employees to make decisions to keep your customers happy. Train your employees on what to do to resolve customer complaints instead of coming to the manager.
- Create a pleasant dining atmosphere, including furniture and fixtures, decorations, lighting, music, and temperature.
- Learn more about your female customers. For family outings and special occasions, women make the decision on where to dine about 75 percent of the time.

With this information, the owners next need to specify the research questions and hypotheses to be examined.

1. What research questions should be examined?
2. What hypotheses should be tested?
3. Should the literature search be expanded? If yes, how?

Hypothesis Testing

Hypothesis An empirically testable though yet unproven statement developed in order to explain phenomena.

Once researchers have developed hypotheses, they can be tested. As we have already seen, **hypotheses** suggest relationships between variables. Suppose we hypothesize that men and women drink different amounts of coffee during the day during finals. The independent variable in this case is gender, while the dependent variable is number of cups of coffee. We collect data and find that the average number of cups of coffee consumed by female students per day during finals is 6.1, and the average number of cups of coffee consumed by males is 4.7. Is this finding meaningful? The answer appears to be straightforward (after all, 6.1 is larger than 4.7), but sampling error could have distorted the results enough so that we conclude there are no real differences between men's and women's coffee consumption.

Intuitively, if the difference between two means is large, one would be more confident there is in fact a true difference between the sample means of the two groups. But another important component to consider is the size of the sample used to calculate the means, because the size of the sample and the variance in the sample affect sample error. To take sample error into account we must place an interval around our estimate of the mean. Once we do this, the two means may not be different enough to conclude that men and women consume different amounts of coffee during finals.

Null hypothesis A statistical hypothesis that is tested for possible rejection under the assumption that it is true.

In hypothesis development, the **null hypothesis** states that there is no relationship between the variables. In this case, the null hypothesis would be there is no difference between male and female coffee consumption. The null hypothesis is the one that is always tested by statisticians and market researchers. Another hypothesis, called the **alternative hypothesis,** states that there is a relationship between two variables. If the null hypothesis is accepted, we conclude that the variables are not related. If the null hypothesis is rejected, we find support for the alternative hypothesis, that the two variables are related.

Alternative hypothesis The hypothesis contrary to the null hypothesis, it usually suggests that two variables are related.

Parameter The true value of a variable.

Sample statistic The value of a variable that is estimated from a sample.

A null hypothesis refers to a population parameter, not a sample statistic. The **parameter** is the actual value of a variable, which can only be known by collecting data from every member of the relevant population (in this case, all male and female college students). The **sample statistic** is an estimate of the population parameter. The data will show that either the two variables are related (reject the null hypothesis) or that once sampling error is considered there is not a large enough relationship to conclude the variables are related. In the latter case, the researcher would not be able to detect a statistically significant difference between the two groups of coffee drinkers. It is important to note that failure to reject the null hypothesis does not necessarily mean the null hypothesis is true. This is because data from another sample of the same population could produce different results.

In marketing research the null hypothesis is developed so that its rejection leads to an acceptance of the alternative hypothesis. Usually, the null hypothesis is notated as H_0 and the alternative hypothesis is notated as H_1. If the null hypothesis (H_0) is rejected, then the alternative hypothesis (H_1) is accepted. The alternative hypothesis always bears the burden of proof.

Marketing Research in Action
The Santa Fe Grill

As mentioned earlier, the owners of the Santa Fe Grill Mexican Restaurant were not happy with the slow growth rate of the restaurant's operations and realized they needed to obtain a better understanding of three important concepts: *customer satisfaction, restaurant store image,* and *customer loyalty.* Using, in part, their practical business knowledge and what they had learned as business students at the University of Nebraska, Lincoln, they developed several key questions:

1. What makes up customer satisfaction?
2. How are restaurant store images created?
3. How does one create customer loyalty?
4. What are the interrelationships between customer satisfaction, store images, and customer loyalty?

Not really knowing where to begin, they contacted one of their past professors, who taught marketing research at the university, to gain some guidance. Their old professor suggested they begin with a literature review of both scholarly and popular press research sources. Using their Internet search skills, they went to Google Scholar (**www.Scholar.Google.com**) and *Business 2.0* (**www.Business2.com**) and found there a wealth of past research and popular press articles on customer satisfaction, store images, and customer loyalty.

After reviewing a number of articles, the owners understood that *customer satisfaction* relates to a restaurant's ability to meet or exceed its customers' dining expectations of a variety of important restaurant attributes such as "food quality," "acceptable service," "competitive prices," "restaurant atmosphere," and "friendly/courteous staff." Regarding *restaurant store image,* they learned that image is really an overall impression expressed in either a positive or negative judgment about the restaurant's operations. In addition, *customer loyalty* reflects customers' willingness to "recommend a restaurant" to their friends, family, and/or neighbors," as well as provide positive word of mouth.

Hands-On Exercise

The owners need your help as follows:

1. Based on your understanding of the material presented in Chapter 3 and the above stated key research questions, should the owners of the Santa Fe Grill go back and restate their questions? If "no," why not? If "yes," why? Suggest how the research questions could be restated.
2. Regarding the owners' desire to understand the interrelationships between *customer satisfaction, restaurant store image,* and *customer loyalty,* develop a set of hypotheses that might be used to investigate these interrelationships.

Summary

Explain why researchers conduct literature reviews.

A literature review is a comprehensive examination of available information that is related to your research topic. When conducting a literature review, researchers locate information relevant to the research problems and issues at hand. Literature reviews have the following objectives: provide background information for the current study; clarify thinking about the research problem and questions you are studying; reveal whether information already exists that addresses the issue of interest; help to define important constructs of interest to the study; and suggest sampling and other methodological approaches that have been successful in studying similar topics.

Describe how to conduct a literature review.

Conducting a literature review is tedious and time consuming, often taking much longer than originally anticipated. The objective of a literature review is to summarize the existing research related to your problem. The review includes findings reported by different authors, their methodology, and how their findings are similar as well as different from your own. For research findings that are similar you likely will point out why. Where the findings are different, you should suggest reasons for this as well. In all cases you should indicate how their findings influenced your own research. A good literature review demonstrates the researcher has an excellent understanding of previous work and how it is related. Citing an extensive list of references is not good enough and could be risky. Researchers must clearly interpret previous research and show the linkages.

Discuss conceptualization and its role in model development.

Literature reviews can also help to conceptualize a model that summarizes the relationships you hope to predict. If you are performing purely exploratory research, you will not need to develop a model before conducting your research. Once you have turned your research objectives into research questions, the information needs can be listed and the data collection instrument can be designed. However, if one or more of your research questions require you to investigate relationships between variables, then you need to conceptualize these relationships. The conceptualization process is aided by developing a picture of your model that shows the predicted causal relationships between variables. To conceptualize and test a model, you must have three elements: variables, constructs, and relationships.

Understand the difference between independent and dependent variables.

A variable is an observable item that is used as a measure on a questionnaire. A construct is an unobservable concept that is measured by a group of related variables. Some examples of commonly measured constructs in marketing include service quality, value, customer satisfaction, and brand attitude. Constructs that represent characteristics of respondents may also be measured, for example, innovativeness, opinion leadership, and deal proneness. Relationships are associations between two or more variables. The relationships are often illustrated visually by drawing conceptual models. When modeling relationships, variables or constructs depicted in relationships can be either independent or dependent variables. An independent variable is the variable or construct that predicts or explains the outcome variable of interest. A dependent variable is the variable or construct researchers are seeking to explain. For example, if technology optimism and household income predict Internet adoption by seniors, then technology optimism and household income are independent variables, and Internet adoption is the dependent variable.

Describe hypothesis testing.

A hypothesis is an empirically testable but unproven statement about relationships between variables. Hypotheses enable researchers to examine relationships between variables. The null hypothesis states that there is no relationship between the two or more variables in your conceptual model. Another hypothesis, called the alternative hypothesis, states that there is a relationship between two variables.

Key Terms and Concepts

Review Questions

1. What are the various reasons to conduct a literature review?
2. What are the major sources of information for a literature review? What are the advantages and disadvantages of using these sources?
3. What should you look for in assessing whether or not an Internet resource is credible?
4. A researcher develops hypotheses which suggest that consumers like ads better when they (1) are truthful, (2) creative, and (3) present relevant information. Picture the conceptual model that would show these relationships. Which variables are the independent and dependent variables?
5. What are relationships? What is a positive relationship? What is a negative relationship? Give an example of a positive and a negative relationship.
6. What is the difference between a parameter and a sample statistic?
7. If you are interested in finding out whether or not young adults (21–34 years old) are more likely to buy products online than older adults (35 or more years old), how would you phrase your null hypothesis? What is the implicit alternative hypothesis accompanying your null hypothesis?

Discussion Questions

1. It is possible to design a study, collect and analyze data, and write a report without conducting a literature review. What are the dangers and drawbacks of conducting your research without doing a literature review? In your judgment, do the drawbacks outweigh the advantages? Why or why not?
2. **EXPERIENCE THE INTERNET.** Visit 4 or 5 of the marketing blogs listed in Exhibit 3.1. Do these blogs have any information that might be relevant to practitioners who are conducting research in the topic areas that the blogs address? Why or why not?
3. **EXPERIENCE THE INTERNET.** Using Google Scholar, identify 20 or so references that are relevant to the topic of service quality. Identify 4 or 5 that you think would be helpful to designing a survey to measure the service quality received at a restaurant. List the title of each of the studies and explain why you think they are relevant to the study you are designing.
4. Imagine that you are getting ready to conduct a study to determine how word-of-mouth affects movie attendance. Explain what general types of resources you would plan to consult in conducting a literature review for this study.
5. Based on your experiences in college, develop a conceptual model that shows the factors that lead to your satisfaction (or dissatisfaction) with a course you are taking.
6. Based on the model you developed in Question 5, make a list of null and alternative hypotheses that you could test to see if your model holds for college students in general. Is each hypothesized relationship a positive or a negative relationship?

Secondary Data and Sources

Chapter 4

1. Understand the role of secondary data in marketing research.
2. Compare internal and external secondary data.
3. Identify sources of internal and external secondary data.
4. Explain syndicated sources of secondary data.
5. Describe the changing focus of secondary data.

Making the Most of an Information-Rich Environment

Dell, Inc., recently responded to a disgruntled customer by building a better box—a shipping box, that is. The customer was one of many that had been invited to the company's usability lab to test the length of time needed to get a new PC up and running. While unpacking a Dell Dimension tower, the customer struggled and struggled with the shipping box. He finally became so frustrated that he picked it up and turned it upside down. The tower fell to the floor and crashed. Although the purpose of the test was to learn how long it took a customer to install a computer, seeing someone destroy a tower was so startling executives quickly decided to redesign the box and its packing material.

Cisco Systems, Inc., a global leader in the networking market, recognized the potential of information and its impact on building customer relationships long before its competitors. After realizing Cisco could not hire enough engineers to support its growing customer base, the company began looking at information solutions. "Our strategy is to empower customers and let them provide us with information they believe is important in maintaining a relationship," says Peter Solvik, senior VP of information systems. Known as Cisco Connect Online, the Web-driven information connection allows customers to provide and access information to and from Cisco for the purposes of helping in the buying process, finding facts about the company's products, providing customer training programs, and so on. Customers also use site features to configure and price their purchases, track order status, manage service contracts, and submit returns. Uniquely, this customer connect system also incorporates an electronic customer council that allows Cisco to conduct online focus groups, collect customer comments via e-mail, and hold chat sessions between customers and corporate officials.[1]

Value of Secondary Data

At first glance, the opening vignette may not appear to fully illustrate the traditional notion of secondary data. Yet it does illustrate an emerging form of secondary data, typically referred to as customer-volunteered information or customer knowledge information. Given new types of information technology, many companies are now using a variety of techniques to collect, store, and categorize customer data for future marketing decisions. Information gathered from electronic customer councils, customer usability labs, e-mail comments, blogs, and chat sessions is increasingly being used to exploit a data-rich environment based on customer interaction. As more data becomes available, many companies are realizing it can be used to make sound marketing decisions. Data of this nature are more readily available and often represents more engaged and authentic customer sentiment than data collected using traditional research methods. As well, the data collection is usually less expensive than traditional primary data collection efforts.

This chapter focuses on the types of secondary data available, how they can be used, the benefits they offer, and the impact of the Internet on the use of secondary data.

Nature and Scope of Secondary Data

Secondary data Data not gathered for the immediate study at hand but for some other purpose.

One of the essential tasks of marketing research is to obtain information that enables management to make the best possible decisions. Before problems are examined, the researcher determines whether useful information already exists, how relevant the information is, and how it can be obtained. Existing sources of information are more widespread than one might expect and should always be considered first before collecting primary data.

Internal secondary data Data collected by the individual company for accounting purposes or marketing activity reports.

The term **secondary data** refers to data gathered for some other purpose than the immediate study. There are two types of secondary data—internal and external. **Internal secondary data** are collected by a company for accounting purposes, marketing programs, inventory management, customer knowledge, and so forth. **Customer knowledge information,** for instance, is provided by customers for marketing purposes as well as for other areas in an organization. Information, for example, may be provided to engineers, logistical support personnel, or information technology departments on issues relating to product improvement, packaging, or Web registration. Data of this type, if properly warehoused and categorized, can be an invaluable form of secondary data for marketing decisions as they relate to customer relationship management (CRM).

Customer knowledge information Information provided by customers that is unsolicited and can be used for marketing planning purposes.

External secondary data is collected by outside organizations such as federal and state governments, trade associations, nonprofit organizations, marketing research services, store audits, or consumer purchase panels. Secondary data also is available from computer data sources. Computerized secondary data sources typically are designed by research companies and include internal and external data combined with online information sources. Examples of these computerized information sources include information vendors, commercial Web sites, mailing lists, and direct marketing clearing and fulfillment services.

External secondary data Data collected by outside agencies such as the federal government, trade associations, or periodicals.

Role of Secondary Data in Marketing Research

The role of secondary data in marketing research has changed in recent years. Traditionally, secondary data was viewed as having limited value. The job of obtaining secondary data often was outsourced to a corporate librarian, syndicated data collection firm, or junior research analyst. The main functions of secondary data research were to provide historical background for a current primary research endeavor and to allow longitudinal trend analysis within an industry. With the increased emphasis on business and competitive intelligence and the ever-increasing availability of information from online databases, secondary data research has gained substantial importance in marketing research.

Secondary research approaches are increasingly used to examine marketing problems because of the relative speed and cost-effectiveness of obtaining the data. The role of the secondary research analyst is being redefined to that of business unit information professional or specialist linked to the information technology area. This individual creates contact and sales databases, prepares competitive trend reports, develops customer retention strategies, and so forth.

Secondary Data and Customer Relationship Management

Customer relationship management (CRM) helps companies learn about customers' needs and behaviors in order to develop stronger relationships with customers. Customer relationship management combines technology with human insights to better understand customer behavior and the value of customers to the organization. For a CRM initiative to be effective an organization first must determine its information needs and what it intends to do with the information. For example, many financial institutions keep track of customer lifecycle stages in order to determine the right time to market appropriate banking products such as mortgages or retirement products. Similarly, companies such as Procter and Gamble maintain lists of expectant mothers so they can target them for baby products.

Companies using CRM examine the different ways customer information comes into the business, where and how the data are stored, and how data are currently being used. For example, one company may interact with customers using mail campaigns, Web sites, brick and mortar stores, call centers, salespersons, and advertising efforts. CRM links these sources of secondary data and data flow between operational units (for example, sales and inventory) and analytical systems sort through the data to identify customer patterns.

While many CRM activities are supported by primary data, the vast network of secondary data collection and storage points is the foundation of the CRM system. Thus, secondary data provide the nucleus for the CRM process.

Secondary Data Research Tasks and the Marketing Research Process

In many areas of marketing research, secondary research plays a subordinate role to primary research. In product and advertising concept testing, focus groups, and customer satisfaction surveys, only primary research can provide answers to marketing problems. But in some situations, secondary data can solve the research problem. For example, secondary data often is the starting point in defining the research that needs to be conducted. If the problem can be solved based on available secondary data alone, then the company can save time, money, and effort. If the secondary data is not sufficient to solve the research problem, then primary data collection needs to be considered.

If the research focus is potential new customers, secondary research adds value to the research process. Researchers may, for example, use internal company documents to profile the current customer base. The existing customer base can then be used to identify significant characteristics of potential customers. Similarly, needs analysis, which identifies problems or requirements of specific customer groups, is another secondary research task. A third type of secondary research involves providing internal support data for the company. Here the focus switches to providing support for primary research activities, sales presentations, and decision-making functions. Marketing departments generate sales using professional presentations and make decisions on product, price, place, and promotion, both of which rely on secondary data. Finally, companies need to know how markets are changing for successful strategic planning. Development of planning tools is a primary task of secondary research. As secondary research continues to increase its role in marketing research, and as the required skills for acquiring new forms of data delivery continue to evolve, the importance and value of secondary data in research will increase.

Use and Evaluation of Secondary Data Sources

A primary reason for using secondary data is to save the researcher time and money. Usually, secondary data collection involves locating the appropriate source or sources, extracting the necessary data, and recording the data for the research purpose. This usually takes several days, but in some cases only a few hours. Primary data, in contrast, can take months to collect. When you consider the process of designing and testing questionnaires, developing a sampling plan, collecting the data, and then analyzing and tabulating it, you can see that primary data collection can be a long and involved procedure.

In addition to taking a long time, primary data collection can cost thousands of dollars. Fees for services rendered by market research firms typically range from $10,000 to $500,000. Clearly, the scope and magnitude of the research project play a significant role in the fee charged for a particular project. Yet with any primary data collection project it is difficult to avoid wages and expenses, transportation and data collection costs, and clerical and field services charges. In contrast, with many secondary data sources such costs are minimal. Expenses associated with secondary data are usually either incurred by the original data source, as with published secondary data sources (the U.S. census, corporate surveys of buying power, state and county demographic data), or shared between the user and the commercial provider of the data. Regardless, obtaining secondary data generally costs significantly less than primary data.

Because of time and cost savings, any research project should first exhaust all potential sources of secondary data. Indeed, by 2010 almost half of all marketing research objectives are expected to be accomplished using secondary data.[2]

As information becomes more abundant, and technology enables greater refinement and categorization, the emphasis on secondary data is likely to increase. In addition, secondary data will be more accurate. Bar coding, optical scanning, and point-of-purchase data often provide companies with all the information they need for many of their marketing decisions.

With the increasing emphasis on secondary data, researchers are developing better procedures to evaluate the quality of information obtained from secondary data sources. The procedures are based on six fundamental principles:

1. **Purpose.** Since most secondary data are collected for purposes other than the one at hand, the data must be carefully evaluated as to how it relates to the current research

objective. Many times the original collection of the data is not consistent with a particular market research study. These inconsistencies often stem from the units of measure employed. For example, much of the information in the *Editors and Publishers Market Guide* is based on averages. Numbers are assigned a weight to account for environmental or situational differences. While the results represent a good average, they may not provide the precision needed for profiling a highly defined target market relative to actual dollars spent on a particular product category.

2. **Accuracy.** When assessing secondary data, researchers need to keep in mind what was actually measured. For example, if actual purchases in a test market were measured, were they first-time trial purchases or repeat purchases? Were the data presented as a total of responses from all respondents, or were they categorized by age, sex, or socioeconomic status?

   Researchers must assess when the secondary data were collected. For example, a researcher tracking the sales of imported Japanese autos in the U.S. market needs to consider changing attitudes, newly imposed tariffs that may restrict imports, and even fluctuations in the exchange rate. With regard to the accuracy of secondary data, researchers must keep in mind the data were collected to answer a different set of research questions than the ones at hand.

3. **Consistency.** When evaluating any source of secondary data, a good strategy is to seek out multiple sources of the same data to assure consistency. For example, when evaluating the economic characteristics of a foreign market, a researcher may try to gather the same information from government sources, private business publications (*Fortune, BusinessWeek*), and specialty import/export trade publications.

4. **Credibility.** Researchers should always question the credibility of the secondary data source. Technical competence, service quality, reputation, training, and expertise of personnel representing the organization are some of the measures of credibility.

5. **Methodology.** The quality of secondary data is only as good as the methodology employed to gather it. Flaws in methodological procedures can produce results that are invalid, unreliable, or not generalizable beyond the study itself. Therefore, the researcher must evaluate the size and description of the sample, the response rate, the questionnaire, and the overall procedure for collecting the data (telephone, Internet, or personal interview).

6. **Bias.** Researchers must determine the underlying motivation or hidden agenda, if any, of the organization that collected the secondary data. It is not uncommon to find secondary data sources published to advance the interests of commercial, political, or other special interest groups. Sometimes secondary data are published to incite controversy or refute other data sources. Researchers must consider whether the organization reporting the data is motivated by a certain purpose. For example, statistics on animal extinction reported by the National Hardwood Lumber Association or, alternatively, by the People for the Ethical Treatmnt of Animals (PETA) should be validated before they can be relied on as unbiased sources of information.

Traditional Internal Sources of Secondary Data

The logical starting point in searching for secondary data is the company's own internal information. Many organizations fail to realize the wealth of information their own records contain. Additionally, internal data are the most readily available and can be accessed at little or no cost at all. But while this appears to be a good rationale for using internal data, researchers must remember that most of the information comes from past business activities. This is not to say that internal data is not usable for future business decisions. As will be evident in the following discussion, internal data sources can be highly effective in helping decision makers plan new-product introductions or new distribution outlets.

Types of Internal Secondary Data

Generally, internal data consists of sales or cost information. Exhibit 4.1 lists key variables found in each of these internal sources of secondary data.

Other types of internal data that exist among company records can be used to complement the information thus far discussed. Exhibit 4.2 outlines other potential sources of internal secondary data.

A lot of internal company information is available for marketing research activities. If maintained and categorized properly, internal data can be used to analyze product performance, customer satisfaction, distribution effectiveness, and target market strategies. These forms of internal data are also useful for planning new-product introductions, product deletions, promotional strategies, competitive intelligence, and customer service tactics.

Exhibit 4.1   Common Sources of Internal Secondary Data

1. **Sales invoices**
   a. Customer name
   b. Address
   c. Class of product/service sold
   d. Price by unit
   e. Salesperson
   f. Terms of sales
   g. Shipment point

2. **Accounts receivable reports**
   a. Customer name
   b. Product purchased
   c. Total unit and dollar sales
   d. Customer as percentage of sales
   e. Customer as percentage of regional sales
   f. Profit margin
   g. Credit rating
   h. Items returned
   i. Reason for return

3. **Quarterly sales reports**
   a. Total dollar and unit sales by:
      Customer   Geographic segment
      Customer segment Sales territory
      Product   Sales rep
      Product segment
   b. Total sales against planned objectives
   c. Total sales against budget
   d. Total sales against prior periods
   e. Actual sales percentage increase/decrease
   f. Contribution trends

4. **Sales activity reports**
   a. Classification of customer accounts
      Mega
      Large
      Medium
      Small
   b. Available dollar sales potential
   c. Current sales penetration
   d. Existing bids/contracts by
      Customer location
      Product

Exhibit 4.2	Additional Sources of Secondary Data

Source	Information
Customer letters	General satisfaction/dissatisfaction data
Customer comment cards	Overall performance data
Mail-order forms	Customer name, address, items purchased, quality, cycle time of order
Credit applications	Detailed biography of customer segments (demographic, socioeconomic, credit usage, credit ratings)
Cash register receipts	Dollar volume, merchandise type, salesperson, vendor, manufacturer
Salesperson expense reports	Sales activities, competitor activities in market
Employee exit interviews	General internal satisfaction/dissatisfaction data, internal company performance data
Warranty cards	Sales volume, names, addresses, zip codes, items purchased, reasons for product return
Past marketing research studies	Data pertaining to the situation in which the marketing research was conducted
Internet-provided information	Customer registration information, tracking, Web site visits, e-mail correspondence

Using and Extracting External Sources of Secondary Data

After searching for internal secondary data, the next logical step for the researcher to focus on is external secondary data. Three primary sources of external secondary data are: (1) published data in periodicals, directories, or indexes; (2) data compiled by outside vendors (syndicated or commercial) that can be acquired on an as-needed basis for a fee; or (3) data contained in online databases. This section will focus on the first two sources of external secondary data: published sources and syndicated/commercial sources. Online technology-based sources will be discussed in a later section.

A major challenge associated with external secondary data is finding and securing the appropriate source. U.S. Department of Defense researchers say there is enough information available today to solve a majority of managers' questions and problems. But 90 percent of that information is not categorized properly.[3] Thus, the problem often is not finding out whether information exists, but finding out where the information resides.

The amount of secondary information is indeed vast. But the information needs of many researchers are connected by a common theme. Data most often sought by researchers includes demographic characteristics, employment data, economic statistics, competitive and supply assessments, regulations, and international market characteristics. Exhibit 4.3 provides examples of specific variables within these categories.

Exhibit 4.3	Key Variables Sought in Secondary Data Search

Demographics

Population growth: actual and projected

Population density

In-migration and out-migration patterns

Population trends by age, race, and ethnic background

Employment Characteristics

Labor force growth

Unemployment levels

Percentage of employment by occupation categories

Employment by industry

Economic Data

Personal income levels (per capita and median)

Type of manufacturing/service firms

Total housing starts

Building permits issued

Sales tax rates

Competitive Characteristics

Levels of retail and wholesale sales

Number and types of competing retailers

Availability of financial institutions

Supply Characteristics

Number of distribution facilities

Cost of deliveries

Level of rail, water, air, and road transportation

Regulations

Taxes

Licensing

Wages

Zoning

International Market Characteristics

Transportation and exporting requirements

Trade barriers

Business philosophies

Legal system

Social customs

Political climate

Cultural patterns

Religious and moral backgrounds

Several key sources of secondary data enable the researcher to create a hierarchy of information sources to guide a secondary data search, regardless of the variables sought. Several broad-to-narrow data sources are described below to help guide the researcher through the jungle of secondary information.

North American Industry Classification System (NAICS)

North American industry classification system (NAICS) A system that codes numerical industrial listings designed to promote uniformity in data reporting procedures for the U.S. government.

An initial step in any secondary data search is to use the numeric listings of the **North American Industry Classification System (NAICS)** codes. NAICS codes were designed to promote uniformity in data reporting by federal and state government sources and private business. The federal government assigns every industry an NAICS code. Businesses within each industry report all activities (sales, payrolls, taxation) according to their code. Currently, there are 99 two-digit industry codes representing everything from agricultural production of crops to environmental quality and housing. Within each two-digit industry classification code is a four-digit industry group code representing specific industry groups. All businesses in the industry represented by a given four-digit code report detailed information about the business to various sources for publication. For example, as shown in

Exhibit 4.4	Sample List of North American Industry Classification System Codes

Numeric Listing

10—Metal Mining

1011 Iron Ores
1021 Copper Ores
1031 Lead & Zinc Ores
1041 Gold Ores
1044 Silver Ores
1061 Ferroalloy Ores except Vanadium
1081 Metal Mining Services
1094 Uranium, Radium & Vanadium Ores
1099 Metal Ores Nec*

12—Coal Mining

1221 Bituminous Coal & Lignite—Surface
1222 Bituminous Coal—Underground
1231 Anthracite Mining
1241 Coal Mining Services

13—Oil & Gas Extraction

1311 Crude Petroleum & Natural Gas
1321 Natural Gas Liquids
1381 Drilling Oil & Gas Wells
1382 Oil & Gas Exploration Services
1389 Oil & Gas Field Services Nec*

14—Nonmetallic Minerals except Fuels

1411 Dimension Stone
1422 Crushed & Broken Limestone
1423 Crushed & Broken Granite
1429 Crushed & Broken Stone Nec*
1442 Construction Sand & Gravel
1446 Industrial Sand

*Not elsewhere classified.

Source: *Ward Business Directory of U.S. Private and Public Companies, 2006.*

Exhibit 4.4, NAICS code 12 is assigned to coal mining and NAICS code 1221 specifies bituminous coal and lignite, surface extraction. It is at the four-digit level where the researcher will concentrate most data searches.

Government Documents

Detail, completeness, and consistency are major reasons for using U.S. government documents. In fact, U.S. Bureau of the Census reports are the statistical foundation for most of the information available on U.S. population and economic activities. Exhibit 4.5 lists some of the common sources of secondary data available from the U.S. government. These include specific census data (e.g., censuses of agriculture or construction), census reports (e.g., the *County and City Data Book*), U.S. Department of Commerce data, and a variety of additional government reports.

There are two notes of caution about census or other secondary data. First, census data is collected only every 10 years with periodic updates, so researchers always need to consider the timeliness of census data. Second, census data can be misleading. Not every person or household is reflected in census data. Those who have recently changed residences or were simply not available for contact at census time are not included in census data.

A final source of information available through the U.S. government is the *Catalog of Government Publications* compiled by Marcive, Inc. (www.marcive.com). This catalog indexes major market research reports for a variety of domestic and international industries, markets, and institutions. It also provides an index of publications available to researchers from July 1976 to the current month and year.

Exhibit 4.5 Common Government Documents Used as Secondary Data Sources

U.S. Census Data

Census of Agriculture
Census of Construction
Census of Government
Census of Manufacturing
Census of Mineral Industries
Census of Retail Trade
Census of Service Industries
Census of Transportation
Census of Wholesale Trade
Census of Housing
Census of Population

U.S. Census Reports

Guide to Industrial Statistics
County and City Data Book
Statistical Abstract of the U.S.
Fact Finders for the Nation
Guide to Foreign Trade Statistics

U.S. Department of Commerce Data

U.S. Industrial Outlook
County Business Patterns
State and Metro Area Data Book
Business Statistics
Monthly Labor Review
Measuring Markets: Federal and State Statistical Data

Additional Government Reports

Aging America: Trends and Population
Economic Indicators
Economic Report of the President
Federal Reserve Bulletin
Statistics of Income
Survey of Current Business

Secondary Sources of Business Information

It is virtually impossible to document all of the sources of secondary data available from businesses. Most sources are, however, classified by some index, directory, or standardized guidebook, so researchers should consult a directory of business information. These directories identify statistical information, trade associations, trade journals, market characteristics, and environmental trends.

A key source of business information is the ABI Inform Database (www.cas.org). This database is available both online and on CD-ROM. It provides indexes and abstracts of business periodicals relating to a broad range of business topics. Electronic access to most business articles is also available. Gathering market information through business sources frequently leads the researcher to these widely used sources of data: *Editors and Publishers Market Guide* and *Source Book of Demographics and Buying Power for Every Zip Code in the U.S.A.* As illustrated in the nearby A Closer Look at Research box, secondary data often come from selected business sources.

Editors and Publishers Market Guide

One source of secondary information on buying potential is the *Editors and Publishers Market Guide*. This guide provides retail sales, population projections, income, and city-by-city information useful in making comparisons. The guide includes information on infrastructure, transportation, principal industries, banks, and retail outlets. The data provides a detailed profile of economic activity within a given geographic area and is used

Secondary Data and the CRM Process: Placing a Value on Customer Information

Organizations are now treating secondary data as a valuable balance sheet asset. Industry leaders in the CRM process are placing a clear value on customer information in order to size, rank, and cost overall CRM investment. Companies that do not articulate a clear business rationale—based on customer information, revenue sources, and exit barrier considerations—for CRM applications and integration priorities are wasting their significant investment.

In directing their CRM investment, catalog retailers such as Lands' End and JC Penney use large amounts of secondary data to calculate the lifetime value of customers. Knowing, for example, that a specific type of customer will likely buy $1,000 in merchandise over 10 transactions allows these companies to place a clear value on that relationship and budget for CRM programs that will retain or enhance customer relationship value by building exit barriers and cross-selling campaigns. Analytical applications that improve data quality, such as data warehousing and data mining, are of course critical components of the process.

for comparison purposes when selecting markets for new stores or product introductions. For more information on this guide, go to their Web site: **http://www.editorandpublisher. com/eandp/resources/market_guide.jsp.**

Source Book of Demographics and Buying Power for Every Zip Code in the U.S.A

This source book provides information on population, socioeconomic characteristics, buying power, and other demographic characteristics for zip code areas across the United States. Each zip code area is analyzed relative to its consumption potential across a variety of product categories, and a purchasing potential index is calculated. The index is based on a national average score of 100.[4] For example, if zip code 55959 generates a score of 110 for furniture consumption, then that zip code area has a 10 percent greater potential to purchase furniture than the U.S. average.

Statistical Sources of Information

Statistical sources of secondary data can lead the researcher to specific statistical publications or can provide actual reprints of data extracted from numerous other secondary data sources. If actual data are located in the sourcebook, rather than in indexed references, these sources can save considerable research time. The following are examples of statistical data sources:

- *Merchandising: "Statistical and Marketing Report"*
- *Standard and Poor's Industrial Surveys*
- *Data Sources for Business and Market Analysis*
- *American Statistics Index*
- *Statistical Reference Index*
- *Federal Statistical Directory*

Commercial Publications and Newspapers

Newspapers and commercial publications (*Time, Newsweek, BusinessWeek, Forbes* and *Fortune*) are important sources of secondary information. Because these publications are circulated on a daily, weekly, or monthly basis, the information they contain is very recent. In addition, many publications are archived enabling the researcher access to historical information. The *Business Periodical Index* is the primary index for commercial publications.

The problem with commercial publications and newspapers is volume. There are probably more than 1,000 business-related commercial publications available. Many of these publications, especially newspapers, are not indexed in traditional reference books. Those that do provide indexing are usually associated with major metropolitan markets. Many of these publications now have archives online, but some of them charge for access.

Continuing Case: Using Secondary Data with the Santa Fe Grill

The owners of the Santa Fe Grill believe secondary data may be useful in better understanding how to run a restaurant. Based on what you have learned in this chapter about secondary data, that should certainly be true.

1.   What kinds of secondary data are likely to be useful?
2.   Conduct a search of secondary data sources for material that could be used by the Santa Fe Grill owners to better understand the problems/opportunities facing them. Use Google, Yahoo, or other search engines to do so.
3.   What key words would you use in the search?
4.   Summarize what you found in your search.

Syndicated Sources of Secondary Data

A major trend in marketing research is toward a greater dependency on syndicated (or commercial) data sources. The rationale for this is that companies can obtain substantial information from a variety of industries at a relatively low cost. Also, because most of the data contained in these sources is collected at the point of purchase, the information represents actual purchase behavior rather than purchase intentions.

The Society of Competitive Intelligence Professionals reports that over 80 percent of marketing research firms purchase and use secondary research reports from commercial vendors. In addition, firms spend more than $15,000 annually for syndicated reports and devote at least 10 hours per week to analyzing the data.[5] Indeed, syndicated reports available online are rapidly replacing traditional paper-based sources.

Characteristics of Syndicated Data Sources

Syndicated (or commercial)
data Data that have been
compiled according to some
standardized procedure;
provides customized data for
companies, such as market
share, ad effectiveness, and
sales tracking.

Syndicated (or commercial) data is information that has been collected and compiled according to some standardized procedure. In most cases the information is collected for a particular business or company, with a specific reason or purpose motivating the data collection procedure. The information is then sold to different companies in the form of tabulated reports prepared specifically for a client's research needs, often tailored to specific reporting units. For example, reports can be organized by geographic region, sales territory, market segment, product class, or brand. For these data sources to be effective, suppliers of commercial/syndicated data must have in-depth knowledge of the industry and generate timely data. Suppliers traditionally have used two methods of data collection: consumer panels and store audits. A third method that is gaining ground—optical-scanner technology—is discussed in a later chapter.

Consumer Panels

Consumer panels consist of large samples of households that have agreed to provide detailed data for an extended period of time. Information provided by these panels typically consists of product purchase information or media habits, often on the consumer package goods industry. But information obtained from optical-scanners is increasing being used as well.

Panels typically are developed by marketing research firms and use a rigorous data collection approach. Respondents are required to record detailed behaviors at the time of occurrence on a highly structured questionnaire. The questionnaire contains a large number of questions related directly to actual product purchases or media exposure. Most often this is an ongoing procedure whereby respondents report data back to the company on a weekly or monthly basis. Panel data are then sold to a variety of clients after being tailored to the client's research needs.

A variety of benefits are associated with panel data. These include (1) lower cost than primary data collection methods; (2) rapid availability and timeliness; (3) accurate reporting of socially sensitive expenditures, for example, beer, liquor, cigarettes, generic brands; and (4) high level of specificity, for instance, actual products purchased or media habits, not merely intentions or propensities to purchase.

There are two types of panel-based data sources: those reflecting actual purchases of products and services and those reflecting media habits. The discussion below provides examples of both types.

Examples of Consumer Panel Data Sources A variety of companies offer panel-based purchasing data. Two of the largest companies are National Family Opinion (NFO) and the NPD Group (**www.npd.com**). NPD collects continuous data from a national sample consisting of approximately 15,000 members. Data collection centers on consumer attitudes and awareness of such products as toys, apparel, textiles, sporting goods, athletic footwear, automotive products, home electronics, and cameras.[6]

Three of NPD's most commonly used data sources are the Consumer Report on Eating Share Trends (CREST), National Eating Trends (NET), and a service that provides data on the food service industry in general. CREST is based on over 14,000 households that report data on restaurant habits. NET provides continuous tracking of in-home food and beverage consumption patterns. ISL, a Canadian subsidiary of the NPD Group, provides similar purchase data through the Consumer Panel of Canada.

National Family Opinion (NFO) maintains a consumer panel of over 450,000 households to conduct product tests, concept tests, and attitude, awareness, and brand-usage studies. The NFO panel offers a proprietary software program called Smart-System. This system enables clients to access and analyze complex information quickly, with easy cross-referencing on major data variables. In addition, NFO maintains highly targeted panels referred to as the Hispanic Panel, the Baby Panel, the Mover Panel, and SIP (Share of Intake Panel on Beverage Consumption). The following list describes additional companies and the consumer panels they maintain:

- Market Facts, Inc., provides panel data for forecasting models, brand equity/loyalty models, and brand tracking information.
- J. D. Power and Associates maintains a consumer panel of car and light-truck owners to provide data on product quality, satisfaction, and vehicle dependability.

- Roper Starch Worldwide provides data on consumption patterns for the 6- to 18-year-old market.
- Creative and Response Research Services has a consumer panel called Kidspeak (**www. kidspeak.com**) that provides advertising and brand tracking among children.

Examples of Media Panel Data Sources Media panels and consumer panels are similar in procedure, composition, and design. They differ only in that media panels primarily measure media consumption habits as opposed to product or brand consumption. As with consumer panels, numerous media panels exist. This section provides examples of the most commonly used syndicated media panels.

Nielsen Media Research is by far the most widely known and accepted source of media panel data. The flagship service of Nielsen is the National Television Index (NIT). Based on a 5,000-household sample, the NIT provides an estimation of national television audiences measuring "ratings" and "share." Ratings refer to the percentage of households that have at least one television set tuned to a program for at least 6 of every 15 minutes a program is aired. "Share" constitutes the percentage of households that have a television tuned to one specific program at one specific time.[7] Data are collected on television, cable, and home video viewing habits through an electronic device, called a people meter, connected to a television set. The people meter continuously monitors and records when a television set is turned on, what channels are being viewed, how much time is spent on each channel, and who is watching. The data are communicated back to the central computer by telephone or the Internet.

The primary purpose of the NIT data is to assist media planners in determining audience volume, demographics, and viewing habits. This information is then used to calculate media efficiency measured as cost per thousand (CPM), that is, how much it costs to reach 1,000 viewers. CPM measures a program's ability to deliver the largest target audience at the lowest cost.

While most data are collected by the people meter, Nielsen still maintains diary panels in selected markets measuring the same media habits. In addition, Nielsen also operates an 800-household sample of Hispanic TV viewers designed to measure Spanish-language media usage in the United States. Arbitron Inc. is primarily a media research firm that conducts ongoing data collection for electronic media. Arbitron is organized into five media research business units.[8] Arbitron Radio provides radio audience data for more than 250 local market areas. Utilizing a 2 million-plus customer panel, Arbitron Radio collects over 1 million weekly listening diaries that are the basis of Arbitron Radio's station rating reports. The data are used primarily by media planners, advertising agencies, and advertisers. Arbitron also sells syndicated data on local media, consumer listening habits, and retail advertising impact data across 58 of the major U.S. markets. Currently, 600 newspapers, radio stations, television stations, and cable systems are predominant users of this syndicated data source.

Store Audits

Store audits Formal examination and verification of how much of a particular product or brand has been sold at the retail level.

Store audits consist of formal examination and verification of how much of a particular product or brand has been sold at the retail level. Based on a collection of participating retailers (typically discount, supermarket, and drugstore retailers), audits are performed on product or brand movement in return for detailed activity reports and cash compensation to the retailer. The audits then operate as a secondary data source. Clients can purchase the data relative to industry, competition, product, or specific brand. Store audits provide two unique benefits: precision and timeliness. Many of the biases of consumer panels are not found in store audits. By design, store audits measure product and brand movement directly at the point of sale (usually at the retail level). Also, sales and competitive activities are reported when the audit is completed, making the data timely and readily available to potential users.

Data Gathering in the Store Audit   Key variables being measured in the store audit typically include beginning and ending inventory levels, sales receipts, price levels, price inducements, local advertising, and point-of-purchase (POP) displays. Collectively, these data allow users of store audit services to generate information on the following factors:

- Product/brand sales in relation to competition.
- Effectiveness of shelf space and POP displays.
- Sales at various price points and levels.
- Effectiveness of in-store promotions and point-of-sale coupons.
- Direct sales by store type, product location, territory, and region.

The Internet as a Growing Source of Secondary Data

The Internet has dramatically accelerated the speed at which anyone can obtain secondary information. Web sites describe products and services and provide information to evaluate corporate structure and marketing positioning strategies. Finding a company's Web page is easy when companies use their name as the URL. Many times, however, several companies have similar names, although operating in different industries. A solution to this problem is to search for competitive companies using "KnowThis" (**www.knowthis.com**), a specialty search engine containing Internet addresses for more than a million companies.

Company management, financial, and marketing information is a necessary component for any business intelligence program and most of the information can be found easily on the Internet. An excellent starting point is a specialty Web site known as "Corporate Information" (**www.corporateinformation.com**). This site contains links to public and private companies in more than 100 countries and recently added a search engine for accessing a database of 100,000 companies.

An additional use of the Internet is to track and monitor current alerts about competitors. Press releases and news stories contain a wealth of information about a competitor's services, products, and markets. A source for this type of information is "Company Sleuth" (**www.companysleuth.com**).

The Future of Secondary Data Sources

This chapter has focused on traditional secondary data sources. But 90 percent of the information referenced here currently exists online. As the technology of information management becomes more acceptable and accessible, more and more secondary data will be available at the push of a computer key. More important, as communication technology converges with computer technology, the amount of secondary data is expected to grow even faster. More actual consumer behavior and purchase information than ever before will become available in a timely and cost-efficient manner.

As more and more organizations begin to realize the full value of database development and information systems management, they will be able to customize secondary data sources.

MARKETING RESEARCH IN ACTION
Santa Fe Grill Considering Expansion

As you may recall from Chapter 1, the Santa Fe Grill is a new restaurant concept that currently operates in Dallas, Texas. The owners of the restaurant, when developing their five-year plan, anticipated the opening of two additional locations in Texas, after five years of successful operation at the Dallas location. The owners were considering expanding to Houston, Texas, and possibly San Antonio, Texas.

After revisiting the five-year plan, the owners realized they lacked data and information relevant to these two cities. In fact, the only information they had were the population size and growth of these two cities. Realizing this, the decision was made to develop an area profile of Houston and San Antonio relative to the restaurant market.

Based on this decision key secondary data must be collected. Population characteristics, economic conditions, competitive trends in the restaurant industry, and market factors appear to be the starting point of the secondary data search. The owners, realizing these factors may be too broad for facilitating an expansion decision, requested the help of a local university marketing research class to conduct a secondary data search for specific information on Houston and San Antonio.

Hands-On Exercise

The owners need your help in designing the approach, collection of data, types of data, and conclusive evidence contained in a secondary research search. Specifically, the following issues should be addressed:

1. Develop a list of the specific variables that need to be examined regarding demographic characteristics, economic characteristics, competitive dimensions of the restaurant market, and other relevant customer data as it pertains to Houston and San Antonio, Texas.
2. Based on the information contained in this chapter, perform a secondary data search on all key variables you identified in your answer to Question 1.
3. Develop a comparative profile of the two cities (Houston, San Antonio) based on your secondary data and provide the owners with a report showing evidence that one, both, or neither of the cities would be desirable for possible restaurant expansion.

Summary

Understand the role of secondary data in marketing research.

The task of a marketing researcher is to solve the problem in the shortest time, at the least cost, with the highest level of accuracy. Therefore, before any marketing research project is conducted, the researcher must seek out existing information that may facilitate a decision or outcome for a company. Existing data are commonly called secondary data. Secondary data frequently are considered the nucleus of the customer relationship management (CRM) process because of the vast amount of customer data that must be collected and stored on a historical basis. Customer knowledge information, or information volunteered by consumers, is often collected on an ongoing basis and consistently stored and monitored as part of CRM initiatives. If secondary data are to be used to assist the decision-making process or problem-solving ability of the manager, they need to be evaluated on six fundamental principles: (1) purpose (how relevant are the data to achieving the specific research objectives at hand?); (2) accuracy (are the data collected, measured, and reported in a manner consistent with quality research practices?); (3) consistency (do multiple sources of the data exist?); (4) credibility (how were the data obtained? what is the source of the data?); (5) methodology (will the methods used to collect the data produce high quality data?); and (6) biases (was the data-reporting procedure tainted by some hidden agenda or underlying motivation to advance some public or private concern?).

Compare internal and external secondary data.

Internal secondary data are usually sorted into three categories. First is company internal accounting and financial information. These typically consist of sales invoices, accounts receivable reports, and quarterly sales reports. Other forms of internal data include past marketing research studies, customer credit applications, warranty cards, and employee exit interviews. Because of the volume of external data available, researchers need to plan the steps of ensuring that the right data are located and

extracted. A simple guideline to follow is: define goals the secondary data need to achieve; specify objectives behind the secondary search process; define specific characteristics of data that are to be extracted; document all activities necessary to find, locate, and extract the data sources; focus on reliable sources of data; and tabulate all the data extracted.

Identify sources of internal and external secondary data.

Internal secondary data comes from within the company, from sources like sales and accounting records. External secondary data can be obtained from a wide variety of sources. The most common forms of external data are North American industry classification system (NAICS) codes, government documents (which include census reports), business directories, trade journals, statistical sources, commercial publications, and newspapers.

Explain syndicated sources of secondary data.

Syndicated (or commercial) data sources consist of data that have been systematically collected and compiled according to some standardized procedure. Suppliers of syndicated data have traditionally used one of two approaches in collecting data: consumer panels and store audits. A third approach, optical-scanner technology, is discussed in a later chapter. With most syndicated data sources, the objective is quite clear: to measure point-of-sale purchase behaviors or to measure media habits.

Describe the changing focus of secondary data.

The computerization of secondary data is revolutionizing the marketing research industry as is the Internet. Online services are making more data available that are more applicable to business needs than ever before. In addition, databases and information systems are bringing the use of secondary data to monumental proportions. Technology will make secondary data more customized and applicable for many businesses.

Key Terms and Concepts

Consumer panels 71

Customer knowledge information 60

External secondary data 60

Internal secondary data 60

North American industry classification system
(NAICS) 66

Secondary data 60

Store audits 72

Syndicated (or commercial) data 70

 Review Questions

1. What characteristic separates secondary data from primary data? What are three sources of secondary data?
2. Explain why a company should use all potential sources of secondary data before initiating primary data collection procedures.
3. List the six fundamental principles used to assess the validity of secondary data.
4. List the three methods of data collection typically used by the suppliers of commercial data sources, and discuss the advantages and disadvantages associated with each.
5. How can information from a sales activity report be used to improve a company's marketing research efforts?
6. How is the Internet changing the nature and use of secondary data?

 Discussion Questions

1. **EXPERIENCE THE INTERNET.** Go online and find the home page for your particular state. For example, **www.mississippi.com** would get you to the home page for the state of Mississippi. Once there, seek out the category that gives you information on county and local statistics. Select the county where you reside and obtain the vital demographic and socioeconomic data available. Provide a demographic profile of the residents in your community.
2. **EXPERIENCE THE INTERNET.** Go to the home page of the U.S. census, **www.census.gov**. Select the category Current Economic Indicators and browse the data provided.
3. What specific industry information could executives at Procter & Gamble obtain from the *Source Book of Demographics and Buying Power for Every Zip Code in the U.S.A.*? How would this information improve Procter & Gamble's marketing strategies?
4. You are planning to open a coffee shop in one of two areas in your local community. Conduct a secondary data search on key variables that would allow you to make a logical decision on which area is best suited for your proposed coffee shop.

Qualitative and Observational Research Designs

Learning Objectives   After reading this chapter, you will be able to:

1. Identify the major differences between qualitative and quantitative research
2. Understand in-depth interviewing and focus groups as questioning techniques.
3. Define focus groups and explain how to conduct them.
4. Explain other qualitative data collection methods such as ethnography, case studies, and projective techniques.
5. Discuss observation methods and explain how they are used to collect primary data.

The Culture Codes

Clotaire Rapaille was hired by Chrysler to help understand how the Jeep Wrangler could be more successfully positioned in the American marketplace. Although Chrysler managers had already conducted plenty of traditional research and were skeptical of Rapaille's methodology, the researcher convinced the company that he could help them to better understand consumers' emotional connections to Jeep.

The research was performed in three stages. In the first hour, Rapaille told participants that he was a visitor from another planet and had never seen a Jeep. He asked group members to explain to an extraterrestrial what a Jeep is and how it is used. In the second hour, they made collages about the Jeep using scissors and pictures cut from magazines. In the last hour, group members lay down on the floor with pillows while soothing music played and the lights were dimmed. This is when participants were asked about their earliest memories of the Jeep.

Rapaille's goal in using a multistage qualitative method is to get past rational, conscious filters into more emotional and unconscious mental territory. Across respondents, several stories and images about the Jeep reoccurred: "being out in the open land . . . going where no ordinary car could go . . . riding free of the restraints of the road." Consistent with these stories, many consumers invoked the image of the American West and the open plains.

Rapaille returned to a skeptical group of Chrysler executives and explained to them that the "Code" for the Jeep in America is "Horse." Thus, designing and positioning the Jeep to be an SUV would be a strategic mistake. "SUVs are not horses. Horses don't have luxury appointments." Chrysler executives weren't impressed because they had done a great deal of research that suggested that consumers wanted something else. But Rapaille asked them to test his theory by changing the Jeep's square headlights to be round instead. His reasoning was that horses have round eyes rather than square ones.

When Chrysler tested the new design, the response from consumers was immediately positive. Sales rose and the new appearance of the Wrangler became its most marketable feature. The company also positioned the car as a horse in its new advertising. In one execution of the ad campaign, a dog falls off a cliff and hangs onto a tree. A child runs for help, passing various vehicles until he reaches a Jeep Wrangler. In this "product as hero" ad, the Jeep is able to negotiate the difficult terrain and rescue the dog. Like a Western hero, the Jeep heads off into the sunset before the child can thank the driver. The campaign was a huge success for Jeep.[1]

Value of Qualitative Research

Management is often faced with situations where important questions cannot be adequately addressed or resolved with secondary information. Meaningful insights can be gained only through the collection of primary data. Recall that primary data are typically collected using a set of formal procedures in which researchers question or observe individuals and record their findings. The method may involve qualitative or quantitative research or both.

As the journey through Phase II of the research process continues (remember Chapter 2, Phase II: Select the Research Design), attention moves from secondary data to collecting primary data. This chapter and the next discuss research designs used in collecting primary data. As noted in earlier chapters, research objectives and information requirements are the keys to determining the appropriate research design for collecting data. For example, qualitative research often is used in exploratory research designs when the research objectives are to gather background information, clarify research problems, and create hypotheses or establish research priorities. Quantitative research can then be used to follow up and quantify the qualitative findings.

Qualitative research results may be sufficient in certain situations. For example, if the research is designed to obtain customer reactions to different advertising approaches while the ads are still in the storyboard phase of development, qualitative research is effective. Qualitative research may also be sufficient when feedback in focus groups or in-depth interviews is consistent, such as overwhelmingly favorable (or unfavorable) toward a new product concept. Last, some topics are more appropriately studied using qualitative research. This is particularly true for complex consumer behaviors that may be affected by factors that are not easily reducible to numbers, such as consumer choices and experiences involving cultural, family, and psychological influences that are difficult to tap using quantitative methods.

Occasionally, qualitative research is conducted as a follow-up to quantitative research. This happens when quantitative findings are contradictory or ambiguous and do not fully answer research questions. This chapter introduces several qualitative research methods used in exploratory research designs. It also covers observation, which can be used to conduct both qualitative and quantitative research. Chapter 6 covers quantitative methods other than observation used with descriptive and causal research designs.

◾ Overview of Qualitative and Quantitative Research Methods

There are differences in qualitative and quantitative approaches, but all researchers interpret data and tell stories about the research topics they study.[2] Prior to discussing qualitative techniques used in exploratory research, we summarize the major differences between qualitative and quantitative research in Exhibit 5.1.

Quantitative Research Methods

Quantitative research
Research that places heavy emphasis on using formal questions and predetermined response options in questionnaires or surveys administered to large numbers of respondents.

Quantitative research uses formal questions and predetermined response options in questionnaires administered to large numbers of respondents. For example, J. D. Power and Associates conducts mail surveys on customer satisfaction among new car purchasers, and American Express uses telephone interviews to complete nationwide surveys on travel behavior. With quantitative methods, research problems are specific and well-defined, and the decision maker and researcher have agreed on the precise information needs.

Quantitative research methods are most often used with descriptive and causal research designs, but are occasionally associated with exploratory designs. For example, a researcher may pilot test questions on a survey to see how well they measure a construct before including them in a larger study. Success in collecting quantitative data is more a function

Exhibit 5.1	Major Differences between Qualitative and Quantitative Research	
Factor	**Qualitative Methods**	**Quantitative Methods**
Goals/Objectives	Discovery/identification of new ideas thoughts, feelings; preliminary understanding of relationships; predictions; understanding of hidden psychological and social processes	Validation of facts, estimates, relationships
Type of Research Type of Questions Time of Execution	Exploratory Open-ended, unstructured, probing Relatively short time frame	Descriptive and causal Mostly structured Typically significantly longer time frame
Representativeness	Small samples, only the sampled individuals	Large samples, with proper sampling can represent population
Type of Analysis	Debriefing, subjective, content analysis, interpretative	Statistical, descriptive, causal predictions
Researcher Skills	Interpersonal communications, observation, interpretation of text or visual data	Statistical analysis, interpretation of numbers
Generalizability	Limited	Generally very good, can infer facts and relationships

of correctly designing and administering the questionnaire than of the communication and interpretive skills of an interviewer or observer.

The main goals of quantitative research are to obtain information to (1) make accurate predictions about relationships between market factors and behaviors, (2) gain meaningful insights into those relationships, (3) validate relationships, and (4) test hypotheses. Quantitative researchers are well trained in construct development, scale measurement, questionnaire design, sampling, and statistical data analysis. In addition, quantitative researchers must be able to translate numerical data into meaningful narrative information, telling a compelling story that is supported by data. Finally, quantitative methods are statistically projectible to the target population of interest and relatively more reliable because every question is asked of all respondents in precisely the same way, and sample sizes are much larger.

Qualitative Research Methods

While qualitative research data collection and analysis can be careful and rigorous, most practitioners regard qualitative research as being less reliable than quantitative research. Qualitative researchers seek to understand research participants rather than to fit their answers into predetermined categories with little room for qualifying or explaining their choices. Thus, **qualitative research** often uncovers unanticipated findings and reactions, and a common objective is to gain preliminary insights into research problems. These preliminary insights are sometimes followed up with quantitative research to verify the qualitative findings.

A second use of qualitative research is to probe more deeply into areas that quantitative research may be too superficial to access, such as subconscious consumer motivations.[3] Qualitative research enables researchers and clients to get closer to their customers and potential customers than does quantitative research. For example, video and textual verbatims (pictures or phrases) enable participants to speak and be heard in their own words in the researcher's report.

Qualitative researchers usually collect detailed data from relatively small samples by asking questions or observing behavior. Researchers trained in interpersonal communications and interpretive skills use open-ended questions and other materials to facilitate in-depth probing of participants' thoughts. Some qualitative research involves analysis of "found" data, or existing text. For example, qualitative researchers who want to better understand teen consumer culture might analyze a sample of MySpace entries posted by teens. In most cases, qualitative data is collected in relatively short time periods. Data analysis typically involves content analysis and interpretation. To increase the reliability and trustworthiness of the interpretation, researchers follow consistent approaches that are extensively documented.

The semistructured format of the questions and the small sample sizes limit the researcher's ability to generalize qualitative data to the population. Nevertheless, qualitative data have important uses in identifying and understanding business problems. For example, qualitative data can be invaluable in providing researchers with initial ideas about specific problems or opportunities, theories and relationships, variables, or the design of scale measurements. Finally, qualitative research can be superior for studying topics that involve complex psychological motivations not easily reduced to survey formats and quantitative analyses.

Qualitative research methods have both advantage and disadvantages. Exhibit 5.2 summarizes the major advantages and disadvantages of qualitative research.

An advantage of qualitative research, particularly for focus groups and in-depth interviews, is it can be completed relatively quickly. Due in part to the use of small samples, researchers can complete investigations in a shorter period of time and sometimes at a lower cost than is true with quantitative methods. Another advantage is the richness of the data.

Qualitative research The collection of data in the form of text or images using open-ended questions, observation, or "found" data.

Exhibit 5.2	Advantages and Disadvantages of Qualitative Research

Advantages of Qualitative Research	Disadvantages of Qualitative Research
Except for ethnography, data can be collected relatively quickly	Lack of generalizability
Richness of the data	Difficulty in estimating the magnitude of phenomena being investigated
Accuracy of recording marketplace behaviors (validity)	Low reliability
Preliminary insights into building models and scale measurements	Difficulty finding well-trained investigators, interviewers, and observers
Insights from qualitative researchers with training in social and behavioral sciences	Reliance on subjective interpretive skills of qualitative researcher

The unstructured approach of qualitative techniques enables researchers to collect in-depth data about respondents' attitudes, beliefs, emotions, and perceptions, all of which may strongly influence their behaviors as consumers.

The richness of qualitative data can often supplement facts gathered through other primary data collection techniques. Qualitative techniques enable decision makers to gain first-hand experiences with customers and can provide revealing information that is contextualized. For example, an ethnographic study of Thanksgiving traditions conducted in consumers' homes during their celebrations discovered the term "homemade" is often applied to dishes that are not made from scratch, but instead use at least some premade, branded ingredients.[4]

Qualitative research methods often provide preliminary insights useful in developing ideas about how variables are related. Similarly, qualitative research can help define constructs or variables and suggest items that can be used to measure those constructs. For example, before they can successfully measure the perceived quality of online shopping experiences from their customers' perspective, retailers must first know the factors or dimensions that are important to their customers when shopping online. Qualitative data also play an important role in identifying marketing problems and opportunities. The in-depth information enhances the researcher's ability to understand consumer behavior. Finally, many qualitative researchers have backgrounds in the social sciences, such as sociology, anthropology, or psychology, and thus bring knowledge of theories from their discipline to enhance interpretation of data. For example, a study of grooming behavior of young adults conducted by an anthropologist described grooming behavior as "ritual magic."[5] The legacy of psychology and psychiatry in developing qualitative techniques is seen in the emphasis on subconscious motivations and the use of probing techniques to uncover motives.[6]

Although qualitative research produces useful information, it has some potential disadvantages, including small sample sizes and the need for well-trained interviewers or observers. The sample size in a qualitative study may be as few as 10 (individual in-depth interviews), and is rarely more than 60 (the number of participants in 5–6 focus groups). Occasionally, companies will undertake large-scale qualitative studies involving thousands of in-depth interviews and hundreds of focus groups, as Forrester Research did to support the development of their e-commerce consulting business,[7] but this is the exception, not the rule. While researchers often handpick respondents to represent their target population, the resulting samples are not representative in the statistical sense. Qualitative researchers emphasize their samples are made up of "relevant" rather than representative consumers. The lack of representativeness of the defined target population may limit the use of qualitative information in selecting and implementing final action strategies.

Qualitative Data Collection Methods

A number of approaches can be used to collect qualitative data. Focus groups are the most frequently used qualitative research method (see Exhibit 5.3). But the use of observation, projective techniques, ethnography, and similar approaches has been growing in recent years.

In-Depth Interviews

In-depth interview A formal process in which a well-trained interviewer asks a subject a set of semistructured questions in a face-to-face setting.

The **in-depth interview,** also referred to as a "depth" or "one-on-one" interview, involves a trained interviewer asking a respondent a set of semistructured, probing questions usually in a face-to-face setting. The typical setting for this type of interview is either the respondent's home or office, or some type of centralized interviewing center convenient for the respondent. Some research firms use hybrid in-depth interviewing techniques involving a combination of Internet and phone interviewing. In these cases, the conversation can be extended over several days giving participants more time to consider their answers.[8] The Internet also enables consumers to be exposed to visual and audio stimuli, thus overcoming a major limitation of phone interviewing.

A unique characteristic of in-depth interviewing is the interviewer uses probing questions to elicit more detailed information on the topic. By turning the respondent's initial response into a question, the interviewer encourages the respondent to further explain the first response, creating natural opportunities for more detailed discussion of the topic. The general rule is that the more a subject talks about a topic, the more likely he or she is to reveal underlying attitudes, motives, emotions, and behaviors.

The major advantages of in-depth interviewing over focus groups include (1) rich detail can be uncovered when focusing on one participant at a time, (2) lower likelihood of

| **Exhibit 5.3** | Qualitative Data Collection Methods |

Primary Qualitative Method—Not Including Observation	2006
Traditional focus groups	51.8%
Hybrids (2 or more methods)	14.3
In-depth interviews	7.8
Netnography	4.2
Ethnography	2.0
Chat-based online focus groups	1.2
Video-based online focus groups	1.0
Other	5.0
None	12.7

Source: *Research Industry Trends—2006 Report*, Pioneer Marketing Research, GreenBook, Rockhopper Research & Dialtech.

participants responding in a socially desirable manner because there are no other participants to impress, and (3) less crosstalk that may inhibit some people from participating in a focus group. In-depth interviewing is a particularly good approach to use with projective techniques, which are discussed later in this chapter.

Skills Required for Conducting In-Depth Interviews   For in-depth interviewing to be effective, interviewers must have excellent interpersonal communications and listening skills. Important interpersonal communication skills include the interviewer's ability to ask questions in a direct and clear manner so respondents understand what they are responding to. Listening skills include the ability to accurately hear, record, and interpret the respondent's answers. Most interviewers ask permission from the respondent to record the interview rather than relying solely on handwritten notes.

Without excellent probing skills, interviewers may allow the discussion of a specific topic to end before all the potential information is revealed. Most interviewers have to work at learning to ask good probing questions. For example, in-depth interviews of business students about what they want in their coursework often reveal that "real world projects" are important learning experiences. But what do they really mean by "real world projects"? What specifically about these projects makes them good learning experiences? What kinds of projects are more likely to be labeled as "real world projects"? It takes time and effort to elicit participants' answers, and ending a sequence of questions relatively quickly, as is the tendency in everyday conversation, is not effective in in-depth interviewing.

Interpretive skills refer to the interviewer's ability to accurately understand the respondent's answers. Interpretive skills are important for transforming the data into usable information. Finally, the personality of the interviewer plays a significant role in establishing a "comfort zone" for the respondent during the question/answer process. Interviewers should be easygoing, flexible, trustworthy, and professional. Participants who feel at ease with an interviewer are more likely to reveal their attitudes, feelings, motivations, and behaviors.

Steps in Conducting an In-Depth Interview   In planning and conducting an in-depth interview, there are a number of steps. Exhibit 5.4 highlights those steps.

Focus Group Interviews

The most widely used qualitative research method in marketing is the focus group, sometimes called the group depth interview. The focus group interview has its roots in the behavioral sciences. **Focus group research** involves bringing a small group of people together for an interactive and spontaneous discussion of a particular topic or concept. Focus groups typically consist of 8 to 12 participants who are guided by a professional moderator through a semistructured discussion that most often lasts about two hours. By encouraging group members to talk in detail about a topic, the moderator draws out as many ideas, attitudes, and experiences as possible about the specified issue. The fundamental idea behind the focus group approach is that one person's response will spark comments from other members, thus creating synergy among participants.

In addition to the traditional face-to-face method, focus groups are now conducted online as well. While body language cannot be assessed online and probing is more difficult, there are advantages to online focus groups. Low incidence populations are easier to reach, more geographically diverse samples can be drawn, response rates can be higher because of increased convenience for participants who can log in from anywhere, software can be used to slow down the responses of more dominant participants, and responses often are more candid because there is less social pressure when participants are not face to face.[9]

Focus group research A formal process of bringing a small group of people together for an interactive, spontaneous discussion on one particular topic or concept.

Exhibit 5.4	Steps in Conducting an In-Depth Interview

Steps	Description and Comments
Step #1:	**Understand Initial Questions/Problems** • Define management's problem situation and questions. • Engage in dialogues with decision makers that focus on bringing clarity and understanding of the research problem.
Step #2:	**Create a Set of Research Questions** • Develop a set of research questions (an interview guide) that focuses on the major elements of the questions or problems. • Arrange using a logical flow moving from "general" to "specific" within topic areas.
Step #3:	**Decide on the Best Environment for Conducting the Interview** • Determine best location for the interview based on the characteristics of the participant and select a relaxed, comfortable interview setting. • Setting must facilitate private conversations without outside distractions.
Step #4:	**Select and Screen the Respondents** • Select participants using specific criteria for the situation being studied. • Screen participants to assure they meet a set of specified criteria.
Step #5:	**Respondent Greeted, Given Interviewing Guidelines, and Put at Ease** • Interviewer meets participant and provides the appropriate introductory guidelines for the interviewing process. • Obtain permission to tape and/or videorecord the interview. • Use the first few minutes prior to the start of the questioning process to create a "comfort zone" for the respondent, using warmup questions. • Begin the interview by asking the first research questions.
Step #6:	**Conduct the In-Depth Interview** • Use probing questions to obtain as many details as possible from the participant on the topic before moving to the next question. • When interview completed, thank respondents for participating, debrief as necessary, and give incentives.
Step #7:	**Analyze Respondent's Narrative Responses** • Summarize initial thoughts after each interview. In particular, write down themes and ideas that may be used later in coding transcripts, a process referred to as memoing. • Follow up on interesting responses that appear in one interview by adding questions to future interviews. • After all data is collected, code each participant's transcripts by classifying responses into categories.
Step #8:	**Write Summary Report of Results** • A summary report is prepared. • The report is similar to writing a report for a focus group.

Exhibit 5.5	Three-Phase Process for Developing a Focus Group Interview

Phase 1: Planning the Focus Group Study
- Researcher must understand the purpose of the study, the problem definition, and specific data requirements.
- Key decisions are who the appropriate participants will be, how to select and recruit participants, how many focus groups will be conducted, and where to have the sessions.

Phase 2: Conducting the Focus Group Discussions
- Moderator's guide is developed that outlines the topics and questions to be used.
- Questions are asked, including follow-up probing.
- Moderator ensures all participants contribute.

Phase 3: Analyzing and Reporting the Results
- Researcher debriefs all the key players involved to compare notes.
- Data obtained from the participants is analyzed using content analysis.
- A formal report is prepared and presented.

Conducting Focus Group Interviews   There is no single approach used by all researchers. But focus group interviews can be divided into three phases: planning the study, conducting the focus group discussions, and analyzing and reporting the results, as shown in Exhibit 5.5.

Phase 1: Planning the Focus Group Study

The planning phase is important to the success of focus groups. In this phase, researchers and decision makers must have a clear understanding of the purpose of the study, a definition of the problem, and specific data requirements. Other important factors in the planning phase relate to decisions about who the participants should be, how to select and recruit respondents, and where to have the focus group sessions.

Focus Group Participants   In deciding who should be included as participants in a focus group, researchers must consider the purpose of the study as well as who can best provide the necessary information. The first step is to consider all of the types of participants that should be represented in the study. Demographics such as age, sex, and product-related behaviors such as purchase and usage behavior are often considered in the sampling plan. The objective is to choose the type of individuals who will best represent the target population of interest. Depending on the research project the target population might include heavy users, opinion leaders, or consumers currently considering a purchase of the product, for example.

The number of groups conducted usually increases with the number of participant variables (for example, age and geographic area) of interest. Most research issues can be covered with 4–8 groups. Use of more than 10 groups seldom uncovers new information on the same topic. Although some differences in opinion between participants are desirable because they facilitate conversation, participants should be separated into different groups when differences are likely to result in opinions being withheld or modified. For example, including top management with middle management in the same employee focus group can inhibit discussion. Similarly, multiple groups are used to obtain information from different market segments. Depending on the topic being discussed, desirable commonalities among participants may include occupation, education, income, age, or sex.

Selection and Recruitment of Participants Selecting and recruiting appropriate participants are important to the success of any focus group. The general makeup of the target population needs to be represented in the focus groups.

To select participants for a focus group, the researcher must first develop a screening form that specifies the characteristics respondents must have to qualify for participation. The first questions are designed to eliminate individuals who might provide biased comments in the discussion or report the results to competitors. The next questions ensure potential respondents meet the demographic criteria and can come at the scheduled time. A final open-ended question is used to evaluate how willing and able the individual might be to talk openly about a particular topic. This question is related to the general topic of the focus groups and gives the potential respondents a chance to demonstrate their communications skills.

Researchers also must choose a method for contacting prospective participants. They can use lists of potential participants supplied either by the company sponsoring the research project or a screening company that specializes in focus group interviewing, or purchased from a list vendor. Other methods include snowball sampling, random telephone screening, and placing ads in newspapers, on bulletin boards, or on the Internet.

Because small samples are inherently unrepresentative, it is usually not possible to recruit a random sample for qualitative methods. Therefore, researchers select sample members purposively or theoretically. Purposive sampling involves selecting sample members because they possess particular characteristics. For example, sample members may be chosen because they are typical members of their category, or because they are extreme members (for example, heavy users or opinion leaders). A stratified purposive sample may be chosen so that various target group members (for example, low income and high income consumers) are included or to provide comparisons between groups. Theoretical sampling occurs when earlier interviews suggest potentially interesting participants not initially considered in the sampling plan. For example, if discussions with parents reveal that teenagers often have input into household technology purchases, a focus group with teens may be added to the research plan.

Size of the Focus Group Most experts agree that the optimal number of participants in any type of focus group interview is from 10 to 12. Any size smaller than eight participants is not likely to generate synergy between participants. In contrast, having too many participants can easily limit each person's opportunity to contribute insights and observations. Recruiters may qualify more than 12 participants for a focus group because inevitably someone will fail to show. But if more than 12 do show up, some participants are paid and sent home so the group will not be too large.

Focus Group Locations Focus groups can be held in the client's conference room, the moderator's home, a meeting room at a church or civic organization, or an office or hotel meeting room, to name a few. While all of the sites listed above are acceptable, in most instances the best location is a professional focus group facility. Such facilities provide specially designed rooms for conducting focus group interviews. Typically, the room has a large table and comfortable chairs for up to 13 people (12 participants and a moderator), a relaxing atmosphere, built-in recording equipment, and a one-way mirror so that researchers and the client can view and hear the discussions without being seen. Also available is videotaping equipment that captures the participants' nonverbal communication behaviors.

Phase 2: Conducting the Focus Group Discussions

The success of the actual focus group session depends heavily on the *moderator's* communication, interpersonal, probing, observation, and interpretive skills. The **focus group moderator** must be able not only to ask the right questions but also to stimulate and control the

Focus group moderator A person who is well trained in the interpersonal communication skills and professional manners required for a focus group.

direction of the participants' discussions over a variety of predetermined topics. The moderator is responsible for creating positive group dynamics and a comfort zone between himself or herself and each group member as well as among the members themselves.

Moderator's guide Detailed outline of topics to stimulate group interactions.

Preparing a Moderator's Guide To ensure that the actual focus group session is productive, a moderator's guide must be prepared. A **moderator's guide** is a detailed outline of the topics and questions that will be used to generate the spontaneous interactive dialogue among group participants. Consider asking questions in different ways and at different levels of generality. A common question is to ask what participants think of a brand or a product. Asking a focus group to talk about the Mercedes Benz, for example, will elicit comments about the quality and styling of the vehicle. But a moderator can also ask the question in a more novel way, for instance, "What does the Mercedes Benz think of you?" This question elicits entirely different information, for example, that the car company thinks participants are the kind of people who are willing to spend a lot of money for the prestige of owning the brand.[10] The level of question is also important. For example, asking participants how they feel about transportation, cars, or luxury cars will all result in different responses than asking more specifically about the Mercedes.[11] The level of questions chosen is dictated by the research problem.

Beginning the Session After the participants sit down, there should be an opportunity (about 10 minutes) for sociable small talk, coupled with refreshments. The purpose of these presession activities is to create a friendly, warm, comfortable environment in which participants feel at ease. The moderator should briefly discuss the ground rules for the session: participants are told that only one person should speak at a time, everyone's opinion is valued, and that there are no wrong answers. If a one-way mirror or audio/video equipment is being used, the moderator informs participants they are being taped and that clients are sitting behind the one-way mirror. Sometimes group members are asked to introduce themselves with a few short remarks. This approach breaks the ice, gets each participant to talk, and continues the process of building positive group dynamics and comfort zones. After completing the ground rules and introductions, the moderator asks the first question, which is designed to engage participants in the discussion.

Main Session Using the moderator's guide, the first topic area is introduced to the participants. It should be a topic that is interesting and easy to talk about. As the discussion unfolds, the moderator must use probing questions to obtain as many details as possible. If there is good rapport between group members and the moderator, it should not be necessary to spend a lot of time merely asking selected questions and receiving answers. In a well-run focus group, participants interact and comment on each other's answers.

Closing the Session After all the prespecified topics have been covered, participants should be asked a closing question that encourages them to express final ideas or opinions. The moderator may present a final overview of the discussion and then ask the participants, "Have we missed anything?" or "Do you think we've missed anything in the discussion?" Responses to these types of closing questions may reveal some thoughts that were not anticipated. Participants should be thanked for participating and given the promised incentive gift or cash.

Phase 3: Analyzing and Reporting the Results

Debriefing analysis An interactive procedure in which the researcher and moderator discuss the subjects' responses to the topics covered in the focus group session.

Debriefing The researchers and the sponsoring client's representatives should conduct debriefing and wrap-up activities as soon as possible after focus group members leave the session. **Debriefing analysis** gives the researcher, client, and moderator a chance to compare notes. Individuals that have heard the discussion need to know how their impressions compare to those of the moderator.

Content analysis The systematic procedure of taking individual responses and grouping them into larger themes, categories, or patterns.

Content analysis Qualitative researchers use content analysis to create meaningful findings from focus group discussions. **Content analysis** requires the researcher to systematically review transcripts of individual responses and categorize them into larger thematic categories. Although first "topline" reactions are shared during debriefing, more formal analysis will reveal greater detail and identify themes and relationships that were not remembered and discussed during debriefing. Qualitative data analysis is discussed in more detail in Chapter 10.

Advantages of Focus Group Interviews

There are five major advantages to using focus group interviews. They stimulate new ideas, thoughts, and feelings about a topic; foster understanding of why consumers act or behave in certain market situations; allow client participation; elicit wide-ranging participant responses; and bring together hard-to-reach informants. Because group members interact with each other, the social influence process that affects consumer behavior and attitudes can be observed. For example, a review of Coca-Cola's research concerning New Coke found the social influence effects revealed in focus groups were more predictive of the failure of New Coke than were individual interviews.[12]

As with any exploratory research design, focus group interviews are not a perfect research method. The major weaknesses of focus groups are inherently similar to all qualitative methods: the findings lack generalizability to the target population, the reliability of the data is limited, and the trustworthiness of the interpretation is based on the care and insightfulness of researchers. Focus groups have an additional drawback: the possibility that group dynamics contaminate results. While the interaction between participants can be a strength of focus group research, "groupthink" is possible as well. *Groupthink* happens when one or two members of the focus group state an opinion and other members just join the bandwagon. Groupthink occurs most often when participants do not have a previously well-formed opinion on issues discussed in the group.

Other Qualitative Data Collection Methods

In addition to in-depth interviews and focus groups, there are several other qualitative data collection methods used by marketing researchers. We provide a brief overview of these methods here.

Ethnography A form of qualitative data collection that records behavior in natural settings to understand how social and cultural influences affect individuals' behaviors and experiences.

Participant observation An ethnographic research technique that involves extended observation of behavior in natural settings in order to fully experience cultural or subcultural contexts.

Ethnography

Most qualitative methods do not allow researchers to actually see consumers in their natural setting. But ethnography, because of this unique strength, is increasingly being used to help researchers better understand how cultural trends influence consumer choices. **Ethnography** is a distinct form of qualitative data collection that seeks to understand how social and cultural influences affect people's behavior and experiences. Ethnography records behavior in natural settings, often involves an extended experience in a cultural or subcultural context called **participant observation,** produces accounts of behaviors that are credible to the persons who are studied, and involves triangulation among multiple sources of data.[13] For example, an ethnographic study of skydiving employed multiple methods, using observation of two skydiving sites over a two-year time period, participant observation of one researcher who made over 700 dives during the research, and in-depth interviews with skydiving participants with varying levels of experience.[14]

There is no one given set of data collection tools used in ethnography. Participant observation is often used because observers can uncover insights by being part of a culture or subculture that informants cannot always articulate in interviews. But some research questions do not require participant involvement to provide answers to questions. In **nonparticipant observation,** the researcher observes without entering into events. For example, Whirlpool's corporate anthropologist, Donna Romero, conducted a study for a line of luxury jetted bathtubs. She interviewed 15 families in their homes and videotaped participants as they soaked in bathing suits. Last, Romero asked participants to create a journal of images that included personal and magazine photos. From her research, Romero concluded that bathing is a "transformative experience . . . it's like getting in touch with the divine for 15 minutes."[15]

Nonparticipant observation An ethnographic research technique that involves extended contact with a natural setting, but without participation by the researcher.

Netnography

Netnography draws on ethnographic techniques. The difference is that netnography uses "found data" on the Internet that is produced by virtual communities. Online communities are often organized around interests in industries, products, brands, sports teams, or music groups, for instance. Moreover, these communities often contain fanatic consumers who are "lead users" or innovators. The data occurs naturally and is thus not affected by the researcher who collects the data. Rob Kozinets, who developed netnography, used the technique to study an online community of coffeephiles. Kozinets concluded the devotion to coffee among the members of <alt.coffee> was almost religious: "Coffee is emotional, human, deeply and personally relevant—and not to be 'commodified' . . . or treated as just another product."[16]

Netnography A research technique that draws on ethnography but uses "found data" on the internet that is produced by virtual communities.

In netnography, researchers must (1) gain entrée into the culture/community, (2) gather and analyze data, (3) ensure trustworthy interpretation, and (4) provide opportunities for feedback from members of the community (see Chapter 10 for interpretation and analysis of qualitative data). Before gaining entrée, researchers must develop research questions and use search to identify online forums that will provide the answers to their research questions. Generally, researchers prefer to collect data from higher traffic forums with larger numbers of discrete message posters and greater between-member interactions.[17]

Case Studies

Case study research focuses on one or a few cases in depth, rather than studying many cases superficially (as does survey research). The case or element studied may be a process (for example, the organizational purchase decision for large-dollar items), a household, an organization, a group, or an industry.[18] It is particularly useful in studying business-to-business purchase decisions because they are made by one or only a few people. Case study research tracks thinking by the same individual using multiple interviews over several weeks and can therefore obtain subconscious thinking and study group interaction over time as problems, projects, and processes are defined and redefined.

Case study An exploratory research technique that intensively investigates one or a few cases in depth.

Projective Techniques

Projective techniques use indirect questioning to encourage participants to freely project beliefs and feelings into a situation or stimulus provided by the researcher. Participants are asked to talk about what "other people" would feel, think, or do; interpret or produce pictures; or project themselves into an ambiguous situation. Indirect questioning methods are designed to more nearly reveal a participant's true thoughts than are direct questions, which often prompt people to give rational, conscious, and socially desirable responses.

Projective techniques were developed by clinical psychologists and can be used in conjunction with focus groups or in-depth interviews. These techniques include word

Projective technique An indirect method of questioning that enables a subject to project beliefs and feelings onto a third party, into a task situation, or onto an inanimate object.

association tests, sentence completion tests, picture tests, thematic appreciation tests (TAT), cartoon or balloon tests, role-playing activities, and the Zaltman Metaphor Elicitation Technique (ZMET). The stimuli should be ambiguous enough to invite individual participant interpretation, but still specific enough to be associated with the topic of interest.

The major disadvantage of projective techniques is the complexity of interpretation. Highly skilled researchers are required and they can be expensive. There is a degree of subjectivity in all qualitative research analyses, but even more so when projective techniques are used. The background and experiences of the researcher influence the interpretation of data collected by projective techniques.

Word association test A projective technique in which the subject is presented with a list of words or short phrases, one at a time, and asked to respond with the first thoughts [word] that comes to mind.

Word Association Tests In **word association,** a respondent is read a word or a preselected set of words, one at a time, and asked to respond with the first thing that comes to her or his mind regarding that word. For example, what comes to your mind when you hear the words "mobile phone," "iPod," or brand names such as "Target" or "Nike"? Researchers study the responses to "map" the underlying meaning of the product or brand to consumers.

Sentence completion test A projective technique where subjects are given a set of incomplete sentences and asked to complete them in their own words.

Sentence Completion Tests In **sentence completion tests,** participants are presented with sentences and asked to complete them in their own words. When successful, sentence completion tests reveal hidden aspects of individuals' thoughts and feelings toward the object studied. From the data collected, researchers interpret the completed sentences to identify meaningful themes or concepts. For example, let's say the local Chili's restaurant in your area wants to find out what modifications to its current image are needed to attract a larger portion of the college student market segment. Researchers could interview college students in the area and ask them to complete the following sentences:

People who eat at Chili's are _____.

Chili's reminds me of _____.

Chili's is the place to be when _____.

A person who gets a gift certificate for Chili's is _____.

College students go to Chili's to _____.

My friends think Chili's is _____.

ZMET (Zaltman Metaphor Elicitation Technique) A visual research technique used in in-depth interviewing that encourages research participants to share emotional and subconscious reactions to a particular topic.

The Zaltman Metaphor Elicitation Technique (ZMET) The **Zaltman Metaphor Elicitation Technique (ZMET)** is the first marketing research tool to be patented in the United States. It is based on the *projective hypothesis,* which holds that a good deal of thought, especially thought with emotional content, is processed in images and metaphors rather than words.[19] In contrast to the visual method used in the ZMET, both surveys and focus groups—the most widely used techniques in marketing research—rely heavily on verbal stimuli. Gerald Zaltman of Olson Zaltman Associates explains that "consumers can't tell you what they think because they just don't know. Their deepest thoughts, the ones that account for their behavior in the marketplace, are unconscious [and] . . . primarily visual."[20]

Several steps are followed in the ZMET. When recruited, participants are told the topic of the study, for example, Coke. Participants are asked to spend a week collecting 10–15 pictures or images that describe their reaction to the topic (in this case, Coke) and to bring the pictures to their interview. Each participant is asked to compare and contrast pictures and to explain what else might be in the picture if the frame were to be widened. Then, participants construct a "mini-movie" which strings together the images they have been discussing and describes how they feel about the topic of interest. At the end of the interview, participants create a "digital image" which is a summary image of their feelings. When the ZMET was used to study Coke, the company discovered something they already knew—that the drink evokes feelings of invigoration and sociability. But it also found something they did not know—that the drink could bring about feelings of calm solitude and relaxation. This paradoxical view of Coke was highlighted in an ad that showed a Buddhist monk meditating in a crowded soccer field, an image taken from an actual ZMET interview.[21]

Continuing Case: Santa Fe Grill

A business consultant with experience in the restaurant industry was hired by the owners of the Santa Fe Grill. After an initial consultation, the business consultant recommended two areas that needed to be examined. The first area focused on the restaurant operations. The proposed variables to be investigated included:

- Prices being charged.
- Menu items being offered.
- Interior decorations and atmosphere.
- Customer counts at lunch and dinner.
- Average amount spent per customer.

The second area to be studied was to learn more about what factors the Santa Fe Grill customers consider in selecting a restaurant at which to dine. Variables to be examined include:

- Food quality.
- Food variety.
- Waiters and other restaurant employees.
- Pricing.
- Atmosphere.
- Dining out habits.
- Customer characteristics.

1. Do the two research projects proposed by the consultant include all the areas that need to be researched? If not, which others need to be studied?
2. Can these topics be fully understood with qualitative research? Or is quantitative research needed as well?

Observation

Observation is used to collect both qualitative and quantitative data. We have already discussed ethnography, which involves extensive researcher observation and results in qualitative data. But observational methods can be quantitative in nature as well. The primary characteristic of observation methods is that researchers must rely on their observation skills rather than relying on respondents' reports of their behavior. That is, researchers watch and record what people or objects do rather than relying on them to report their behavior.

A great deal of information about the behavior of people and objects can be observed: physical actions (consumers' shopping patterns or automobile driving habits), expressive behaviors (tone of voice and facial expressions), verbal behavior (phone conversations), temporal behavior patterns (amount of time spent shopping online or on a particular Web site), spatial relationships and locations (number of vehicles that move through a traffic light or movements of people at a theme park), physical objects (which brand name items are purchased at supermarkets or which make/model SUVs are driven), and so on. Observational data can be added to data collected using other research designs by providing direct evidence about individuals' actions.

Observation The systematic activities of witnessing and recording the behavioral patterns of objects, people, and events.

Observation involves systematic watching and recording of the behavioral patterns of objects, people, events, and other phenomena. Observation methods require two elements: a behavior or event that is observable and a system of recording it. Behavior patterns are recorded using trained human observers or devices such as videotapes, cameras, audiotapes, computers, handwritten notes, or some other recording mechanism. The main weakness of observation methods is they cannot be used to obtain information on attitudes, preferences, beliefs, emotions, and similar information. Researchers see what people do, but not why they do it. Some research efforts combine observation with other methods to overcome this limitation. One example of a combined methodological approach is usability studies. Moderators give participants activities to complete at a Web site, and then talk to them about any problems they are having in completing their task.

Observation can be described in terms of four characteristics: (1) directness, (2) awareness, (3) structure, and (4) type of observing mechanism. Exhibit 5.6 is an overview of the characteristics and their impact.

Exhibit 5.6	Unique Characteristics of Observation

Characteristic	Description
Directness	The degree to which the researcher or trained observer actually observes the behavior or event as it occurs. Observation can be either direct or indirect.
Awareness	The degree to which individuals consciously know their behavior is being observed and recorded. Observation can be either disguised or undisguised.
Structure	The degree to which the behavior, activities or events to be observed are known to the researcher before doing the observations. Observation can be either structured or unstructured.
Observing Mechanism	How the behavior, activities, or events are observed and recorded. Alternatives include trained human observers and mechanical or electronic devices.

Types of Observation Methods

The type of observation method refers to how behaviors or events will be observed. Researchers can choose between human observers and mechanical or electronic devices. With human observation, the observer is either a person hired and trained by the researcher or is a member of the research team. To be effective, the observer must have a good understanding of the research objectives and excellent observation and interpretation skills. For example, a marketing research professor could use observation skills to capture not only students' classroom behavior but also nonverbal communication exhibited by students during class (for example, facial expressions, body postures, movement in chairs, hand gestures). This enables them to determine, in real time, if students are paying attention to what is being discussed, when students become confused about a concept, or if boredom begins to set in.

Mechanical/electronic observation Data collection using some type of mechanical device to capture human behavior, events, or marketing phenomena.

In many situations the use of mechanical or electronic devices is more suitable than a person in collecting the data. **Mechanical/electronic observation** uses a mechanical or electronic device to capture human behavior, events, or marketing phenomena. Devices commonly used include video cameras, traffic counters, optical scanners, eye tracking monitors, pupilometers, audio voice pitch analyzers, and psychogalvanometers. The devices often reduce the cost and improve the flexibility and accuracy of data collection. For example, when the Department of Transportation conducts traffic-flow studies, air pressure lines are laid across the road and connected to a counter box that is activated every time a vehicle's tires roll over the lines. Although the data is limited to the number of vehicles passing by within a specified time span, this method is less costly and more accurate than using human observers to record traffic flows. Other examples of situations where mechanical/electronic observation would be appropriate include security cameras at ATM locations to detect problems customers might have in operating an ATM, optical scanners and bar-code technology (which relies upon the universal product code or UPC) to count the number and types of products purchased at a retail establishment, turnstile meters to count the number of fans at major sporting or entertainment events, and placing "cookies" on computers to track Internet usage behavior (clickstream analysis).

Advances in technology are making electronic observation techniques more useful and cost-effective. For example, AC Nielsen upgraded its U.S. Television Index (NTI) system by integrating its People Meter technology into the NTI system. The People Meter is a technology-based rating system that replaces handwritten diaries with electronic measuring devices. When the TV is turned on, a symbol appears on the screen to remind viewers to indicate who is watching the program using a handheld electronic device similar to a TV remote control. Another device attached to the TV automatically sends prespecified information (for example, viewer's age, sex, program tuned to, time of program) to Nielsen's computers. Data are used to generate overnight ratings for shows as well as demographic profiles of the audience for various shows.

Scanner-based panel A group of participating households which have a unique bar-coded card as an identification characteristic for inclusion in the research study.

Scanner technology, a type of electronic observation, is rapidly replacing traditional consumer purchase diary methods. **Scanner-based panels** involve a group of participating households that are assigned a unique bar-coded card that is presented to the clerk at the checkout register. The household's code number is matched with information obtained from scanner transactions during a defined period. Scanner systems enable researchers to observe and develop a purchase behavior database on each household. Researchers also can combine offline tracking information with online-generated information for households providing more complete customer profiles. Studies that mix online and offline data can show, for instance, if panel members who are exposed to an online ad or Web site made an offline purchase after their exposure. Scanner data provide week-by-week information on

Stores Call on the Secret Service

Mystery shopping employs trained "spies" pretending to be customers. Mystery shoppers observe a wide array of store employee behaviors in different retail settings. Mystery shopping has been used for over 60 years and the industry tops $700 million in revenue according to the National Center for Professional Mystery Shoppers and Merchandisers based in Tampa, Florida. John Swinburn, Executive Director of the Mystery Shopping Providers Association, tells how the industry has grown from an informal network of homemakers jotting down notes to something more sophisticated. Today, companies want detailed, instant feedback so they can quickly make changes. With increased competition, many retailers find it more challenging to survive, and information from secret shoppers can give them an edge.

The following story illustrates the power of mystery shoppers. A man sat at a bar with his underage daughter—who was served alcohol without being carded—and listened as the bartender bad-mouthed her employer. The bartender was quitting soon and didn't plan to tell her boss. Little did she know that the customer, Doug Kelly, is a spy of sorts. The bartender couldn't have told a worse person because Kelly filed a detailed report and sent it to her employer, noting the indiscretions. It turned out that Doug Kelly is a co-owner and president of Kelly Customer Impressions, Inc., a mystery shopping firm owned by the bartender's employer. Doug and his trained staff visit restaurants, stores, hotels, and cruise ships and report their observations and experiences to management. When doing mystery shopping at a restaurant, for example, mystery shoppers pretend to be regular customers, but watch for whether a hostess greets them with a smile, how quickly food arrives, whether they get proper change for their bill and even how much soap is in the restroom. They record how they were treated during their dining experience, including names of employees and how they were dressed, and then submit detailed reports. Companies that hire these special spies feel mystery shopping information helps them see problems early.

Chris Lewis, Managing Partner of the Bayshore Company, which owns four Radisson hotels along the west coast of Florida explains the rationale for hiring mystery shoppers. In the hotel business, as in many other retail businesses, the most dangerous customer is the moderately satisfied customer. The customers who are really angry will always tell you. The ones who are really happy will always tell you. The customers who are only moderately satisfied and do not complain just don't come back. This is why companies spend the money to obtain mystery-shopping information.

how products are doing in individual stores and track sales against price changes and local ads or promotion activities. They also facilitate longitudinal studies covering longer periods of time.

Scanner technology is also used to observe and collect data from the general population. Market research companies work with drugstores, supermarkets, and other types of retail stores to collect data at check-out counters. The data include products purchased, time of day, day of week, and so forth. Data on advertising campaigns as well as in-store promotions is integrated with the purchase data to determine effectiveness of various marketing strategies.

Perhaps the fastest growing observation approach is tracking clickstream behavior on the Internet. Online merchants, content sites, search engines, and ad servers such as Doubleclick all collect information about online behavior. These companies maintain databases with customer profiles and can predict probable response rates to ads, the time of day and day of week the ads are likely to be most effective, the various stages of potential buyers in the consideration process for a particular product or service, and the type and level of engagement with a Web site.

Selecting the Observation Method

The first step in selecting the observation method is to understand the information requirements and consider how the information will be used. Without this understanding, selecting the observation method is significantly more difficult. First researchers must answer the following questions:

1. What types of behavior are relevant to the research problem?
2. How simple or complex are the behaviors?
3. How much detail of the behavior needs to be recorded?
4. What is the most appropriate setting to observe the behavior—natural or artificial?

Then the various methods of observing behaviors must be evaluated. Issues to be considered include:

1. How complex is the required setting?
2. Is a setting available to observe the behaviors or events?
3. To what extent are the behaviors or events repetitious and frequently exhibited?
4. What degree of directness and structure is needed to observe the behaviors or events?
5. How aware should the subjects be that their behaviors are being observed?
6. Are the observable behaviors or events complex enough to require the use of a mechanical/electronic device to observe the behavior? If so, which method would be most appropriate?

The researcher can now determine the proposed method's ability to accurately observe and record the behavior or activity. The costs involved—time, money, and manpower—also must be determined and evaluated. Finally, potential ethical issues associated with the proposed observation method must be considered.

Benefits and Limitations of Observation Methods

Observation methods have strengths and weaknesses, as summarized in Exhibit 5.7. Among the major benefits is that observation enables collection of actual behavior or activities rather than reported activities. This is especially true in situations where individuals are observed in a natural setting using a disguised technique. In situations where the behaviors or events are complex and unstructured, mechanical/electronic observation techniques such as video cameras are useful. In addition, observation methods reduce recall error, response bias, and refusal to participate, as well as interviewer errors. Finally, data often can be collected in less time and at a lower cost than through other types of procedures.

Exhibit 5.7	Benefits and Limitations of Observation	
Benefits of Observation	**Limitations of Observation**
Accuracy of recording actual behavior	Difficult to generalize findings
Reduces many types of data collection	Cannot explain behaviors or events unless combined with another method
Provides detailed behavioral data	Problems in setting up and recording behavior(s) or events

MARKETING RESEARCH IN ACTION
The Future of For-Profit Higher Education

As over 74 million Gen Y's reach college age and beyond, surging demand for higher education is forcing state universities and community colleges to cap enrollment. For-profit institutions have stepped in to fill the growing need.

The following dialogue is part of an in-depth interview on higher education and where it is heading recently conducted by *American Demographics* reporter Sandra Yin with Sean Gallagher, senior analyst with Eduventures, a consulting firm in Boston that serves the education industry. The dialogue relates only to the for-profit higher education portion of the topic. **AD** is the *American Demographics* reporter and **SG** is Sean Gallagher.

AD: How much will for-profit higher education grow over the next five years?

SG: It is forecasted that total growth from 2005 to 2010 will be about 91 percent based on current growth in enrollment and increases in pricing.

AD: What factors will contribute to this continued growth?

SG: The growth drivers vary. One is the demographic bulge of Gen Y. Another is more people recognize the economic value of a degree. Also, what formerly could be learned through on-the-job training may now require a degree. For example, one might need an associate degree to do specific kinds of health-care work. Because of automation and computers vocational disciplines like auto repair have become more technical than ever.

AD: What distinguishes for-profit schools from the nonprofits?

SG: They are managed as businesses, with all profits coming from tuition. Program offerings are aligned with market demand and employers' needs as well as convenience, accessibility, and flexible scheduling of courses. For-profits often centralize the development of their curriculum and syndicate it throughout their campuses.

Hands-On Exercise

Using the qualitative dialogue from the above in-depth interview, complete the following:

1. Conduct a "content analysis" of Sean Gallagher's response to the questions posed by Sandra Yin of *American Demographics* and identify message themes. Be sure you include support for each of the themes.
2. Given the specific topic of the above interview, what other questions might have been asked to create a richer database?
3. What specific conclusions, if any, could you draw from your analysis of the above interview?

Summary

Identify the major differences between qualitative and quantitative research.

In business problem situations where secondary information alone cannot answer management's questions, primary data must be collected and transformed into usable information. Researchers can choose between two general types of data collection methods: qualitative or quantitative. There are many differences between these two approaches with respect to their research objectives and goals, type of research, type of questions, time of execution, generalizability to target populations, type of analysis, and researcher skill requirements.

Qualitative methods may be used to generate exploratory, preliminary insights into decision problems or address complex consumer motivations that may be difficult to study with quantitative research. Qualitative methods are also useful to understand the impact of culture or subculture on consumer decision making and to probe unconscious or hidden motivations that are not easy to access using quantitative research. Qualitative researchers collect detailed amounts of data from relatively small samples by questioning or observing what people do and say. These methods require the use of researchers well trained in interpersonal communication, observation, and interpretation. Data typically are collected using open-ended or semistructured questioning formats that allow for probing attitudes or behavior patterns or human/mechanical/electrical observation techniques for current behaviors or events. In netnography, qualitative researchers analyze text and images produced in online communities. While qualitative data can be collected quickly (except in ethnography), it requires good interpretive skills to transform into useful findings. As well, the small nonrandom samples that are typically used make generalization to a larger population of interest questionable.

In contrast, quantitative or survey research methods place heavy emphasis on using formal, structured questioning practices where the response options have been predetermined by the researcher. These questions tend to be administered to large numbers of respondents. Quantitative methods are directly related to descriptive and causal types of research projects where the objectives are either to make more accurate predictions about relationships between market factors and behaviors or to validate the existence of relationships. Quantitative researchers are well trained in scale measurement, questionnaire design, sampling, and statistical data analyses.

Understand in-depth interviewing and focus groups as questioning techniques.

An in-depth interview is a formal process of asking a subject a set of semistructured, probing questions in a face-to-face setting. Focus groups involve bringing a small group of people together for an interactive and spontaneous discussion of a particular topic or concept. While the success of in-depth interviewing depends heavily on the interpersonal communication and probing skills of the interviewer, success in focus group interviewing relies more on the group dynamics of the members, the willingness of members to engage in an interactive dialogue, and the moderator's abilities to keep the discussion on track.

In-depth interviewing and focus groups are both guided by similar research objectives: (1) to provide data for defining and redefining marketing problem situations; (2) to provide data for better understanding the results from previously completed quantitative survey studies; (3) to reveal and understand consumers' hidden or unconscious needs, wants, attitudes, feelings, behaviors, perceptions, and motives regarding services, products, or practices; (4) to generate new ideas about products, services, or delivery methods; and (5) to discover new constructs and measurement methods.

Define focus groups and explain how to conduct them.

A focus group is a small group of people (8 to 12) brought together for an interactive, spontaneous discussion. The three phases of a focus group study are planning the study, conducting the actual focus group discussions, and analyzing and reporting the results. In the planning of a focus group, critical decisions have to be made regarding who should participate, how to select and recruit the appropriate participants, what size the group should be, what incentives to offer to encourage and reinforce participants' willingness and commitment to participate, and where the group sessions should be held.

Explain other qualitative data collection methods such as ethnography, case studies, and projective techniques.

There are several useful qualitative data collection methods other than in-depth interviews and focus groups. These methods include ethnography and case studies, which both involve extended contact with research settings. Researchers may also use projective techniques such as word association tests, sentence completion, picture and cartoon tests, thematic apperception tests, and the ZMET, which use indirect techniques to access consumers' feelings, emotions, and unconscious motivations. These techniques are used less frequently than are focus groups but are still considered useful approaches.

Discuss observation methods and explain how they are used to collect primary data.

Observation methods can be used by researchers in all types of research designs (exploratory, descriptive, causal).

In addition to the general advantages of observation, major benefits are the accuracy of collecting data on actual behavior, reduction of confounding factors, and the amount of detailed behavioral data that can be recorded. The unique limitations of observation methods are lack of generalizability of the data, inability to explain current behaviors or events, and the complexity of observing the behavior.

 ## Key Terms and Concepts

Review Questions

1. What are the major differences between quantitative and qualitative research methods? What skills must a researcher have to develop and implement each type of design?

2. Compare and contrast the unique characteristics, main research objectives, and advantages/disadvantages of the in-depth and focus group interviewing techniques.

3. Explain the pros and cons of using qualitative research in each of the following situations:
   a. Adding carbonation to Gatorade and selling it as a true soft drink.
   b. Finding new consumption usages for Arm & Hammer baking soda.
   c. Inducing customers who have stopped shopping at Sears to return to Sears.
   d. Advising a travel agency that wants to enter the cruise ship vacation market.

4. What are the characteristics of a good focus group moderator? What is the purpose of a moderator's guide?

5. Why is it important to have 6 to 12 participants in a focus group? What difficulties might exist in meeting that objective?

6. Why are the screening activities so important in the selection of focus group participants? Develop a screening form that would allow you to select participants for a focus group on the benefits and costs of leasing new automobiles.

7. What are the advantages and disadvantages of "online" focus group interviews compared to "offline" group interviews? How are focus group participants recruited, and what are the common difficulties associated with the recruitment of these people?

8. What are the advantages and disadvantages of ethnography as compared to other qualitative techniques?

9. Develop a word association test that will provide some insight into the following information research question: "What are college students' perceptions of their university's Student Union?"

10. What are the major advantages and disadvantages of observation studies as compared to surveys?

11. Discuss why disguised observation is an appropriate data collection technique for investigating how parents discipline their children when shopping at a supermarket.

◨ Discussion Questions

1. What type of exploratory research design (observation, projective technique, in-depth interview, focus group, case study, ethnography, netnography, ZMET) would you suggest for each of the following situations and why?

   a. A jewelry retailer wants to better understand why men buy jewelry for women and how they select what they buy.

   b. An owner of a McDonald's store is planning to build a playland and wants to know which play equipment is most interesting to children.

   c. Victoria's Secret wants to better understand women's body images.

   d. The senior design engineer for the Ford Motor Company wishes to identify meaningful design changes to be integrated into the 2008 Ford Taurus.

   e. Apple wants to better understand how teenagers discover and choose popular music to download.

   f. Nike wants to better understand the concepts of customization and personalization to support the online product customization services provided by NikeID.

2. Develop a moderator's guide that could be used in a focus group interview to investigate the following question: What does "cool" mean to teens and how do teens decide what products are "cool"?

3. Thinking about how most participants are recruited for focus groups, identify and discuss three ethical issues the researcher and decision maker must consider when using a focus group research design to collect primary data and information.

4. Conduct an in-depth interview and write a brief summary report that would allow you to address the following decision question: "What do students want from their educations?"

5. OutBack Steak, Inc., is concerned about the shifting attitudes and feelings of the public toward the consumption of red meat. Chris Sullivan, CEO and co-founder of OutBack Steak, Inc., thinks that the "red meat" issues are not that important because his restaurants also serve fish and chicken entrees. Select any two "projective interviewing" techniques that you feel would be appropriate in collecting data for the above situation. First, defend your choice of each of your selected projective interviewing techniques. Second, describe in detail how each of your two chosen techniques would be applied to Sullivan's research problem at hand.

6. What type of observational techniques would you suggest for each of the following situations and why?

   a. The director of on-campus housing at your university proposes some significant style changes to the physical configuration of the current on-campus dorm rooms for freshmen and new transfer students.

   b. The senior design engineer for DaimlerChrysler wants to identify meaningful design changes for the 2008 Jeep.

   c. A retail supermarket manager would like to know the popularity of a new brand of cereal that is produced by General Mills.

   d. Fidelity.com wants to test the usability of their Web site for investors who are 65 and older.

Descriptive and Causal Research Designs

Learning Objectives   After reading this chapter, you will be able to:

1. Explain the purpose and advantages of survey research designs.
2. Describe the types of survey methods.
3. Discuss the factors influencing the choice of survey methods.
4. Explain experiments and the types of variables used in causal designs.
5. Define test marketing and evaluate its usefulness in marketing research.

The Excelsior Hotel Preferred Guest Card

Several years ago, Excelsior Hotel implemented a strategy to attract and retain business travelers. The central feature was a VIP hotel card program for business travel customers offering privileges to cardholders not available to other hotel patrons. The program was similar to the airline industry's "frequent flier" programs. To become a member of the preferred guest program, a business traveler had to fill out an application at any of the hotel's properties. There were no costs to join and no annual card fee to members. Excelsior Hotel's corporate accounting records indicated the initial costs associated with the program were approximately $55,000 and annual operating costs were about $85,000. At the end of the program's third year, the membership was 17,000.

At a recent corporate management team meeting, the CEO asked the following questions concerning the Preferred Guest Card Program: "Is the guest card strategy working? Does it give us a competitive advantage?" "Has the program increased the hotel's market share of business travelers?" "Is the company making money from the program?" "Is the program helping to create loyalty among our business customers?" Taken by surprise by this line of questions, the Corporate VP of Marketing replied by saying those were great questions but he had no answers at that time. After having his assistants examine corporate records, the Marketing VP realized all he had was a current membership listing and the total program costs to date of about $310,000. No information was available on the attitudes and behaviors of cardholders and his best estimate of revenue benefits was about $85,000 a year.

The vice president then contacted Alex Smith, senior project director at Marketing Resource Group (MRG). After a meeting they identified two major problems:

1. Excelsior Hotel needed information to determine whether or not the company should continue the Preferred Guest Card program.
2. The Ad agency needed attitudinal, behavioral, motivational, and demographic information to design promotional strategies to attract new members, retain current cardholders, and increase the card usage.

Before undertaking a survey, they decided to conduct qualitative exploratory research using in-depth interviews with the General Managers of several Excelsior Hotel properties and focus group sessions with Excelsior Hotel Preferred Guest Cardholders. This additional information was used to develop the following research questions:

- What are the card usage patterns among Excelsior Hotel Preferred Guest Cardholders?
- What is business travelers' awareness of the card program?
- How important is the card as a factor in selecting a hotel for business purposes?
- Which features of the card program are most valued? Least valued?
- Should Excelsior Hotel charge an annual fee for card membership?
- What are the differences between heavy users, moderate users, light users, and nonusers of the card?

Can qualitative research adequately answer these questions, or is quantitative research needed?

Value of Descriptive and Causal Survey Research Designs

Some research problems require primary data that can only be gathered by questioning a large number of respondents representative of the target population. Chapter 5 covered qualitative methods involving smaller samples. This chapter discusses quantitative methods of collecting primary data, including survey designs used in descriptive and causal research.

We begin this chapter by discussing the relationship between descriptive research designs and survey methods. We then provide an overview of the main objectives of survey research methods. The next section examines in detail the various types of survey methods and the factors influencing survey method selection. The remainder of the chapter reviews causal research designs, including experiments and test marketing.

Descriptive Research Designs and Surveys

Before we discuss methods for conducting descriptive research, it is necessary to understand the relationships among descriptive research designs, quantitative research, and survey methods. Selection of a descriptive research design is based on three factors: (1) the nature of the initial problem or opportunity, (2) the research questions, and (3) the research objectives. When the research problem/opportunity is either to describe characteristics of existing market situations or to evaluate current marketing mix strategies, then a descriptive research design is the appropriate choice. If research questions include issues such as who, what, where, when, and how for target populations or marketing strategies, then a descriptive research design also is most appropriate. Finally, if the task is to identify relationships between variables or determine whether differences exist between groups, then descriptive research designs are generally best.

Two general approaches are used to collect data for descriptive research: asking questions and observation. Descriptive designs frequently use data collection methods which

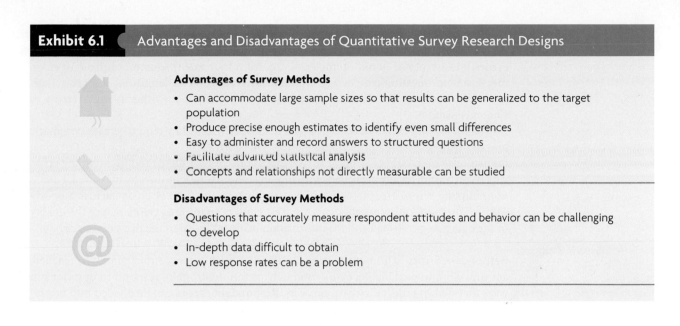

Exhibit 6.1   Advantages and Disadvantages of Quantitative Survey Research Designs

Advantages of Survey Methods

- Can accommodate large sample sizes so that results can be generalized to the target population
- Produce precise enough estimates to identify even small differences
- Easy to administer and record answers to structured questions
- Facilitate advanced statistical analysis
- Concepts and relationships not directly measurable can be studied

Disadvantages of Survey Methods

- Questions that accurately measure respondent attitudes and behavior can be challenging to develop
- In-depth data difficult to obtain
- Low response rates can be a problem

involve asking respondents structured questions about what they think, feel, and do. Thus, descriptive research designs often result in the use of survey research methods to collect quantitative data from large groups of people through the question/answer process. But with the emergence of scanner data and tracking of Internet behavior, observation is being used more often in descriptive designs.

The term "descriptive" is sometimes used to describe qualitative research, but the meaning is different than when the word is used to describe quantitative research. Qualitative research is descriptive in the sense that it provides vivid and detailed textual descriptions of consumers, consumption contexts, and culture. Quantitative studies are descriptive in the sense that they use numbers and statistics to summarize demographics, attitudes, and behaviors.

Survey research methods
Research procedures for collecting large amounts of raw data using question-and-answer formats.

Survey research methods are a mainstay of quantitative marketing research and are most often associated with descriptive and causal research designs. The main goal of quantitative survey research methods is to provide facts and estimates from a large, representative sample of respondents. The advantages and disadvantages of quantitative survey research designs are summarized in Exhibit 6.1.

Types of Errors in Surveys

Sampling error Any type of bias in a survey study that is attributable to mistakes made in either the selection process of prospective sampling units or determining the size of a sample required to ensure its representativeness of the larger defined target population.

Errors can reduce the accuracy and quality of data collected by researchers. Survey research errors can be classified as being either sampling errors or nonsampling errors.

Sampling Error

Any survey research design that involves collecting data from a sample will have some error. **Sampling error** is the difference between the findings based on the sample and the true values for a population. Sampling error is caused by the method of sampling used and the size of the sample, and it can be reduced by increasing sample size and using the appropriate sampling method. We learn more about sampling error in Chapter 7.

Nonsampling Errors

Nonsampling error A type of bias that occurs in a research study regardless of whether a sample or census is used.

Errors that occur in survey research design not related to sampling are called **nonsampling errors.** Most types of nonsampling errors are from four major sources: respondent error, measurement/questionnaire design errors, incorrrect problem definition, and project administration errors. We discuss respondent errors here and the other types of errors in Chapters 8 and 9.

Nonsampling errors have several characteristics. First, they tend to create systematic bias in the data. Second, nonsampling errors are controllable. They are the result of some human mishap in either design or survey execution. Third, unlike random sampling error, which can be statistically measured, nonsampling errors cannot be directly measured. Finally, nonsampling errors are interactive in nature. That is, one type of error, such as a poorly worded question, causes respondent mistakes. Thus, nonsampling errors reduce the quality of the data being collected and the information being provided to the decision maker.

Respondent error The type of nonsampling errors that can occur when selected perspective respondents cannot be initially reached to participate in the survey process, do not answer accurately, or demonstrate an unwillingness to participate in the survey.

Respondent Errors This type of error occurs when respondents either cannot be reached, are unwilling to participate, or intentionally or unintentionally respond to questions in ways that do not reflect their true answers. **Respondent errors** can be divided into nonresponse error and response error.

Nonresponse error is a systematic bias that occurs when the final sample differs from the planned sample. Nonresponse error occurs when a sufficient number of the preselected prospective respondents in the sample refuse to participate or cannot be reached. Nonresponse is caused by many factors. Some people do not trust the research sponsor or have little commitment about responding,[1] while others resent what is perceived as an invasion of their privacy. The differences between people who do and those who do not respond can be striking. For example, some research has shown that for mail surveys, respondents tend to be more educated than nonrespondents and have higher scores on related variables such as income. In addition, women are more likely than men to respond.[2] Methods for improving response rates include multiple callbacks, follow-up mailings, incentives, enhancing the credibility of the research sponsor, and shorter questionnaires.[3]

Nonresponse error An error that occurs when the portion of the defined target population not represented or underrepresented in the response pool is systematically and significantly different from those that did respond.

When researchers ask questions, respondents search their memory, retrieve thoughts, and provide them as responses. Sometimes respondents give the correct answer, but other times they give what they believe is the socially desirable response—whatever makes them look more favorable—or they may simply guess. Respondents may also forget when reporting their past behavior, as human memory is also a source of response errors. When respondents have impaired memory and do not respond accurately, this is termed **response error** or *faulty recall*. Memory is subject to selective perception (noticing and remembering what we want to) and time compression (remembering events as being more recent than they actually were). Respondents sometimes use averaging to overcome memory retrieval problems, for example, telling the interviewer what is typically eaten for dinner on Sunday, rather than what was actually consumed on the previous Sunday.

Response error Error caused by faulty memory or other mental distortions.

◼◗ Types of Survey Methods

Improvements in information technology and telecommunications have created new survey approaches. Nevertheless, survey methods can be classified as person-administered, self-administered, or telephone-administered. Exhibit 6.2 provides an overview of the major types of survey methods.

Exhibit 6.2	Major Types of Survey Research Methods

Type of Survey Research	Description
Person-Administered	
In-home interview	An interview takes place in the respondent's home or, in special situations, within the respondent's work environment (in-office).
Mall-intercept Interview	Shopping patrons are stopped and asked for feedback during their visit to a shopping mall.
Telephone-Administered	
Traditional telephone interview	An interview takes place over the telephone. Interviews may be conducted from a central telephone location or the interviewer's home.
Computer-assisted telephone interview (CATI)	A computer is used to assist in a telephone interview.
Wireless phone surveys	Wireless phones are used to collect data. The surveys may be text-based or Web-based.
Self-Administered	
Mail survey	Questionnaires are distributed to and returned from respondents via the postal service or overnight delivery.
Online surveys	The Internet is used to ask questions and record responses from respondents.
Mail panel survey	Surveys are mailed to a representative sample of individuals who have agreed in advance to participate.
Drop-off survey	Questionnaires are left with the respondent to be completed at a later time. The surveys may be picked up by the researcher or returned via mail.

Person-Administered Surveys

Person-administered surveys
Data collection techniques that require the presence of a trained human interviewer who asks questions and records the subject's answers.

In-home interview A structured question-and-answer exchange conducted in the respondent's home.

Person-administered survey methods have a trained interviewer who asks questions and records the subject's answers. Exhibit 6.3 highlights some of the advantages and disadvantages associated with person-administered surveys.

In-Home Interviews   An **in-home interview** is a face-to-face structured question-and-answer exchange conducted in the respondent's home. Interviews are also occasionally conducted in office environments. This method has several advantages. The interviewer can explain confusing or complex questions and use visual aids. Respondents can try new products or watch potential ad campaigns and evaluate them. In addition, respondents are in a comfortable, familiar environment, thus increasing the likelihood of respondents' willingness to answer the survey's questions.

Frequently, in-home interviewing is accomplished through door-to-door canvassing of geographic areas. This canvassing process is one of the disadvantages of in-home interviewing.

Interviewers who are not well supervised may skip homes they find threatening or even fabricate interviews. In-home and in-office interviews are expensive and time-consuming.

Mall-Intercept Interviews   The expense of in-home interviews has forced many researchers to conduct their surveys in a central location, frequently within regional shopping centers. A **mall-intercept interview** is a face-to-face personal interview that takes place in a shopping mall. Mall shoppers are stopped and asked to complete a survey. The survey may take place in a common area of the mall or in the researcher's on-site offices.

Mall-intercept interviews share the advantages of in-home and in-office interviews, except the environment is not as unfamiliar to the respondent. But mall-intercepts are less expensive and more convenient for the researcher. A researcher spends little time or effort in securing a person's agreement to participate in the interview because both are already at a common location.

The disadvantages of mall-intercept interviews are similar to those of in-home or in-office interviews except that interviewer travel time is reduced. Moreover, mall patrons are not likely to be representative of the target population, even if they are screened. Typically, mall-intercept interviews must use some form of nonprobability sampling, which adversely affects the ability to generalize survey results.

Mall-intercept interview A face-to-face personal interview that takes place in a shopping mall.

Exhibit 6.3	Advantages and Disadvantages of Person-Administered Surveys

Advantages	
Adaptability	Trained interviewers can quickly adapt to respondents' differences.
Rapport	Not all people are willing to talk with strangers when asked to answer a few questions. Interviewers can help establish a "comfort zone" during the questioning process and make the process of taking a survey more interesting to respondents.
Feedback	During the questioning process, interviewers can answer respondents' questions and increase the respondents' understanding of instructions and questions and capture additional verbal and nonverbal information.
Quality of responses	Interviewers can help ensure respondents are screened to represent the target population Respondents are more truthful in their responses when answering questions in a face-to-face situation as long as questions are not likely to result in social desirability biases.

Disadvantages	
Possible recording error	Interviewers may incorrectly record responses to questions.
Interviewer-respondent interaction error	Respondents may interpret the interviewer's body language, facial expression, or tone of voice as a clue to how to respond to a question.
High expense	Overall cost of data collection using an interviewer is higher than other data collection methods.

Telephone-Administered Surveys

Telephone interviews are a major source of market information. Compared to face-to-face interviews, **telephone interviews** are less expensive, faster, and more suitable for gathering data from large numbers of respondents. Interviewers working from their homes or from central locations use telephones to ask questions and record responses.

Telephone survey methods have a number of advantages over face-to-face survey methods. One advantage is that interviewers can be closely supervised if they work out of a central location. Supervisors can record calls and review them later, and they can listen in on calls. Reviewing or listening to interviewers ensures quality control and can identify training needs.

Although there is the added cost of telephone calls, they are still less expensive than face-to-face interviews. Telephone interviews facilitate interviews with respondents across a wide geographic area. The data can be collected relatively quickly, as well. Another advantage of telephone surveys is that they enable interviewers to call back respondents who did not answer the telephone or who found it inconvenient to grant interviews when first called. Using the telephone at a time convenient to the respondent facilitates collection of information from many individuals who would be almost impossible to interview personally. A last advantage is that random digit dialing can be used to select a random sample.

The telephone method also has several drawbacks. One disadvantage is that pictures or other nonaudio stimuli cannot be presented over the telephone. Some research firms overcome this disadvantage by using the Internet to show visual stimuli during telephone interviewing. A second disadvantage is that some questions become more complex when administered over the telephone. For example, imagine a respondent trying to rank 8–10 products over the telephone, a task that is much less difficult in a mail survey. Third, telephone surveys tend to be shorter than personal interviews because some respondents hang up when a telephone interview becomes too lengthy. Telephone surveys also are limited, at least in practice, by national borders; the telephone is seldom used in international research.

Many people are annoyed by telephone research because it interrupts their privacy, their dinner, or their relaxation time. Moreover, the increased use of telemarketing and the illegal and unethical act of "sugging," or selling under the guise of research, has contributed to a poor perception of telephone interviewing among the public.

Computer-Assisted Telephone Interviews (CATI)   Most research firms have computerized the central location telephone interviewing process. With faster, more powerful computers and affordable software, even very small research firms can use **computer-assisted telephone interviewing** (CATI) systems. Interviewers are equipped with a "hands-free" headset and seated in front of a keyboard, "touch-screen" computer terminal, or personal computer.

Most CATI systems have one question per screen. The interviewer reads each question and records the respondent's answer. The program automatically skips questions that are not relevant to a particular respondent. CATI systems overcome most of the problems associated with manual systems of callbacks, complex quota samples, skip logic, rotations, and randomization.

Although the major advantage of CATI is lower cost per interview, there are other advantages as well. Sometimes people need to stop in the middle of an interview but are willing to finish at another time. Computer technology can send inbound calls to a particular interviewer who "owns" the interview and who can complete the interview at a later time. Not only is there greater efficiency per call, there also can be cost savings.

CATI eliminates the need for separate editing and data entry tasks associated with manual systems. The possibility for coding or data entry errors is eliminated with CATI because it is impossible to accidentally record an improper response from outside the set of prelisted responses established for a given question.

Results can be tabulated in real time at any point of the study. Quick preliminary results can be beneficial in determining when certain questions can be eliminated because enough information has been obtained or when some additional questions are needed because of unexpected patterns uncovered in the earlier part of the interviewing process. Use of CATI systems continues to grow because decision makers have embraced the cost savings, quality control, and timesaving aspects of these systems.

Wireless phone survey A method of conducting a marketing survey in which the data are collected on standard wireless phones.

Wireless Phone Surveys In a **wireless phone survey,** data are collected from wireless phone users. Wireless phone surveys are currently in their infancy. But some research firms are starting to experiment with them because they have two specific advantages over Internet and phone surveys: immediacy and portabililty. Wireless phone surveys provide immediacy in the sense that consumers can fill out surveys close to the moments of shopping, decision making, and consuming. For example, wireless phone surveys have been used to (1) capture impulse purchases as they are made and consumed, (2) collect data about side effects in real time from patients who are participating in pharmacological testing, and (3) survey wireless customers. A company named Kinesis Survey Research offers researchers the option of attaching a miniature bar code reader to a mobile phone that will discretely collect and store bar codes of purchased items. Finally, wireless phone panels may be especially appropriate for surveying teens, early adopters, and impulse buyers.[4]

Researchers primarily survey in either text-based or Web-based formats. In short messaging (SMS) format, the respondent can access the survey and display it as text messages on a wireless phone screen. The SMS format is used for simple polling and very short surveys. In Europe, mobile phone penetration rates are high and SMS usage is higher than in the United States, so SMS is often preferred to wireless Web surveys.[5]

In the United States, wireless Web surveys are used more often than SMS. As compared to SMS, the wireless Web facilitates a continuous session, with no time delay between questions and receipt of responses. Wireless Web surveys tend to be cheaper for both the recipient and administrator of the survey. Wireless Web surveys also permit some functionality associated with CATI and Internet surveys to be used, including conditional branching and display of images. When CATI abilities are added to wireless Web surveys, the result is called CAMI, or computer-aided mobile interviewing.[6]

Marketing researchers usually do not call wireless phone users to solicit participation as they do over landlines. One reason is that FCC regulations prevent the use of autodialing. Thus, when potential respondents are called, each one must be dialed by hand. Second, wireless phone respondents incur a cost when taking a survey. Third, wireless phone respondents could be anywhere when they are called, meaning they are likely to be distracted by other activities, and may disconnect in the middle of the call. Safety is a potential issue since respondents could be driving when they get the call from researchers.[7] Typically respondents are recruited using a solicitation method other than the mobile phone, such as landlines, the Internet, mall-intercept, or in-store. Wireless panels are created from participants who have "opted in" or agreed to participate in advance.

We have already mentioned that immediacy is an advantage of wireless Web surveys. A second advantage of wireless surveys is their ability to reach mobile-phone-only households, which are increasing. For example, between 2000 and 2005, the number of landlines in Kansas declined by 19 percent; in New York state, Michigan, and Louisiana by about 13 percent; and in Oregon, New Jersey, Connecticut and Illinois by about 11 percent.[8] Thus, one motivation for the market research industry to use wireless phone surveys is their need to obtain representative samples.[9] Wireless-only households are skewed in sex, race, income, and age. Therefore, utilizing wireless phone surveys along with other methods enables research firms to reach consumers they otherwise could not include in their surveys.

Wireless phone surveys face several challenges. Because of limited screen space, wireless phone surveys are not suitable for research that involves long and/or complex questions and responses. Second, even though mobile phones have some capacity to handle graphics, that capacity is somewhat limited. Third, wireless panels currently provide relatively small sample sizes. In spite of these challenges, this method of surveying is expected to increase over the next decade.

Self-Administered Surveys

A **self-administered survey** is a data collection technique in which the respondent reads survey questions and records his or her own responses without the presence of a trained interviewer. The advantages and disadvantages of self-administered surveys are shown in Exhibit 6.4. We discuss four types of self-administered surveys: mail surveys, mail panels, drop-off, and Internet.

Self-administered survey A data collection technique in which the respondent reads the survey questions and records his or her own answers without the presence of a trained interviewer.

Exhibit 6.4	Advantages and Disadvantages of Self-Administered Surveys
Advantages	
Low cost per survey	With no need for an interviewer or computerized assistance device, self-administered surveys are by far the least costly method of data acquisition.
Respondent control	Respondents are in total control of how fast, when, and where the survey is completed, thus the respondent creates his/her own comfort zone.
No interviewer-respondent bias	There is no chance of introducing interviewer bias or interpretive error based on the interviewer's body language, facial expression, or tone of voice.
Anonymity in responses	Respondents are more comfortable in providing honest and insightful responses because their true identity is not revealed.
Disadvantages	
Minimize flexibility	The type of data collected is limited to the specific questions initially put on the survey. It is impossible to obtain additional in-depth data because of the lack of probing and observation capabilities.
High nonresponse rates	Most respondents will not complete and return the survey.
Potential response errors	The respondent may not fully understand a survey question and provide incorrect responses or mistakenly skip sections of the survey. Respondents may unconsciously commit errors while believing they are responding accurately.
Slow data acquisition	The time required to obtain the data and enter it into a computer file for analysis can be significantly longer than other data collection methods.
Lack of monitoring capability	Not having an interviewer present can increase misunderstanding of questions and instructions.

Mail Surveys   Mail surveys typically are sent to respondents using the postal service. An alternative, for example, in business-to-business surveys where sample sizes are much smaller, is to send questionnaires out by overnight delivery. But overnight delivery is much more expensive.

Direct mail surveys A self-administered questionnaire that is delivered to selected respondents and returned to the researcher by mail.

Direct mail surveys are inexpensive to implement. There are no interviewer-related costs such as compensation, training, travel, or search costs. The costs include postage, printing, and the cost of the incentive. Another advantage is that mail surveys can reach even hard-to-interview people.

One major drawback is lower response rates than with face-to-face or telephone interviews, which creates nonresponse bias. Another problem is that of misunderstood or skipped questions. People who simply do not understand a question may record a response the researcher did not intend. Finally, mail surveys are slow since there can be a significant time lag between when the survey is mailed and when it is returned.

Mail Panel Surveys   To overcome some of the drawbacks of the mail surveys, a researcher may choose a mail panel survey method. A **mail panel survey** is a questionnaire sent to a group of individuals who have agreed to participate in advance. The panel can be tested prior to the survey so the researcher knows the panel is representative. This prior agreement usually results in high response rates. In addition, mail panel surveys can be used for longitudinal research. That is, the same people can be questioned several times over an extended period. This enables the researcher to observe changes in panel members' responses over time.

Mail panel survey A questionnaire sent to a group of individuals who have agreed in advance to participate.

The major drawback to mail panels is that members are often not representative of the target population at large. For example, individuals who agree to be on a panel may have a special interest in the topic or may simply have a lot of time available.

Drop-Off Surveys   A popular combination technique is the **drop-off survey.** In this method, a representative of the researcher hand-delivers survey forms to respondents. Completed surveys are returned by mail or picked up by the representative. The advantages of drop-off surveys include the availability of a person who can answer general questions, screen potential respondents, and create interest in completing the questionnaire. The disadvantage of drop-offs is they are more expensive than mail surveys.

Drop-off survey A self-administered questionnaire that a representative of the researcher hand-delivers to selected respondents; the completed surveys are returned by mail or picked up by the representative.

Online Survey Methods   The most frequently used survey method today in marketing research is **Internet surveys** (see Exhibit 6.5). Why has the administration of online surveys grown so rapidly in a relatively short time? There are several reasons. An important advantage for Internet surveys is that it they are cheaper per respondent than any other survey method. There is no cost of copying surveys or buying postage, and no interviewer cost. Surveys are self-administered, and no coding is necessary; thus the results are ready for statistical analysis almost immediately.

Internet survey A self-administered questionnaire that is placed on a Web site for prospective respondents to read and complete.

The ability of Internet surveys to reach hard-to-reach samples is also another important reason for their growth. Some market research firms maintain large panels of respondents that can be used to identify specific targets, for example, allergy sufferers or doctors. One of the largest online panels, Harris Interactive, has a worldwide panel that numbers in the millions; they have specialty panels that include executives, teens, and gays, lesbians, and transgender individuals. Access to hard-to-reach samples is also possible through community, blog, or social networking sites dedicated to specific demographic or interest groups, such as seniors, for instance, or fans of *The Simpsons,* coffee lovers, or Texas Instrument calculator enthusiasts, just to name a few.[10]

Other advantages of online surveys include the improved functional capabilities of Web site technologies over pen and pencil surveys. One functional improvement is the

Exhibit 6.5	Usage of Types of Survey Methods	
	Internet	36.8%
	CATI	25.3
	Hybrid (2 or more methods)	12.0
	Face-to-face intercepts	11.5
	Mail	3.3
	Other	4.1

Source: *Research Industry Trends 2006 Report*, Pioneer Marketing Research, GreenBook, Dialtek and Rockhopper Research.

ability to randomize the order of questions within a group, so that the effects of question order on responses is removed. Another important improvement over mail surveys is that missing data can be eliminated. Whenever respondents skip questions, they are prompted to answer them before they can move to the next screen. Third, marketing research firms are now learning how to use the improved graphic and animation capabilities of the Web. For example, ranking questions can be completed by respondents by clicking and dragging the items into the appropriate order. Words that might describe the respondent's personality, a brand, a product, or a retailer can be animated to move from left to right, with the respondent clicking on the appropriate words as they pass by on their screen. Pictures and videos can be used, so that full-color 3D pictures and videos of store interiors, products, ads, or movie reviews can be shown in the context of online surveys. Graphic improvements to survey design make tasks more realistic and more engaging for respondents.

In addition to using online panels created by marketing research firms, companies may survey their own customers using their existing e-mail lists to send out invitations to participate in surveys. Small businesses can use online survey creation software offered by businesses like **Zoomerang.com** and **Surveymonkey.com** to design an online survey and collect data relatively easily and inexpensively. Some online retailers use research contests both to gather information and increase customer engagement with their company. For instance, graphic designers post pictures of possible T-shirts at **www.Threadless.com**. The designs that garner the most votes are printed and offered for sale on the site.

While the benefits of online surveys include low cost per completed interview, quick data collection, and the ability to use visual stimuli, Internet samples are rarely representative and nonresponse bias can be high. About 70 percent of individuals in the United State have home access to the Internet, which limits the ability to generalize to the general population. **Propensity scoring** can be used to adjust the results to look more like those a representative sample would have produced, but the accuracy of this procedure must be evaluated. With propensity scoring the responses of underrepresented sample members are weighted more heavily to adjust for sampling inadequacies. For example, if respondents who are 65 or older are only half as likely to be in an Internet sample as their actual incidence in the population, each senior who responds would be counted twice in the sample.

Propensity scoring
Weighting underrepresented respondents more heavily in results.

Selecting the Appropriate Survey Method

Researchers weigh various factors when choosing a survey method. The following sections describe situational, task, and respondent factors affecting choice of survey method.

Situational Factors

In an ideal situation, researchers could focus solely on the collection of accurate data. We live in an imperfect world, however, and researchers must cope with the competing objectives of budget, time, and data quality. In choosing a survey research method, the goal is to produce usable data in as short a time as possible at the lowest cost. But there are trade-offs. It is easy to generate large amounts of data in a short time if quality is ignored. But excellent data quality often can be achieved only through expensive and time-consuming methods. In selecting the survey method, the researcher commonly considers a number of situational factors in combination.

Budget The budget includes all the resources available to the researcher. While budgets are commonly thought of in terms of dollar amount, other resources such as staff size can also constrain research efforts. Budget determinations are frequently much more arbitrary than researchers would prefer. However, it is rare the budget is the sole determinant of the survey method. Much more commonly, the budget is considered along with data quality and time in selecting a survey method.

Completion Time Frame Long time frames give researchers the luxury of selecting the method that will produce the highest quality data. In many situations, however, the affordable time frame is much shorter than desired, forcing the researcher to choose a method that may not be ideal. Some surveys, such as direct mail or personal interviews, require relatively long time frames. Other methods, such as Internet surveys, telephone surveys, or mall intercepts, can be done more quickly.

Quality Requirements Data quality is a complex issue that encompasses issues of scale measurement, questionnaire design, sample design, and data analysis. A brief overview of three key issues will help explain the impact of data quality on the selection of survey methods.

Completeness of Data *Completeness* refers to the depth and breadth of the data. Having complete data allows the researcher to paint a total picture, fully describing the information from each respondent. Incomplete data will lack some amount of detail, resulting in a picture that is somewhat vague or unclear. Personal interviews and Internet surveys tend to be complete, while mail surveys may not be. In some cases, the depth of information needed to make an informed decision will dictate that a personal survey is the appropriate method.

Data Generalizability Data that are *generalizable* accurately represent the population being studied. Data collected from mail surveys are frequently less generalizable than those collected from phone interviews or personal interviews due to low response rates. Small sample size will limit the generalizability of data collected using any technique.

Data Precision *Precision* refers to the degree of exactness of the data in relation to some other possible response. For example, if all a car company needs to know is that bright colors are preferred, then less precise data will suffice. If, however, the car company needs to know that red is preferred by a two-to-one margin, then precise data are needed. Mail and Internet surveys can frequently deliver precise results, but may not always produce the most generalizable results. Telephone surveys may be generalizable but may lack precision due to short questions and short interview times.

Task Factors

Researchers ask respondents to engage in tasks that take time and effort. Task factors include: (1) task difficulty; (2) required stimuli; (3) amount of information asked from respondents; and (4) sensitivity of the research topic.

Difficulty of the Task Answering some kinds of survey questions can be somewhat difficult for respondents. For example, product or brand preference testing may involve comparing and rating many similar products and therefore can be laborious for the respondents. **Task difficulty** is an important factor to consider—and to try to alleviate. In general, more complex survey environments require more highly trained individuals to conduct the interviews. Regardless of the difficulty of the survey task, the researcher should try to make it as easy as possible for respondents to answer the questions.

Task difficulty How hard a survey respondent needs to work to complete a survey.

Stimuli Needed to Elicit the Response Frequently, researchers need to expose respondents to some type of stimulus in order to elicit a response. Common examples of stimuli are products (as in taste tests) and promotional visuals (as in advertising research). An interviewer is often needed in situations where respondents must touch or taste something. The Internet and personal surveys can be used whenever visual stimuli are required in the research.

The actual form of the personal interview may vary. It is not always necessary to design a one-on-one interview. For example, people may come in groups to a central location for taste testing, or people in mall-intercepts can be shown videos to obtain their opinions on advertising.

Amount of Information Needed from the Respondent Generally speaking, if a large amount of detailed information is required from respondents, the need for personal interaction with a trained interviewer increases. As with any survey method, however, collecting more data lowers response rates and increases respondent fatigue. The survey researcher's goal is to achieve the best match between the survey method and the amount of information needed.

Research Topic Sensitivity In some cases, the research problem requires researchers to ask socially or personally sensitive questions. **Topic sensitivity** is the degree to which a specific survey question leads the respondent to give a socially acceptable response. When asked about a sensitive issue, some respondents will feel they should give a socially acceptable response even if they actually feel or behave otherwise. Phone and face-to-face interaction increases the tendency to report socially desirable attitudes and behavior. Undesirable behaviors such as cigarette smoking are likely to be underreported during personal interviews while desirable behaviors such as recycling are likely to be overreported. Even behaviors that are seemingly benign may be under- or overreported based on the social desirability of the behavior. For example, when Quaker Oats conducted a study using both an online survey and mall-intercept survey, they found that the online sample reported significantly more daily snacking behavior. Quaker Oats concluded that the online respondents were more honest.[11] In addition, some respondents simply refuse to answer questions they consider too personal or sensitive. Others may even terminate the interview.

Topic sensitivity The degree to which a survey question leads the respondent to give a socially acceptable response.

Respondent Factors

Since most marketing research projects target prespecified groups of people, the third major factor in selecting the appropriate survey method is the respondents' characteristics. The extent to which members of the target group of respondents share common characteristics influences the survey method selected.

Diversity *Diversity* of respondents refers to the degree to which respondents share characteristics. The more diverse the respondents the fewer similarities they share. The less diverse the respondents the more similarities they share. For example, if the defined target population is specified as people who own or have access to a fax machine, then diversity is low and a fax survey can be an effective and cost-efficient method. However, if the defined target population does not have convenient access to a fax machine fax surveys will fail.

There are cases in which the researcher may assume a particular personal characteristic or behavior is shared by many people in the defined target population, when in fact very few share that characteristic. For example, the rates of unlisted telephone numbers vary significantly by geographic area. In some areas (e.g., small rural towns in Illinois), the rate of unlisted numbers is very low (< 10%), while in others (e.g., large cities like New York or Los Angeles), the rate is very high (>50%).

Respondent Participation Over the years, researchers have developed strategies to increase participation levels. One frequently used strategy is offering an incentive. Incentives can include both monetary "gifts" such as a dollar bill and nonmonetary items such as a pen, a coupon to be redeemed for a food product, or entry into a drawing. Another strategy to increase participation would be to personally deliver the questionnaire to potential respondents. In survey designs that involve group situations, researchers can use social influence to increase participation, for example, mentioning that neighbors or colleagues have already participated.

Experiments and Test Marketing

Exploratory and descriptive research designs are useful for many types of studies. But they do not examine causal links between marketing variables. In contrast, *experiments* are causal research designs and can identify cause-and-effect relationships between variables and determine why events occur.

Test marketing, a special type of experimental design, is used to assess customer attitudes toward new product ideas, service delivery alternatives, or marketing communication strategies. Test marketing consists of controlled field experiments conducted in limited market areas on selected marketing indicators. Its main objectives are to predict sales, identify consumer reactions, and anticipate adverse consequences of marketing programs.

The Nature of Experimentation

Variable A concept that can have more than one value.

Marketing research often involves measurement of variables. A **variable** is a concept or construct that can vary or have more than one value. In marketing, variables include demographics such as age and income, attitudes such as brand loyalty and customer satisfaction, and behaviors such as media consumption and purchase and product usage.

When conducting an experiment, researchers attempt to identify the relationships between variables of interest. Let's consider, for example, the following research question: "How long does it take a customer to receive an order from the drive-through at a Wendy's fast-food restaurant?" The time it takes to receive a food order is a variable that can be measured quantitatively. That is, the different values of the time variable are determined by some method of measurement. But how long it takes a particular customer to receive a food order is complicated by a number of other variables. For instance, what if there were 10 cars waiting in line, or it was 12:00 noon, or it was raining? Other factors such as the number of drive-up windows, the training level of order takers, and the number of customers waiting also are variables. Consequently, all of these variables can have an effect on the order time variable.

Other variables include the make of the car the person is driving, the number of brothers or sisters they have, and the quantity of food ordered. The first two variables are unlikely to have an effect on order time. But there is likely to be a relationship between the quantity of items in the order and waiting time. If it is true that the quantity of food ordered increases customer wait time at a drive-through, the researcher can conclude that there is a relationship between food quantity ordered and waiting time. In causal research designs involving experiments, the focus is on determining if there is systematic change in one variable as another variable changes.

Experimental research is primarily a hypothesis testing method which examines hypotheses about relationships between independent and dependent variables. Researchers develop hypotheses and then design an experiment to test the hypothesis. To do so, researchers must identify the *independent* variables that might bring about changes in one or more *dependent* variables. Experiments and other causal designs are most appropriate when the researcher wants to find out why certain events occur and why they happen under certain conditions and not others.

Experiments enable marketing researchers to control the research situation so that causal relationships among the variables can be examined. In a typical experiment the independent variable is manipulated (changed) and its effect on another variable (dependent variable) is measured and evaluated. Researchers attempt to measure or control the influence of any variables other than the independent variable that could affect the dependent variable; these are **control variables.** Any variables that might affect the outcome of the experiment and which are not measured or controlled are called **extraneous variables.** After the experiment, the researcher measures the dependent variable to see if it has changed. If it has, the researcher concludes that the change in the dependent variable is caused by the independent variable.

Validity Concerns with Experimental Research

To use causal research designs, researchers must understand *validity*. There often are numerous uncontrollable variables with experimental designs. Their presence can make it difficult to determine whether the results of the experiment are valid. That is, was the change in the dependent variable caused by the independent variable or something else? **Validity** is the extent to which the conclusions drawn from the experiment are true.

Internal Validity   **Internal validity** refers to the extent to which the research design accurately identifies causal relationships. In other words, internal validity exists when the researcher can rule out competing explanations for the conclusions about the relationship. The following example illustrates the importance of ruling out competing hypotheses and thus establishing internal validity. A bakery in White Water, Wisconsin, wanted to know whether or not putting additional frosting on its cakes would cause customers to like the cakes better. Researchers used an experiment to test the hypothesis that customers prefer additional frosting on their cakes. However, when the amount of frosting was increased, it also made the cakes more moist. Customers reacted favorably to this change. But was the favorable reaction caused by the moistness of the cakes or by the additional frosting?

External Validity   **External validity** means the results of the experiment can be generalized to the target population. For example, imagine that a food company wants to find out if its new dessert would appeal to a market segment between the ages of 18 and 35. It would be too costly to ask every 18- to 35-year-old in the United States to taste the product. But using experimental design methods the company can randomly select individuals in the target

Experimental research An empirical investigation that tests for hypothesized relationships between dependent variables and manipulated independent variables.

Control variables Variables that the researcher does not allow to vary freely or systematically with independent variables; control variables should not change as the independent variable is manipulated.

Extraneous variables Any variables that experimental researchers do not measure or control that may affect the dependent variable.

Validity The extent to which the conclusions drawn from the experiment are true.

Internal validity The extent to which the research design accurately identifies causal relationships.

External validity The extent to which a causal relationship found in a study can be expected to be true for the entire target population.

population (aged 18–35) and assign them to different treatment groups, varying one component of the dessert for each group. Respondents in each treatment group would then taste the new dessert. If 60 percent of the respondents indicated they would purchase the product, and if in fact 60 percent of the targeted population did purchase the new product when it was marketed, then the results of the study would be considered externally valid.

Comparing Laboratory and Field Experiments

Lab experiment Experiment conducted in an artificial setting.

Marketing researchers use two types of experiments—laboratory and field. **Laboratory (lab) experiments** are conducted in an artificial setting. If a researcher recruits participants for an experiment where several different kinds of ads are shown and asks them to come to a research facility to view and evaluate the TV ads, this would be a laboratory experiment. The setting is different than would be natural for viewing TV ads, which would be in the home, and is therefore considered artificial. Laboratory experiments enable the researcher to control the setting and therefore achieve high internal validity. But the trade-off is that laboratory experiments lack external validity.

Field experiments Causal research designs that manipulate the independent variables in order to measure the dependent variable in a natural test setting.

Field experiments are performed in natural or "real" settings. Field experiments are often conducted in retail environments such as malls or supermarkets. These settings provide a high level of realism. But high levels of realism mean the independent and extraneous variables are difficult to control. Problems with control occur in several ways. For example, conducting a field experiment of a new product in a supermarket requires the retailer's permission to put the product in the store. Given the large number of new-product introductions each year, retailers are becoming more hesitant about adding new products. Even if the retailer cooperates, proper display and retailer support are needed to conduct the experiment.

Besides realism and control, there are at least three other issues to consider when deciding whether to use a field experiment: time frames, costs, and competitive reactions. Field experiments take longer to complete than laboratory experiments. The planning stage—which can include determining which test market cities to use and which retailers to approach with product experiments, securing advertising time, and coordinating the distribution of the experimental product—adds to the length of time needed to conduct field experiments. Field experiments are more expensive to conduct than laboratory experiments because of the high number of independent variables that must be manipulated. For example, the cost of an advertising campaign alone can increase the cost of the experiment. Other items adding to the cost of field experiments are coupons, product packaging development, trade promotions, and product sampling. Because field experiments are conducted in a natural setting, competitors can learn about the new product almost as soon as it is introduced and respond by using heavy promotional activity to invalidate the results of the experiment or by rushing similar products to market. If secrecy is desired, then laboratory experiments are generally more effective.

Test Marketing

Test marketing Using controlled field experiments to gain information on specified market performance indicators.

The most common type of field experiment is test marketing. **Test marketing** is the use of experiments to obtain information on market performance indicators. Test marketing measures the sales potential of a product and evaluates variables in the product's marketing mix. The cost of conducting test marketing experiments can be high. But with the failure rate of new consumer products estimated to be between 80 and 90 percent, many companies believe the expense of conducting test marketing can help them avoid the more expensive mistake of an unsuccessful product rollout. Read the following *Marketing Research in Action* to see how the Lee Apparel Company used test marketing procedures to build a unique customer database to successfully launch a new brand of women's jeans.

Marketing Research in Action
Riders Fits New Database into Brand Launch

The Lee Apparel Company used market test data from a field experiment to build a customer database and help successfully launch a new brand of jeans. A few years ago, the company decided to market a new apparel line of jeans under the name Riders. The management team seized the opportunity to begin building a customer database. Unlike the typical process of building a customer database around promotions, merchandising, and advertising efforts that directly benefit retailers, their goal was to use marketing dollars to build both the brand and the database. The initial launch of the Riders apparel line went well with rollouts in the company's Midwest and Northeast regional markets. The initial positioning strategy called for the products to be priced slightly higher than competitive brands and marketed at mass-channel retailers like Ames, Bradlee's, Caldor, Target, and Venture. During the first year, the communication program emphasized the line's "comfortable fit," and within two years the rollouts went national, using major retail channels like Wal-Mart.

Initially, Riders used a spring promotion called "Easy Money" to generate product trial and to gather name, address, and demographic information about the line's first customers. This data was collected using a rebate card and certificate from the retailer. Upon completing and mailing the rebate card to Riders, the customer was rewarded with a check in the mail. This initial market test provided valuable data on each customer, such as the exact type of product purchased, how much was spent, whom they bought for, where they heard of the Riders brand, and their lifestyle interests. As part of the test market, Riders supported the effort with point-of-purchase (POP) displays and promotions in Sunday newspaper circulars. In addition, the management team funded the promotion and handled all development, redemption, and fulfillment in-house. Results of the first test market were as follows: a total of $1.5 million in certificates were distributed yielding a 2.1 percent response, or just over 31,000 customer names. About 20 percent of the buyers bought more than one item.

Another part of the test market design was the follow-up phone survey among new customers three months after the initial promotion. Of the customers surveyed, 62 percent had purchased Riders products. The survey provided detailed information to salespeople and consumers. Riders then repeated the test market design adding a postcard mailing to existing database names. The promotional effort netted over 40,000 new customer names and information for the database. It also proved the responsiveness of database customers—3.8 percent of the database customers who received the postcard promotion came into the store to make a purchase, compared to a 2.8 percent response to the POP and circular ads.

To build a successful customer database from test market designs, the critical first step is figuring out the most efficient way to gather the names. The second step is deciding how you want to use the information with customers, prospects, and retailers. Finally, you begin the process of testing and evaluating the relationships and applying what you have learned to build customer loyalty.

Focus on Retail Partnerships

The main goal of the test marketing was to create valuable information that could be used to build relationships with Riders consumers and those retail accounts Riders depended on for distribution. The growing philosophy within the Riders brand management team was

"The more we know about our customers, the better the decisions we'll be able to make in dealing both with them and with our retailers." Moreover, the detailed information such as hard dollar results of each promotion as well as the demographic profiles is shared with retailers, as is the research showing the consumer behavior benefits. For example, a tracking study found that purchase intent of database customers was twice that of nondatabase customers in a given trade area. Unaided brand awareness likewise was high (100 percent, compared to 16 percent of the general population), and awareness of Riders advertising was 53 percent compared to 27 percent.

The Riders team believed so strongly in tying database information with promotional efforts that they insisted that a database component be part of any chain-specific promotions. Management hoped to convince the retailers to build their own database capabilities to share their information. For example, retail account information can identify more product and promotion opportunities. Riders believed the real payoff comes when both manufacturer and retailer use data, from either source, to do a better job of attracting and keeping the key asset for both channel members—the customer. Riders must continue convincing retailers that putting Riders merchandise on their shelves is bringing people into their stores. From test marketing to creating complete customer databases, the Riders team has begun to put a major part of its marketing investment into image-building advertising strategies focused on print and television media.

For instance, they say, "The more we know about our customers and their preferences, the better we'll be able to hone our advertising messages and media buys, pinpoint what kind of promotions work best, and understand what new products we ought to be developing. As competitive pressures continue to mount, Riders expects detailed customer information to become more valuable in helping define the brand position clearly. Defining ourselves and what's different about Riders products is going to be an increasingly important element in drawing customers who have a great many choices to stores where Riders products are on the shelves. Although it initially began with test markets guiding the development of a complete customer database program, it's now the databases that are guiding the inclusion of key elements in our test market research. Riders' ultimate goal is creating a tool that is going to make its products more attractive to retailers and to consumers."

Hands-on Exercise

Using your knowledge from reading about market tests, answer the following questions:

1. What was Lee Apparel Company's overall goal for conducting such an extensive test market of its new line of jeans under the brand name "Riders"? In your opinion, did the company achieve its goal? Why or why not?
2. Identify and explain the strengths and weaknesses associated with the test market process used by the Lee Apparel Company.
3. In your opinion, should the company give consideration to the development and implementation of Internet-based test marketing strategies? Why or why not?

◗ Summary

Explain the purpose and advantages of survey research designs.

The main advantages of using descriptive survey research designs to collect primary data from respondents are large sample sizes are possible; generalizability of results; ability to distinguish small differences between diverse sampled groups; ease of administering; and the ability to identify and measure factors that are not directly measurable (such as customer satisfaction). In contrast, disadvantages of descriptive survey research designs include the difficulty of developing accurate survey instruments, inaccuracy in construct definition and scale measurement, and limits to the depth of the data that can be collected.

Describe the types of survey methods.

Survey methods are generally divided into three generic types. One is the person-administered survey, in which there is significant face-to-face interaction between the interviewer and the respondent. The second is the telephone-administered survey. In these surveys the telephone is used to conduct the question-and-answer exchanges. Computers are used in many ways in telephone interviews, especially in data recording and telephone-number selection. The third type is the self-administered survey. In these surveys, there is little, if any, actual face-to-face contact between the researcher and prospective respondent. The respondent reads the questions and records his or her answers.

Discuss the factors influencing the choice of survey methods.

There are three major factors affecting the choice of survey method: situational, task, and respondent factors. With situational factors, consideration must be given to elements such as available resources, completion time frame, and data quality requirements. Also, the researcher must consider the overall task requirements and ask questions like "How difficult are the tasks?" "What stimuli (e.g. ads or products) will be needed to evoke responses?" "How much information is needed from the respondent?" and "To what extent do the questions deal with sensitive topics?" Finally, researchers must consider the diversity of the prospective respondents, their likely incidence rate, and the degree of survey participation. Maximizing the quantity and quality of data collected while minimizing the cost and time of the survey generally requires the researcher to make trade-offs.

Explain experiments and the types of variables used in causal designs.

Experiments enable marketing researchers to control the research situation so that causal relationships among the variables can be examined. In a typical experiment the independent variable is manipulated (changed) and its effect on another variable (dependent variable) is measured and evaluated. During the experiment the researcher attempts to eliminate or control all other variables that might impact the relationship being measured. After the manipulation, the researcher measures the dependent variable to see if it has changed. If it has, the researcher concludes that the change in the dependent variable is caused by the manipulation of the independent variable.

To conduct causal research, the researcher must understand the four types of variables in experimental designs (independent, dependent, extraneous, control) as well as randomization of test subjects and the role that theory plays in creating experiments. The most important goal of any experiment is to determine which relationships exist among different variables (independent, dependent). Functional (cause–effect) relationships require measurement of systematic change in one variable as another variable changes.

Define test marketing and evaluate its usefulness in marketing research.

Test markets are a specific type of field experiment commonly conducted in natural field settings. Data gathered from test markets provide both researchers and practitioners with invaluable information concerning customers' attitudes, preferences, purchasing habits/patterns, and demographic profiles. This information can be useful in predicting new product/service acceptance levels and advertising and image effectiveness, as well as in evaluating current marketing mix strategies.

Key Terms and Concepts

Review Questions

1. Identify and discuss the advantages and disadvantages of using quantitative survey research methods to collect primary data in marketing research.
2. What are the three critical components for determining data quality? How does achieving data quality differ in person-administered surveys and self-administered surveys?
3. Explain why survey designs that include a trained interviewer are more appropriate than computer-assisted survey designs in situations where the task difficulty and stimuli requirements are extensive.
4. Explain the major differences between in-home interviews and mall-intercept interviews. Make sure you include their advantages and disadvantages.
5. How might measurement and design errors affect respondent errors?
6. Develop three recommendations to help researchers increase the response rates in direct mail and telephone-administered surveys.
7. What is "nonresponse"? Identify four types of nonresponse found in surveys.
8. What are the advantages and disadvantages associated with "online" surveys?
9. How might a faulty problem definition error affect the implementation of a mail survey?
10. Explain the difference between internal validity and external validity.
11. What are the advantages and disadvantages of field experiments?

Discussion Questions

1. Develop a list of the factors used to select from person-administered, telephone-administered, self-administered, and computer-assisted survey designs. Then discuss the appropriateness of those selection factors across each type of survey design.

2. What impact, if any, will advances in telecommunication and computer technologies have on survey research practices? Support your thoughts.

3. **EXPERIENCE THE INTERNET.** Go to the latest Gallup Poll survey (www.gallup.com) and evaluate the survey design being used. Write a two-page report that summarizes the design's strengths and weaknesses.

4. Comment on the ethics of the following situations:

   a. A researcher plans to use invisible ink to code his direct mail questionnaires to identify those respondents who return the questionnaire.

   b. A telephone interviewer calls at 10:00 P.M. on a Sunday and asks to conduct an interview.

   c. A manufacturer purchases 100,000 e-mail addresses from a national e-mail distribution house and plans to e-mail out a short sales promotion under the heading of "We Want to Know Your Opinions."

5. The store manager of a local independent grocery store thought customers might stay in the store longer if slow, easy-to-listen-to music were played over the store's intercom system. After some thought, the manager considered whether he should hire a marketing researcher to design an experiment to test the influence of music tempo on shoppers' behaviors. Answer the following questions:

   a. How would you operationalize the independent variable?

   b. What dependent variables do you think might be important in this experiment?

   c. Develop a hypothesis for each of your dependent variables.

Part 3

Gathering
and
Collecting
Accurate
Data

Sampling: Theory and Methods

Chapter 7

1. Explain the role of sampling in the research process.
2. Distinguish between probability and nonprobability sampling.
3. Understand factors to consider when determining sample size.
4. Understand the steps in developing a sampling plan.

The Web: A Growing Trend for Mobile Searching

As mobile phone and Internet technologies continue to advance, opportunities for searching the Web through mobile phones are just around the corner. According to Ron Rogowski, Senior Analyst at Forrester Research, an independent technology and market research company that predicts technology's impact on business and consumers, many businesses and consumers aren't ready to engage the Web through their mobile phones. Recent Forrester studies show that 80 percent of marketers use or plan to use search engine marketing (SEM), yet less than a third of retail marketers and one-half of consumer-product/goods marketers expect to use mobile search in their marketing mixes. Media companies are most receptive, with about 70 percent planning to use mobile search in their promotion mixes. In contrast, consumers are less ready to adopt the idea of mobile search. Among today's 190 million cell phone subscribers, only about 5 percent have ever used their phones for Web searches, less than half the number who buy a ringtone each month.

Two of the reasons for the slow acceptance of mobile search activities are (1) searching on a two-inch mobile screen is not yet a good user experience and (2) consumers mistakenly believe a mobile search should be the same as an Internet search. From the findings in another study, Tony Phillip, CEO of UpSNAP, a search firm that offers free weather, sports scores, and subscription content, reminds consumers that mobile search is not the Internet on a phone and people need to think of a mobile search as one alternative to finding a specific, quick hit.

From a marketing research perspective, there are two key questions to be asked about studies on mobile search. First, *"What respondents should be included in a study about consumer acceptance of mobile search?"* And second, *"How many respondents should be included in each study?"* These might be difficult questions to answer for companies that do not have good customer demographics, attitudes, and behavior databases. But specialty research firms like Survey Sampling International, LLC (SSI), one of the premier international marketing research firms specializing in selecting high-quality samples for over

1,500 clients each year, can help. SSI (**www.ssisamples.com**) has the technology and skills to generate a wide variety of samples for targeting consumers and/or businesses based on lifestyles, topics of interest, and demographics such as age, presence of children, occupation, marital status, education level, and income. The firm is well respected for its Internet, RDD, telephone, B2B, and mail sampling designs. As you read this chapter, you will learn the importance of knowing whom to sample, how many elements to sample, and the different methods available to researchers for drawing high-quality, reliable samples.

Value of Sampling in Marketing Research

Sampling is a concept we practice in our everyday activities. Consider, for example, going on a job interview. Making a good first impression in a job interview is important because based on the initial exposure (i.e., sample) people often make judgments about the type of person we are. Similarly, people sit in front of their TV with a remote control in their hand and rapidly flip through a number of different channels, stopping a few seconds to take a sample of the program on each channel until they find a program worth watching. Next time you have a free moment, go to a bookstore like Barnes and Noble and observe sampling at its best. People at a bookstore generally pick up a book or magazine, look at its cover, and read a few pages to get a feel for the author's writing style and content before deciding whether to buy the book. When people go automobile shopping, they want to test-drive a particular car for a few miles to see how the car feels and performs before deciding whether to buy it. One commonality in all these situations is that a decision is based on the assumption that the smaller portion, or sample, is representative of the larger population. From a general perspective, **sampling** involves selecting a relatively small number of elements from a larger defined group of elements and expecting the information gathered from the small group will enable accurate judgments about the larger group.

Sampling Selection of a small number of elements from a larger defined target group of elements and expecting that the information gathered from the small group will enable judgments to be made about the larger group.

Census A research study that includes data about every member of the defined target population.

Sampling as a Part of the Research Process

Sampling is often used when it is impossible or unreasonable to conduct a census. With a **census** primary data is collected from every member of the target population. The best example of a census is the U.S. Census, which takes place every 10 years.

It is easy to see that sampling is less time-consuming and less costly than conducting a census. For example, American Airlines may want to find out what business travelers like and dislike about flying with them. Gathering data from 2,000 American business travelers would be much less expensive and time-consuming than surveying several million travelers. No matter what type of research design is used to collect data, decision makers are concerned about the time and cost required, and shorter projects are more likely to fit the decision maker's time frames.

Samples also play an important indirect role in designing questionnaires. Depending on the research problem and the target population, sampling decisions influence the type of research design, the survey instrument, and the actual questionnaire. For example, by having a general idea of the target population and the key characteristics that will be used to draw the sample of respondents, researchers can customize the questionnaire to ensure that it is of interest to respondents and provides high-quality data.

The Basics of Sampling Theory

Population

Population The identifiable set of elements of interest to the researcher and pertinent to the information problem.

A **population** is an identifiable group of **elements** (for example, people, products, organizations) of interest to the researcher and pertinent to the information problem. For example, Mazda Motor Corporation could hire J. D. Power and Associates to measure customer satisfaction among automobile owners. The population of interest could be all people who own automobiles. It is unlikely, however, that J. D. Power and Associates could draw a sample that would be truly representative of such a broad, heterogeneous population—any data collected would probably not be generalizable about customer satisfaction that would be of use to Mazda. This lack of specificity unfortunately is common in marketing research. Most businesses that collect data are not really concerned with total populations, but with a prescribed segment. In this chapter we use a modified definition of population: defined target population. A **defined target population** consists of the complete group of elements (people or objects) that are identified for investigation based on the objectives of the research project. A precise definition of the target population is essential and is usually done in terms of elements, sampling units, and time frames. **Sampling units** are target population elements actually available to be used during the sampling process.

Element A person or object from the defined target population from which information is sought.

Defined target population The complete set of elements identified for investigation.

Sampling units The target population elements available for selection during the sampling process.

Sampling Frame

Sampling frame The list of all eligible sampling units.

After defining the target population, the researcher develops a list of all eligible sampling units, referred to as a **sampling frame.** Some common sources of sampling frames are lists of registered voters and customer lists from magazine publishers or credit card companies. There also are specialized commercial companies (for instance, Survey Sampling, Inc.; American Business Lists, Inc.; and Scientific Telephone Samples) that sell databases containing names, addresses, and telephone numbers of potential population elements. Although the costs of obtaining sampling lists will vary, a list typically can be purchased for between $150 and $300 per 1,000 names.[1]

Regardless of the source, it is often difficult and expensive to obtain accurate, representative, and current sampling frames. It is doubtful, for example, that a list of individuals who have eaten a taco from a Taco Bell in a particular city in the past six months will be readily available. In this instance, a researcher would have to use an alternative method such as random-digit dialing (if conducting telephone interviews) or a mall-intercept interview to generate a sample of prospective respondents.

Factors Underlying Sampling Theory

To understand sampling theory, you must know sampling-related concepts. Sampling concepts and approaches are often discussed as if the researcher already knows the key population parameters prior to conducting the research project. However, because most business environments are complex and rapidly changing, researchers often do not know these parameters prior to conducting research. For example, retailers that have added online shopping alternatives for consumers are working to identify and describe the people who are making their retail purchases over the Internet rather than at traditional "brick and mortar" stores. Experts estimate that the world's online population exceeds 450 million people,[2] but the actual number of online retail shoppers is still difficult to estimate. One of the major goals of researching small, yet representative, samples of members of a defined target population is that the results of the research will help to predict or estimate what the true population parameters are within a certain degree of confidence.

If business decision makers had complete knowledge about their defined target populations, they would have perfect information about the realities of those populations, thus eliminating the need to conduct primary research. Moreover, better than 95 percent of today's marketing problems exist primarily because decision makers lack information about their problem situations and who their customers are, as well as customers' attitudes, preferences, and marketplace behaviors.

Tools Used to Assess the Quality of Samples

There are numerous opportunities to make mistakes that result in some type of bias in any research study. This bias can be classified as either *sampling error* or *nonsampling error*. Random sampling errors could be detected by observing the difference between the sample results and the results of a census conducted using identical procedures. Two difficulties associated with detecting sampling error are (1) a census is very seldom conducted in survey research and (2) sampling error can be determined only after the sample is drawn and data collection is completed.

Sampling error is any bias that results from mistakes in either the selection process for prospective sampling units or in determining the sample size. Moreover, random sampling error tends to occur because of chance variations in the selection of sampling units. Even if the sampling units are properly selected, those units still might not be a perfect representation of the defined target population, but they generally are reliable estimates. When there is a discrepancy between the statistic estimated from the sample and the actual value from the population, a sampling error has occurred. Sampling error can be reduced by increasing the size of the sample. In fact, doubling the size of the sample can reduce the sampling error, but increasing the sample size primarily to reduce the standard error may not be worth the cost.

Nonsampling error occurs regardless of whether a sample or a census is used. These errors can occur at any stage of the research process. For example, the target population may be inaccurately defined causing population frame error; inappropriate question/scale measurements can result in measurement error; a questionnaire may be poorly designed causing response error; or there may be other errors in gathering and recording data or when raw data are coded and entered for analysis. In general, the more extensive a study the greater the potential for nonsampling errors. Unlike sampling error, there are no statistical procedures to assess the impact of nonsampling errors on the quality of the data collected. Nonsampling errors usually are related to the accuracy of the data, whereas sampling errors relate to the representativeness of the sample to the defined target population.

> **Sampling error** Any type of bias that is attributable to mistakes in either drawing a sample or determining the sample size.

> **Nonsampling error** A bias that occurs in a research study regardless of whether a sample or census is used.

Continuing Case: The Santa Fe Grill

The business consultant has recommended a survey of Santa Fe Grill customers. To interview the customers, the consultant has suggested several approaches for collecting the data. One is to ask customers to complete the questionnaires at their table either before or after they get their food. Another is to stop them on the way out of the restaurant and ask them to complete a questionnaire. A third option is to give it to them and ask that they complete it at home and mail it back. A fourth option is to load software on the computer, write a program to randomly select customers, and when they pay their bill give them instructions on how to go to a Web site and complete the survey. The last option, however, is most expensive because it is expensive to do the computer programming to set the survey up on the Internet.

The consultant has been brainstorming with other restaurant industry experts on how to best collect the data. He does not yet have any options with which he feels comfortable suggesting to the owners.

1. Which of the data collection options is best? Why?
2. Should data be collected from customers of competitive restaurants? If yes, what are some possible ways to collect data from their customers?

◼◤ Probability and Nonprobability Sampling

Probability sampling
Sampling designs in which each sampling unit in the sampling frame has a known, nonzero probability of being selected for the sample.

Nonprobability sampling
Sampling designs in which the probability of selection of each sampling unit is not known. The selection of sampling units is based on the judgment or knowledge of the researcher and may or may not be representative of the target population.

Simple random sampling A method of probability sampling in which every sampling unit has an equal, nonzero chance of being selected. Results generated by using simple random sampling can be projected to the target population with a prespecified margin of error.

There are two basic sampling designs: probability and nonprobability. Exhibit 7.1 lists the different types of both sampling methods.

In **probability sampling,** each sampling unit in the defined target population has a known probability of being selected for the sample. The actual probability of selection for each sampling unit may or may not be equal depending on the type of probability sampling design used. Specific rules for selecting members from the population for inclusion in the sample are determined at the beginning of a study to ensure (1) unbiased selection of the sampling units and (2) proper sample representation of the defined target population. Probability sampling enables the researcher to judge the reliability and validity of data collected by calculating the probability the sample findings are different from the defined target population. The observed difference can be partially attributed to the existence of sampling error. The results obtained by using probability sampling designs can be generalized to the target population within a specified margin of error.

In **nonprobability sampling,** the probability of selecting each sampling unit is not known. Therefore, sampling error is not known. Selection of sampling units is based on intuitive judgment or researcher knowledge. The degree to which the sample is representative of the defined target population depends on the sampling approach and how well the researcher executes the selection activities.

Probability Sampling Designs

Simple Random Sampling **Simple random sampling** is a probability sampling procedure. With this approach, every sampling unit has a known and equal chance of being selected. For example, an instructor could draw a sample of 10 students from among

Exhibit 7.1	Types of Probability and Nonprobability Sampling Methods

Probability Sampling Methods	Nonprobability Sampling Methods
Simple random sampling	Convenience sampling
Systematic random sampling	Judgment sampling
Stratified random sampling	Quota sampling
Cluster sampling	Snowball sampling

30 students in a marketing research class. The instructor could write each student's name on a separate, identical piece of paper and place all of the names in a hat. Each student would have an equal, known probability of selection. Many software programs including SPSS have an option to select a random sample.

Advantages and Disadvantages   Simple random sampling has several advantages. The technique is easily understood and the survey's results can be generalized to the defined target population with a prespecified margin of error. Another advantage is that simple random samples produce unbiased estimates of the population's characteristics. This method guarantees that every sampling unit has a known and equal chance of being selected, no matter the actual size of the sample, resulting in a valid representation of the defined target population. The primary disadvantage of simple random sampling is the difficulty of obtaining a complete and accurate listing of the target population elements. Simple random sampling requires that all sampling units be identified. For this reason, simple random sampling works best for small populations where accurate lists are available.

Systematic Random Sampling   **Systematic random sampling** is similar to simple random sampling but requires that the defined target population be ordered in some way, usually in the form of a customer list, taxpayer roll, or membership roster. In research practices, systematic random sampling has become a popular method of drawing samples. Compared to simple random sampling, systematic random sampling is less costly because it can be done relatively quickly. When executed properly, systematic random sampling creates a sample of objects or prospective respondents that is very similar in quality to a sample drawn using simple random sampling.

> **Systematic random sampling** A method of probability sampling that is similar to simple random sampling but requires that the defined target population be naturally ordered in some way.

To use systematic random sampling, the researcher must be able to secure a complete listing of the potential sampling units that make up the defined target population. But unlike simple random sampling there is no need to give the sampling units any special code prior to drawing the sample. Instead, sampling units are selected according to their position using a skip interval. The *skip interval* is determined by dividing the number of potential sampling units in the defined target population by the number of units desired in the sample. The required skip interval is calculated using the following formula:

$$\text{Skip interval} = \frac{\text{Defined target population list size}}{\text{Desired sample size}}$$

For instance, if a researcher wants a sample of 100 to be drawn from a population of 1,000, the skip interval would be 10 (1,000/100). Once the skip interval is determined, the researcher would then randomly select a starting point and take every 10th unit until he or she had proceeded through the entire target population list. Exhibit 7.2 displays the steps that a researcher would take in drawing a systematic random sample.

Advantages and Disadvantages   Systematic sampling is frequently used because it is a relatively easy way to draw a sample while ensuring randomness. The availability of lists and the shorter time required to draw a sample versus simple random sampling makes systematic sampling an attractive, economical method for researchers. The greatest weakness of systematic random sampling is the possibility of hidden patterns in the data that create bias. Another difficulty is that the number of sampling units in the target population must be known. When the size of the target population is large or unknown, identifying the number of units is difficult and estimates may not be accurate.

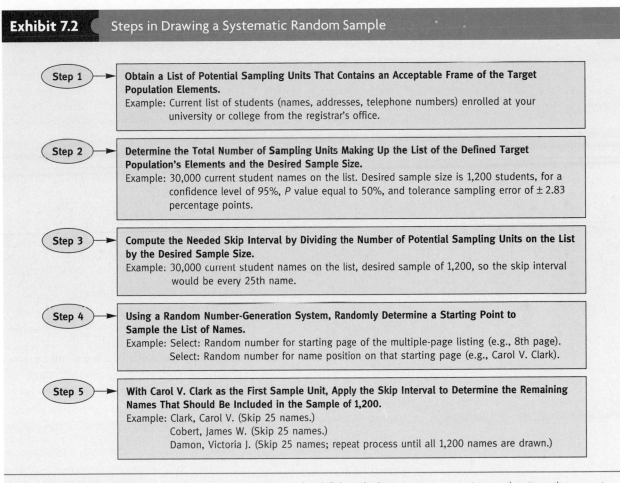

Exhibit 7.2 Steps in Drawing a Systematic Random Sample

Step 1 → **Obtain a List of Potential Sampling Units That Contains an Acceptable Frame of the Target Population Elements.**
Example: Current list of students (names, addresses, telephone numbers) enrolled at your university or college from the registrar's office.

Step 2 → **Determine the Total Number of Sampling Units Making Up the List of the Defined Target Population's Elements and the Desired Sample Size.**
Example: 30,000 current student names on the list. Desired sample size is 1,200 students, for a confidence level of 95%, *P* value equal to 50%, and tolerance sampling error of ± 2.83 percentage points.

Step 3 → **Compute the Needed Skip Interval by Dividing the Number of Potential Sampling Units on the List by the Desired Sample Size.**
Example: 30,000 current student names on the list, desired sample of 1,200, so the skip interval would be every 25th name.

Step 4 → **Using a Random Number-Generation System, Randomly Determine a Starting Point to Sample the List of Names.**
Example: Select: Random number for starting page of the multiple-page listing (e.g., 8th page).
Select: Random number for name position on that starting page (e.g., Carol V. Clark).

Step 5 → **With Carol V. Clark as the First Sample Unit, Apply the Skip Interval to Determine the Remaining Names That Should Be Included in the Sample of 1,200.**
Example: Clark, Carol V. (Skip 25 names.)
Cobert, James W. (Skip 25 names.)
Damon, Victoria J. (Skip 25 names; repeat process until all 1,200 names are drawn.)

Note: The researcher must visualize the population list as being continuous or "circular"; that is, the drawing process must continue past those names that represent the Z's an include names representing the A's and B's so that the 1,200th name drawn will basically be the 25th name prior to the first drawn name (i.e., Carol V. Clark).

Stratified random sampling
A method of probability sampling in which the population is divided into different subgroups and samples are selected from each structure.

Stratified Random Sampling **Stratified random sampling** involves the separation of the target population into different groups, called strata, and the selection of samples from each stratum. Stratified random sampling is similar to segmentation of the defined target population into smaller, more homogeneous sets of elements.

To ensure that the sample maintains the required precision, representative samples must be drawn from each of the smaller population groups (stratum). Drawing a stratified random sample involves three basic steps:

1. Dividing the target population into homogeneous subgroups or strata.
2. Drawing random samples from each stratum.
3. Combining the samples from each stratum into a single sample of the target population.

As an example, if researchers are interested in the market potential for home security systems in a specific geographic area, they may wish to divide the homeowners into several different strata. The subdivisions could be based on such factors as assessed value of the

A Closer Look at Research IN THE FIELD

Which Is Better, Proportionately or Disproportionately Stratified Samples?

The owners of the Santa Fe Grill have a list of 3,000 potential customers broken down by age. Using a statistical formula, they have decided that a proportionately stratified sample of 200 customers will produce information that is sufficiently accurate for decision making. The number of elements to be chosen from each stratum using a proportionate sample based on age is shown in the fourth column of the table. But if they believe the sample size in each stratum should be relative to its

economic importance, and the 18 to 49 age group are the most frequent diners and spend the most when dining out, then the number of selected elements would be disproportionate to stratum size as illustrated in the table's fifth column. The numbers in the disproportionate column would be determined based on the judgment of each stratum's economic importance.

Should proportionate or disproportionate sampling be used? That is, should the decision be based on economic importance, or some other criteria?

(1) Age Group	(2) Number of Elements in stratum	(3) % of Elements in Stratum	Number of Elements Selected for the Sample	
			(4) Proportionate Sample Size	(5) Disproportionate Sample Size
18–25	600	20	40 = 20%	50 = 25%
26–34	900	30	60 = 30%	50 = 25%
35–49	270	9	18 = 9%	50 = 25%
50–59	1020	34	68 = 34%	30 = 15%
60 and Older	210	7	14 = 7%	20 = 10%
Total	3000	100	200	200

homes, household income, population density, or location (e.g., sections designated as high- and low-crime areas).

Two common methods are used to derive samples from the strata: proportionate and disproportionate. In *proportionately stratified sampling,* the sample size from each stratum is dependent on that stratum's size relative to the defined target population. Therefore, the larger strata are sampled more heavily because they make up a larger percentage of the target population. In *disproportionately stratified sampling,* the sample size selected from each stratum is independent of that stratum's proportion of the total defined target population. This approach is used when stratification of the target population produces sample sizes for subgroups that differ from their relative importance to the study. For example, stratification of manufacturers based on number of employees will usually result in a large segment of manufacturers with fewer than 10 employees and a very small proportion with, say, 500 or more employees. The economic importance of those firms with 500 or more employees would dictate taking a larger sample from this stratum and a smaller sample from the subgroup with fewer than 10 employees than indicated by the proportionality method.

Advantages and Disadvantages Dividing the target population into homogeneous strata has several advantages, including: (1) the assurance of representativeness in the sample; (2) the opportunity to study each stratum and make comparisons between strata; and (3) the ability to make estimates for the target population with the expectation of greater precision and less error. The primary difficulty encountered with stratified sampling is determining the basis for stratifying. Stratification is based on the target population's characteristics of interest. Secondary information relevant to the required stratification factors might not be readily available, therefore forcing the researcher to use less desirable criteria as the factors for stratifying the target population. Usually the larger the number of relevant strata, the more precise the results. Inclusion of irrelevant strata, however, will waste time and money without providing meaningful results.

Cluster Sampling   Cluster sampling is similar to stratified random sampling, but is different in that the sampling units are divided into mutually exclusive and collectively exhaustive subpopulations called clusters. Each cluster is assumed to be representative of the heterogeneity of the target population. Examples of possible divisions for cluster sampling include customers who patronize a store on a given day, the audience for a movie shown at a particular time (for example, the matinee), or the invoices processed during a specific week. Once the cluster has been identified, the prospective sampling units are selected for the sample by either using a simple random sampling method or canvassing all the elements (a census) within the defined cluster.

A popular form of cluster sampling is *area sampling*. In area sampling, the clusters are formed by geographic designations. Examples include metropolitan statistical areas (MSAs), cities, subdivisions, and blocks. Any geographical unit with identifiable boundaries can be used. When using area sampling, the researcher has two additional options: the one-step approach or the two-step approach. When deciding on a one-step approach, the researcher must have enough prior information about the various geographic clusters to believe that all the geographic clusters are basically identical with regard to the specific factors that were used to initially identify the clusters. By assuming that all the clusters are identical, the researcher can focus his or her attention on surveying the sampling units within one designated cluster and then generalize the results to the population. The probability aspect of this particular sampling method is executed by randomly selecting one geographic cluster and performing a census on all the sampling units in that cluster.

Advantages and Disadvantages   Cluster sampling is widely used because of its cost-effectiveness and ease of implementation. In many cases, the only representative sampling frame available to researchers is one based on clusters (for example, states, counties, MSAs, census tracts). These lists of geographic regions, telephone exchanges, or blocks of residential dwellings usually can be easily compiled, thus avoiding the need of compiling lists of all the individual sampling units making up the target population.

Cluster sampling methods have several disadvantages. A primary disadvantage of cluster sampling is the clusters often are homogeneous. The more homogeneous the cluster, the less precise the sample estimates. Ideally, the people in a cluster should be as heterogeneous as those in the population.

Another concern with cluster sampling is the appropriateness of the designated cluster factor used to identify the sampling units within clusters. While the defined target population remains constant, the subdivision of sampling units can be modified depending on the selection of the factor used to identify the clusters. As a result, caution must be used in selecting the factor to determine clusters in area sampling situations.

Nonprobability Sampling Designs

Convenience Sampling   Convenience sampling is a method in which samples are drawn based on pure convenience. For example, interviewing of individuals at shopping malls or other high-traffic areas is a common method of generating a convenience sample. The assumption is that the individuals interviewed at the shopping mall are similar to the overall defined target population with regard to the characteristic being studied. In reality, it is

---

Cluster sampling A method of probability sampling where the sampling units are selected in groups (or clusters) rather than individually. Once the cluster has been identified, the elements to be sampled are drawn by simple random sampling or all of the units may be included in the sample.

Convenience sampling A method of nonprobability sampling where the samples are drawn on the basis of the convenience of the researcher or interviewer; also referred to as *accidental sampling*. Convenience sampling is often used in the early stages of research because it allows a large number of respondents to be interviewed in a short period of time.

difficult to accurately assess the representativeness of the sample. Given self-selection and the voluntary nature of participating in the data collection, researchers should consider the impact of nonresponse error when using sampling based on convenience only.

Advantages and Disadvantages   Convenience sampling enables a large number of respondents to be interviewed in a relatively short time. For this reason, it is commonly used in the early stages of research, including construct and scale measurement development as well as pretesting of questionnaires. But using convenience samples to develop constructs and scales can be risky. For example, assume a researcher is developing a measure of service quality and in the preliminary stages uses a convenience sample of 300 undergraduate business students. While college students are consumers of services, serious questions should be raised about whether they are truly representative of the general population. By developing constructs and scales using a convenience sample of college students, the constructs might be unreliable if used to study a broader target population. Another major disadvantage of convenience samples is that the data are not generalizable to the defined target population. The representativeness of the sample cannot be measured because sampling error estimates cannot be calculated.

Judgment sampling A nonprobability sampling design that selects participants for a sample based on an experienced individual's belief that the participants will meet the requirements of the research study.

Judgment Sampling   In **judgment sampling,** sometimes referred to as purposive sampling, respondents are selected because the researcher believes they meet the requirements of the study. For example, sales representatives may be interviewed rather than customers to determine whether customers' wants and needs are changing or to assess the firm's product or service performance. Similarly, consumer packaged goods companies such as Procter & Gamble may select a sample of key accounts to obtain information about consumption patterns and changes in demand for selected products, for example, Crest toothpaste or Cheer laundry detergent. The assumption is that the opinions of a group of experts are representative of the target population.

Advantages and Disadvantages   If the judgment of the researcher is correct, the sample generated by judgment sampling will be better than one generated by convenience sampling. As with all nonprobability sampling procedures, however, you cannot measure the representativeness of the sample. Thus, data collected from judgment sampling should be interpreted cautiously.

Quota sampling The selection of participants based on specific quotas regarding characteristics such as age, race, gender, income, or specific behaviors. Quotas are usually determined by specific research objectives.

Quota Sampling   **Quota sampling** involves the selection of prospective participants according to prespecified quotas for either demographic characteristics (e.g. age, race, gender, income), specific attitudes (e.g. satisfied/dissatisfied, liking/disliking, great/marginal/no quality), or specific behaviors (e.g. regular/occasional/rare customer, product user/ nonuser). The purpose of quota sampling is to assure that prespecified subgroups of the population are represented.

Advantages and Disadvantages   The major advantage of quota sampling is that the sample generated contains specific subgroups in the proportions desired by researchers. Use of quotas ensures that the appropriate subgroups are identified and included in the survey. Also, quota sampling reduces selection bias by field workers. An inherent limitation of quota sampling is that the success of the study is dependent on subjective decisions made by researchers. Since it is a nonprobability sampling method, the representativeness of the sample cannot be measured. Therefore, generalizing the results beyond the sampled respondents is questionable.

Snowball sampling A nonprobability sampling method in which a set of respondents is chosen and they help the researcher identify additional people to be included in the study.

Snowball Sampling   **Snowball sampling** involves identifying a set of respondents who can help the researcher identify additional people to include in the study. This method of sampling is also called *referral sampling*, because one respondent refers other potential respondents. Snowball sampling typically is used in situations where (1) the defined target population is small and unique, and (2) compiling a complete list of sampling units is very difficult. Consider, for example, researching the attitudes and behaviors of people who volunteer their time to charitable organizations like the Children's Wish Foundation. While traditional sampling methods require an extensive search effort both in time and cost to find a sufficient number of prospective respondents, the snowball method yields better results at a much lower cost. Here the researcher interviews a qualified respondent, then solicits his or her help to identify other people with similar characteristics. While membership in these types of social circles might not be publicly known, intra-circle knowledge is very accurate. The underlying logic of this method is that rare groups of people tend to form their own unique social circles.

Advantages and Disadvantages Snowball sampling is a reasonable method of identifying respondents who are members of small, hard-to-reach, uniquely defined target populations. As a nonprobability sampling method, it is most useful in qualitative research. But snowball sampling allows bias to enter the study. If there are significant differences between people who are known in certain social circles and those who are not, there may be problems with this sampling technique. Like all other nonprobability sampling approaches, the ability to generalize the results to members of the target population is limited.

Determining the Appropriate Sampling Design

Determining the best sample design involves consideration of several factors. In Exhibit 7.3 we provide an overview of the major factors that should be considered.

Exhibit 7.3 Factors to Consider in Selecting the Sampling Design

Selection Factors	Questions
Research objectives	Do the research objectives call for the use of qualitative or quantitative research designs?
Degree of accuracy	Does the research call for making predictions or inferences about the defined target population, or only preliminary insights?
Resources	Are there light budget constraints with respect to both dollars and human resources that can be allocated to the research project?
Time frame	How quickly does the research project have to be completed?
Knowledge of the target population	Are there complete lists of the defined target population elements? How easy or difficult is it to generate the required sampling frame of prospective respondents?
Scope of the research	Is the research going be international, national, regional, or local?
Statistical analysis needs	To what extent are accurate statistical projections and/or testing of hypothesized differences in the data required?

◼️ Continuing Case: The Santa Fe Grill

The business consultant has recommended a survey of customers. The restaurant is open seven days a week for lunch and dinner. The consultant is considering both probability and nonprobability sampling methods as ways to collect customer data.

1. Which of the sampling options is best for the survey of the Santa Fe Grill customers? Why?
2. What are some possible sampling methods to collect data from customers of competitive restaurants?

◼️ Determining Sample Sizes

Determining the sample size is not an easy task. The researcher must consider how precise the estimates must be and how much time and money are available to collect the required data, since data collection is generally one of the most expensive components of a study. Sample size determination differs between probability and nonprobability designs.

Probability Sample Sizes

Three factors play an important role in determining sample sizes with probability designs:

1. *The variability of the population characteristic under investigation.* The greater the variability of the characteristic the larger the sample size necessary.
2. *The level of confidence desired in the estimate.* The higher the level of confidence desired the larger the sample size needed.
3. *The degree of precision desired in estimating the population characteristic.* The more precise the required sample results, that is, the smaller the desired error, the larger the sample size.

There are separate formulas for determining sample size based on a predicted population mean and a population proportion. The formulas are used to estimate the sample size for a simple random sample. When the situation involves estimating a population mean, the formula for calculating the sample size is:

$$n = (Z^2_{B,CL})\left(\frac{\sigma^2}{e^2}\right)$$

where

$Z_{B,CL}$ = The standardized *z*-value associated with the level of confidence
σ_μ = Estimate of the population standard deviation (σ) based on some type of prior information
e = Acceptable tolerance level of error (stated in percentage points)

In situations where estimates of a population proportion are of concern, the standardized formula for calculating the needed sample size would be

$$n = (Z^2_{B,CL})\left(\frac{[P \times Q]}{e^2}\right)$$

where

$Z_{B,CL}$ = The standardized *z*-value associated with the level of confidence

P = Estimate of expected population proportion having a desired characteristic based on intuition or prior information

Q = $[1 - P]$, or the estimate of expected population proportion not holding the characteristic of interest

e = Acceptable tolerance level of error (stated in percentage points)

When the defined target population size in a consumer study is 500 elements or less, the researcher should consider taking a census of the population rather than a sample. The logic behind this is based on the theoretical notion that at least 384 sampling units need to be included in most studies to have a 95 percent confidence level and a sampling error of ± 5 percentage points.

Sample sizes in business-to-business studies present a different problem than in consumer studies where the population almost always is very large. With business-to-business studies the population frequently is only 200 to 300 individuals. What then is an acceptable sample size? In such cases an attempt is made to contact and complete a survey from all individuals in the population. An acceptable sample size may be as small as 30 percent or so but the final decision would be made after examining the profile of the respondents. For example, you could look at position titles to see if you have a good cross-section of respondents from all relevant categories. You likely will also determine what proportion of the firm's annual business is represented in the sample to avoid having only smaller firms or accounts that do not provide a representative picture of the firm's customers. Whatever approach you use, in the final analysis you must have a good understanding of who has responded so you can accurately interpret the study's findings.

Nonprobability Sample Sizes

Sample size formulas cannot be used for nonprobability samples. Determining the sample size for nonprobability samples is usually a subjective, intuitive judgment made by the researcher based on either past studies, industry standards, or the amount of resources available. Regardless of the method, the sampling results cannot be used to make statistical inferences about the true population parameters. The best that can be offered is directional ideas about the target population.

Steps in Developing a Sampling Plan

Sampling plan The blueprint or framework used to ensure that the data collected are, in fact, representative of a larger defined target population structure.

After understanding the key components of sampling theory, the methods of determining sample sizes, and the various designs available, the researcher is ready to use them to develop a sampling plan. A **sampling plan** is the blueprint to ensure the data collected are representative of the population. A good sampling plan includes the following steps: (1) define the target population, (2) select the data collection method, (3) identify the sampling frames needed, (4) select the appropriate sampling method, (5) determine necessary sample sizes and overall contact rates, (6) create an operating plan for selecting sampling units, and (7) execute the operational plan.

Step 1: Define the Target Population In any sampling plan, the first task of the researcher is to determine the group of people or objects that should be investigated. With the problem and research objectives as guidelines, the characteristics of the target population should be identified. An understanding of the target population helps the researcher to successfully draw a representative sample.

Step 2: Select the Data Collection Method Using the problem definition, the data requirements, and the research objectives, the researcher chooses a method for collecting the data from the population. Choices include some type of interviewing approach (for instance, personal or telephone), a self-administered survey, or perhaps observation. The method of data collection guides the researcher in selecting the sampling frame(s).

Step 3: Identify the Sampling Frame(s) Needed A list of eligible sampling units must be obtained. The list includes information about prospective sampling units (individuals or objects) so the researcher can contact them. An incomplete sampling frame decreases the likelihood of drawing a representative sample. Sampling lists can be created from a number of different sources (e.g., customer lists from a company's internal database, random-digit dialing, an organization's membership roster, or purchased from a sampling vendor).

Step 4: Select the Appropriate Sampling Method The researcher chooses between probability and nonprobability methods. If the findings will be generalized, a probability sampling method will provide more accurate information than will nonprobability sampling methods. As noted earlier, in determining the sampling method, the researcher must consider seven factors: (1) research objectives, (2) desired accuracy, (3) availability of resources, (4) time frame, (5) knowledge of the target population, (6) scope of the research, and (7) statistical analysis needs.

Step 5: Determine Necessary Sample Sizes and Overall Contact Rates In this step of a sampling plan, the researcher decides how precise the sample estimates must be and how much time and money are available to collect the data. To determine the appropriate sample size, decisions have to be made concerning (1) the variability of the population characteristic under investigation, (2) the level of confidence desired in the estimates, and (3) the precision required. The researcher also must decide how many completed surveys are needed for data analysis.

At this point the researcher must consider what impact having fewer surveys than initially desired would have on the accuracy of the sample statistics. An important question is, "How many prospective sampling units will have to be contacted to ensure the estimated sample size is obtained, and at what additional costs?"

Step 6: Create an Operating Plan for Selecting Sampling Units The researcher must decide how to contact the prospective respondents in the sample. Instructions should be written so that interviewers know what to do and how to handle problems contacting prospective respondents. For example, if the study data will be collected using mall-intercept interviews, then interviewers must be given instructions on how to select respondents and conduct the interviews.

Step 7: Execute the Operational Plan This step is similar to collecting the data from respondents. The important consideration in this step is to maintain consistency and control.

MARKETING RESEARCH IN ACTION
Developing a Sampling Plan for a New Menu Initiative Survey

Owners of the Santa Fe Grill realize that in order to remain competitive in the restaurant industry, new menu items need to be introduced periodically to provide variety for current customers and to attract new customers. Recognizing this, the owners of the Santa Fe Grill believe three issues need to be addressed using marketing research. One is, should the menu be changed to include items beyond the traditional Southwestern cuisine? For example, should they add items that would be considered standard American, Italian, or European cuisine? Two, regardless of the cuisine to be explored, how many new items (for example, appetizers, entrées, or desserts), should be included on the survey? And three, what type of sampling plan should be developed for selecting respondents, and who should those respondents be? Should they be current customers, new customers, and/or old customers?

Hands-On Exercise

Understanding the importance of sampling and the impact it will have on the validity and accuracy of the research results, the owners have asked the local university if a marketing research class could assist them in this project. Specifically, the owners have posed the following questions that need to be addressed:

1. How many questions should the survey contain to adequately address all possible new menu items, including the notion of assessing the desirability of new cuisines? In short, how can it be determined that all necessary items will be included on the survey without the risk of ignoring menu items that may be desirable to potential customers?
2. How should the potential respondents be selected for the survey? Should patrons be interviewed while they are dining? Should patrons be asked to participate in the survey upon exiting the restaurant? Or should a mail or telephone approach be used to collect information from patrons/nonpatrons?

    Based on the above questions, your task is to develop a procedure to address the following issues:

3. How many new menu items can be examined on the survey? Remember, all potential menu possibilities should be assessed but you must have a manageable number of questions so the survey can be performed in a timely and reasonable manner. Specifically, from a list of all possible menu items that can be included on the survey, what is the optimal number of menu items that should be used? Is there a sampling procedure one can use to determine the maximum number of menu items to place on the survey?
4. Determine the appropriate sample design. Develop a sample design proposal for the Santa Fe Grill that addresses the following: Should a probability or nonprobability sample be used? Given your answer, what type of sampling design should be employed (simple random, stratified, convenience, etc.)? Given the sample design suggested, how will potential respondents be selected for the study? Finally, determine the necessary sample size and suggest a plan for selecting the sampling units.

Summary

Explain the role of sampling in the information research process.

Sampling uses a portion of the population to make estimates about the entire population. The fundamentals of sampling are used in many of our everyday activities. For instance, we sample before selecting a TV program to watch, test-drive a car before deciding whether to purchase it, and take a bite of food to determine if our food is too hot or if it needs additional seasoning. The term *target population* is used to identify the complete group of elements (e.g., people or objects) that are identified for investigation. The researcher selects sampling units from the target population and uses the results obtained from the sample to make conclusions about the target population. The sample must be representative of the target population if it is to provide accurate estimates of population parameters.

Sampling is frequently used in marketing research projects instead of a census because sampling can significantly reduce the amount of time and money required in data collection. When data collection destroys or contaminates the elements being studied, sampling usually is the only alternative. Sampling is useful in identifying, developing, and understanding new marketing constructs, as well as in developing the scales used to collect primary data. Decisions concerning sampling indirectly affect the design of questionnaires.

Distinguish between probability and nonprobability sampling.

In probability sampling, each sampling unit in the defined target population has a known probability of being selected for the sample. The actual probability of selection for each sampling unit may or may not be equal depending on the type of probability sampling design used. In nonprobability sampling, the probability of selection of each sampling unit is not known. The selection of sampling units is based on some type of intuitive judgment or knowledge of the researcher.

Probability sampling enables the researcher to judge the reliability and validity of data collected by calculating the probability the findings based on the sample will differ from the defined target population. This observed difference can be partially attributed to the existence of sampling error. Each probability sampling method—simple random, systematic random, stratified, and cluster—has its own inherent advantages and disadvantages.

In nonprobability sampling, the probability of selection of each sampling unit is not known. Therefore, potential sampling error cannot be accurately known either. Although there may be a temptation to generalize nonprobability sample results to the defined target population, for the most part the results are limited to the people who provided the data in the survey. Each nonprobability sampling method—convenience, judgment, quota, and snowball—has its own inherent advantages and disadvantages.

Understand factors to consider when determining sample size.

Researchers consider several factors when determining the appropriate sample size. The amount of time and money available often affect this decision. In general, the larger the sample, the greater the amount of resources required to collect data. Three factors that are of primary importance in the determination of sample size are (1) the variability of the population characteristic under consideration, (2) the level of confidence desired in the estimate, and (3) the degree of precision desired in estimating the population characteristic. The greater the variability of the characteristic under investigation, the higher the level of confidence required. Similarly, the more precise the required sample results, the larger the necessary sample size.

Statistical formulas are used to determine the required sample size in probability sampling. Sample sizes for nonprobability sampling designs are determined using subjective methods such as industry standards, past studies, or the intuitive judgments of the researcher. The size of the defined target population does not affect the size of the required sample unless the population is small relative to the sample size.

Understand the steps in developing a sampling plan.

A sampling plan is the blueprint or framework needed to ensure that the data collected are representative of the defined target population. A good sampling plan will include, at least, the following steps: (1) define the target population, (2) select the data collection method, (3) identify the sampling frames needed, (4) select the appropriate sampling method, (5) determine necessary sample sizes and overall contact rates, (6) create an operating plan for selecting sampling units, and (7) execute the operational plan.

Key Terms and Concepts

Census 128

Cluster sampling 135

Convenience sampling 135

Defined target population 129

Element 129

Judgment sampling 136

Nonprobability sampling 131

Nonsampling error 130

Population 129

Probability sampling 131

Quota sampling 136

Sampling 128

Sampling error 130

Sampling frame 129

Sampling plan 139

Sampling units 129

Simple random sampling 131

Snowball sampling 136

Stratified random sampling 133

Systematic random sampling 132

Review Questions

1. Why do many research studies place heavy emphasis on correctly defining a target population rather than a total population?

2. Identify, graph, and explain the relationship between sample sizes and estimated standard error measures. What does the estimated standard error really measure in survey research?

3. The vice president of operations at Busch Gardens knows that 70 percent of the patrons like roller-coaster rides. He wishes to have an acceptable margin of error of no more than ±2 percent and wants to be 95 percent confident about the attitudes toward the "Gwazi" roller coaster. What sample size would be required for a personal interview study among on-site patrons?

Discussion Questions

1. Summarize why a current telephone directory is not a good source from which to develop a sampling frame for most research studies.

2. **EXPERIENCE THE INTERNET.** Go to www.surveysampling.com and select from the menu "the frame." Once there, select "archive" and go to a particular year (e.g., 2006) and review the articles available on the topic of sampling. Select two articles and write a brief summary on how sampling affects the ability to conduct accurate market research.

Measurement and Scaling

Chapter 8

1. Understand the role of measurement in marketing research.
2. Explain the four basic levels of scales.
3. Describe scale development and its importance in gathering primary data.
4. Discuss comparative and noncomparative scales.

Fast Food, Side by Side: Restaurant Location and Loyalty

Among the more important problems facing the Burger King Corporation is selecting sites for new restaurants that will attract sufficient customer loyalty for the new store to be profitable. Since Burger King has many more major competitors today than just McDonald's or Wendy's, its traditional strategy of locating restaurants no closer than about three miles to a McDonald's, on streets with high traffic, in neighborhoods with schools, and in areas of predominantly middle-income families is no longer feasible.

The traditional location selection process did not include formal marketing research or assessing the significance of customer loyalty, but instead relied heavily on the experience and knowledge of the Burger King senior management team. Since the site-location model did not consider these criteria, sales forecasts for new restaurants often were inaccurate. To correct the problem, the marketing research department combined customer survey data with traditional sales and geographic data from existing Burger King restaurants. New research objectives included measuring customer loyalty and its impact on the relationship between the site-location criteria and sales, as well as considering other criteria that would more accurately predict sales.

To better understand customer loyalty, Burger King turned to Burke's (www. burke.com) Customer Satisfaction Division and its Customer Loyalty Index measures. New research showed that while traffic density was a significant indicator of sales, neither the proximity of schools nor income levels of the surrounding area were good indicators. Moreover, customers preferred places where several fast-food establishments were clustered together so that more choice was available. In the process, management learned that customer loyalty was a complex construct that required better understanding of consumers' satisfaction, positive word-of-mouth recommendations, and consideration of behavioral intentions.

The importance of construct and measurement development is evident from the Burger King experience. First, not knowing the critical criteria for locating a business often leads to intuitive guesswork and counterproductive results. Second, making accurate location decisions requires identifying and precisely measuring the constructs (e.g., attitudes, emotions, intentions) consumers consider important in creating customer loyalty. Read the *Marketing Research in Action* at the end of this chapter to see how Burke, Inc., measures customer loyalty.

Value of Measurement in Information Research

Measurement is an integral part of the modern world, yet the beginnings of measurement lie in the distant past. Before a farmer could sell his corn, potatoes, or apples, both he and the buyer had to decide on a common unit of measurement. Over time this particular measurement became known as a bushel or four pecks or, more precisely, 2,150.42 cubic inches. In the early days, measurement was achieved simply by using a basket or container of standard size that everyone agreed was a bushel.

From such simple everyday devices as the standard bushel basket, we have progressed in the physical sciences to an extent that we are now able to measure the rotation of a distant star, the altitude of a satellite in microinches, or time in picoseconds (1 trillionth of a second). Today, precise physical measurement is critical to airline pilots flying through dense fog or to physicians controlling a surgical laser.

In most marketing situations, however, the measurements are applied to things that are much more abstract than altitude or time. For example, most decision makers would agree that it is important to have information about whether or not a firm's customers are going to like a new product or service prior to introducing it. In many cases, such information makes the difference between business success and failure. Yet, unlike time or altitude, people's preferences can be very difficult to measure accurately. The Coca-Cola Company introduced New Coke after incompletely conceptualizing and measuring consumers' preferences, and consequently suffered substantial losses.

Because accurate measurement is essential to effective decision making, this chapter provides a basic understanding of the importance of measuring customers' attitudes and behaviors and other marketplace phenomena. We describe the measurement process and the decision rules for developing scale measurements. The focus is on measurement issues, construct development, and scale measurements. The chapter also discusses popular scales that measure attitudes and behavior.

Overview of the Measurement Process

Measurement The systematic process of quantifying information about constructs, concepts, or objects.

Measurement is the process of developing methods to systematically characterize or quantify information about persons, events, ideas, or objects of interest. As part of the measurement process, researchers assign either numbers or labels to phenomena they measure. For example, when gathering data about consumers who shop for automobiles online, a researcher may collect information about their attitudes, perceptions, past online purchase behaviors, and demographic characteristics. Then, numbers are used to represent how individuals responded to questions in each of these areas.

The measurement process consists of two tasks: construct selection/development and scale measurement. To collect accurate data, researchers must understand what they are attempting to measure before choosing the appropriate scale measurements. The goal of the construct development process is to precisely identify and define what is to be measured. In turn, the scale measurement process determines how to precisely measure each construct. For example, a 10-point scale results in a more precise measure than a 2-point scale. We begin with construct development and then move to scale measurement.

Construct Development

Construct An unobservable concept that is measured indirectly by a group of related variables.

Marketing constructs must be clearly defined. Recall that a **construct** is an unobservable concept that is measured indirectly by a group of related variables. Thus, constructs are made up of a combination of several related indicator variables that together define the concept being measured. Each individual indicator has a scale measurement. The construct being studied is indirectly measured by obtaining scale measurements on each of the indicators and adding them together to get an overall score for the construct. For example, customer satisfaction is a construct while respondents' positive (or negative) feelings about a specific aspect of their shopping experience, such as attitude toward the store's employees, is an indicator variable.

Construct development A process in which researchers identify characteristics of a concept.

Construct development begins with an accurate definition of the purpose of the study and the research problem. Without a clear initial understanding of the research problem, the researcher is likely to collect irrelevant or inaccurate data, thereby wasting a great deal of time, effort, and money. **Construct development** is the process in which researchers identify characteristics that define the concept being studied by the researcher. Once the characteristics are identified, the researcher must then develop a method of indirectly measuring the concept.

At the heart of construct development is the need to determine exactly what is to be measured. Objects that are relevant to the research problem are identified first. Then the objective and subjective properties of each object are specified. When data is needed only about a concrete issue, the research focus is limited to measuring the object's objective properties. But when data is needed to understand an object's subjective (abstract) properties, the researcher must identify measurable subcomponents that can be used as indicators of the object's subjective properties. Exhibit 8.1 shows examples of objects and their concrete and abstract properties. A rule of thumb is that if an object's features can be directly measured using physical characteristics, then those features are concrete variables and not abstract constructs. Abstract constructs are not physical characteristics and are measured indirectly.

Scale Measurement

Scale measurement The process of assigning descriptors to represent the range of possible responses to a question about a particular object or construct.

The quality of responses associated with any question or observation technique depends directly on the scale measurements used by the researcher. **Scale measurement** involves assigning a set of scale descriptors to represent the range of possible responses to a question about a particular object or construct. The *scale descriptors* are a combination of labels, such as "Strongly Agree" or "Strongly Disagree," and numbers, such as 1–7, that are assigned using a set of rules.

Scale points Designated degrees of intensity assigned to the responses in a given questioning or observation method.

Scale measurement assigns degrees of intensity to the responses. The degrees of intensity are commonly referred to as **scale points.** For example, a retailer might want to know how important a preselected set of store or service features is to consumers in deciding where to shop. The level of importance attached to each store or service feature would be determined by the researcher's assignment of a range of intensity descriptors (scale points)

Exhibit 8.1	Examples of Concrete and Abstract Properties of Objects and Constructs

Objects

Consumer	**Concrete properties:** age, sex, marital status, income, brand last purchased, dollar amount of purchase, types of products purchased, color of eyes and hair
	Abstract properties: attitudes toward a product, brand loyalty, high-involvement purchases, emotions (love, fear, anxiety), intelligence, personality
Organization	**Concrete properties:** name of company, number of employees, number of locations, total assets, Fortune 500 rating, computer capacity, types and numbers of products and service offerings
	Abstract properties: competence of employees, quality control, channel power, competitive advantages, company image, consumer-oriented practices

Marketing Constructs

Brand loyalty	**Concrete properties:** the number of times a particular brand is purchased, the frequency of purchases of a particular brand, amount spent
	Abstract properties: like/dislike of a particular brand, the degree of satisfaction with the brand, overall attitude toward the brand
Customer satisfaction	**Concrete properties:** identifiable attributes that make up a product, service, or experience
	Abstract properties: liking/disliking of the individual attributes making up the product, positive feelings toward the product
Service quality	**Concrete properties:** identifiable attributes of a service encounter, for example amount of interaction, personal communications, service provider's knowledge
	Abstract properties: expectations held about each identifiable attribute, evaluative judgment of performance
Advertising recall	**Concrete properties:** factual properties of the ad (for example, message, symbols, movement, models, text), aided and unaided recall of ad properties
	Abstract properties: favorable/unfavorable judgments, attitude toward the ad

to represent the possible degrees of importance associated with each feature. If labels are used as scale points to respond to a question, they might include the following: definitely important, moderately important, slightly important, and not at all important. If numbers are used as scale points, then a 10 could mean very important and a 1 could mean not important at all.

All scale measurements can be classified as one of four basic scale levels: nominal, ordinal, interval, and ratio. We discuss each of the scale levels next.

Nominal Scales

Nominal scale The type of scale in which the questions require respondents to provide only some type of descriptor as a response.

A **nominal scale** is the most basic and least powerful scale design. With nominal scales the questions require respondents only to provide some type of descriptor as the response. Responses do not contain a level of intensity. Thus, a ranking of the set of responses is not possible. Nominal scales allow the researcher only to categorize the responses into mutually exclusive subsets that do not have distances between them. Thus, the only possible mathematical calculation is to count the number of responses in each category and to report the mode. Some examples of nominal scales are given in Exhibit 8.2.

Ordinal Scales

Ordinal scale A scale that allows a respondent to express relative magnitude between the answers to a question.

An **ordinal scale** is more powerful than a nominal scale. It enables respondents to express relative magnitude between the answers to a question, and responses can be rank ordered in a hierarchical pattern. Thus, you can determine relationships between responses such as "greater than/less than," "higher than/lower than," "more often/less often," "more important/less important" or "less agreement/more agreement." The mathematical calculations appropriate with ordinal scales include the mode and the median.

Ordinal scales cannot be used to determine the level of difference between rankings. That is, a respondent can indicate they prefer Coke over Pepsi, but you do not know how much more they prefer Coke. Exhibit 8.3 gives examples of ordinal scales.

Interval Scales

Interval scale A scale that demonstrates absolute differences between each scale point.

Interval scales can measure absolute differences between scale points. Thus, in addition to the mode and median, the mean and standard deviation of the respondents' answers can be calculated. This means that researchers can report findings not only about differences in rules (better than or worse than), but also about the absolute differences between the data. Exhibit 8.4 gives several examples of interval scales.

Exhibit 8.2   Examples of Nominal Scales

Example 1:
Please indicate your marital status.
____ Married   ____ Single   ____ Separated   ____ Divorced   ____ Widowed

Example 2:
Do you like or dislike chocolate ice cream?
____ Like   ____ Dislike

Example 3:
Which of the following supermarkets have you shopped at in the last 30 days? Please check all that apply.
____ Albertson's   ____ Winn-Dixie   ____ Publix   ____ Safeway   ____ Wal-Mart

Exhibit 8.3	Examples of Ordinal Scales

Example 1:

Among the banking methods listed below, please indicate your top three preferences using a "1" to represent your first choice, a "2" for your second preference, and a "3" for your third choice of methods. Write the numbers in the space next to your selected methods. Please no ties—do not assign the same number to two methods.

_____ Inside the bank   _____ Bank by mail

_____ Drive-in (drive-up) windows   _____ Bank by telephone

_____ ATM   _____ Internet banking

Example 2:

Which one statement best describes your opinion of the quality of an Intel PC processor? (Please check just one statement.)

_____ Higher than AMD's PC processor

_____ About the same as AMD's PC processor

_____ Lower than AMD's PC processor

Ratio Scales

Ratio scale A scale that allows the researcher not only to identify the absolute differences between each scale point but also to make absolute comparisons between the raw responses.

Ratio scales are the highest level scale because they enable the researcher not only to identify the absolute differences between each scale point but also to make absolute comparisons between the responses. For example, in collecting data about how many cars are driven by households in Atlanta, Georgia, a researcher knows that the difference between driving one car and driving three cars is always going to be two. Furthermore, when comparing a one-car family to a three-car family, the researcher can assume that the three-car family will have significantly higher total car insurance and maintenance costs than the one-car family.

Ratio scales are designed to enable a "true natural zero" or "true state of nothing" response to be a valid response to a question. Generally, ratio scales ask respondents to provide a specific numerical value as their response, regardless of whether or not a set of scale

Exhibit 8.4	Examples of Interval Scales

Example 1:

How likely are you to recommend the Santa Fe Grill to a friend?	Definitely Will Not Recommend					Definitely Will Recommend	
	1	2	3	4	5	6	7

Example 2:

Using a scale of 1–10, with "10" being Highly Satisfied and "1" being Not Satisfied At All, how satisfied are you with the banking services you currently receive from (read name of primary bank) ?   Answer: _____

Exhibit 8.5	Examples of Ratio Scales

Example 1:

Please circle the number of children under 18 years of age currently living in your household.

    0   1   2   3   4   5   6   7   If more than 7, please specify: _____.

Example 2:

In the past seven days, how many times did you go shopping at a retail shopping mall?

_____ # of times

Example 3:

In years, what is your current age?

_____ # of years old

points is used. In addition to the mode, median, mean, and standard deviation, you can make comparisons between levels. Thus, if you are measuring weight, a familiar ratio scale, you can then say a person weighing 200 pounds is twice as heavy as one weighing only 100 pounds. Exhibit 8.5 shows examples of ratio scales.

Evaluating Measurement Scales

All measurement scales should be evaluated for reliability and validity. *Scale reliability* refers to the extent to which a scale can reproduce the same or similar measurement results in repeated trials. Thus, reliability is a measure of consistency in measurement. Random error produces inconsistency in scale measurements that leads to lower scale reliability. But researchers can improve reliability by carefully designing scaled questions. Since reliable scales are not necessarily valid, researchers also need to be concerned about validity.

Scale validity assesses whether a scale measures what it is supposed to measure. Thus, validity is a measure of accuracy in measurement. *Face validity* is based on the researcher's evaluation of whether the statements look like they measure what they are supposed to measure. Thus, researchers use their intuitive judgment to determine face validity. Face validity is considered a minimally adequate evaluation of validity.

■ Developing Scale Measurements

Designing high-quality scales requires (1) understanding the defined research problem, (2) establishing detailed data requirements, (3) identifying and developing the constructs, and (4) knowing that a complete measurement scale consists of three components—the question, the attributes, and the scale point descriptors. After the problem and data requirements are understood, the researcher must develop constructs. Next, the appropriate scale format (nominal, ordinal, interval, or ratio) must be selected. If the problem requires interval data, but the researcher asks the questions using a nominal scale, the wrong level of data will be collected and the final information that can be generated may not be helpful in addressing the research problem.

Criteria for Scale Development

Questions must be phrased carefully to produce accurate data. To do so, the researcher must develop appropriate scale descriptors to be used as the scale points.

Understanding of the Questions   The researcher must consider the intellectual capacity and language ability of individuals that will be asked to respond to the scales. Researchers should not automatically assume that respondents understand the questions and response choices. Appropriate language must be used in both the questions and the answers. Simplicity in word choice and straightforward, simple sentence construction improve understanding. All scaled questions should be pretested to evaluate their level of understanding.

Discriminatory power The scale's ability to differentiate between the categorical scale responses (or points).

Discriminatory Power of Scale Descriptors   The **discriminatory power** of scale descriptors is the scale's ability to differentiate between the scale responses. Researchers must decide how many scale points are necessary to represent the relative magnitudes of a response scale. The more scale points, the greater the discriminatory power of the scale.

There is no absolute rule about the number of scale points that should be used in creating a scale. For most respondents, scales should not be more than seven points because it may be difficult to make a choice when there are more than seven levels. This is particularly true for respondents with lower education levels and less experience in responding to scales. But the authors have found with more educated respondents a 10-point scale works quite well.

Balanced versus Unbalanced Scales   Researchers must consider whether to use a balanced or unbalanced scale. A *balanced scale* has an equal number of positive (favorable) and negative (unfavorable) response alternatives. An example of a balanced scale is:

> Based on your experiences with your new vehicle since owning and driving it, to what extent are you presently satisfied or dissatisfied with the overall performance of the vehicle? Please check only one response.
>
> _____ Completely satisfied (no dissatisfaction)
> _____ Generally satisfied
> _____ Slightly satisfied (some satisfaction)
> _____ Slightly dissatisfied (some dissatisfaction)
> _____ Generally dissatisfied
> _____ Completely dissatisfied (no satisfaction)

An *unbalanced scale* has a larger number of response options on one side, either positive or negative. For most research situations a balanced scale is recommended because unbalanced scales often introduce bias. One exception is when the attitudes of respondents are likely to be predominantly one-sided, either positive or negative. When this situation is expected, researchers typically use an unbalanced scale. For example, when respondents are asked to rate the importance of evaluative criteria in choosing to do business with a particular company, they often rate all criteria listed as very important. An example of an unbalanced scale is:

> Based on your experiences with your new vehicle since owning and driving it, to what extent are you presently satisfied with the overall performance of the vehicle? Please check only one response.

_____ Completely satisfied

_____ Definitely satisfied

_____ Generally satisfied

_____ Slightly satisfied

_____ Dissatisfied

Forced or Nonforced Choice Scales A scale that does not have a neutral descriptor to divide the positive and negative answers is referred to as a *forced-choice scale*. It is forced because the respondent can select only a positive or a negative answer and not a neutral one. In contrast, a scale that includes a center neutral response is referred to as a *nonforced* or *free-choice scale*. Exhibit 8.6 presents several different examples of both "even-point, forced-choice" and "odd-point, nonforced choice" scales.

Some researchers believe scales should be designed as "odd-point, nonforced" scales[1] since not all respondents will have enough knowledge or experience with the topic to be able to accurately assess their thoughts or feelings. If respondents are forced to choose, the scale may produce lower-quality data. With nonforced choice scales, however, the so-called neutral scale point provides respondents an easy way to express their feelings.

Many researchers believe there is no such thing as a neutral attitude or feeling—that these mental aspects almost always have some degree of a positive or negative orientation attached to them. A person either has an attitude or does not have an attitude about a given

Exhibit 8.6	**Examples of Forced-Choice and Nonforced Choice Scales**

Even-Point, Forced-Choice Rating Scales

Purchase Intention (Buy—Not Buy)

____ Definitely will buy ____ Probably will buy ____ Probably will not buy ____ Definitely will not buy

Personal Beliefs/Opinions (Agreement—Disagreement)

Definitely agree	Generally agree	Slightly agree	Neither agree nor disagree	Slightly disagree	Generally disagree	Definitely disagree
_____	_____	_____	_____	_____	_____	_____

Odd-Point, Nonforced Choice Rating Scales

Purchase Intention (Buy—Not Buy)

Definitely will buy	Probably will buy	Neither will nor will not buy	Probably will not buy	Definitely will not buy
_____	_____	_____	_____	_____

Personal Beliefs/Opinions (Agreement—Disagreement)

Definitely agree	Generally agree	Slightly agree	Neither agree nor disagree	Slightly disagree	Generally disagree	Definitely disagree
_____	_____	_____	_____	_____	_____	_____

object. Likewise, a person will either have a feeling or not have a feeling. An alternative approach to handling situations in which respondents may feel uncomfortable about expressing their thoughts or feelings because they have no knowledge of or experience with the object would be to incorporate a "Not Applicable" response choice.

Desired Measures of Central Tendency and Dispersion The type of statistical analyses that can be performed on data depends on the level of the data collected, whether nominal, ordinal, interval, or ratio. In Chapters 12 and 13 we show how the level of data collected influences the type of analysis. Here we focus on how the scale's level affects the choice of how we measure central tendency and dispersion. **Measures of central tendency** locate the center of a distribution of responses and are basic summary statistics. The mean, median, and mode measure central tendency using different criteria. The *mean* is the arithmetic average of all the data responses. The *median* is the sample statistic that divides the data so that half the data are above the statistic value and half are below. The *mode* is the value most frequently given among all of the responses.

    Measures of dispersion describe how the data are dispersed around a central value. These statistics enable the researcher to report the variability of responses on a particular scale. Measures of dispersion include the frequency distribution, the range, and the estimated standard deviation. A *frequency distribution* is a summary of how many times each possible response to a scale question/setup was recorded by the total group of respondents. This distribution can be easily converted into percentages or histograms. The *range* represents the distance between the largest and smallest response. The *standard deviation* is the statistical value that specifies the degree of variation in the responses.

    Given the important role these statistics play in data analysis, an understanding of how different levels of scales influence the use of a particular statistic is critical in scale design. Exhibit 8.7 displays these relationships. Nominal scales can only be analyzed using frequency distributions and the mode. Ordinal scales can be analyzed using medians and ranges as well as modes and frequency distributions. For interval or ratio scales, the most appropriate statistics to use are means and standard deviations. In addition, interval and ratio data can be analyzed using modes, medians, frequency distributions, and ranges.

Measures of central tendency The basic sample statistics that are generated through analyzing data; these are the mode, the median, and the mean.

Measures of dispersion The sample statistics that allow a researcher to report the variability of the data collected from scale measurements; they are the frequency distribution, the range, and the estimated sample standard deviation.

| **Exhibit 8.7** | Relationships between Scale Levels and Measures of Central Tendency and Dispersion |

| | **Basic Levels of Scales** | | | |
Measurements	Nominal	Ordinal	Interval	Ratio
Central Tendency				
Mode	**Appropriate**	Appropriate	Appropriate	Appropriate
Median	Inappropriate	**More Appropriate**	Appropriate	Appropriate
Mean	Inappropriate	Inappropriate	**Most Appropriate**	**Most Appropriate**
Dispersion				
Frequency Distribution	**Appropriate**	Appropriate	Appropriate	Appropriate
Range	Inappropriate	**More Appropriate**	Appropriate	Appropriate
Estimated Standard Deviation	Inappropriate	Inappropriate	**Most Appropriate**	**Most Appropriate**

Now that we have presented the basics of construct development as well as the rules for developing scale measurements, we are ready to discuss attitudinal and behavioral scales frequently used by marketing researchers.

◐ Scales to Measure Attitudes and Behaviors

Scales are the "rulers" that measure customer attitudes, behaviors, and intentions. Well-designed scales result in better measurement of marketplace phenomena and thus provide more accurate information to marketing decision makers. Several types of scales have proven useful in different situations. This section discusses three scale formats: Likert scales, semantic differential scales, and behavioral intention scales. Exhibit 8.8 shows the general steps in the construct development/scale measurement process. These steps are followed in developing most types of scales, including the three discussed here.

Likert Scale

Likert scale An ordinal scale format that asks respondents to indicate the extent to which they agree or disagree with a series of statements about a given object.

A **Likert scale** asks respondents to indicate the extent to which they either agree or disagree with a series of statements about a subject. Usually the scale format is balanced between agreement and disagreement scale descriptors. Named after its original developer, Rensis Likert, this scale initially had five scale descriptors: "strongly agree," "agree," "neither agree nor disagree," "disagree," "strongly disagree." The Likert scale is often expanded beyond the original five-point format to a seven-point scale, and most researchers treat the scale format as an interval scale. Likert scales are best for research designs that use self-administered surveys, personal interviews, or online surveys. Exhibit 8.9 provides an example of a 6-point Likert scale in a self-administered survey.

Semantic Differential Scale

Semantic differential scale A unique bipolar ordinal scale format that captures a person's attitudes or feelings about a given object.

Another rating scale used quite often in marketing research is the **semantic differential scale.** This scale is unique in its use of bipolar adjectives (good/bad, like/dislike, competitive/noncompetitive, helpful/unhelpful, high quality/low quality, dependable/undependable) as the endpoints of a continuum. Only the endpoints of the scale are labeled. Usually there

Exhibit 8.8	Construct/Scale Development Process	
Steps		**Activities**
1. Identify and define construct		Determine construct dimensions/factors
2. Create initial pool of attribute statements		Conduct qualitative research, collect secondary data, identify theory
3. Assess and select reduced set of items/statements		Use qualitative judgment and item analysis
4. Design scales and pretest		Collect data from pretest
5. Complete statistical analysis		Evaluate reliability and validity
6. Refine and purify scales		Eliminate poorly designed statements
7. Complete final scale evaluation		Most often qualitative judgment, but may involve further reliability and validity tests

Exhibit 8.9 Example of a Likert Scale

For each of the statements, please check the one response that best expresses the extent to which you agree or disagree with that statement.

Statements	Definitely Agree	Somewhat Agree	Slightly Agree	Slightly Disagree	Somewhat Disagree	Definitely Disagree
I buy many things with a credit card.	____	____	____	____	____	____
I wish we had a lot more money.	____	____	____	____	____	____
My friends often come to me for advice.	____	____	____	____	____	____
I am never influenced by advertisements.	____	____	____	____	____	____

will be one object and a related set of attributes, each with its own set of bipolar adjectives. In most cases, semantic differential scales use either five or seven scale points.

Means for each attribute can be calculated and mapped on a diagram with the various attributes listed, creating a "perceptual image profile" of the object. Semantic differential scales can be used to develop and compare profiles of different companies, brands, or products. Respondents can also be asked to indicate how an ideal product would rate, and then researchers can compare ideal and actual products.

To illustrate semantic differential scales, assume the researcher wants to assess the credibility of Tiger Woods as a spokesperson in advertisements for the Nike brand of personal grooming products. A credibility construct consisting of three dimensions is used: (1) expertise, (2) trustworthiness, and (3) attractiveness. Each dimension is measured using five bipolar scales (see measures of two of these dimensions in Exhibit 8.10).

Exhibit 8.10 Example of a Semantic Differential Scale Format for Tiger Woods as a Credible Spokesperson[2]

We would like to know your opinions about the expertise, trustworthiness, and attractiveness you believe Tiger Woods brings to Nike advertisements. Each dimension below has five factors that may or may not represent your opinions. For each listed item, please check the space that best expresses your opinion about that item.

Expertise:

Knowledgeable	____	____	____	____	____	____	____	Unknowledgeable
Expert	____	____	____	____	____	____	____	Not an expert
Skilled	____	____	____	____	____	____	____	Unskilled
Qualified	____	____	____	____	____	____	____	Unqualified
Experienced	____	____	____	____	____	____	____	Inexperienced

Trustworthiness:

Reliable	____	____	____	____	____	____	____	Unreliable
Sincere	____	____	____	____	____	____	____	Insincere
Trustworthy	____	____	____	____	____	____	____	Untrustworthy
Dependable	____	____	____	____	____	____	____	Undependable
Honest	____	____	____	____	____	____	____	Dishonest

Non-Bipolar Descriptors A problem encountered in designing semantic differential scales is the inappropriate narrative expressions of the scale descriptors. In a well-designed semantic differential scale, the individual scales should be truly bipolar. Sometimes researchers use a negative pole descriptor that is not truly an opposite of the positive descriptor. This creates a scale that is difficult for the respondent to correctly interpret. Consider, for example, the "expert/not an expert" scale in the "expertise" dimension. While the scale is dichotomous, the words "not an expert" do not allow the respondent to interpret any of the other scale points as being relative magnitudes of that phrase. Other than that one endpoint described as "not an expert," all the other scale points would have to represent some intensity of "expertise," thus creating a skewed scale toward the positive pole.

Researchers must be careful when selecting bipolar descriptors to make sure the words or phrases are truly extremely bipolar in nature and allow for creating symmetrical scales. For example, the researcher could use descriptors such as "complete expert" and "complete novice" to correct the above-described scale descriptor problem.

Exhibit 8.11 shows a semantic differential scale used by Midas Auto Systems to collect attitudinal data on performance. The same scale can be used to collect data on several competing automobile service providers and each of the semantic differential profiles can be displayed together.

Behavioral Intention Scale

One of the most widely used scale formats in marketing research is the **behavioral intention scale.** In using this scale the decision maker is attempting to assess the likelihood that people will behave in some way regarding a product or service. For example, market researchers may measure purchase intent, attendance intent, shopping intent, or usage intent.

Behavioral intention scale
A special type of rating scale designed to capture the likelihood that people will behave in some way regarding a product or service.

Exhibit 8.11	Example of a Semantic Differential Scale for Midas Auto Systems

From your personal experiences with Midas Auto Systems' service representatives, please rate the performance of Midas on the basis of the following listed features. Each feature has its own scale ranging from "one" (1) to "six" (6). Please circle the response number that best describes how Midas has performed on that feature. For any feature(s) that you feel is (are) not relevant to your evaluation, please circle the (NA)—Not applicable—response code.

Cost of Repair/Maintenance Work	(NA)	Extremely High	6	5	4	3	2	1	Very Low, Almost Free
Appearance of Facilities	(NA)	Very Professional	6	5	4	3	2	1	Very Unprofessional
Customer Satisfaction	(NA)	Totally Dissatisfied	6	5	4	3	2	1	Truly Satisfied
Promptness in Delivering Service	(NA)	Unacceptably Slow	6	5	4	3	2	1	Impressively Quick
Quality of Service Offerings	(NA)	Truly Terrible	6	5	4	3	2	1	Truly Exceptional
Understands Customer's Needs	(NA)	Really Understands	6	5	4	3	2	1	Doesn't Have a Clue
Credibility of Midas	(NA)	Extremely Credible	6	5	4	3	2	1	Extremely Unreliable
Midas's Keeping of Promises	(NA)	Very Trustworthy	6	5	4	3	2	1	Very Deceitful
Midas Services Assortment	(NA)	Truly Full Service	6	5	4	3	2	1	Only Basic Services
Prices/Rates/Charges of Services	(NA)	Much Too High	6	5	4	3	2	1	Great Rates
Service Personnel's Competence	(NA)	Very Competent	6	5	4	3	2	1	Totally Incompetent
Employee's Personal Social Skills	(NA)	Very Rude	6	5	4	3	2	1	Very Friendly
Midas's Operating Hours	(NA)	Extremely Flexible	6	5	4	3	2	1	Extremely Limited
Convenience of Midas's Locations	(NA)	Very Easy to Get to	6	5	4	3	2	1	Too Difficult to Get to

In general, behavioral intention scales have been found to be reasonably good predictors of consumers' choices of frequently purchased and durable consumer products.[3]

Behavioral intention scales are easy to construct. Consumers are asked to make a subjective judgment of their likelihood of buying a product or service or taking a specified action. An example of scale descriptors used with a behavioral intention scale is "definitely will," "probably will," "not sure," "probably will not," and "definitely will not." When designing a behavioral intention scale, a specific time frame should be included in the instructions to the respondent. Without an expressed time frame, it is likely respondents will bias their response toward the "definitely would" or "probably would" scale categories.

Behavioral intentions are often a key variable of interest in marketing research studies. To increase the specificity of scale points, the researcher can use descriptors that indicate the percentage chance they will buy a product or engage in a behavior of interest. The following set of scale points could be used: "definitely will (90% to 100% chance)"; "probably will (50% to 89% chance)"; probably will not (10% to 49% chance)"; and "definitely will not (less than 10% chance)." Exhibit 8.12 shows what the shopping intention scale might look like.

No matter what kind of scale is used to capture people's attitudes and behaviors, there often is no one best or guaranteed approach. While there are established scale measures for obtaining the components that make up respondents' attitudes and behavioral intentions, the data provided from these scale measurements should not be interpreted as being completely predictive of behavior. Unfortunately, knowledge of an individual's attitudes may not predict actual behavior. Intentions are better than attitudes at predicting behavior, but the strongest predictor of future behavior is past behavior.

Exhibit 8.12 Retail Store: Shopping Intention Scale for Casual Clothes

When shopping for casual wear for yourself or someone else, how likely are you to shop at each of the following types of retail stores? **(Please check one response for each store type.)**

Type of Retail Store	Definitely Would Shop At (90–100% chance)	Probably Would Shop At (50–89% chance)	Probably Would Not Shop At (10–49% chance)	Definitely Would Not Shop At (less than 10% chance)
Department Stores (e.g., Macy's, Dillard's)	❑	❑	❑	❑
Discount Department Stores (e.g., Wal-Mart, Kmart, Target)	❑	❑	❑	❑
Clothing Specialty Shops (e.g., Wolf Brothers, Surrey's George Ltd.)	❑	❑	❑	❑
Casual Wear Specialty Stores (e.g., The Gap, Banana Republic, Aca Joe's)	❑	❑	❑	❑

Comparative and Noncomparative Rating Scales

Noncomparative rating scale
A scale format that requires a judgment without reference to another object, person, or concept.

Comparative rating scale
A scale format that requires a judgment comparing one object, person, or concept against another on the scale.

Graphic rating scale A scale measure that uses a scale point format that presents the respondent with some type of graphic continuum as the set of possible responses to a given question.

A **noncomparative rating scale** is used when the objective is to have a respondent express his or her attitudes, behavior, or intentions about a specific object (e.g., person or phenomenon) or its attributes without making reference to another object or its attributes. In contrast, a **comparative rating scale** is used when the objective is to have a respondent express his or her attitudes, feelings, or behaviors about an object or its attributes on the basis of some other object or its attributes. Exhibit 8.13 gives several examples of graphic rating scale formats, which are among the most widely used noncomparative scales.

Graphic rating scales use a scaling descriptor format that presents a respondent with a graphic continuum as the set of possible responses to a question. For example, the first graphic rating scale displayed in Exhibit 8.13 is used in situations where the researcher wants to collect "usage behavior" data about an object. Or as another example, imagine that Yahoo wants to determine how satisfied Internet users are with its search engine without making reference to any other available search engine alternatives such as Google. In using this type of scale, the respondents would simply place an "X" along the graphic line, which would be labeled with extreme narrative descriptors, in this case "Not At All Satisfied" and "Very Satisfied," together with numeric descriptors, 0 and 100. The remainder of the line is sectioned into equal-appearing numeric intervals.

Another popular type of graphic rating scale descriptor design utilizes smiling faces. The smiling faces are arranged in order and depict a continuous range from "very happy" to "very sad" without providing narrative descriptors of the two extreme positions. This visual graphic rating design can be used to collect a variety of attitudinal and emotional data. It is most popular in collecting data from children. Graphic rating scales can be constructed easily and are simple to use.

Turning now to comparative rating scales, Exhibit 8.14 illustrates rank-order and constant sum scale formats. A common characteristic of comparative scales is that they can be

---

Exhibit 8.13 Examples of Graphic Rating Scales

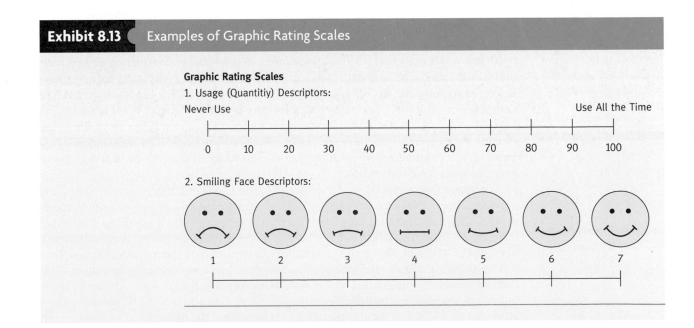

Graphic Rating Scales

1. Usage (Quantitiy) Descriptors:

Never Use   Use All the Time

0   10   20   30   40   50   60   70   80   90   100

2. Smiling Face Descriptors:

1   2   3   4   5   6   7

Exhibit 8.14	Examples of Comparative Rating Scales

Rank-Order Scale

Thinking about the different types of music, please rank your top three preferences of types of music you enjoy listening to by writing in your first choice, second choice, and third choice on the lines provided below.

First Preference: _____

Second Preference: _____

Third Preference: _____

Constant Sum Scale

Below is a list of seven banking features. Please allocate 100 points among the features. Your allocation should represent the importance each feature has to you in selecting "your" bank. The more points you assign to a feature, the more importance that feature has in your selection process. If the feature is "not at all important" in your process, you should not assign it any points. When you have finished, please double-check to make sure your total adds to 100.

Banking Features	**Number of Points**
Convenience/location	____
Banking hours	____
Good service charges	____
The interest rates on loans	____
The bank's reputation	____
The interest rates on savings	____
Bank's promotional advertising	____
	100 points

used to identify and directly compare similarities and differences between products/services, brands, or product attributes.

Rank-order scales A scale formate that allows respondents to indicate order of preference.

Rank-order scales use a format that enables respondents to compare objects by indicating their order of preference or choice from first to last. Rank-order scales are easy to use as long as respondents are not asked to rank too many items. Use of rank-order scales in traditional or computer-assisted telephone interviews may be difficult, but it is possible as long as the number of items being compared is kept to four or five. When respondents are asked to rank objects or attributes of objects, problems can occur if the respondent's preferred objects or attributes are not listed. Another limitation is that only ordinal data can be obtained using rank-order scales.

Constant sum scales Require the respondent to allocate a given number of points, usually 100, among several attributes or features based on their importance to the individual; this format requires a person to evaluate each separate attribute or feature relative to all the other listed ones.

Constant sum scales ask respondents to allocate a given number of points. The points are often allocated based on the importance of product features to respondents. Respondents are asked to determine the value of each separate feature relative to all the other listed features. The resulting values indicate the relative magnitude of importance each feature has to the respondent. This scaling format usually requires that the individual values must add up to 100. Consider, for example, the constant sum scale displayed in Exhibit 8.14. Bank of America could use this type of scale to identify which banking attributes are more important to customers in influencing their decision as to where to bank. More than 5–7 attributes should not be used to allocate points because of the difficulty in adding to reach 100 points.

◀■ Other Scale Measurement Issues

Attention to scale measurement issues will increase the usefulness of research results. Several additional design issues related to scale measurement are reviewed below.

Single-Item and Multiple-Item Scales

Single-item scale design A scale format that collects data about only one attribute of an object or construct.

Multiple-item scale design A scale format that simultaneously collects data on several attributes of an object or construct.

A **single-item scale** involves collecting data about only one attribute of the object or construct being investigated. One example of a single-item scale would be age. The respondent is asked a single question about his or her age and supplies only one possible response to the question. In contrast, many marketing research projects that involve collecting attitudinal, emotional, and behavioral data use some type of multiple-item scale. A **multiple-item scale** is one that includes several statements relating to the object or construct being examined. Each statement has a rating scale attached to it and the researcher typically will sum the ratings on the individual statements to obtain a summated or overall rating for the object or construct.

The decision to use a single-item versus a multiple-item scale is made when the construct is being developed. Two factors play a significant role in the process—the number of dimensions of the construct and the reliability and validity. First, the researcher must assess the various factors or dimensions that make up the construct under investigation. For example, studies of service quality often measure five dimensions: empathy, reliability, responsiveness, assurance, and tangibles. If a construct has several different, unique dimensions the researcher must measure each of those subcomponents. Second, researchers must consider reliability and validity. In general, multiple-item scales are more reliable and more valid. Thus, multiple-item scales generally are preferred over single-item scales.

Clear Wording

When phrasing the question setup element of the scale, use clear wording and avoid ambiguity. Also avoid using "leading" words or phrases in any scale measurement's question. Regardless of the data collection method (personal, telephone, computer-assisted interviews, or online surveys), all necessary instructions for both respondent and interviewer are part of the scale measurement's setup. All instructions should be kept simple and clear. When determining the appropriate set of scale point descriptors, make sure the descriptors are relevant to the type of data being sought. Scale descriptors should have adequate discriminatory power, be mutually exclusive, and make sense to the respondent.

Screening Questions

Screening questions should be used in any type of interview. Their purpose is to identify qualified prospective respondents and prevent unqualified respondents from being included in the study. For example, if you are interested in studying online shoppers, you must include a screening question that ensures that the potential respondent has made an online purchase in a recent time frame. Screening questions need to be separately administered before the beginning of the main interview.

Skip Questions

Skip questions are also called "conditional" or "branching" questions. If they are needed, the instructions must be clearly communicated to the respondent or interviewer. Skip questions are used if the next question or set of questions should be responded to only by a respondent who meets a particular condition. A simple expression of a skip command might be: "If you answered "yes" to Question 5, skip to Question 9." Skip questions help ensure that only specifically qualified respondents answer certain items. This type of question can be automatically executed using either Internet data collection or computer-assisted phone interviewing.

MARKETING RESEARCH IN ACTION
What Can You Learn from a Customer Loyalty Index?

The idea that loyal customers are especially valuable is not new. Loyal customers repeatedly purchase products or services. They recommend a company to others. And they stick with a business over time. Loyal customers are worth the special effort it may take to keep them. But how can you provide that special treatment if you don't know your customers and how their loyalty is won and lost?

To better understand the concept of customer loyalty, we can first define what customer loyalty is not. Customer loyalty is not customer satisfaction. Satisfaction is a necessary component of loyal or secure customers. However, just because customers are satisfied with your company does not mean they will continue to do business with you in the future.

Customer loyalty is not a response to trial offers or incentives. Customers who respond to a special offer or incentive may be just as quick to respond to your competitors' incentives.

Customer loyalty is not high market share. Many businesses mistakenly look at their sales numbers and market share and think, "We wouldn't be enjoying high levels of market share if our customers didn't love us." However, this may not be true. Many other factors can drive up market share, including poor performance by competitors or pricing issues.

Customer loyalty is not repeat buying or habitual buying. Many repeat customers may be choosing your products or services because of convenience or habit. However, if they learn about a competitive product that they think may be less expensive or better quality, they may quickly switch to that product.

So what does customer loyalty mean? Customer loyalty is a composite of a number of qualities. It is driven by customer satisfaction, yet it also involves a commitment on the part of the customer to make a sustained investment in an ongoing relationship with a brand or company. Finally, customer loyalty is reflected by a combination of attitudes and behaviors. These attitudes include:

- The intention to buy again and/or buy additional products or services from the same company.
- A willingness to recommend the company to others.
- A commitment to the company demonstrated by a resistance to switching to a competitor.

Customer behaviors that reflect loyalty include:

- Repeat purchasing of products or services.
- Purchasing more and different products or services from the same company.
- Recommending the company to others.

Burke Customer Satisfaction Associates (www.burke.com) developed a Secure Customer Index (SCI) using the combined scores on three components of customer loyalty.[4] They ask, for example: "Overall, how satisfied were you with your visit to this restaurant?" To examine likelihood to recommend: "How likely would you be to recommend this restaurant to a friend or associate?" And finally, to examine likelihood of repeat purchases, they ask, "How likely are you to choose to visit this restaurant again?" (See Exhibit 8.15.)

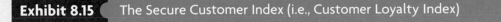

Exhibit 8.15   The Secure Customer Index (i.e., Customer Loyalty Index)

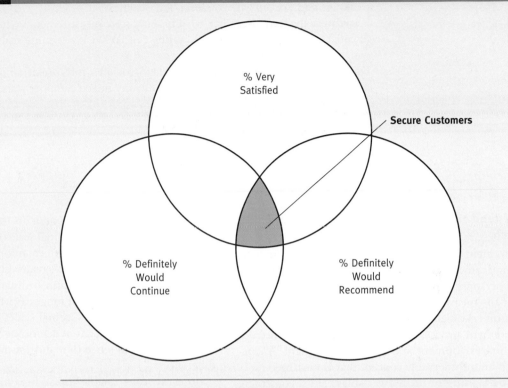

With these three components, and the appropriate scales for each, "secure customers" are defined as those giving the most positive responses across all three components. All other customers would be considered vulnerable or at risk of defecting to a competitor.

Companies are increasingly able to link customer satisfaction and customer loyalty to bottom-line benefits. By examining customer behaviors over time and comparing them to SCI scores, a strong connection can be shown between secure customers and repeat purchasing of products or services. In comparing cases across customer and industry types, Burke has found other illustrations that show a connection between the index scores and financial or market performance.

Using a customer loyalty index helps companies better understand their customers. By listening to customers, implementing change, and continuously monitoring the results, companies can focus their improvement efforts with the goal of winning and keeping customers.

Hands-on Exercise

Using the material from the chapter and the above information, answer each of the following questions:

1. In your judgment, what level of scale design would be the most appropriate in creating the necessary scale measurements for collecting primary data on each construct?
2. For each construct, design an example of the actual scale measurement that could be used by Burke Customer Satisfaction Associates to collect the data.

3. What are several weaknesses associated with how Burke Customer Satisfaction Associates measured its Secure Customer Index (SCI)? Make sure you clearly identify each weakness and explain why you feel it is a weakness.

4. If you were the lead researcher, what types of scale measurement would you have used to collect the needed data for calculating SCI? Why? Write some scale measurements you would use.

5. Do you agree or disagree with the Burke Associates' interpretation of the value they provide their clients using the Customer Loyalty Index? Support your response.

Summary

Understand the role of measurement in marketing research.

Measurement is the process of developing methods to systematically characterize or quantify information about persons, events, ideas, or objects of interest. As part of the measurement process, researchers assign either numbers or labels to phenomena they measure. The measurement process consists of two tasks: construct selection/development and scale measurement. A construct is an unobservable concept that is measured indirectly by a group of related variables. Thus, constructs are made up of a combination of several related indicator variables that together define the concept being measured. Construct development is the process in which researchers identify characteristics that define the concept being studied by the researcher.

When developing constructs, researchers must consider the abstractness of the construct and its dimensionality, as well as reliability and validity. Once the characteristics are identified, the researcher must then develop a method of indirectly measuring the concept. Scale measurement is the process of assigning a set of descriptors to represent the range of possible responses a person may give in answering a question about a particular object or construct.

Explain the four basic levels of scales.

The four basic levels of scales are nominal, ordinal, interval, and ratio. Nominal scales are the most basic and provide the least amount of data. They assign labels to objects/respondents but do not show relative magnitudes between them. Nominal scales ask respondents about their religious affiliation, gender, type of dwelling, occupation, last brand of cereal purchased, and so on. To analyze nominal data researchers use modes and frequency distributions.

Ordinal scales require respondents to express relative magnitude about a topic. Ordinal scales enable researchers to create a hierarchical pattern among the responses (or scale points) that indicate "greater than/less than" relationships. Data derived from ordinal scale measurements include medians and ranges as well as modes and frequency distributions. Ordinal scales determine relative position, but they cannot determine how much more or how much less since they do not measure absolute differences.

Interval scales enable researchers to show absolute differences between scale points. With interval data, means and standard deviations can be calculated, as well as the mode, median, frequency distribution, and range. Ratio scales enable researchers to identify absolute differences between each scale point and to make absolute comparisons between the respondents' responses. Ratio questions are designed to allow "true natural zero" or "true state of nothing" responses. Ratio scales also can develop means, standard deviations, and other measures of central tendency and variation.

Describe scale development and its importance in gathering primary data.

There are three important components to scale measurement: (1) question/setup; (2) dimensions of the object, construct, or behavior; and (3) the scale point descriptors. Some of the criteria for scale development are the intelligibility of the questions, the appropriateness of the primary descriptors, and the discriminatory power of the scale descriptors. Likert scales use agree/disagree scale descriptors to obtain a person's attitude toward a given object or behavior. Semantic differential scale formats are used to obtain perceptual image profiles of an object or behavior. This scale format is unique in that it uses a set of bipolar scales to measure several different attributes of a given object or behavior. Behavioral intention scales measure the likelihood that people will purchase an object or service, or visit a store. Scale point descriptors such as "definitely would," "probably would," "probably would not," and "definitely would not" are often used with intentions scales.

Discuss comparative and noncomparative scales.

Comparative scales require the respondent to make a direct comparison between two products or services, whereas noncomparative scales rate products or services independently. Data from comparative scales is interpreted in relative terms. Both types of scales are generally considered interval or ratio and more advanced statistical procedures can be used with them. One benefit of comparative scales is they enable researchers to identify small differences between attributes, constructs, or objects. In addition, comparative scales require fewer theoretical assumptions and are easier for respondents to understand and respond to than are many noncomparative scales.

Key Terms and Concepts

Behavioral intention scale 157

Comparative rating scale 159

Constant sum scales 160

Construct 147

Construct development 147

Discriminatory power 152

Graphic rating scales 159

Interval scale 149

Likert scale 155

Measurement 146

Measures of central tendency 154

Measures of dispersion 154

Multiple-item scale design 161

Nominal scale 149

Noncomparative rating scale 159

Ordinal scale 149

Rank-order scales 160

Ratio scale 150

Scale measurement 147

Scale points 147

Semantic differential scale 155

Single-item scale design 161

Review Questions

1. What is measurement?
2. Among the four basic levels of scales, which one provides the researcher with the most information?
3. Explain the main differences between interval and ratio scale measurements.
4. What are the major differences between ordinal and interval scales? In your response include an example of each type of scale.
5. Explain the major differences between "rating" and "ranking" scales. Which is a better scale measurement technique for collecting attitudinal data on salesforce performance of people who sell commercial laser printers? Why?
6. What are the benefits and limitations of comparative scale measurements? Design a paired-comparison scale that will enable you to determine brand preference between Bud Light, Miller Lite, Coors Light, and Old Milwaukee Light beers.

Discussion Questions

1. Develop a semantic differential scale that can identify the perceptual profile differences between Outback Steakhouse and Longhorn Steakhouse restaurants.

2. Design a behavioral intention scale that can answer the following research question: "To what extent are college students likely to purchase a new automobile within six months after graduating?" Discuss the potential shortcomings of your scale design.

3. For each of the scales shown below (A, B, and C), answer the following questions:

   a. What type of data is being collected?
   b. What level of scale measurement is being used?
   c. What is the most appropriate measure of central tendency?
   d. What is the most appropriate measure of variation (or dispersion)?
   e. What weakness, if any, exists with the scale?

A. How do you pay for your travel expenses?

   _____ Cash   _____ Company charge
   _____ Check   _____ Personal charge
   _____ Credit card   _____ Other _____

B. How often do you travel for business or pleasure purposes?

For Business	For Pleasure
_____ 0–1 times per month	_____ 0–1 times per year
_____ 2–3 times per month	_____ 2–3 times per year
_____ 4–5 times per month	_____ 4–5 times per year
_____ 6 or more times per month	_____ 6 or more times per year

C. Please check the one category that best approximates your total family annual income, before taxes. (Please check only one category.)

_____ Under $10,000	_____ $30,001–$40,000	_____ $60,001–$70,000
_____ $10,000–$20,000	_____ $40,001–$50,000	_____ $70,001–$100,000
_____ $20,001–$30,000	_____ $50,001–$60,000	_____ Over $100,000

4. For each of the listed concepts or objects, design a scale measurement that would enable you to collect data on that concept/object.

   a. An excellent long-distance runner.
   b. A person's favorite Mexican restaurant.
   c. Size of the listening audience for a popular country and western radio station.
   d. Consumers' attitudes toward the Colorado Rockies professional baseball team.
   e. The satisfaction a person has toward his or her automobile.
   f. Purchase intentions for a new tennis racket.

5. Identify and discuss the key issues a researcher should consider when choosing a scale for capturing consumers' expressions of satisfaction?

6. AT&T is interested in capturing consumer response to its new wireless cell phone services. Determine and justify what service attributes should be used to capture the performance of its wireless cell phone service. Design two scale measurements that would allow AT&T to accurately collect the data.

7. The local Ford dealership is interested in collecting data to answer the following research question: *"How likely are young adults to purchase a new automobile within a year after graduating from college?"* Design a nominal, ordinal, interval, and ratio scale measurement that will enable the dealership to collect the required data. In your opinion, which one of your designs would be most useful to the dealership and why?

Designing the Questionnaire

Chapter 9

Learning Objectives   After reading this chapter, you will be able to:

1. Describe the steps in questionnaire design.
2. Discuss the questionnaire development process.
3. Summarize the characteristics of good questionnaires.
4. Compose a cover letter.
5. Explain the importance of other documents used with questionnaires.

Can Surveys Be Used to Develop University Residence Life Plans?

University administrators implemented a "Residence Life" program to identify factors likely to enrich the academic and social experiences of on-campus students. The main goals were to ensure the university offered high-quality on-campus living experiences with facilities and programs for attracting new students to the university, increasing on-campus housing occupancy rates, and improving retention levels of students, thus increasing the likelihood that students would renew their on-campus housing contracts for multiple years. MPC Consulting Group, Inc., a national firm specializing in on-campus housing programs, was retained to oversee the project. The firm had an excellent reputation, but seldom conducted primary marketing research.

After clarifying the objectives of the project, MPC determined that a self-administered survey instrument would be used to obtain students' information, attitudes, and feelings regarding on-campus living experiences. The survey would be administered using the university's newly acquired "Blackboard" electronic e-mail system. The rationale for using this method was that all 43,000 students had access and it would save time and costs. MPC's consulting team brainstormed a list of 59 questions to be asked of both on-campus and off-campus students currently enrolled at the university. The questionnaire's design began by asking about personal demographic characteristics followed by some questions concerning students' current housing situations and an evaluation of those conditions. Next, questions were asked about the importance of a list of preselected housing characteristics, then questions about students' intentions of living on-campus versus off-campus and reasons for those intentions. After asking about marital status and children, questions were asked on the desirability of types of housing structures and amenities. The survey ended with personal thoughts about the need for child care services.

When placed on "Blackboard" for access, the questionnaire took 24 screens with six different "screener" questions requiring respondents to skip back and forth between computer screens depending on how they responded to the screening questions. After being in the field three weeks, only 17 students had responded, and eight of those surveys were incomplete. University officials were disappointed in the response rate and asked MPC three simple but critical questions: (1) "Why such a low response rate?" (2) "Was the survey a good or bad instrument for capturing the needed information?" and (3) "What was the value of the data for addressing the given goals?"

Based on your knowledge and understanding of good information research practices to this point, give your answers to the three questions. What are the potential problems (weaknesses) that were created by MPC's process described above?

Value of Questionnaires in Marketing Research

This chapter focuses on the importance of questionnaire design and the process that should be undertaken in the development of data collection instruments. Understanding questionnaire design will require integration of many of the concepts discussed in earlier chapters.

Most surveys are designed to be descriptive or predictive. Descriptive research designs use questionnaires to collect data that can be turned into knowledge about a person, object, or issue. For example, the U.S. Census Bureau uses descriptive survey questionnaires to collect attributes and behavioral data that can be translated into facts about the U.S. population (e.g., income levels, marital status, age, occupation, family size, usage rates, consumption quantities). In contrast, predictive survey questionnaires require the researcher to collect a wider range of data that can be used in predicting changes in attitudes and behaviors as well as in testing hypotheses.

You may never actually design a questionnaire. But you likely will be in the position of determining whether a survey is good or bad. Thus, you should know the activities and principles involved in designing survey questionnaires. A **questionnaire** is a document consisting of a set of questions and scales to gather primary data. Good questionnaires enable researchers to collect reliable and valid information. Advances in communication systems, the Internet, and software have influenced how questions are asked and recorded. Yet the principles followed in designing questionnaires remain essentially unchanged. Whether developing a survey to use online or offline, the steps researchers follow in designing questionnaires are similar.

Questionnaire A document consisting of a set of questions and scales to gather primary data.

Questionnaire Design

Researchers follow a systematic approach when they design questionnaires. Exhibit 9.1 lists the steps followed in developing survey questionnaires. Discussion of the steps is based on a study conducted for American Bank in Baton Rouge, the capital city of Louisiana. The bank would like to expand regionally. To improve decision making, information is needed on banking habits and patterns, satisfaction and commitment, as well as demographic and lifestyle characteristics of current and potential customers.

Step 1: Confirm Research Objectives

In the initial phase of the development process, the research objectives are agreed upon by the researcher and bank management. The research objectives are listed below:

1. To collect data on selected demographic characteristics that can be used to create a profile of current American Bank customers as well as potential future customers.

Exhibit 9.1	Steps in Questionnaire Design

Step 1: Confirm research objectives

Step 2: Select appropriate data collection method

Step 3: Develop questions and scaling

Step 4: Determine layout and evaluate questionnaire

Step 5: Obtain initial client approval

Step 6: Pretest, revise, and finalize questionnaire

Step 7: Implement the survey

2. To collect data on selected lifestyle dimensions that can be used to better understand current American Bank customers and their banking habits and those of potential customers.

3. To identify preferred banking services, as well as attitudes and feelings toward those services.

4. To identify demographic and lifestyle characteristics of market segments as well as satisfaction with and commitment to current primary banking relationship.

Step 2: Select Appropriate Data Collection Method

To select the data collection method, the researcher first must determine the data requirements to achieve each of the objectives as well as the type of respondent demographic information desired. In doing so the researcher should follow a general-to-specific order. The data requirements and flow for the American Bank study are described below:

Section I: Banking Services

a. The bank most often patronized by customers; that is the primary banking relationship.

b. Bank characteristics perceived as important in selecting a bank (convenience/location, banking hours, good service charges, interest rates on savings accounts, knew a person at the bank, bank's reputation, bank's promotional advertisements, interest rates on loans, and Internet banking services).

c. Personal savings accounts held by household members at financial institutions.

d. Preferences for and usage of selected banking methods (inside the bank, drive-up window, 24-hour ATM, electronic banking, bank by mail, bank by phone).

Section II: Lifestyle Dimensions   Includes belief statements to classify bank customer's lifestyles in terms of segments such as financial optimist, financially dissatisfied, information exchanger, credit or debit card user, family oriented, price conscious, and so forth.

Section III: Banking Relationships   Includes questions to examine satisfaction and commitment to current primary banking relationship.

Section IV: Demographic Characteristics   Includes characteristics such as sex, length of time in area and at current residence, employment status, marital status, spouse or partner's current employment status, number of dependent children, education, age, occupation, income, and zip code.

The researcher considered several approaches to data collection, including random telephone calls and Internet surveys. On the basis of the research objectives, information requirements, and the desire for a random sample of current bank customers, bank management and the researcher decided that an initial phone contact followed by a direct mail survey would be the best method of collecting data for current customers along with a telephone survey for potential customers.

Step 3: Develop Questions and Scaling

Questionnaire design is systematic and includes a series of logical activities. Researchers select the appropriate scales as well as design the questionnaire format to meet the data requirements. To do so, the researcher decides question format (unstructured or structured), wording of and instructions for responding to questions and scales, and type of data required (nominal, ordinal, interval, or ratio). Constructs and scaling were discussed in a previous chapter. We discuss the other topics in the following sections.

Unstructured questions
Open-ended questions formatted to allow respondents to reply in their own words.

Question Format **Unstructured questions** are open-ended questions that allow respondents to reply in their own words. There is no predetermined list of responses available to aid or limit respondents' answers. Open-ended questions are more difficult to code for analysis. Perhaps more importantly, these questions require more thinking and effort on the part of respondents. As a result, with quantitative surveys there are generally only a few open-ended questions. Unless the question is interesting to respondents, open-ended questions are often skipped.

Structured questions
Closed-ended questions that require the respondent to choose from a predetermined set of responses or scale points.

Structured questions are closed-ended questions that require the respondent to choose from a predetermined set of responses or scale points. Structured formats reduce the amount of thinking and effort required by respondents, and the response process is faster. In quantitative surveys, structured questions are used much more often than unstructured ones. They are easier for respondents to fill out and easier for researchers to code. Examples of structured questions are shown in Exhibit 9.2.

Wording Researchers must carefully consider the words used in creating questions and scales. Ambiguous words and phrases as well as vocabulary that is difficult to understand must be avoided.

Words and phrases can influence a respondent's answer to a given question. For example, small changes in wording can produce quite different answers to questions. The following illustrates this point:

1. Do you think anything <u>could</u> be done to make it more convenient for students to register for classes at your university or college?
2. Do you think anything <u>should</u> be done to make it more convenient for students to register for classes at your university or college?
3. Do you think anything <u>will</u> be done to make it more convenient for students to register for classes at your university or college?

Questions and Scaling Questions and scale format directly impact survey design. To collect accurate data researchers must devise good questions and select the correct type of scale. Several types of scales were discussed in the previous chapter. Whenever possible, metric scales should be used. Also, researchers must be careful to maintain consistency in scales used and coding to minimize confusion among respondents in answering questions.

Exhibit 9.2	Examples of Structured Questions

Personal Interview

HAND RESPONDENTS THE CARD. Please look at this card and tell me the letters that indicate what toppings, if any, you typically add to a pizza other than cheese when ordering a pizza for yourself from Pizza Hut. Interviewer: Record all mentioned toppings by circling the letters below, and make sure you probe for any other toppings.

[a] anchovies	[b] bacon	[c] barbecue beef
[d] black olives	[e] extra cheese	[f] green olives
[g] green peppers	[h] ground beef	[i] ham
[j] hot peppers	[k] mushrooms	[l] onions
[m] pepperoni	[n] sausage	[o] some other topping: _____

Telephone Interview (Traditional or Computer Assisted)

I'm going to read you a list of pizza toppings. As I read each one, please tell me whether or not that topping is one that you usually add to a pizza when ordering a pizza for yourself from Pizza Hut. Interviewer: Read each topping category slowly and record all mentioned toppings by circling their corresponding letter below, and make sure you probe for any other toppings.

[a] anchovies	[b] bacon	[c] barbecue beef
[d] black olives	[e] extra cheese	[f] green olives
[g] green peppers	[h] ground beef	[i] ham
[J] hot peppers	[k] mushrooms	[l] onions
[m] pepperoni	[n] sausage	[o] some other topping: _____

Self-Administered Survey (Online or Offline)

Among the pizza toppings listed below, what toppings, if any, do you usually add to a pizza other than cheese when ordering a pizza for yourself from Pizza Hut? Check as many boxes as apply.

❏ anchovies	❏ bacon	❏ barbecue beef
❏ black olives	❏ extra cheese	❏ green olives
❏ green peppers	❏ ground beef	❏ ham
❏ hot peppers	❏ mushrooms	❏ onions
❏ pepperoni	❏ sausage	❏ some other topping: _____

Bad questions Any questions that prevent or distort communication between the researcher and the respondent.

Once a particular question or scale is selected, the researcher must ensure they are introduced properly and easy to respond to accurately. **Bad questions** prevent or distort communications between the researcher and the respondent. If the respondent cannot answer a question in a meaningful way, it is a bad question. Some examples of bad questions are those that are:

1. *Unanswerable* either because the respondent does not have access to the information needed or because none of the answer choices apply to the respondent. An example would be: "What was your parents' yearly after-tax income two years ago?"
2. *Leading (or loaded)* in that the respondent is directed to a response that would not ordinarily be given if all possible response categories or concepts were provided, or if all

the facts were provided for the situation. An example of this would be: "We care about the customer service you receive from our business. How would you rate the quality of service you received?"

3. *Double-barreled* in that they ask the respondent to address more than one issue at a time. An example would be: "Do you drink Pepsi with breakfast, lunch, and dinner?"

When designing specific questions and scales, researchers should act as if they are two different people: one thinking like a technical, systematic researcher and the other like a respondent. The questions and scales must be presented in a logical order. After creating a title for the questionnaire, the researcher includes a brief introductory section and any general instructions prior to asking the first question. Questions should be asked in a natural general-to-specific order to reduce the potential for sequence bias.

At the beginning of the demographic section a statement similar to the following is used: *"The survey is almost completed. There are only a few more questions."* This is a "transition phrase" that serves two purposes. First, it communicates to the respondents that a change in their thinking process is about to take place. They can clear their minds before thinking about their personal data. Second, it indicates the task of completing the survey is almost over. The questionnaire used in the banking survey is shown in Exhibit 9.3.

Prior to developing the layout for the survey questionnaire, the researcher should assess the reliability and validity of the scales, such as the items in "Section II: General Opinions" of Exhibit 9.3. Once this is completed, the focus is on preparing instructions and making required revisions. See Exhibit 9.4 for a summary of general guidelines for evaluating questions.

Step 4: Determine Layout and Evaluate Questionnaire

In good questionnaire design, questions flow from general to more specific information and end with demographic data. Questionnaires begin with an *introductory section* that gives the respondent an overview of the research. The section also includes general instructions for filling out the survey. Next the researcher reviews the information requirements for each research objective and arranges them from general to specific. The end result of this process is the second section of the questionnaire which focuses on the research questions. This is called the *research questions section.* The last section includes demographic questions for the respondents. The questionnaire ends with a thank-you statement.

Demographic questions are placed at the end of a questionnaire because they often ask personal information and many people are reluctant to provide this information to strangers. Until the "comfort zone" is established between the interviewer and respondent, asking personal questions could easily bring the interviewing process to a halt.

Questionnaire formatting and layout should make it easy for respondents to read and follow instructions. It also should look professional and be visually appealing. If the researcher fails to consider questionnaire layout the quality of the data is substantially reduced.

The value of a well-constructed questionnaire is difficult to estimate. The main function of a questionnaire is to capture people's true thoughts and feelings about issues or objects. Data collected using questionnaires should improve understanding of the problem or opportunity that motivated the research. In contrast, bad questionnaires can be costly in terms of time, effort, and money.

After preparing the questionnaire but before submitting it to the client for approval, the researcher should review the document carefully. The focus is on determining whether

Exhibit 9.3   Consumer Banking Opinion Survey

Thank you for participating in this study. Your participation will help us determine what people think about the products and services offered by banks. The results will provide insights on how to better serve the banking customers. Your attitudes and opinions are important to this study. All of your answers will be kept strictly confidential.

DIRECTIONS: PLEASE READ EACH QUESTION CAREFULLY. ANSWER THE QUESTION BY FILLING IN THE APPROPRIATE BOX(ES) THAT REPRESENT YOUR RESPONSES.

SECTION I: GENERAL BANKING HABITS

1. Which one of the following banks is the one you use most often in conducting banking or financial transactions? Please check only one box.

   ❏ American Bank   ❏ Capital Bank   ❏ Hibernia National Bank

   ❏ Baton Rouge Bank   ❏ City National Bank   ❏ Louisiana National Bank

   ❏ Some other bank; please specify: _____

2. How important were each of the following factors to you in selecting the bank mentioned in Q.1 above?

   Please check only one response for each factor.

Factor	Extremely Important	Important	Somewhat Important	Not at All Important
Convenient locations	❏	❏	❏	❏
Banking hours	❏	❏	❏	❏
Reasonable service charges	❏	❏	❏	❏
Interest rates on savings	❏	❏	❏	❏
Personally knew someone at the bank	❏	❏	❏	❏
Bank's reputation	❏	❏	❏	❏
Bank's promotional advertising	❏	❏	❏	❏
Interest rate on loans	❏	❏	❏	❏
Internet banking services	❏	❏	❏	❏

   If there was some other reason (factor) you considered important in selecting your bank mentioned in Q.1, please specify : _____

3. At which of the following financial institutions do you or some member of your immediate household have a personal savings account? Please check as many or as few as necessary.

Financial Institutions	Both You and Some Other Member	Some Other Member	Yourself
A credit union	❏	❏	❏
American Bank	❏	❏	❏
Baton Rouge Bank	❏	❏	❏
City National Bank	❏	❏	❏
Hibernia National Bank	❏	❏	❏
Louisiana National Bank	❏	❏	❏
Another institution (Please specify): _____			

continued

Exhibit 9.3   Consumer Banking Opinion Survey, *continued*

4. We would like to know your feelings about each of the following banking methods. For each banking method listed, please check the response that best describes your preference for using that method. Please check only one response for each banking method.

Banking Methods	Definitely Like Using	Somewhat Like Using	Somewhat Dislike Using	Definitely Dislike Using
Inside the bank	❑	❑	❑	❑
Drive-in (Drive-up)	❑	❑	❑	❑
24-hour machine	❑	❑	❑	❑
Bank by phone	❑	❑	❑	❑
Bank by mail	❑	❑	❑	❑
Online banking	❑	❑	❑	❑

5. Now we would like to know to what extent you actually use each of the following banking methods. Please check only one response for each banking method.

Banking Methods	Usually	Occasionally	Rarely	Never
Inside the bank	❑	❑	❑	❑
Drive-in (Drive-up)	❑	❑	❑	❑
24-hour machine	❑	❑	❑	❑
Bank by phone	❑	❑	❑	❑
Bank by mail	❑	❑	❑	❑
Internet banking	❑	❑	❑	❑

SECTION II: GENERAL OPINIONS

A list of general statements is included in this section. There are no right or wrong answers to the statements. We are just interested in your opinions.

6. Next to each statement, please fill in the one response that best expresses the extent to which you agree or disagree with the statement. Remember, there are no right or wrong answers—we just want your opinions.

Statements	Definitely Agree	Somewhat Agree	Neither Agree or Disagree	Somewhat Disagree	Definitely Disagree
I often seek out the advice of my friends regarding a lot of different things.	❑	❑	❑	❑	❑
I buy many things with credit cards.	❑	❑	❑	❑	❑
I wish we had a lot more money.	❑	❑	❑	❑	❑
Security is most important to me.	❑	❑	❑	❑	❑
I am definitely influenced by advertising.	❑	❑	❑	❑	❑
I like to pay cash for everything I buy.	❑	❑	❑	❑	❑

Exhibit 9.3	*continued*

Statements	Definitely Agree	Somewhat Agree	Neither Agree or Disagree	Somewhat Disagree	Definitely Disagree
My neighbors or friends often come to me for advice on many different matters.	❑	❑	❑	❑	❑
It is good to have charge accounts.	❑	❑	❑	❑	❑
I will probably have more money to spend next year than I have now.	❑	❑	❑	❑	❑
A person can save a lot of money by shopping around for bargains.	❑	❑	❑	❑	❑
For most products or services, I try the ones that are most popular.	❑	❑	❑	❑	❑
Unexpected situations often catch me without enough money in my pocket.	❑	❑	❑	❑	❑
Five years from now, my income will probably be much higher than it is now.	❑	❑	❑	❑	❑

SECTION III: BANKING RELATIONSHIPS

Please indicate your view on each of the following questions. Check the box that most closely represents your feelings.

	Not Very Satisfied				Highly Satisfied
7. How satisfied are you with the bank you do most of your business with? (i.e., your primary banking relationship)	❑	❑	❑	❑	❑

	Not Very Likely				Highly Likely
8. How likely are you to continue doing business with your current primary bank?	❑	❑	❑	❑	❑
9. How likely are you to recommend your primary bank to a friend?	❑	❑	❑	❑	❑

SECTION IV: CLASSIFICATION DATA

The next few questions ask for your demographic information. We ask these questions so we can properly generalize survey results to the greater population. Your answers help us to ensure that we have sufficient diversity among our respondents.

10. What is your sex? ❑ Female ❑ Male

continued

Exhibit 9.3 Consumer Banking Opinion Survey, *continued*

11. Approximately how long have you lived at your current address?
   ❑ Less than 1 year   ❑ 4 to 6 years   ❑ 11 to 20 years
   ❑ 1 to 3 years   ❑ 7 to 10 years   ❑ Over 20 years

12. What is your current employment status?
   ❑ Employed full-time   ❑ Employed part-time   ❑ Not currently employed
   ❑ Retired

13. What is your current marital status?
   ❑ Married   ❑ Single (never married)
   ❑ Single (widowed, divorced, or separated)

14. **IF MARRIED,** please indicate your spouse's current employment status.
   ❑ Employed full-time   ❑ Employed part-time   ❑ Not currently employed   ❑ Retired

15. **IF YOU HAVE CHILDREN,** please indicate the number of children under 18 years of age in your household.
   0   1   2   3   4   5   6   7   8   More than 8; please specify: _____
   ❑   ❑   ❑   ❑   ❑   ❑   ❑   ❑   ❑

16. Which one of the following categories best represents your last completed year in school?
   ❑ Post-graduate studies or advanced degree   ❑ Completed high school
   ❑ Graduate studies or degree   ❑ Some high school
   ❑ Completed college (4-year degree)   ❑ Completed grammar school
   ❑ Some college or technical school   ❑ Some grammar school

17. What is your current age?
   ❑ Under 18   ❑ 26 to 35   ❑ 46 to 55   ❑ 66 to 70
   ❑ 18 to 25   ❑ 36 to 45   ❑ 56 to 65   ❑ Over 70

18. Which one of the following categories best describes the type of work you do?
   ❑ Government (Federal, State, City)   ❑ Legal   ❑ Financial   ❑ Insurance
   ❑ Petrochemical   ❑ Manufacturing   ❑ Transportation   ❑ Consulting
   ❑ Educational   ❑ Medical   ❑ Retailing   ❑ Wholesaling
   ❑ Some other area, please specify: _____

19. In which of the following categories does your total annual family income, before taxes, fall?
   ❑ Under $10,000   ❑ $30,001 to $50,000
   ❑ $10,000 to $15,000   ❑ $50,001 to $75,000
   ❑ $15,001 to $20,000   ❑ $75,001 to $100,000
   ❑ $20,001 to $30,000   ❑ Over $100,000

20. What is the five-digit zip code of your residence address?   ❑ ❑ ❑ ❑ ❑

THANK YOU VERY MUCH FOR PARTICIPATION IN THIS STUDY!
YOUR TIME AND OPINIONS ARE APPRECIATED.

Exhibit 9.4	Guidelines for Evaluating the Adequacy of Questions

1. Questions should be simple, straightforward, and avoid technical or sophisticated words.
2. Questions should avoid qualifying phrases.
3. Question response categories (scale points) should be mutually exclusive.
4. Questions and scale statements should be meaningful to the respondent.
5. Questions and scales should avoid an arrangement of response categories that might bias the respondent's answers.
6. Questions and scales should not have double-barreled items.

each question is necessary and if the overall length is acceptable. Also, the researcher checks to make sure the survey meets the research objectives, the scale format and instructions work well, and the questions move from general to specific. A summary of the major considerations in questionnaire design is given in Exhibit 9.5.

Step 5: Obtain Initial Client Approval

Copies of the questionnaire should be given to all parties involved in the project. This is the client's opportunity to provide suggestions of topics overlooked or to ask any questions. Researchers must obtain final approval of the questionnaire prior to pretesting. If changes are necessary, this is where they should occur. Changes at a later point will be more expensive and may not be possible.

Step 6: Pretest, Revise, and Finalize Questionnaire

The final evaluation of the questionnaire is obtained from a pretest. For pretests, the survey questionnaire is given to a small, representative group of respondents that are asked to fill

Exhibit 9.5	Considerations in Questionnaire Design

1. Confirm the research objectives before starting to design the questionnaire.
2. Determine data requirements to complete each research objective.
3. The introduction section should include a general description of the study.
4. Instructions should be clearly expressed.
5. Questions and scale measurements should follow a logical order—that is, one that appears logical to the respondent rather than to the researcher or practitioner.
6. Begin an interview or questionnaire with simple questions that are easy to answer, and then gradually lead up to the more difficult questions. Use a general-to-specific questions and topic sequence.
7. Ask personal questions at the end of the interview or survey.
8. Place questions that involve personal opinions, attitudes, and beliefs toward the end of the interview or survey, but before demographics.
9. Avoid asking questions using a different measurement format in the same section of the questionnaire.
10. End the interview or survey with a thank-you statement.

out the survey and provide feedback to researchers. The number of respondents is most often between 20 and 30 individuals. In a pretest, respondents are asked to pay attention to words, phrases, instructions, and question sequence. They are asked to point out anything that is difficult to follow or understand. Returned questionnaires are checked for signs of boredom or tiring on the part of the respondent. These signs include skipped questions or circling the same answer for all questions within a group.

The pretest helps the researcher determine how much time respondents will need to complete the survey, whether to add or revise instructions, and what to say in the cover letter. If problems or concerns arise in the pretest, modifications must be made and approved by the client prior to moving to the next step.

Step 7: Implement the Survey

The focus here is on the process followed to collect the data using the agreed-upon questionnaire. The process varies depending on whether the survey is self-administered or interviewer-completed. For example, self-completed questionnaires must be distributed to respondents and methods used to increase response rates. Similarly, with Internet surveys the format, sequence, skip patterns, and instructions must be thoroughly checked after the questionnaire is posted to the Web. Thus, the final step in the process involves following up to ensure all previous decisions are properly implemented.

◼◼◼ The Role of a Cover Letter

Cover letter A written communication to a prospective respondent designed to enhance that person's willingness to complete and return the survey in a timely manner.

A **cover letter** is used with a self-administered questionnaire. The primary role of the cover letter is to obtain the respondent's cooperation and willingness to participate in the research project. With personal or telephone interviews, interviewers use a verbal statement that includes many of the points covered by a mail or drop-off cover letter. Self-administered surveys often have low response rates (25 percent or less). Good cover letters increase response rates. Exhibit 9.6 provides guidelines for developing cover letters.

◼◼◼ Other Documents Used in Collecting Data

When data are collected using interviews, supervisor and interviewer instructions must be developed as well as screening forms, rating cards, and call record sheets. These documents ensure the data collection process is successful. In this section we summarize each of these forms.

Supervisor Instructions

Supervisor instruction form A form that serves as a blueprint for training people to execute the interviewing process in a consistent fashion.

Many researchers collect data using interviews conducted by field interviewing companies. A **supervisor instruction form** serves as a blueprint for training people to complete the interviewing process in a consistent fashion. The instructions outline the process for conducting the study and are important to any research project that uses personal or telephone interviews. They include detailed information on the nature of the study, start and completion dates, sampling instructions, number of interviewers required, equipment and facility requirements, reporting forms, quotas, and validation procedures. Exhibit 9.7 displays a sample page from a set of supervisor instructions for a restaurant study.

Exhibit 9.6	Guidelines for Developing Cover Letters

Factors	Description
1. Personalization	Cover letters should be addressed to the prospective respondent. The research firm's professional letterhead stationery should be used.
2. Identification of the organization	Clear identification of the name of the research firm conducting the survey or interview. A disguised approach is most often used but an undisguised approach that reveals the actual client (or sponsor) of the study may be used.
3. Clear statement of the study's purpose and importance	Describe the general topic of the research and emphasize its importance to the prospective respondent.
4. Anonymity and confidentiality	Give assurances that the prospective respondent's name will not be revealed. Explain how the respondent was chosen, and stress that his or her input is important to the study's success.
5. General time frame of doing the study	Communicate the overall time frame of the survey or study.
6. Reinforce the importance of respondent's participation	Communicate the importance of the prospective respondent's participation.
7. Acknowledge reasons for nonparticipation in survey or interview	Point out "lack of leisure time," "surveys classified as junk mail," and "forgetting about survey" reasons for not participating, and defuse them.
8. Time requirements and incentive	Communicate the approximate time required to complete the survey. Discuss incentive, if any.
9. Completion date and where and how to return the survey	Communicate to the prospective respondent all instructions for returning the completed questionnaire.
10. Advance thank-you statement for willingness to participate	Thank the prospective respondent for his or her cooperation.

Interviewer Instructions

Interviewer instructions The vehicle for training the interviewer on how to select prospective respondents, screen them for eligibility, and conduct the actual interview.

Interviewer instructions are used for training interviewers to correctly select a prospective respondent for inclusion in the study, screen prospective respondents for eligibility, and properly conduct the actual interview. The instructions include detailed information about the nature of the study, start and completion dates, sampling instructions, screening procedures, quotas, number of interviews required, guidelines for asking questions, use of rating cards, recording responses, reporting forms, and verification form procedures.

Screening Forms

Screening forms A set of preliminary questions that are used to determine the eligibility of a prospective respondent for inclusion in the survey.

Screening forms ensure the respondents interviewed for a study are representative of the defined target population. **Screening forms** are a set of preliminary questions used to confirm the eligibility of a prospective respondent for inclusion in the survey. Screening forms also are used to ensure that certain types of respondents are not included in the study. This occurs most frequently when a person's direct occupation or a family member's occupation in a particular industry eliminates the person from inclusion in the study. For example, a study of the perceived quality of automobiles manufactured by Ford Motor Company

Exhibit 9.7	Supervisor Instructions for a Restaurant Study Using Personal Interviews
Purpose:	To determine students' dining-out patterns and attitudes toward selected restaurants located within one mile of campus.
Number of Interviewers:	A total of 90 trained student interviewers (30 interviewers per class, three different classes).
Location of Interviews:	Interviews will be conducted over a two-week period beginning March 10 and ending March 24, 2007. They will be conducted between the hours of 8:00 A.M. and 9:00 P.M., Monday through Friday. The locations of the interviews will be outside the campus buildings housing the 14 colleges making up the university plus the Library and Student Union. There will be three shifts of interviewers, 30 interviewers per shift, working the time frames of 8:00 A.M. to 12:00 noon or 12:01 P.M. to 5:00 P.M. or 5:01 P.M. to 9:00 P.M.
Quota:	Each interviewer will conduct and complete 30 interviews, with a maximum of 5 completed interviews for each of the following named restaurants: Mellow Mushroom, Pizza Hut, Domino's Pizza, Chili's, Outback Steakhouse, and any five "local restaurants." All completed interviews should come from their assigned location and time period.
	For each shift of 30 interviewers, there will be a minimum of 150 completed interviews for each of the five named restaurants in the study and maximum of 150 completed interviews representing the set of "local restaurants."
Project Materials:	For this study, you are supplied with the following materials: 2,701 personal questionnaires, 91 interviewer instruction-screening-quota forms, 91 sets of "Rating Cards" with each set consisting of six different rating cards, 91 "Verification of Interview" forms, and 1 interviewer scheduling form.
Preparation:	Using your set of materials, review all material for complete understanding. Set a two-hour time frame for training your 90 student interviewers on how they should select a prospective respondent, screen for eligibility, and conduct the interviews. Make sure each interviewer understands the embedded "interviewer's instructions" in the actual questions making up the survey. In addition, assign each interviewer to a specified location and time frame for conducting the interviews. Make sure all locations and time frames are properly covered. Prepare a backup plan for anticipated problems.

would exclude people who work for Ford Motor Company, or an automobile dealership that sells Ford vehicles. Individuals who work for marketing research firms or advertising agencies also are routinely excluded from participation in studies.

Quota Sheets

Quota sheets A tracking form that enables the interviewer to collect data from the right type of respondents.

Quota sheets are tracking forms that enable the interviewer to collect data from the right type of respondents. When a particular quota for a subgroup of respondents is filled, a quota sheet indicates to the interviewer they no longer should interview people from that subgroup. In the retail banking example, each interviewer completed 30 interviews, with 5 each from customers of six different banks: Bank of America, Sun Trust Bank, Citicorp, Chase, First Union, and "Other Banks." Once the quota was reached for a particular bank, any prospective respondent who indicated that Chase was his or her primary bank would be excluded from participating in the survey.

Rating cards Cards used in personal interviews that display the set of actual scale points and descriptions used to respond to a specific question in the survey. These cards serve as a tool to help the interviewer and respondent speed up the data collection process.

Rating Cards

When collecting data using personal interviews, the researcher may need rating cards. A **rating card** displays the scale points and their descriptions for specific questions on the survey. Whenever there is a question that asks the respondent to express some degree of intensity as part of the response, the interviewer provides the respondent with a rating card that shows the possible scale responses. Before asking the question, the interviewer will hand the respondent the rating card and explain how to use the information on the card to respond to the question. Exhibit 9.8 is an example of a question and the appropriate rating card for a restaurant survey that used personal interviews.

Exhibit 9.8	Question/Scale Format and Rating Card Used in a Restaurant Survey

RATING CARD A
(Importance Scale for Q2)

Rating Numbers	Description
6_____	**Extremely Important** Consideration to me
5_____	**Definitely Important** Consideration to me
4_____	**Generally Important** Consideration to me
3_____	**Somewhat Important** Consideration to me
2_____	**Slightly Important** Consideration to me
1_____	**Not At All Important** Consideration to me

INTERVIEWER INSTRUCTIONS

Q2 Let's begin. I am going to read to you some restaurant characteristics which may or may not be important to you in selecting a restaurant to eat at. The situation you should think about is when are considering eating at a restaurant that is *not* a "fast food" restaurant and serves both food and alcoholic beverages.

Using this rating card **(HAND RESPONDENT RATING CARD A),** please tell me the number that best describes how important you feel each characteristic is to you in selecting a restaurant to eat at.

To what extent is **(READ FIRST FEATURE)** an important consideration to you in selecting a restaurant to each at?

INTERVIEWER: MAKE SURE YOU READ AND RECORD THE ANSWER FOR ALL LISTED FEATURES. DO NOT PERMIT TIES.

Rating Number	Feature	Rating Number	Feature
_____	Convenience of location	_____	Speed of service
_____	Quality of food	_____	Menu variety
_____	Friendly waiters	_____	Knowledgeable waiters
_____	Inexpensive food prices	_____	Drink specials
_____	Atmosphere	_____	Type of music
_____	Mostly students go there	_____	Few students go there

ON COMPLETION TAKE BACK RATING CARD A

Call Record Sheets

Call record sheet A recording document that gathers basic summary information about an interviewer's performance efficiency (e.g., number of contact attempts, number of completed interviews, length of time of interview).

Call record sheets, also referred to as either reporting or tracking sheets, are used to help the researcher estimate the efficiency of the interviewers' performance. The form typically collects information on the number of attempts to contact potential respondents made by each interviewer and the results of those attempts. Call record sheets are used in data collection methods that require the use of an interviewer. The types of information gathered from call record sheets include number of calls or contacts made per hour, number of contacts per completed interview, length of time of the interview, completions by quota categories, number of terminated interviews, reasons for termination, and number of callback attempts.

Your understanding of the activities needed to develop a survey instrument completes the third phase of the research process—gathering and collecting accurate data—and prepares you to move into the last phase—data preparation and analysis. Chapter 11 covers coding, editing, and preparing data for analysis.

MARKETING RESEARCH IN ACTION
Designing a Questionnaire to Survey Santa Fe Grill Customers

This illustration extends the chapter discussion on questionnaire design. Read through this example and use the actual screening questions (Exhibit 9.9) and questionnaire (Exhibit 9.10) to answer the questions at the end.

In early 2007, two recent college business graduates (one majored in finance and the other in management) came together with a new restaurant concept for a Southwestern casual dinning experience that focuses on a Mexican theme with a variety of good food items and a friendly family-oriented atmosphere. After six months of planning and creating detailed business and marketing plans, the two entrepreneurs were able to get the necessary capital to build and open their restaurant, the Santa Fe Grill.

After the initial six months of success, they noticed that revenues, traffic flow, and sales were declining and realized that they knew very little about their patrons. Neither of the owners had taken any marketing courses beyond basic marketing in college, so they turned to a friend who worked in marketing for some advice. Initially they were advised to hire a marketing research firm to collect some primary data about people's dining-out habits and patterns. Looking into marketing research firms, they quickly found out that these firms wanted more money than they were willing to pay to conduct the research. So they went to a Barnes & Noble bookstore and purchased a practitioner's book on how to do marketing research studies. Using their new understanding of how to do research and design questionnaires, the owners decided to use an experience intercept research design (randomly stopping customers as they were leaving the Santa Fe Grill), trained interviewers to qualify the respondents using a set of three screening questions (see Exhibit 9.9), and a 13-question, self-administered survey to actually collect the needed data. In addition, the following six research objectives were used to guide the design of their survey instrument shown in Exhibit 9.10.

Research Objectives:

1. To identify the factors people consider important in making casual dining restaurant choice decisions.
2. To determine the characteristics customers use to describe the Santa Fe Grill restaurant.
3. To develop a psychographic and demographic profile of Santa Fe Grill's customer base.
4. To determine the patronage and positive word-of-mouth advertising patterns toward the Santa Fe Grill restaurant.
5. To assess the customer's willingness to return to the Santa Fe Grill in the future.
6. To assess the degree to which customers are satisfied with their Santa Fe Grill restaurant experience.

Exhibit 9.9   Screening and Rapport Questions for the Santa Fe Grill Restaurant Study

Hello. My name is _____ and I work for DSS Research. We are talking to individuals today (tonight) about dining out habits.

"Do you regularly eat out at casual dining restaurants?"   __ Yes __ No

"Have you eaten at other Mexican restaurants in the last six months?"   __ Yes __ No

"Is your gross annual household income $15,000 or more?"   __ Yes __ No

If respondent answers **Yes** to all three questions, then say:

We would like you to answer a few questions about your experience today (tonight) at the Santa Fe Grill restaurant, and we hope you will be willing to give us your opinions. The survey will only take a few minutes and it will be very helpful to management in better serving its customers.

If the person says yes, give them a clipboard with the questionnaire on it, briefly explain the questionnaire, and show them where to complete the survey.

Exhibit 9.10   The Santa Fe Restaurant Dining-Out Survey

Please read all questions carefully. If you do not understand a question, ask the interviewer to help you. In the first section a number of statements are given about interests and opinions. Using a scale from 1 to 7, with 7 being "Strongly Agree" and 1 being "Strongly Disagree," please indicate the extent to which you agree or disagree that a particular statement describes you. Circle only one number for each statement.

Section 1: Lifestyle Questions

1. I often try new and different things.

   Strongly Disagree   Strongly Agree

   1   2   3   4   5   6   7

2. I like parties with music and lots of talk.

   Strongly Disagree   Strongly Agree

   1   2   3   4   5   6   7

3. People come to me more often than I go to them for information about products.

   Strongly Disagree   Strongly Agree

   1   2   3   4   5   6   7

4. I try to avoid fried foods.

   Strongly Disagree   Strongly Agree

   1   2   3   4   5   6   7

5. I like to go out and socialize with people.

   Strongly Disagree   Strongly Agree

   1   2   3   4   5   6   7

Exhibit 9.10 *continued*

6. Friends and neighbors often come to me for advice on products and brands.

Strongly Disagree   Strongly Agree

1   2   3   4   5   6   7

7. I am self-confident about myself and my future.

Strongly Disagree   Strongly Agree

1   2   3   4   5   6   7

8. I usually eat balanced, nutritious meals.

Strongly Disagree   Strongly Agree

1   2   3   4   5   6   7

9. When I see a new product in stores, I buy it.

Strongly Disagree   Strongly Agree

1   2   3   4   5   6   7

10. I am careful about what I eat.

Strongly Disagree   Strongly Agree

1   2   3   4   5   6   7

11. I try new brands before my friends and neighbors do.

Strongly Disagree   Strongly Agree

1   2   3   4   5   6   7

Section 2: Perceptions Measures

Listed below is a set of characteristics that could be used to describe the Santa Fe Grill Mexican restaurant. Using a scale from 1 to 7, with 7 being "Strongly Agree" and 1 being "Strongly Disagree," to what extent do you agree or disagree that the Santa Fe Grill:

12. has friendly employees

Strongly Disagree   Strongly Agree

1   2   3   4   5   6   7

13. is a fun place to eat

Strongly Disagree   Strongly Agree

1   2   3   4   5   6   7

14. has large size portions

Strongly Disagree   Strongly Agree

1   2   3   4   5   6   7

15. has fresh food

Strongly Disagree   Strongly Agree

1   2   3   4   5   6   7

16. has reasonable prices

Strongly Disagree   Strongly Agree

1   2   3   4   5   6   7

continued

Exhibit 9.10   The Santa Fe Restaurant Dining-Out Survey, *continued*

17. has an attractive interior

Strongly
Disagree

Strongly
Agree

1   2   3   4   5   6   7

18. has excellent food taste

Strongly
Disagree

Strongly
Agree

1   2   3   4   5   6   7

19. has knowledgeable employees

Strongly
Disagree

Strongly
Agree

1   2   3   4   5   6   7

20. serves food at the proper temperature

Strongly
Disagree

Strongly
Agree

1   2   3   4   5   6   7

21. has quick service

Strongly
Disagree

Strongly
Agree

1   2   3   4   5   6   7

Section 3: Relationship Measures

Please indicate your view on each of the following questions:

22. How satisfied are you with the
Santa Fe Grill?

Not Satisfied
At All

Very
Satisfied

1   2   3   4   5   6   7

23. How likely are you to return to the
Santa Fe Grill in the future?

Definitely Will
Not Return

Definitely Will
Return

1   2   3   4   5   6   7

24. How likely are you to recommend
Santa Fe Grill to a friend?

Definitely Will
Not Recommend

Definitely Will
Recommend

1   2   3   4   5   6   7

25. How often do you patronize the
Santa Fe Grill?

1 = Very Infrequently
2 = Somewhat Infrequently
3 = Occasionally
4 = Somewhat Frequently
5 = Very Frequently

Section 4: Selection Factors

Listed below are some reasons many people use in selecting a restaurant where they want to dine. Think about your visits to casual dining restaurants in the last three months and please rank each attribute from 1 to 4, with 1 being the most important reason for selecting the restaurant and 4 being the least important reason. There can be no ties so make sure you rank each attribute with a different number.

Exhibit 9.10 *continued*

Attribute	Ranking
26. Prices	
27. Food Quality	
28. Atmosphere	
29. Service	

Section 5: Classification Questions

Please circle the number that classifies you best.

30. Distance driven

1 Less than 1 mile
2 1–3 miles
3 More than 3 Miles

31. Do your recall seeing any advertisements in the last 60 days for the Santa Fe Grill?

0 No
1 Yes

32. Your gender

0 Male
1 Female

33. Number of children at home

1 None
2 1–2
3 More than 2 children at home

34. Your age in years

1 18–25
2 26–34
3 35–49
4 50–59
5 60 and Older

35. Your annual gross household income

1 $15,000–$30,000
2 $30,001–$50,000
3 $50,001–$75,000
4 $75,001–$100,000
5 More than $100,000

Thank you very much for your help. Please give your questionnaire back to the Interviewer.

Interviewer: Check answers to questions 22, 23, and 24. If respondent answers 1, 2, or 3 ask the following questions:

You indicated you are not too satisfied with the Santa Fe Grill. Could you please tell me why?

Record answer here: _____

_____

You indicated you are not likely to return to the Santa Fe Grill. Could you please tell me why?

Record answer here: _____

_____

continued

Exhibit 9.10   The Santa Fe Restaurant Dining-Out Survey, *continued*

You indicated you are not likely to recommend the Santa Fe Grill. Could you please tell me why?

Record answer here: _____

_____

Could I please have your name and phone number for verification purposes?

_____   _____
Name   Phone #

I hereby attest that this is a true and honest interview and complete to the best of my knowledge. I guarantee that all information relating to this interview shall be kept strictly confidential.

_____   _____
Interviewer's Signature   Date and Time completed

Hands-On Exercise

1. Based on the research objectives, does the owners' self-administered questionnaire, in its current form, correctly illustrate sound questionnaire design principles? Please explain why or why not.
2. Overall, is the current survey design able to capture the required data needed to address all the stated research objectives? Why or why not? If changes are needed, how would you change the survey's design?
3. Evaluate the "screener" used to qualify the respondents. Are there any changes needed? Why or why not?
4. Redesign questions 26–29 on the survey using a rating scale that will enable you to obtain the "degree of importance" a customer might attach to each of the four listed attributes in selecting a restaurant to dine at.

◗ Summary

Describe the steps in questionnaire design.

Researchers follow a systematic approach to designing questionnaires. The steps include: confirm research objectives; select appropriate data collection method; develop questions and scaling; determine layout and evaluate questionnaire; obtain initial client approval; pretest, revise, and finalize questionnaire; and implement the survey.

Discuss the questionnaire development process.

A number of design considerations and rules of logic apply to the questionnaire development process. The process requires knowledge of sampling plans, construct development, scale measurement, and types of data. A questionnaire is a set of questions/scales designed to collect data and generate information to help decision makers solve business problems. Good questionnaires enable researchers to gain a true report of the respondent's attitudes, preferences, beliefs, feelings, behavioral intentions, and actions. Through carefully worded questions and clear instructions, a researcher has the ability to focus a respondent's thoughts and ensure answers that faithfully represent respondent's attitudes, beliefs, intentions, and knowledge. By understanding good communication principles, researchers can avoid bad questions that might result in unrealistic information requests, unanswerable questions, or leading questions that prohibit or distort the respondent's answers.

Summarize the characteristics of good questionnaires.

Survey information requirements play a critical role in the development of questionnaires. For each objective, the researcher must choose types of scale formats (nominal, ordinal, interval, or ratio); question formats (open-ended and closed-ended); and the appropriate scaling. Researchers must be aware of the impact that different data collection methods (personal, telephone, self-administered, computer-assisted) have on the wording of both questions and response choices. With good questionnaires, the questions are simple, expressed clearly, logical, meaningful to the respondent, and move from general to specific topics.

Compose a cover letter.

The primary role of a cover letter should be to obtain the respondent's cooperation and willingness to participate in the project. Ten factors should be examined in developing cover letters. Observing these guidelines will increase response rates.

Explain the importance of other documents used with questionnaires.

When data are collected using interviews, supervisor and interviewer instructions must be developed as well as screening forms, rating cards, and call record sheets. These documents ensure the data collection process is successful. Supervisor instructions serve as a blueprint for training people to complete the interviewing process in a consistent fashion. The instructions outline the process for conducting the study and are important to any research project that uses personal or telephone interviews. Interviewer instructions are used to train interviewers to correctly select a prospective respondent for inclusion in the study, screen prospective respondents for eligibility, and properly conduct the actual interview. Screening forms are a set of preliminary questions used to confirm the eligibility of a prospective respondent for inclusion in the survey. Quota sheets are tracking forms that enable the interviewer to collect data from the right type of respondents. Rating cards help respondents to better understand scaling and call record sheets enable interviewers' performance to be evaluated. All of these documents help improve data collection efforts.

◗ Key Terms and Concepts

Bad questions 173

Call record sheets 184

Cover letter 180

Interviewer instructions 181

Questionnaire 170

Quota sheets 182

Rating cards 183

Screening forms 181

Structured questions 172

Supervisor instruction form 180

Unstructured questions 172

◗ Review Questions

1. Discuss the advantages and disadvantages of using unstructured (open-ended) and structured (closed-ended) questions in developing an online, self-administered survey instrument.
2. Explain the role of a questionnaire in the research process. What should be the role of the client during the questionnaire development process?
3. What are the guidelines for deciding the format and layout of a questionnaire?
4. What makes a question bad? Develop three examples of bad questions. Then, using the information in Exhibit 9.4, rewrite your examples so they could be judged as good questions.
5. Discuss the value of a good questionnaire design.
6. Discuss the main benefits of including a brief introductory section in questionnaires.
7. Unless needed for screening purposes, why shouldn't demographic questions be asked up front in questionnaires?
8. Discuss the critical issues involved in pretesting a questionnaire.

◗ Discussion Questions

1. Discuss the guidelines for developing cover letters. What are some of the advantages of developing good cover letters? What are some of the costs of a bad cover letter?
2. Using the questions asked in evaluating any questionnaire design (see Exhibit 9.5), evaluate the Santa Fe Grill restaurant questionnaire. Write a one-page assessment.

Part 4

Data Preparation, Analysis, and Reporting the Results

Analyzing and Reporting Qualitative Research

Chapter 10

Learning Objectives After reading this chapter, you will be able to:

1. Contrast qualitative and quantitative data analysis.
2. Explain the steps in qualitative data analysis.
3. Describe the processes of categorizing and coding data as well as developing theory.
4. Clarify how credibility is established in qualitative data analysis.
5. Discuss the steps involved in writing a qualitative research report.

Wireless Communication's Impact on Social Behavior

Mobile phones were once all business. But today they are all in the family. A recent survey of Americans between the ages of 18 and 64 conducted by Knowledge Networks, a market research firm in Cranford, New Jersey, revealed that most respondents underscore "family" as the top reason to go wireless. Young respondents, more so than older ones, cite "reaching friends" as their second leading reason to go wireless, with "work-related calls" being the overall third most important reason for having a wireless phone. The survey also reported some interesting descriptive information. For example, men tend to make more calls on mobile phones per day (8.3 calls) than women (5.5 calls). Although both put family first, women were more partial to calling friends, whereas men were three times as likely to use their phones for work. In addition, 65 percent of African-Americans had mobile phones, compared to 62 percent of Caucasians. Hispanics remain well behind in mobile phone usage, with just 54 percent penetration.

While the above describes the type of information that results from conducting traditional surveys, the findings are limited to aggregate descriptive interpretations and meaning. In contrast, qualitative research on wireless phone usage offers greater opportunities to gain more in-depth understanding of what lies beyond those descriptive numbers. For example, with over 190 million Americans owning mobile phones, the phones reach further into our lives. They are beginning to create a deeper impression of the American psyche. Robbie Blinkoof, principal anthropologist and managing partner at Context-Based Research Group in Baltimore, Maryland, and other ethnographers believe that wireless communication is beginning to have a notable impact on Americans' social behavior—one that could have a long-lasting effect on society and the world around us. For instance, recent ethnographic studies have yielded significant clues about cell phone users' communication habits. In general, observed changes relate to how mobile phone customers form relationships and define a sense of time and place. In one study, researchers watched newly wired users at work and play, and found that one of the biggest differences was these users became more accessible to their social network. Mobile phones supported entire social networks and relationships. Participants were more flexible in how they arranged their schedules and gradually more willing to speak on a mobile phone in public, sustaining social ties for purely psychological and emotional value. In another ethnographic study, context researchers observed changes in how the subjects related to mobile life. Participants were far more concerned with wireless as an enabler rather than a toy. They had to learn to use the wireless features they needed while ignoring those they didn't. Other interpretive findings were: wireless phones give people new opportunities for spontaneity, people can change their plans at the last minute more easily, or call friends and colleagues to tell them they are running behind schedule. Also, wireless phones create flexibility by loosening time parameters, enabling people to merely suggest a time and place to meet and to pin down a location as they approach the meeting time.

Nature of Qualitative Data Analysis

In this chapter, you will learn the processes used by researchers to interpret qualitative data and form insights about their meaning. Researchers often think of data analysis as involving numbers. But the data qualitative researchers analyze consists of text (and sometimes images) rather than numbers. Some researchers criticize qualitative research as "soft," lacking rigor, and being inferior. But measurement and statistical analysis do not ensure that research is useful or accurate. What increases the likelihood of good research is a deliberate, thoughtful, knowledgeable approach whether qualitative or quantitative research methods are used. While the reliability and validity of quantitative analysis can be evaluated numerically, the trustworthiness of qualitative analysis depends fundamentally on the rigor of the process used for collecting and analyzing the data.

As we explained in Chapter 5, when magnitude of response and statistical projectability are important, quantitative research should be used to verify and extend qualitative findings. But when the purpose of a research project is to better understand psychoanalytical or cultural phenomena, quantitative research may not offer a great deal of insight or depth. For these topics, qualitative research and analysis often is superior to quantitative research in providing useful knowledge for decision makers.

This chapter details a process that can be followed to ensure qualitative data analyses are careful and rigorous. In this chapter we first compare qualitative and quantitative analysis. Next we describe the steps involved in qualitative data analysis. Topics such as categorization, coding, and assessing trustworthiness or credibility are explained. The chapter concludes by providing guidelines on writing a qualitative research report.

Qualitative versus Quantitative Analysis

All marketing researchers construct stories that are based on the data they have collected. The goal of these stories, whether they are based on qualitative or quantitative data, is to provide actionable answers to research questions. Yet, there are many differences between the processes of analyzing and interpreting qualitative and quantitative data. The most apparent difference stems from the nature of the data itself. Qualitative data is textual (and occasionally visual), rather than numerical. While the goal of quantitative analysis is quantifying the magnitude of variables and relationships, or explaining causal relationships, understanding is the goal of qualitative analysis. A second contrast between the two kinds of analysis is that qualitative analyses tend to be ongoing and iterative. This means the data is analyzed as it is collected, which may affect further data collection efforts in terms of who is sampled and what questions are asked. Another difference between the methods is that quantitative analyses are guided entirely by the researchers while good qualitative researchers employ member checking. **Member checking** involves asking key informants to read the researcher's report to verify that the story they are telling about the focal problem or situation is accurate.

Qualitative data analysis is largely inductive. The categories, themes, and patterns analysts describe in their reports emerge from the data, rather than being defined prior to data collection, as in quantitative analyses. Because an inductive process is used, the theory that emerges is often called grounded theory.[1] The categories and corresponding codes for categories are developed as researchers work through the texts and images and find what is there. Of course, rarely is the development of categories and theory completely inductive. Researchers bring with them knowledge, theory, and training that suggests categories, themes, and theories which might exist in the data they have collected.

There is no one process for analyzing qualitative data, although the three-step process described in this chapter has been useful to the thinking of many qualitative researchers. Some researchers prefer a more impressionistic approach to qualitative analysis and do not go through transcripts and other documents with the degree of care that we suggest here. Nevertheless, "careful and deliberate analysis remains crucial to sound qualitative research."[2]

Qualitative researchers differ in their beliefs about the use of quantifying their data. Some feel that quantification is completely useless and likely misleading. But others find that quantification can be useful in both counting responses and in model development.[3] We discuss tabulation (counting) later in this chapter.

Qualitative researchers use different techniques for data collection. These differences affect the kinds of analyses that can be performed with the data. Ethnographic analysis usually results in a **thick description** that contextualizes behavior within a culture or subculture.[4] In marketing research, thick description explains consumer behavior more fully than other methods because it connects that behavior to the larger social context in which it occurs. For example, a thick description of urban culture would contextualize the purchase and display of the Timberland brand, stylish tire rims, and Courvoisier—products and brands that have symbolic properties in the urban subculture that would not be immediately understandable to outsiders.

Focus group and in-depth interview data typically do not produce thick descriptions because the data gathered are not as extensive and are not collected in context. As in thick description, however, analysts use the collected and transcribed textual data to develop themes, categories, and relationships between variables. Categories are usually developed as the transcripts (and images) are reviewed by researchers. Codes are attached to the categories, which are then used to mark the portions of text (or images) where the category is mentioned.

In this chapter, we review the process of analyzing qualitative data. We explain the process of data reduction, data display, and conclusion making/verification. We also explain how qualitative researchers develop analyses that are credible, which means the analyses are authentic and believable. Finally, we explain how to write a qualitative research report.

Member checking Asking key informants to read the researcher's report to verify that the analysis is accurate.

Thick description An ethnographic research report that contextualizes behavior within a culture or subculture.

The Process of Analyzing Qualitative Data

After data is collected, researchers engage in a three-step process of analysis: data reduction, data display, and conclusion drawing/verification.[5] The three steps and relationships between the steps and data collection efforts are pictured in Exhibit 10.1.

Managing the Data Collection Effort

In online focus groups and netnography, the text is produced automatically and is immediately available for analysis. For other methods, audiotapes or videotapes have to be transcribed. Notes and memory may be used to fill in sections of the transcript that are inaudible and to make corrections to the transcription. Qualitative researchers also enter any of their observations and notes, including notes from debriefing sessions, into the data set. Ethnographers take field notes that contain their observations. These field notes also become part of the data set. Any pictures taken by researchers or brought to interviews by participants (as in the ZMET) become part of the data set as well. Material should be indexed and related material should be cross-indexed.

Step 1: Data Reduction

The amount of data collected in a qualitative study can be extensive. Researchers must make decisions about how to categorize and represent the data. This results in *data reduction*. The most systematic method of analysis is to read through transcripts and develop categories to represent the data. When similar topics are encountered, they are coded similarly. Researchers may simply write codes in the margins of their transcripts. But increasingly software such as QSR NVIVO and Atlas/ti is used to track the passages that are coded. Computer coding enables researchers to view all similarly coded passages at the same time,

---

Exhibit 10.1 | Components of Data Analysis: An Interactive Model

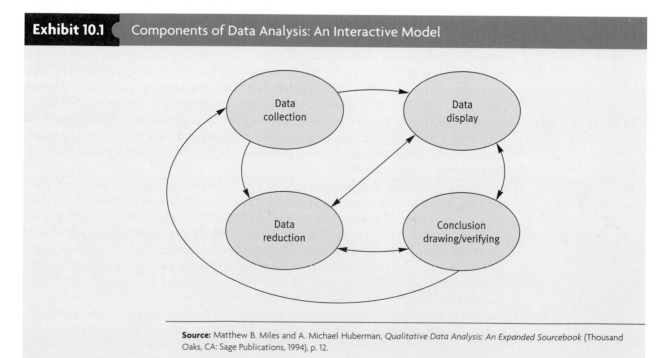

Source: Matthew B. Miles and A. Michael Huberman, *Qualitative Data Analysis: An Expanded Sourcebook* (Thousand Oaks, CA: Sage Publications, 1994), p. 12.

Data reduction The categorization and coding of data that is part of the theory development process in qualitative data analysis.

Categorization Placing portions of transcripts into similar groups based on their content.

which facilitates comparison and deeper coding. Computer coding also makes it easier to study relationships in the data. **Data reduction** consists of several interrelated processes: categorization and coding; theory development; and iteration and negative case analysis.

Data Reduction: Categorization and Coding The first step in data reduction is **categorization.** Researchers categorize sections of the transcript into categories and label them with names and sometimes code numbers. There may be some categories that are determined before the study because of existing researcher knowledge and experience. However, most often the codes are developed inductively as researchers move through transcripts and discover new themes of interest and code new instances of categories that have already been discovered. The sections that are coded can be one word long or several pages. The same sections of data can be categorized in multiple ways. If a passage refers to several different themes that have been identified by researchers, the passage will be coded for all the different relevant themes. Some portions of the transcripts will not contain information that is relevant to the analysis and will not be coded at all.[6] A **code sheet** is a piece of paper with all the codes (see Exhibit 10.2 for an example from a Senior Internet adoption study). The coded data may be entered into a computer, but the first round of coding usually occurs in the margins (Exhibit 10.3). The **codes** can be words or numbers that refer to categories on the coding sheet.

Code sheet A sheet of paper that lists the different themes or categories for a particular study.

Codes Labels or numbers that are used to track categories in a qualitative study.

An example of the process of data coding comes from an online shopping study based on data collected from both online and offline focus groups. One theme that emerged from the data was the importance of freedom and control as desirable outcomes when shopping online.[7] The following are some examples of passages that were coded as representing the freedom and control theme:

- "You're not as committed [online]. You haven't driven over there and parked and walked around so you have a little more flexibility and can get around a lot faster."
- "When I go to a store and a salesperson's helping me for a long time and it's not really what I wanted . . . I'll oblige them, they spent all this time with me . . . but . . . online, I know I will get to the point and be ready to order but I know I don't have to, I can come back anytime I want to."
- "You can sit on your arse and eat while you shop. You kin even shop nekked!"
- "For me, online browsing is similar [to offline browsing], but I have more of a sense of freedom. I'll browse stores I might not go into offline . . . Victoria's Secret comes to mind . . . also I'll go into swank stores that I might feel intimidated in going into offline . . . when you're a 51-year-old chubby gramma, online Victoria's Secret just feels a bit more comfortable."

Abstraction Collapsing some categories or themes into a larger category or higher order conceptual construct.

Categories may be modified and combined as data analysis continues. The researcher's understanding evolves during the data analysis phase and often results in revisiting, recoding, and recategorizing data. In the process of **abstraction,** some categories are collapsed into higher order conceptual constructs.[8] For instance, in a study of senior adoption of the Internet, researchers initially had separate categories for "curiosity," "lifelong learning," "proactive coping," and "life involvement." After reviewing the data, researchers believed the concepts were related to each other and reviewed research in psychology, which also suggested the categories previously labeled as curiosity, lifelong learning, self-efficacy, and life involvement could be subsumed in a category called "self-directed values and behavior."[9]

Not all categories can be combined with others. The decision to combine categories is based on the perception that subcategories are related to each other in some meaningful way and that the higher order construct has theoretical significance.[10]

Exhibit 10.2 Initial Code Sheet, Senior Adoption of the Internet Study

I. Antecedents

A. Observability
   1. Seeing others use the Internet
   2. Having an "a-ha" experience
   3. Marketing influences
B. Trialability
   1. Family
   2. Community centers
   3. Friends
   4. Work
C. Complexity
   1. Physical challenges
   2. Learning challenges
   3. Initial fear
D. Relative Advantage
   1. Cultural currency
   2. Ability to engage in hobbies
   3. Finding information
   4. Communication
   5. Creativity
E. Compatibility
   1. Openness to experience/life involvement
   2. Technology optimism
   3. Self-efficacy/proactive coping
   4. Financial resources
   5. Time in retirement
   6. Previous experience w/computing

II. Processes

1. Attend formal classes
2. Consult published sources
3. Mentors
4. Bricolage (learning by doing)
5. Ancillary systems (e.g., handwritten notes)
6. Flow
7. Multitasking

III. Uses

1. Communication (email, jokes, support groups)
2. Gather info
   a. health
   b. hobbies
   c. places
   d. news
   e. financial
   f. product
   g. travel
3. Banking
4. Shop selectively
5. Later life uses (keeper of the meaning, generativity, integrity)
6. Intended uses
7. Acting as an intermediary/proxy
8. Entertainment
9. Word processing, etc.
10. Creativity

IV. Outcomes

A. Connectedness
   1. Companionship
   2. Social support
   3. Linkages to places visited, lived
B. Self-efficacy/Independence
C. Cultural Currency
   1. Computer skills
   2. Increased knowledge
D. Excitement
E. Evangelism
F. Fun
G. Self-extension

V. Coping Strategies

A. Security—personal info
B. Protecting privacy
C. Flow/ limiting flow
D. Ease
E. Satisficing

Codes for Senior Characteristics

B	= Broadband	S	= Self-adopted
M	= Modem	O	= Other adopted
OO	= Old Old 75+	SA	= Self-assisted
Y	= Young Old 65–74		

Exhibit 10.3	Coding Transcripts in the Margins

Moderator: **What's a typical session like? You sit down at the computer and . . .**

III 1

Nisreen: I sit down at the computer and then I go into my emails. I check my emails and I make the replies. Then I want to find out about certain things, then I find out about those things and then I go to World News. Then I go to the different countries I'm interested in, then I go to the newspapers. I get the news about Pakistan III 2D right now. I go into Asia and then I go into Pakistan and then I get the news right there before I think my III 2C relatives know in Pakistan. I know the news before that. So isn't it wonderful?

Moderator: **Yes. It really is. It's amazing.** IV D

IV A

Nisreen: My cousin in Australia . . . before he thought he was leaving Australia from Sydney and I knew all about it, it's faster than telegram. It's so wonderful. I almost feel like I'm sitting on a magic carpet and I press a button IV D and boom, I'm there. IV C

Moderator: **That's interesting. Just reading the paper makes you feel like you are there.** IV F

III 2D

Nisreen: And then I want to read the viewpoint of different newspapers, so I go into different countries like India, Bangladesh or Pakistan or the Middle East. In the Middle East I used to be a voluntary assistant of the, III 2C "Perspective," which is the only women's magazine in the Middle East. At that time, Jordan was a very peaceful place. The rest of the world was up in arms and that kind of thing. So you see, I feel like I'm in IV A touch with the whole world. It's such a wonderful feeling at my age to be in touch with the world. I wish IV C2 more and more . . . because I think in the near future, that would be the order of the day. I know my bank tells me, my utility.

In the senior Internet adoption study (see again Exhibit 10.2), the set of self-directed values and behaviors identified through analysis of the transcripts were strongly related to adoption and extent of Internet usage by seniors. Thus, the construct possessed theoretical significance.

Comparison The process of developing and refining theory and constructs by analyzing the differences and similarities in passages, themes, or types of participants.

Data Reduction: Comparison **Comparison** of differences and similarities is a fundamental process in qualitative data analysis. There is an analogy to experimental design, in which various conditions or manipulations (for instance, price levels, advertising appeals) are compared to each other or to a control group. Comparison first occurs as researchers identify categories. Each potential new instance of a category or theme is compared to already coded instances to determine if the new instance belongs in the existing category. When all transcripts have been coded and important categories and themes identified, instances within a category will be scrutinized so that the theme can be defined and explained in more detail. For example, in a study of employee reactions to their own employers' advertising, the category "effectiveness of advertising with consumers" was a recurring theme. Because of the importance of advertising effectiveness in determining employees' reactions to the ad, employees' views of what made ads effective were compared and contrasted. Employees most often associated the following qualities with effective organizational ads to consumers: (1) likely to result in short-term sales, (2) appealing to the target audience (3) attention grabbing, (4) easily understandable, and (5) portrays the organization and its products authentically.[11]

Comparison processes are also used to better understand the differences and similarities between two constructs of interest. In the study of online shopping, two types of shopping motivations emerged from analyses of transcripts: goal-oriented behavior (shopping to buy or find information about specific products) and experiential behavior (shopping to shop). Comparison of shopper motivations, descriptions, and desired outcomes from each type of behavior reveals that consumers' online shopping behavior is different depending on whether or not the shopping trip is goal-oriented or experiential.[12]

Comparisons can also be made between different kinds of informants. In a study of high-risk leisure behavior, skydivers with different levels of experience were interviewed. As a result of comparing more and less experienced skydivers, the researchers were able to show that motivations changed and evolved—for example, from thrill, to pleasure, to flow—as skydivers continued their participation in the sport.[13] Similarly, in a study of Post-Socialist Eastern European women who were newly exposed to cosmetics and cosmetics brands, researchers compared women who embraced cosmetics to those who were either ambivalent about cosmetics or who rejected them entirely.[14]

Integration The process of moving from the identification of themes and categories to the development of theory.

Axial coding Specifying the conditions, context, or variables that lead to a particular category or construct, and the outcomes from the construct.

Data Reduction: Theory Building Integration is the process through which researchers build theory that is grounded, or based on the data collected. The idea is to move from the identification of themes and categories to the development of theory.

Two techniques are useful for developing theory: axial coding and selective coding.[15] In **axial coding,** researchers can specify the conditions, context, or variables that lead to a particular category or construct; the actions needed for informants to carry out the construct; and the outcomes from the construct. In axial coding researchers learn that particular conditions, contexts, and outcomes cluster together. For example, self-directed seniors (conditions) tend to be technology optimists (conditions) who adopt the Internet (a central concept of interest). They either adopt themselves, or if they have high levels of technology discomfort, get help to adopt (actions or strategies to carry out the construct). Adoption can lead to heavier or lighter use (outcome). Self-directed seniors are not only more likely to adopt the Internet, they use it more often after adoption (outcome).

Recursive A relationship in which a variable can both cause and be caused by the same variable.

In qualitative research, relationships may or may not be conceptualized and pictured in a way that looks like the traditional causal model employed by quantitative researchers. For instance, relationships may be portrayed as circular or **recursive.** In recursive relationships, variables may both cause and be caused by the same variable. A good example is the relationship between job satisfaction and financial compensation. Job satisfaction tends to increase performance and thus compensation earned on the job, which in turn increases job satisfaction.

Selective coding Building a storyline around one core category or theme; the other categories will be related to or subsumed to this central overarching category.

Qualitative researchers may look for one core category or theme to build their storyline around, a process referred to as **selective coding.** All other categories will be related to or subsumed to this central category or theme. Selective coding is evident in the following studies that all have an overarching viewpoint or frame:

- A study of personal Web sites finds that posting a Web site is an imaginary digital extension of self.
- A study of an online Newton (a discontinued Apple PDA) user group finds several elements of religious devotion in the community.
- A study of Hispanic consumer behavior in the United States uses the metaphor of boundary crossing to explore Hispanic purchase and consumption.[16]

Given its role as an integrating concept, it is not surprising that selective coding generally occurs in the later stages of data analysis. Once the overarching theme is developed, researchers review all their codes and cases to better understand how they relate to the larger category, or central storyline that has emerged from their data.

Data Reduction: Iteration and Negative Case Analysis   **Iteration** means working through the data in a way that permits early ideas and analyses to be modified by choosing cases and issues in the data that will permit deeper analyses. The iterative process may uncover issues that the already collected data do not address. In this case, the researcher will collect data from more informants, or may choose specific types of informants that he or she believes will answer questions that have arisen during the iterative process. The iterative procedure may also take place after an original attempt at integration. Each of the interviews (or texts or images) may be reviewed to see whether it supports the larger theory that has been developed. This iterative process can result in revising and deepening constructs as well as the larger theory based on relationships between constructs.

An important element of iterative analysis is note taking or **memoing.** Researchers should write down their thoughts and reactions as soon after each interview, focus group, or site visit as time will allow. Researchers may want to write down not only what participants say they feel, but whether or not what they say is credible.

Perhaps most important, during the iterative process researchers use **negative case analysis,** which means that they deliberately look for cases and instances that contradict the ideas and theories that they have been developing. Negative case analysis helps to establish boundaries and conditions for the theory that is being developed by the qualitative researcher. The general stance of qualitative researchers should be skepticism toward the ideas and theory they have created based on the data they have collected.[17] Otherwise they are likely to look for evidence that confirms their preexisting biases and early analysis. Doing so may result in important alternative conceptualizations that are legitimately present in the data being completely overlooked.

Iterative and negative case analyses begin in the data reduction stage. But they continue through the data display and conclusion drawing/verification stages. As analysis continues in the project, data displays are altered. Late in the life of the project, iterative analysis and negative case analysis provide verification for and qualification of the themes and theories developed during the data reduction phase of research.

Data Reduction: The Role of Tabulation   The use of tabulation in qualitative analyses is controversial. Some analysts feel that any kind of tabulation will be misleading. After all, the data collected are not like survey data where all questions are asked of all respondents in exactly the same way. Each focus group or in-depth interview asks somewhat different questions in somewhat different ways. Moreover, frequency of mention is not always a good measure of research importance. A unique answer from a lone wolf in an interview may be worthy of attention because it is consistent with other interpretation and analysis, or because it suggests a boundary condition for the theory and findings.[18]

Exhibit 10.4 shows a tabulation from the study of senior adoption of the Internet. The most frequently coded response was "communication," followed by "self-directed values/behavior." While this result may seem meaningful, a better measure of the importance of communications to seniors over the Internet is likely to be found using surveys. But the result does provide some guidance. All 27 participants in the study mentioned the use of the Internet for communication, so researchers are likely to investigate this theme in their analysis even if the tabulations are not included in the final report. Note that qualitative researchers virtually never report percentages. For example, they seldom would report 4 out of 10 that are positive about a product concept as 40 percent. Using percentages would inaccurately imply that the results are statistically projectible to a larger population of consumers.

Iteration   Working through the data several times in order to modify early ideas and to be informed by subsequent analyses.

Memoing   Writing down thoughts as soon as possible after each interview, focus group, or site visit.

Negative case analysis   Deliberately looking for cases and instances that contradict the ideas and theories that researchers have been developing.

Exhibit 10.4	Tabulation of Most Frequently Appearing Categories in the Senior Adoption of the Internet Study

Themes	Passages	Documents (Participants)
Communication—uses	149	27
Self-directed values and behavior	107	23
Shopping/conducting biz—uses	66	24
Gather information—uses	65	25
Classes to learn the Internet	64	22
Future intended uses	63	20
Mentors/teachers helping to learn	55	20
Difficulty in learning	50	20
Self-efficacy/proactive coping—outcome	46	16
Later life cycle uses (e.g. genealogy)	45	19
Entertainment—uses	43	24
Excitement about the Internet	40	14
Adopting to facilitate hobbies	40	15
Technology optimism	40	18
Proactive coping	38	19
Health information on Internet—uses	34	19
Bricolage (Linkering to learn the Internet)	34	20

Tabulation can also keep researchers honest. For example, researchers involved in the senior Internet adoption study were initially impressed by informants who made the decision to adopt the Internet quickly and dramatically when someone showed them an Internet function that supported a preexisting interest or hobby (coded as "a-ha"). But the code only appeared three times across the 27 participants in the study. While researchers may judge the theme worthy of mention in their report, they are unlikely to argue that "a-ha" moments are central in the senior adoption decision process. Counting responses can help keep researchers honest in the sense that it provides a counterweight to biases they may bring to the analysis.[19]

Another way to use tabulation is to look at co-occurrences of themes in the study. Exhibit 10.5 shows the number of times selected concepts were mentioned together in the same coded passage. In the table, categories most often mentioned together with curiosity were technology optimism, proactive coping skills ("I can figure it out even if it makes me feel stupid sometimes"), and cultural currency (adopting to keep up with the times). The co-mentions with curiosity suggest that qualitative analysts would consider the idea that curious people are more likely to be technology optimists, to be interested in keeping up with the times, and to have strong proactive coping skills. But interpreting these numbers too literally is risky. Further iterative analysis is required to develop these conceptual ideas and to support (or refute) their credibility. Whenever the magnitude of a finding is important

| Exhibit 10.5 | Relationships between Categories: Co-Mentions of Selected Constructs in the Senior Adoption of the Internet Study |

	Curiosity	Technology Optimism	Proactive Coping Skills	Cultural Currency
Curiosity	**107***			
Technology Optimism	16	**40**		
Proactive Coping Skills	19	10	**38**	
Cultural Currency	12	8	7	**26**

*Diagonal contains total number of mentions of each concept.

to decision makers, well-designed quantitative studies are likely to provide better measures than are qualitative studies.

Some researchers suggest a middle ground for reporting tabulations of qualitative data. They suggest using "fuzzy numerical qualifiers" such as "often," "typically," or "few" in their reports.[20] Marketing researchers usually include a section in their reports about limitations of their research. A caution about the inappropriateness of estimating magnitudes based on qualitative research typically is included in the limitations section of the report. Therefore, when reading qualitative findings, readers would be cautioned that any numerical findings presented should not be read too literally.

Step 2: Data Display

Qualitative researchers typically use visual displays to summarize data. Data displays are important because they help reduce and summarize the extensive textual data collected in the study in a way that conveys major ideas in a compact fashion. There is no one way to display and present data in qualitative analysis. Any perusal of qualitative reports will find a wide variety of formats, each developed in response to the combination of research problem, methodology (ethnography, case study, focus group, or in-depth interview, for instance), and focus of analysis. Coming up with ideas for useful data displays is a creative task that can be both fun and satisfying. Some data displays provide interim analysis and thus may not be included in the final report. In any case, the displays will probably change over the course of analysis as researchers interpret and reread their data and modify and qualify their initial impressions. The displays also evolve as researchers seek to better display their findings.

Displays may be tables or figures. Tables have rows or row by column formats that cross themes and/or informants. Figures may include flow diagrams; traditional box and arrow causal diagrams (often associated with quantitative research); diagrams that display circular or recursive relationships; trees that display consumers' taxonomies of products, brands, or other concepts; consensus maps, which picture the collective connections that informants make between concepts or ideas; and checklists that show all informants and then indicate whether or not each informant possesses a particular attitude, value, behavior,

Exhibit 10.6	Eight Central Paradoxes of Technological Products

Paradox	Description
Control/chaos	Technology can facilitate regulation or order, and technology can lead to upheaval or disorder
Freedom/enslavement	Technology can facilitate independence or fewer restrictions, and technology can lead to dependence or more restrictions
New/obsolete	New technologies provide the user with the most recently developed benefits of scientific knowledge, and new technologies are already or soon to be outmoded as they reach the marketplace
Competence/incompetence	Technology can facilitate feelings of intelligence or efficacy, and technology can lead to feelings of ignorance or ineptitude
Efficiency/inefficiency	Technology can facilitate less effort or time spent in certain activities, and technology can lead to more effort or time in certain activities
Fulfills/creates needs	Technology can facilitate the fulfillment of needs or desires, and technology can lead to the development or awareness of needs or desires previously unrealized
Assimilation/isolation	Technology can facilitate human togetherness, and technology can lead to human separation
Engaging/disengaging	Technology can facilitate involvement, flow, or activity, and technology can lead to disconnection, disruption, or passivity

Source: David Glen Mick and Susan Fournier, "Paradoxes of Technology: Consumer Cognizance, Emotions and Coping Strategies," *Journal of Consumer Research* 25 (September 1998), p. 126.

ideology, or role, for instance. While displays of qualitative findings are quite diverse, some common types of displays are:

- A table that explains central themes in the study. For example, a study of technology products uncovered eight themes that represent the paradoxes or issues in technology adoption and use (see Exhibit 10.6).
- A diagram that suggests relationships between variables. An example of a diagram that pictures relationships between themes comes from the earlier-mentioned study of skydiving (see Exhibit 10.7). The diagram pictures how three sets of motivations evolve over time as skydivers become more experienced. The arrows are double-sided because movement to a higher level is not complete, since skydivers revisit and experience the lower-level motivations.
- A table with a comparison of key categories in the study. An example is a table that compares goal-oriented and experiential shopping in an online environment (see Exhibit 10.8).

| Exhibit 10.7 | Evolution of Motives for High-Risk Consumption in Relation to Risk Acculturation and Experience |

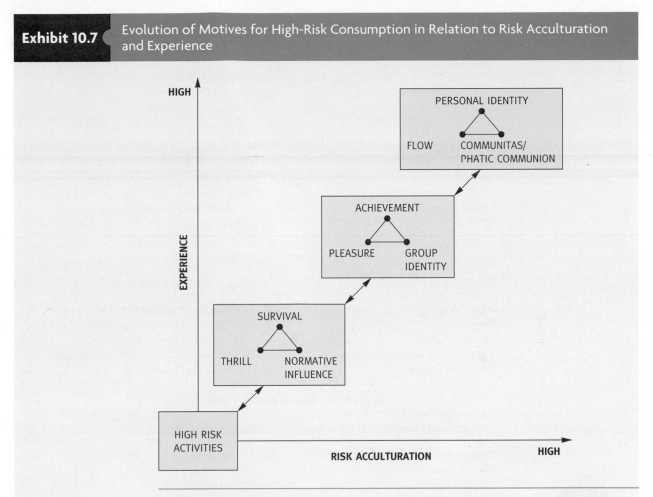

Source: Richard L. Celsi, Randy L. Rose, and Tom W. Leigh, "An Exploration of High Risk Leisure Consumption through Skydiving," *Journal of Consumer Research* 20 (June 1993), p. 14.

- A matrix including quotes for various themes from representative informants. An example of this is a table from the previously mentioned study of involvement with cosmetics and brand attitudes in Post-Socialist Europe, which shows attitudes of women who are ambivalent about cosmetics (see Exhibit 10.9). Other tables included in the study contain parallel verbatims for women who have embraced cosmetics and women who have rejected cosmetics.
- A consensus map that shows the relationships between ideas and concepts informants collectively express. In an example based on a ZMET study of the issues that surround privacy, the data display appeared online, and users could drill down and see representative verbatims for each concept and for the connections between concepts (see Exhibit 10.10).

Step 3: Conclusion Drawing/Verification

The iterative process and negative case analysis continues through the verification phase of the project. The process includes checking for common biases that may affect researcher conclusions. A list of the most common biases to watch out for is shown in Exhibit 10.11. In addition to actively considering the possibility of bias in the analysis, researchers also must establish credibility for their findings. We explain credibility next.

Exhibit 10.8 Goal-Oriented versus Experiential Behavior in Online Shopping

Focus Group Participant Descriptors of:

Goal-Oriented Shopping	Experiential Shopping
Accomplishment	Enjoyment
Going to specific site	Surfing/trying new sites
Looking for specific product	Looking for new things
Saving time	Killing time
I have a purpose in mind	I look for ideas
I make repeat purchases	I check my favorite sites regularly
Finding the best price for a specific item	Bargain hunting for what's on sale

Focus Group Participant Desires when:

Goal-Oriented Shopping	Experiential Shopping
I want to get in-and-out quickly (fewest clicks)	I want a welcoming site that draws me in
Do-it-myself	I can interact with other consumers
Don't waste my time	Show me lots of choices
I want immediate response to questions	I like to browse sites related to my hobby
I want ease of use	I want a unique experience

Focus Group Participant Descriptors of:

Freedom and Control	Fun
Control what information I receive	Read reviews (but don't believe them)
No salespeople	I get drawn in
No lines/crowds	Excitement of bidding
Only brands/sites I know	Window shopping
I can come back anytime/delay purchase	I'm impulsive
I have options	I have to limit myself
Show me what I want	Surprise me

Source: Mary Wolfinbarger and Mary C. Gilly, "Shopping Online for Freedom, Control and Fun," *California Management Review* 43, no.2 (Winter 2001), p. 39.

Verification/Conclusion Drawing: Credibility in Qualitative Research Quantitative researchers establish credibility in data analysis by demonstrating their results are reliable (measurement and findings are stable, repeatable, and generalizable) and valid (the research measures what it was intended to measure). In contrast, the credibility of qualitative data analysis is based on the rigor of "the actual strategies used for collecting, coding, analyzing, and presenting data when generating theory."[21] The essential question in developing credibility in qualitative research is "How can [a researcher] persuade his or her audiences that the research findings of an inquiry are worth paying attention to?"[22]

The terms *validity* and *reliability* have to be redefined in qualitative research. For example, in qualitative research the term **emic validity** means that the analysis presented in the report resonates with people inside the studied culture or subculture, a form of validity established by member checking. Similarly, **cross-researcher reliability** means the text and images are

Emic validity An attribute of qualitative research that affirms that key members within a culture or subculture agree with the findings of a research report.

Cross-researcher reliability The degree of similarity in the coding of the same data by different researchers.

Exhibit 10.9	Post-Socialist Eastern European Women's Product Involvement and Brand Commitment: Informants Who Were Ambivalent about Cosmetics	
	Alexandra	**Laura**
Cosmetics use and involvement	3.1: Normally I wash my hair twice a week. But . . . I knew we would meet, so I washed it yesterday. It depends on my mood. I use corrector and cream powder in winter when I am not so brown, but in the summer. . . . It is disgusting. If I go to a movie I don't. So, I always say, "Okay, you have to have a nice look, but you don't have to prepare for the next beauty contest every morning."	3.8: Only if something bad happened, a disaster, and then I wouldn't think about appearance. Mascara, this is something that I always use, and powder everyday for my face. I like it. . . . Mascara, I can put that on myself. But I can't put on makeup. I can give advice, but I don't know how to do it for myself. Maybe I am too stressed, I won't get the effect that I want. I feel better without makeup.
Consumer as interpreter	3.2: When I'll be the grandparent then it will be okay for the parent, because I've changed my way of thinking. I will give it to my children.	3.9: I buy things that I don't really need. I know that I don't need it, but it, and then I am sorry. . . . Those things can wait.
Cultural ideologies and intermediaries	3.3: I mean during the socialist communist regime there wasn't a choice. People weren't conscious about cosmetics. The only thing that was important was to have a workplace and to meet the requirement of the socialist men and women.	3.10: Romanian women are more attractive than five years ago because they have the chance to find out new things from TV and magazines—how to put on makeup and how to dress. For instance, my mother doesn't take care of herself. . . . You know we didn't learn how to use cosmetics from her. We watched TV, read books. My mother didn't tell me anything.
Local context and social networks	3.4: There is *Cosmopolitan* in Hungarian, but it is not as good as in English. It is thinner, and there are only advertisements in it and about sex and that is all. I am lucky because we have an English teacher at the university, and they subscribe to this magazine, and I can read it. And there are fashion models, as well and cooking advice and so on. So, it is much nicer.	3.11: They judge you according to appearance. Even in the job, women discuss . . . and then you also have to buy it, because you want to be at the same level. I saw this, and after they buy the products, they show off. Look what I have. Those who cannot buy suffer, even if they don't admit it. It is painful. . . . After the Revolution, I guess this is when it started—with jeans.
Ideological positions	3.5: We have to forget about communism, and we have to change our way of thinking, but it is very, very hard to change the thinking of the whole country.	3.12: If you look good, you get a good guy, a good job, even though you are not very smart. But many have problems because of this . . . it is risky to look good. Everyone wants to look better than the other. They think that if you are dressed according to the latest fashion, everyone will think that you have money and have a good life.
Involvement with branded products	3.6: If I have money I get cosmetics at a pharmacy, If I don't have much money I go to a drugstore. Usually [pharmacists] have creams that they do themselves. They are good ones because they know what to put in them, but they don't have names. And they are cheaper. . . . The name isn't important to me, what is important is quality. If I find an unknown product, but it is	3.13: I saw many women that want to use branded products, not because they know it is good, but because they saw a commercial, or they want to show off. They don't think it is possible that the products don't fit you. Branded products might not fit you. At some point, we had Pantene shampoos. All the commercial breaks had ads with Pantene. I didn't want to buy. I got it as a gift and used

	Exhibit 10.9 Post-Socialist Eastern European Women's Product Involvement and Brand Commitment: Informants Who Were Ambivalent about Cosmetics *continued*	
	Alexandra	**Laura**
Brand commitment and brand experimentation	good for me, I buy it. . . . And I don't trust these [products] . . . it would be cheaper to buy them, but I haven't heard about them. I don't trust them. 3.7: This is my favorite. I just found it. . . . It is brand new. I tried Wash & Go. It was advertised very frequently, and everybody ran to the shops and bought it. But I said, "OK, it's very popular, but it is not good for me [it tangled my hair]."	it, and I wasn't happy with it. I didn't like. It might be a good brand, but it didn't fit me, so brand is not enough. 3.14: I prefer L'Oreal, and Avon and Oriflame have good body lotion. I still like to try other things. I like to try only things that I have heard of.

Source: Robin A. Coulter, Linda L. Price, and Lawrence Feick, "Rethinking the Origins of Involvement and Brand Commitment: Insights from Postsocialist Europe," *Journal of Consumer Research* 30 (September 2003), p. 159.

coded similarly among multiple researchers. However, many qualitative researchers prefer terms such as "quality," "rigor," "dependability," "transferability," and "trustworthiness" to the traditionally quantitative terms "validity" and "reliability." Moreover, some qualitative researchers completely reject any notions of validity and reliability, believing there is no single "correct" interpretation of qualitative data.[23] In this chapter, we use the term **credibility** to describe the rigor and believability established in qualitative analysis.

Credibility The degree of rigor, believability, and trustworthiness established by qualitative research.

Triangulation is the technique most often associated with credibility in qualitative research.[24] Triangulation requires that research inquiry be addressed from multiple perspectives. Several kinds of triangulation are possible:

Triangulation Addressing the topic of analysis from multiple perspectives, including using multiple methods of data collection and analysis, multiple data sets, multiple researchers, multiple time periods, and different kinds of relevant research informants.

- Multiple methods of data collection and analysis.
- Multiple data sets.
- Multiple researchers analyzing the data, especially if they come from different backgrounds or research perspectives
- Data collection in multiple time periods.
- Providing selective breadth in informants so that different kinds of relevant groups that may have different and relevant perspectives are included in the research.

Credibility is also increased when key informants and other practicing qualitative researchers are asked to review the analyses. As earlier mentioned, soliciting feedback from key informants or member checking strengthens the credibility of qualitative analysis. Seeking feedback from external expert reviewers, called **peer review,** also strengthens credibility. Key informants and external qualitative methodology and topic area experts often question the analyses, push researchers to better clarify their thinking, and occasionally change key interpretations in the research. When member checking and peer review are utilized in a qualitative design, it is reported in the methodological section of the report.

Peer review A process in which external qualitative methodology or topic area specialists are asked to review the research analysis.

Exhibit 10.10   Consensus Map of the Concept of Privacy along with Drilldown of the Relationship between Scrutiny and Invasion

Consensus Map for Consumer Thoughts about Privacy

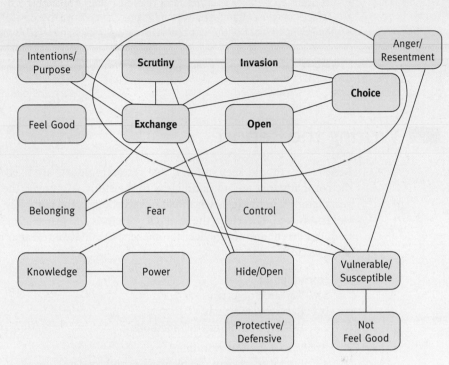

The Reasoning Process Involving Scrutiny and Invasion

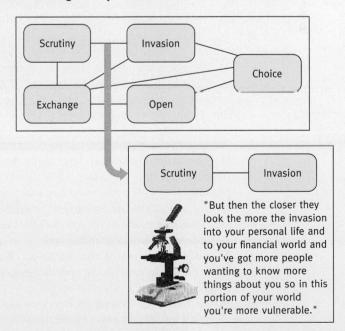

"But then the closer they look the more the invasion into your personal life and to your financial world and you've got more people wanting to know more things about you so in this portion of your world you're more vulnerable."

Source: Gerald Zaltman, *How Consumers Think: Essential Insights into the Mind of the Market* (Boston: Harvard Business School Press, 2003), pp. 152 and 154.

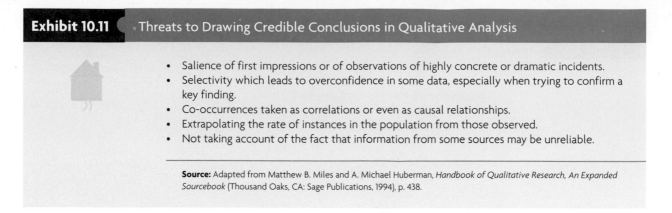

Exhibit 10.11 Threats to Drawing Credible Conclusions in Qualitative Analysis

- Salience of first impressions or of observations of highly concrete or dramatic incidents.
- Selectivity which leads to overconfidence in some data, especially when trying to confirm a key finding.
- Co-occurrences taken as correlations or even as causal relationships.
- Extrapolating the rate of instances in the population from those observed.
- Not taking account of the fact that information from some sources may be unreliable.

Source: Adapted from Matthew B. Miles and A. Michael Huberman, *Handbook of Qualitative Research, An Expanded Sourcebook* (Thousand Oaks, CA: Sage Publications, 1994), p. 438.

Writing the Report

Researchers should keep in mind that research reports are likely to be read by people in the company that are not familiar with the study. Moreover, the study may be reviewed years later by individuals who were not working at the company at the time the research was conducted. Therefore, the research objectives and procedures should be well explained both to current and future decision makers. Qualitative research reports typically contain three sections:[25]

1. Introduction
   a. Research objectives
   b. Research questions
   c. Description of research methods
2. Analysis of the Data/Findings
   a. Literature review and relevant secondary data
   b. Findings displayed in tables or charts
   c. Interpretation and summary of the findings.
3. Conclusions and Recommendations.

The introductory portion of the report should present the research problem, objectives of the research, and the methodology used. As do quantitative researchers, qualitative researchers report the procedures they used to collect and analyze data. The methodology section of a qualitative report usually contains:

- Topics covered in questioning and other materials used in questioning informants.
- If observational methods are used, the locations, dates, times, and context of observation.
- Number of researchers involved and their level of involvement in the study. Any diversity in background or training of researchers may be highlighted as positive for the study because multiple viewpoints have been brought to the analysis.
- Procedure for choosing informants.
- Number of informants and informant characteristics, such as age, gender, location, level of experience with the product/service. This information is often summarized in a table.
- The number of focus groups, interviews, or transcripts.
- The total number of pages of the transcripts, number of pictures, videos, number and page length of researcher memos.

- Any procedures used to ensure that the data collection and analysis were systematic, for example, coding, iterative analysis of transcripts, member checking, peer reviews, and so forth.
- Procedures used for negative case analyses and how the interpretation was modified.
- Limitations of qualitative methodology in general, and any limitations that are specific to the particular qualitative method used.

Two examples of explaining the general limitations of qualitative methodology in a report are:

"The reader is cautioned that the findings reported here are qualitative, not quantitative in nature. The study was designed to explore *how* respondents feel and behave rather than to determine *how many* think or act in specific ways."

"Respondents constitute a small nonrandom sample of relevant consumers and are therefore not statistically representative of the universe from which they have been drawn."[26]

Analysis of the Data/Findings

The sequence of reported findings should be written in a way that is logical and persuasive. Secondary data may be brought into the analysis to help contextualize the findings. For instance, in the senior adoption of the Internet study, the percentage and demographics of senior adopters was covered in the report to contextualize the qualitative findings. Also, general topics precede more specific topics. For example, a discussion of findings related to seniors' general attitudes toward and adoption of technology will precede the discussion of senior Internet adoption.

Verbatims Quotes from research participants that are used in research reports.

Data displays that summarize, clarify, or provide evidence for assertions should be included with the report. **Verbatims,** or quotes from research participants, should be used judiciously in the textual report as well as in data displays. When they are well chosen, verbatims are a particularly powerful way to underscore important points because they express consumer viewpoints in their own voice. Video verbatims can be used in live presentations. Of course, the power of verbatims is a double-edged sword. Colorfully stated, interesting verbatims do not always make points that are well grounded in the body of data collected. Researchers need to take care that they do not select, analyze, and present verbatims that are memorable rather than revealing of patterns in their data.

Conclusions and Recommendations

Researchers should provide information that is relevant to the research problem articulated by the client. As two qualitative researchers stated, "A psychoanalytically rich interpretation of personal hygiene and deodorant products is ultimately of little value to the client if it cannot be linked to a set of actionable marketing implications—for example, a positioning which directly reflects consumer motivations or a new product directed at needs not currently addressed."[27] As with quantitative research, knowledge of both the market and the client's business is useful in translating research findings into managerial implications.

When the magnitude of consumer response is important to the client, researchers are likely to report what they have found and suggest follow-up research. Even so, qualitative research should be reported in a way that reflects an appropriate level of confidence in the findings. Exhibit 10.12 lists three examples of forceful, but realistic, recommendations based on qualitative research.

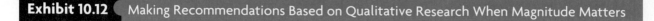

Exhibit 10.12 Making Recommendations Based on Qualitative Research When Magnitude Matters

- "The qualitative findings give reason for optimism about market interest in the new product concept . . . We therefore recommend that the concept be further developed and formal executions be tested."
- "While actual market demand may not necessarily meet the test of profitability, the data reported here suggest that there is widespread interest in the new device."
- "The results of this study suggest that ad version #3 is most promising because it elicited more enthusiastic responses and because it appears to describe situations under which consumers actually expect to use the product."

Source: Alfred E. Goldman and Susan Schwartz McDonald, *The Group Depth Interview* (Englewood Cliffs, N J: Prentice Hall, 1987), p. 176.

Continuing Case: Santa Fe Grill: Using Qualitative Research

The business consultant hired by the owners of the Santa Fe Grill has recommended a quantitative survey of lunch and dinner customers. He has not recommended any qualitative research. The owners are not experts in research methods, but they do know the difference in qualitative and quantitative research. They are wondering if some kind of qualitative research approach would be better to understand the challenges facing them. Or perhaps both qualitative and quantitative research should be undertaken?

1. Could observation be used to collect qualitative information?
2. If yes, when and how could observation be used?
3. Are there topics that could be explored better using focus groups?
4. If yes, suggest topics to be used in the focus group studies.

MARKETING RESEARCH IN ACTION
Hotel Travelers' Cheers and Jeers at Their Experiences

Recently, ethnographers at *American Demographics* (AD) investigated the following research question: "What are travelers' good and bad experiences with the hospitality industry?" Using content analysis and procedures for triangulation, researchers sifted through a sample of nearly 2,000 letters submitted by consumers to hotels and resorts through Planetfeedback, a division of Intelliseek, a Cincinnati-based market research firm. Of all the letters submitted to Planetfeedback's online forum, 78 percent were complaints and 16 percent were compliments, with the remaining 6 percent being either questions or suggestions. Through qualitative analysis, the researchers identified several themes, including "personalized service," "fair deal," "extra perks," "cleanliness/hygiene," "unsatisfactory facilities," and "poor customer service." Here is what they discovered: travelers overwhelmingly agree that hotel housekeeping needs to clean up its act. Among the 150 letters submitted on the topic of "cleanliness/hygiene," almost all of them were complaints. The billing and check-in departments also received a large share of complaints. Despite the efforts of the hospitality industry to personalize reservations and add amenities, nothing wins guests over like a friendly staff. The highest percentage of complimentary letters fell into the "hotel staff performance" category. Here are some examples of what consumers wrote:

Customer 1

"I would like to compliment the employees of your Peoria, IL hotel. They greet me by name; ask how my day has been and if they can do anything to help me out. They always phone after I've gone to my room to see that it's adequate. When I've neglected to get a reservation, they have been kind enough to reserve a room for me at another hotel. That's going the extra mile for a guest!"

Customer 2

"My partner and I are very price-conscious and tend to shop around for the best hotel rates. On one of the popular travel Web sites, I found a much cheaper rate than I was quoted by your hotel on the phone or on your own site. I pointed this out to the staff and they honored the Web rate, plus they knocked an additional 10 percent off. The entire process was very efficient."

Customer 3

"When we arrived at your hotel, we asked about receiving a room upgrade, never imagining we could afford it—and we received it for free. We were absolutely thrilled. The employees at the front desk went out of their way to make it a pleasant stay for our family and us. It really made our day, month, and probably our year."

Customer 4

"When we returned to our room, the beds were not made, towels were not replaced, and were wet on the floor, and the waste receptacles were overflowing. The front desk person informed us that there was a form in the room that we were supposed to fill out to identify the level of housekeeping we needed. It seems that a minimum level of cleaning should be assumed in the absence of any formal request form."

Customer 5

"My husband has a heart condition and is supposed to exercise every day. I chose your hotel in St. Louis because it had an exercise facility. When we got there, the equipment was rusty and nonfunctional."

Customer 6

"I called your toll-free reservation line and was quoted $92.65 per night. When I checked out of the hotel, I was billed $92.65 for Friday night but $143.65 for Saturday night. The attendant called the 800-number and handed me the phone. The representative took my number and told me someone from Guest Relations would call me. I did not receive a call. I am very upset by the brush-off."

Hands-On Exercise

1. Using your understanding of the chapter material and the theme topics presented above, reanalyze each of the given examples and categorize them into what you believe to be the most appropriate "theme."
2. Using the six customer examples, is there any evidence that would allow you to determine if "triangulation" of the data occurs? If yes, explain how. If no, why not?
3. What other possible "themes," if any, could be identified from the given customers' letters? Make sure you label the topics and support your choices.

Summary

Contrast qualitative and quantitative data analysis.

There are many differences between qualitative and quantitative data analysis. The data that are analyzed in qualitative research include text and images, rather than numbers. In quantitative research, the goal is to quantify the magnitude of variables and relationships, or explain causal relationships. In qualitative analysis, the goal of research is deeper understanding. A second difference is that qualitative analysis is iterative, with researchers revisiting data and clarifying their thinking during each iteration. Third, quantitative analysis is driven entirely by researchers, while good qualitative research employs member checking, or asking key informants to verify the accuracy of research reports. Last, qualitative data analysis is inductive, which means that the theory grows out of the research process rather than preceding it, as it does in quantitative analysis.

Explain the steps in qualitative data analysis.

After data collection, there are three steps in analyzing qualitative data. Researchers move back and forth between these steps iteratively rather than going through them one step at a time. The steps are data reduction, constructing data displays, and drawing/verifying conclusions. Data reduction consists of several interrelated processes: categorization and coding, theory development and iteration, and negative case analysis. Categorization is the process of coding and labeling sections of the transcripts or images into themes. Then, the categories can be integrated into a theory through iterative analysis of the data. Data displays are the second step. Data displays picture findings in tables or figures so that the data can be more easily digested and communicated. After a rigorous iterative process, researchers can draw conclusions and verify their findings. During the verification/conclusion drawing stage, researchers work to establish the credibility of their data analysis.

Describe the processes of categorizing and coding data as well as developing theory.

During the categorization phase, researchers develop categories based both on preexisting theory and the categories that emerge from the data. They code the data in margins and develop a code sheet that shows the various labels that they are developing. The codes are revised and revisited as the theory develops. In the process of abstraction, related categories are collapsed into higher order conceptual constructs. Comparison of differences and similarities between instances of a category, between related categories, and between different participants is particularly useful in better defining constructs and refining theory.

Integration is the process of moving from identification of themes and categories to the investigation of relationships between categories. Two techniques are used in the integration/theory development process. One is axial coding in which researchers specify the conditions, context, or variables that lead to a particular category or construct; the actions needed for informants to carry out the construct; and the outcomes from the construct. In axial coding researchers learn that particular conditions, contexts, and outcomes cluster together. In selective coding, researchers develop an overarching theme or category around which to build their storyline.

Clarify how credibility is established in qualitative data analysis.

Credibility in data analysis is established through (1) careful, iterative analysis in categorization and theory development, (2) the use of negative case analysis, and (3) triangulation. In negative case analysis, researchers systematically search the data for information that does not conform to their theory. This helps to establish the credibility of their analysis and to identify boundary conditions for their theory. Triangulation is especially important in developing credibility for qualitative data analyses. There are several forms of triangulation, including using multiple methods of data collection and analysis; multiple data sets; multiple researchers; data collection in multiple time periods; and informants with different perspectives and experiences. Credibility is also enhanced with member checking, which is soliciting feedback about the accuracy of the analysis from key informants. In peer review, qualitative methodology experts are asked to critique the qualitative report.

Discuss the steps involved in writing a qualitative research report.

A qualitative report has three sections: (1) Introduction, (2) Analysis of the Data/Findings, and (3) Conclusions and Recommendations, or Marketing Implications. In the introductory portion of the report, the objectives of the research and methodology are explained. In the data analysis section, the reported findings are written in a way that is logical and persuasive. Data displays and verbatims may be used to enhance the communication of the findings. The Conclusion includes the marketing implications section. In this part of the report, researchers provide information that is relevant to the research problem articulated by the client.

 Key Terms and Concepts

 Review Questions

1. How is quantitative and qualitative data analysis different?
2. Describe the three steps in qualitative data analysis and explain how and why these steps are iterative.
3. What are the interrelated steps in data reduction?
4. How do you build theory in qualitative analysis?
5. What is negative case analysis and why is it important to the credibility of qualitative analysis?
6. What are the different kinds of data displays? Give some specific examples of how they may be used in qualitative data analysis.
7. What are some of the threats to drawing credible conclusions in qualitative data analysis?
8. What is triangulation and what is its role in qualitative analysis?
9. What are the various ways that credibility can be established in qualitative analysis?

 Discussion Questions

1. Compare and contrast reliability and validity in quantitative analysis with the concept of credibility used in qualitative analysis? Do you believe the concepts are really similar? Why or why not?
2. Let's say your college has as a goal increasing the participation in student activities on campus. To help in this effort, you are doing an ethnographic study to better understand why students do or do not participate in student activities. How would you plan for triangulation in this study?
3. **EXPERIENCE THE INTERNET.** Ask permission from three people to analyze the content of their MySpace, Facebook, or similar site (of course, you should promise them anonymity). If the sites are

extensive, you may need a plan to sample a portion of the Web site (at least 5–10 representative pages). As you go through the sites, develop a coding sheet. What did you learn about MySpace sites from your coding? What content categories are the most frequently occurring? What do you conclude based on the fact that these categories are the most frequently occurring at these three Web sites? Are there any implications of your findings for advertisers that are considering advertising on MySpace?

4. An anthropology professor over the age of 50 took a year of leave, and spent the year undercover as a student at her college. She did not take classes in her own department, but instead signed up, attended classes, took exams, and wrote papers just like any other freshmen. She lived in the dorm for a year. At the end of a year, she wrote a book entitled *My Freshman Year*,[28] which details her findings. In reporting the research methodology of her study, what methodological strengths and weaknesses should the anthropology professor address?

5. Conduct 3–4 in-depth interviews with college students who are not business majors. You will be conducting an investigation of the associations that college students make with the word "marketing." You can ask students to bring 5–10 images of any type (pictures, cutouts from magazines) that most essentially picture what they think marketing is all about. You may also conduct a word association exercise with the students. During the interview, you may want to tell informants that you are an alien from another planet and have never heard of marketing. Based on your interviews, develop a consensus map that shows the concepts that students relate to marketing. Draw a circle around the most frequently occurring connections in your diagram. What did you learn about how college students view marketing?

6. You are conducting a small-scale qualitative project about the nature of product dissatisfaction. You will need to follow the steps below.

   a. Write a 2-page narrative about a time that you purchased a product or service with which you were very dissatisfied. You should include in your narrative the following points: (1) the product or service; (2) your expectations when you bought the product or service; (3) any interactions with salespeople or customer service people before, during, or after the purchase; (4) the feelings and emotions that accompanied your dissatisfaction; and (5) the outcomes of your dissatisfaction. You may include other details as well.

   b. Collect narratives written by four of your classmates. You are now going to engage in axial coding of the narratives. Create a matrix. Across the top you will list the product or service, the conditions that led to dissatisfaction, any actions that are related to the creation of dissatisfaction, and the outcomes of dissatisfaction (you may separate the emotions accompanying dissatisfaction from other outcomes in two or more separate outcome columns). Down the left side you will name each person (using a pseudonym).

   c. If you were to engage in selective coding, what overarching theme or perspective do you think would integrate your categories?

   d. What did you learn about dissatisfaction? What are the managerial implications of your findings, that is, how can companies lessen or prevent dissatisfaction? Be as complete as possible in drawing managerial implications.

Preparing Data for Quantitative Analysis

Chapter 11

1. Describe the process for data preparation and analysis.
2. Discuss validation, editing, and coding of survey data.
3. Explain data entry procedures as well as how to detect errors.
4. Describe data tabulation and analysis approaches.

Wal-Mart and Scanner Technology

Each item you purchase in almost any retail store is scanned into a computer. The bar code enables the store to know exactly what products are selling and when. Store managers can also keep accurate control of inventory, so they can easily order more products when they run low. Probably the ultimate example of scanning use is Wal-Mart, where scanners have been vital. Wal-Mart does not own the products on its shelves; they remain there on consignment by the manufacturers. With its scanning system, however, Wal-Mart always knows what is there, what is selling, and what needs replenishment. The scanner has pushed back the law of diminishing returns and made it possible to build and manage larger inventories than would have been possible a few years ago.

The same equipment that scans product codes can also scan a bar-coded customer card so the customer is associated with his or her purchase in a central database. This process takes a second or two per transaction and requires only that the customer produce the card at purchase time.

Scanner technology is widely used in the marketing research industry. Questionnaires can be prepared through any of a number of word processing software packages and printed on a laser printer. Respondents can complete the questionnaire with any type of writing instrument. With the appropriate software and scanning device, the researcher can scan the completed questionnaires and the data are checked for errors, categorized, and stored within a matter of seconds. When a researcher expects to receive 400 to 500 completed surveys, scanner technology can be worth its weight in gold.[1]

Value of Preparing Data for Analysis

Converting information from a questionnaire so it can be transferred to a data warehouse is referred to as data *preparation*. This process usually follows a four-step approach, beginning with data *validation*, then editing and coding, followed by data entry and data tabulation. Error detection begins in the first phase and continues throughout the process. The purpose of data preparation is to take data in its raw form and convert it to establish meaning and create value for the user.

The process of data preparation and analysis starts after the data is collected. Several interrelated tasks must be completed to ensure the data is accurately reported. The stages of data preparation and analysis are shown in Exhibit 11.1. This chapter discusses the data preparation process and Chapters 12 and 13 provide an overview of data analysis for quantitative research.

Exhibit 11.1	Overview of Data Preparation and Analysis

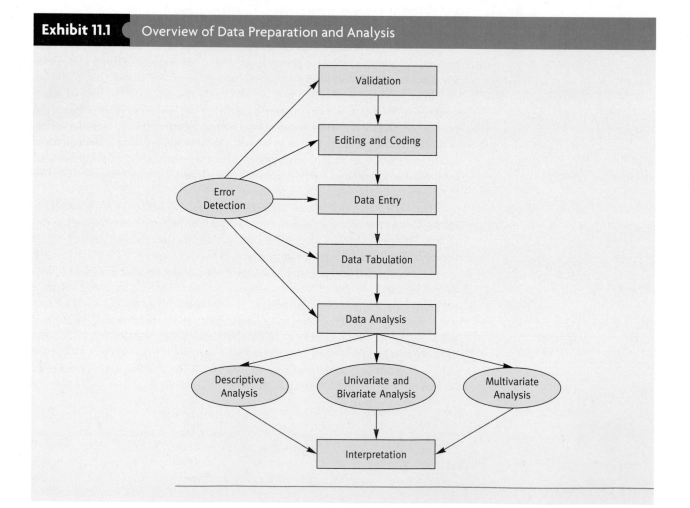

Validation

Data validation The process of determining, to the extent possible, whether a survey's interviews or observations were conducted correctly and are free of fraud or bias.

Curbstoning Cheating or falsification in the data collection process.

The purpose of **data validation** is to determine if surveys, interviews, and observations were conducted correctly and are free of bias. Data collection often is not easy to monitor closely. To facilitate accurate data collection, each respondent's name, address, and phone number may be recorded. While this information is not used for analysis, it does enable the validation process to be completed.

In the marketing research industry submitting false data is referred to as **curbstoning.** As the name implies, curbstoning is when interviewers find an out-of-the-way location, such as a curbstone, and fill out the survey themselves rather than follow procedures with an actual respondent. Because of the potential for such falsification, data validation is an important step in the data acquisition process.

Most marketing research professionals will target between 10 and 30 percent of completed interviews for "callbacks." Specifically for telephone, mail, and personal interviews, a certain percentage of respondents from the completed interviews will be recontacted by the research firm to make sure the interview was conducted correctly. Normally through telephone recontact, respondents will be asked several short questions as a way of validating the returned interview. Generally, the process of validation covers five areas:

1. **Fraud.** Was the person actually interviewed, or was the interview falsified? Did the interviewer contact the respondent simply to get a name and address, and then proceed to fabricate responses? Did the interviewer use a friend to obtain the necessary information?

2. **Screening.** Many times an interview must be conducted only with qualified respondents. To ensure accuracy of the data collected, many respondents will be screened according to some preselected criteria, such as household income level, recent purchase of a specific product or brand, or even sex or age. For example, the interview procedure may require that only female heads of households with an annual household income of $25,000 or more be interviewed. In this case, a validation callback would verify each of these factors.

3. **Procedure.** In many marketing research projects it is critical that data be collected according to a specific procedure. For example, many customer exit interviews must occur in a designated place as the respondent leaves a certain retail establishment. In this particular example a validation callback may be necessary to ensure the interview took place at the proper setting, not some social gathering area like a party or a park.

4. **Completeness.** In order to speed through the data collection process, an interviewer may ask the respondent only a few of the questions. In such cases, the interviewer asks the respondent a few questions from the beginning of the questionnaire and then skips to the end, omitting questions from other sections. The interviewer may then make up answers to the remaining questions. To determine if the interview is valid, the researcher could recontact a sample of respondents and ask about questions from different parts of the questionnaire.

5. **Courtesy.** Respondents should be treated with courtesy and respect during the interviewing process. Situations can occur, however, where the interviewer may inject a tone of negativity into the interviewing process. To ensure a positive image, respondent callbacks are common to determine whether the interviewer was courteous. Other aspects of the interviewer checked during callbacks include appearance, communication, and interpersonal skills.

◀◼ Editing and Coding

Following validation, the data must be edited for mistakes. **Editing** is the process of checking the data for mistakes made by either the interviewer or the respondent. By scanning each completed interview, the researcher can check several areas of concern: (1) asking the proper questions, (2) accurate recording of answers, (3) correct screening of respondents, and (4) complete and accurate recording of open-ended questions.

Asking the Proper Questions

One aspect of the editing process especially important to interviewing methods is to make certain the proper questions were asked of the respondent. As part of the editing process, the researcher will check to make sure all respondents were asked the proper questions. In cases where they were not, respondents are recontacted to obtain a response to omitted questions.

Accurate Recording of Answers

Completed questionnaires sometimes have missing information. The interviewer may have accidentally skipped a question or not recorded it in the proper location. With a careful check of all questionnaires, these problems can be identified. In such cases, if it is possible, respondents are recontacted and the omitted responses recorded.

Correct Screening Questions

The first three items on the questionnaire in Exhibit 11.2 are actually screening questions that determine whether the respondent is eligible to complete the survey. During the editing phase, the researcher makes certain only qualified respondents were included. It is also critical in the editing process to establish that the questions were asked and (for self-administered surveys) answered in the proper sequence. If the proper sequence is not followed, the respondent must be recontacted to verify the accuracy of the recorded data.

Responses to Open-Ended Questions

Responses to open-ended questions often provide very meaningful data. Open-ended questions may provide greater insight into the research questions than forced-choice questions. A major part of editing the answers to open-ended questions is interpretation. Exhibit 11.3 shows some typical responses to an open-ended question and thus points to problems associated with interpreting these questions. For example, one response to the question, "Why are you coming to the Santa Fe Grill more often?" is simply, "They have good service." This answer by itself is not sufficient to determine what the respondent means by "good service." The interviewer needed to probe for a more specific response. For example, are the employees friendly, helpful, courteous? Do they appear neat and clean? Do they smile when taking an order? Probes such as these would enable the researcher to better interpret the "good service" answer. In cases such as these, the individual doing the editing must use judgment in classifying responses. At some point the responses must be placed in standard categories. Answers that are incomplete are considered useless.

The Coding Process

Coding involves grouping and assigning values to responses to the survey questions. It is the assignment of numerical values to each individual response for each question on the survey. Typically, the codes are numerical—a number from 0 to 9—because numbers are

Exhibit 11.2	The Santa Fe Grill Questionnaire

Hello. My name is _____ and I work for DSS Research. We are talking to individuals today/tonight about dining out habits.

"Do you regularly eat out at casual dining restaurants?"   __ Yes   __ No

"Have you eaten at other Mexican restaurants in the last six months?"   __ Yes   __ No

"Is your gross annual household income $15,000 or more?"   __ Yes   __ No

If respondent answers "Yes" to all three questions, then say:

We would like you to answer a few questions about your experience today/tonight at the Santa Fe Grill restaurant, and we hope you will be willing to give us your opinions. The survey will only take a few minutes and it will be very helpful to management in better serving its customers.

If the person says yes, give them a clipboard with the questionnaire on it, briefly explain the questionnaire, and show them where to complete the survey.

DINING OUT SURVEY

Please read all questions carefully. If you do not understand a question, ask the interviewer to help you. In the first section a number of statements are given about interests and opinions. Using a scale from 1 to 7, with 7 being "Strongly Agree" and 1 being "Strongly Disagree," please indicate the extent to which you agree or disagree a particular statement describes you. Circle only one number for each statement.

Section 1: Life Style Questions

1. I often try new and different things.

   Strongly Disagree   Strongly Agree

   1   2   3   4   5   6   7

2. I like parties with music and lots of talk.

   Strongly Disagree   Strongly Agree

   1   2   3   4   5   6   7

3. People come to me more often than I go to them for information about products.

   Strongly Disagree   Strongly Agree

   1   2   3   4   5   6   7

4. I try to avoid fried foods.

   Strongly Disagree   Strongly Agree

   1   2   3   4   5   6   7

5. I like to go out and socialize with people.

   Strongly Disagree   Strongly Agree

   1   2   3   4   5   6   7

6. Friends and neighbors often come to me for advice about products and brands.

   Strongly Disagree   Strongly Agree

   1   2   3   4   5   6   7

continued

Exhibit 11.2   The Santa Fe Grill Questionnaire, continued

7. I am self-confident about myself and my future.

Strongly Disagree   Strongly Agree

1   2   3   4   5   6   7

8. I usually eat balanced, nutritious meals.

Strongly Disagree   Strongly Agree

1   2   3   4   5   6   7

9. When I see a new product in stores, I often buy it.

Strongly Disagree   Strongly Agree

1   2   3   4   5   6   7

10. I am careful about what I eat.

Strongly Disagree   Strongly Agree

1   2   3   4   5   6   7

11. I often try new brands before my friends and neighbors do.

Strongly Disagree   Strongly Agree

1   2   3   4   5   6   7

Section 2: Perceptions Measures

Listed below is a set of characteristics that could be used to describe the Santa Fe Grill Mexican restaurant. Using a scale from 1 to 7, with 7 being "Strongly Agree" and 1 being "Strongly Disagree," to what extent do you agree or disagree the Santa Fe Grill:

12. has friendly employees

Strongly Disagree   Strongly Agree

1   2   3   4   5   6   7

13. is a fun place to eat

Strongly Disagree   Strongly Agree

1   2   3   4   5   6   7

14. has large size portions

Strongly Disagree   Strongly Agree

1   2   3   4   5   6   7

15. has fresh food

Strongly Disagree   Strongly Agree

1   2   3   4   5   6   7

16. has reasonable prices

Strongly Disagree   Strongly Agree

1   2   3   4   5   6   7

17. has an attractive interior

Strongly Disagree   Strongly Agree

1   2   3   4   5   6   7

Exhibit 11.2 *continued*

18. has excellent food taste

Strongly Disagree   Strongly Agree

1   2   3   4   5   6   7

19. has knowledgeable employees

Strongly Disagree   Strongly Agree

1   2   3   4   5   6   7

20. serves food at the proper temperature

Strongly Disagree   Strongly Agree

1   2   3   4   5   6   7

21. has quick service

Strongly Disagree   Strongly Agree

1   2   3   4   5   6   7

Section 3: Relationship Measures

Please indicate your view on each of the following questions:

22. How satisfied are you with the Santa Fe Grill?

Not Satisfied At All   Very Satisfied

1   2   3   4   5   6   7

23. How likely are you to return to the Santa Fe Grill in the future?

Definitely Will Not Return   Definitely Will Return

1   2   3   4   5   6   7

24. How likely are you to recommend Santa Fe Grill to a friend?

Definitely Will Not Recommend   Definitely Will Recommend

1   2   3   4   5   6   7

25. How often do you patronize the Santa Fe Grill?

1 = Occasionally (Less than once a month)
2 = Frequently (1–3 times a month)
3 = Very Frequently (4 or more times a month)

Section 4: Selection Factors

Listed below are some factors (reasons) many people use in selecting a restaurant where they want to dine. Think about your visits to casual dining restaurants in the last three months and please rank each attribute from 1 to 4, with 1 being the most important reason for selecting the restaurant and 4 being the least important reason. There can be no ties so make sure you rank each attribute with a different number.

Attribute	Ranking
26. Prices	
27. Food Quality	
28. Atmosphere	
29. Service	

continued

Exhibit 11.2   The Santa Fe Grill Questionnaire, *continued*

Section 5: Classification Questions

Please circle the number that classifies you best.

30. Distance Driven

1	Less than 1 mile
2	1–3 miles
3	More than 3 Miles

31. Do your recall seeing any advertisements in the last 60 days for the Santa Fe Grill?

0	No
1	Yes

32. Your Gender

0	Male
1	Female

33. Number of Children at Home

1	None
2	1–2
3	More than 2 children at home

34. Your Age in Years

1	18–25
2	26–34
3	35–49
4	50–59
5	60 and Older

35. Your Annual Gross Household Income

1	$15,000–$30,000
2	$30,001–$50,000
3	$50,001–$75,000
4	$75,001–$100,000
5	More than $100,000

Thank you very much for your help.

Interviewer: Check answers to questions 22, 23, and 24. If respondent answers 1, 2, or 3 ask the following questions.

You indicated you are not too satisfied with the Santa Fe Grill. Could you please tell me why?

Record answer here:

_____

You indicated you are not likely to return to the Santa Fe Grill. Could you please tell me why?

Record answer here:

_____

You indicated you are not likely to recommend the Santa Fe Grill. Could you please tell me why?

Record answer here:

_____

Exhibit 11.2	*continued*

Could I please have your name and phone number for verification purposes?

_____   _____
          Name   Phone #

I hereby attest that this is a true and honest interview and complete to the best of my knowledge. I guarantee that all information relating to this interview shall be kept strictly confidential.

_____   _____
    Interviewer's Signature   Date and Time completed

quick and easy to input and computers work better with numbers than alphanumerical values. Like editing, coding can be tedious if certain issues are not addressed prior to collecting the data. A well-planned and constructed questionnaire can reduce the amount of time spent on coding and increase the accuracy of the process if it is incorporated into the design of the questionnaire. The Santa Fe Grill questionnaire shown in Exhibit 11.2 has built-in coded responses for all questions except the open-ended ones asked by the interviewer at the end of the survey. In the "Lifestyle Questions," for example, a respondent has the option of responding from 1 to 7, based on his or her level of agreement or disagreement

Exhibit 11.3	Responses to Open-Ended Questions

10. Why are you eating at the Santa Fe Grill more often?

- They have good service.
- Found out how good the food is.
- I enjoy the food.
- We just moved here and where we lived there were no good Mexican restaurants.
- That part of town is building up so fast.
- They have a couple of offers in the newspaper.
- It is right beside where my husband works.
- Tastes better—grilled.
- They started giving better value packages.
- We really like their chicken sandwiches, so we go more often now.
- The good food.
- Only because they only put one in within the last year.
- Just opened lately.
- It is located right by Wal-Mart.
- Just moved into area and they have good food.
- There is one in the area where I work.

with a particular statement. Thus, if the respondent circled "5" as his or her choice, then the value of "5" would become the coded value for a particular question.

In contrast, open-ended questions pose unique problems to the coding process. An exact list of potential responses cannot be prepared ahead of time for open-ended questions. Thus, a coding process must be prepared after data is collected. But the value of the information obtained from open-ended questions often outweighs the problems of coding the responses.

Researchers typically use a four-step process to develop codes for responses. The procedure begins by generating a list of as many potential responses as possible. Responses are then assigned values within a range determined by the actual number of separate responses identified. When reviewing responses to the open-ended questions, the researcher attaches a value from the developed response list. If responses do not appear on the list, the researcher adds a new response and corresponding value to the list or places the response into one of the existing categories.

Consolidation of responses is the second phase of the four-step process. Exhibit 11.4 illustrates several actual responses to the question, "Why are you dining less frequently at the _____ restaurant?" Four of these—related to not liking the food—can be consolidated into a single response category because they all have the same shared meaning. Developing consolidated categories is a subjective decision that should be made only by an experienced research analyst with input from the project's sponsor.

Exhibit 11.4	Illustration of Response Consolidation for Open-Ended Questions

Q10a. Why are you dining less frequently at the _____ restaurant?

Respondent # 72113

- I am a state employee. I look for bargains. Need more specials.
- Because I'm no longer close to a _____.

Respondent # 72114

- I do not like the food.

Respondent # 72116

- They never get my order right.
- I got tired of the hamburgers. I don't like the spices.
- Prices are too high.
- Family doesn't like it.
- My husband didn't like the way the burgers tasted.
- They should give more with their combos than they do. More fries.
- Because they always got our orders wrong and they are rude.
- The order is never right.
- Health reasons.
- I work longer hours, and don't think about food.
- Cannot eat the food.
- We started eating at _____.
- The location of my work moved so I am not near a _____.

The third step of the process is to assign a numerical value as a code. While at first this may appear to be a simple task, the structure of the questionnaire and the number of responses per question need to be considered. For example, if a question has more than 10 responses, then double-digit codes need to be used, such as "01," "02," . . . "11." Another good practice is to assign higher-value codes to positive responses than to negative responses. For instance, "no" responses are coded 0 and "yes" responses coded 1; "dislike" responses are coded as 1 and "like" responses coded as 5. Coding makes subsequent analysis easier. For example, the researcher will find it easier to interpret means or averages if higher values occur as the average moves from "dislike" to "like."

If correlation or regression is used in data analysis, then for categorical data there is another consideration. The researcher may wish to create "dummy" variables in which the coding is "0" and "1." To learn more about dummy coding, go to our Web site at **www.mhhe.com/hairessentials1e**.

Assigning a coded value to missing data is very important. For example, if a respondent completes a questionnaire except for the very last question and a recontact is not possible, how do you code the response to the unanswered question? A good practice in this situation is to first consider how the response is going to be used in the analysis phase. In certain types of analysis, if the response is left blank and has no numerical value, the entire questionnaire (not just the individual question) will be deleted. The best way to handle the coding of omitted responses is first to check on how your data analysis software treats missing data. This should be the guide for determining whether omissions are coded or left blank.

The fourth step in the coding process is to assign a coded value to each response. This is probably the most tedious process because it is done manually. Unless an optical scanning approach is used to enter the data, this task is almost always necessary to avoid problems in the data entry phase.

Each questionnaire is assigned a numerical value. The numerical value typically is a three-digit code if there are fewer than 1,000 questionnaires to code, and a four-digit code if there are 1,000 or more. For example, if 452 completed questionnaires were returned, the first would be coded 001, the second 002, and so on, finishing with 452.

▰ Data Entry

Data entry Those tasks involved with the direct input of the coded data into some specified software package that ultimately allows the research analyst to manipulate and transform the data into useful information.

Data entry follows validation, editing, and coding. **Data entry** is the procedure used to enter the data into a computer file for subsequent data analysis. Data entry is the direct input of the coded data into a file that enables the research analyst to manipulate and transform the data into useful information.

There are several ways of entering coded data into an electronic file. With CATI and Internet surveys, the data are entered simultaneously with data collection and a separate step is not required. However, if the data are entered manually, most likely they are entered using a personal computer (PC) and a spreadsheet interface.

Scanning technology also can be used to enter data. This approach enables the computer to read alphabetic, numeric, and special character codes through a scanning device. Respondents use a number two pencil to fill in responses, which are then scanned directly into a computer file.

Online surveys are becoming increasingly popular for completing marketing research studies. Indeed, online surveys now represent almost 40 percent of all data collection approaches. Not only are they often faster to complete, but they eliminate entirely the data entry process.

Error Detection

Error detection identifies errors from data entry or other sources. The first step in error detection is to determine whether the software used for data entry and tabulation performs "error edit routines" that identify the wrong type of data. For example, say that for a particular field on a given data record, only the codes of 1 or 2 should appear. An error edit routine can display an error message on the data output if any number other than 1 or 2 has been entered. Such routines can be quite thorough. A coded value can be rejected if it is too large or too small for a particular scaled item on the questionnaire. In some instances, a separate error edit routine can be established for every item on the questionnaire.

Another approach to error detection is for the researcher to review a printed representation of the entered data. Exhibit 11.5, for example, shows the coded values for observations 398–427 in the Santa Fe Grill database. In this example the top row indicates

---

Exhibit 11.5 SPSS Data View of Coded Values for Santa Fe Grill Observations

Santa Fe Grill database_N = 427_new.sav - SPSS Data Editor

File　Edit　View　Data　Transform　Analyze　Graphs　Utilities　Window　Help

1 : id　1

	id	x_s1	x_s2	x_s3	x1	x2	x3	x4	x5	x6	x7	x8	x9
398	398	1	1	1	6	3	4	5	5	4	3	5	5
399	399	1	1	1	4	3	3	4	3	3	3	5	5
400	400	1	1	1	6	4	5	3	4	5	4	3	6
401	401	1	1	1	6	4	5	3	4	5	4	3	6
402	402	1	1	1	4	3	4	2	.	4	4	2	7
403	403	.	1	1	3	4	7	3	4	7	5	5	2
404	404	1	1	1	6	.	.	4	.	.	4	4	6
405	405	1	1	1	4	4	5	2	4	5	.	3	5
406	406	1	1	1	4	6	7	2	4	7	4	.	7
407	407	1	1	.	5	4	5	3	2	5	2	3	.
408	408	.	1	1	6	.	6	4	4	.	4	5	4
409	409	1	1	1	.	5	6	2	5	5	2	2	7
410	410	1	1	1	5	5	6	3	4	6	2	2	7
411	411	1	.	1	4	4	5	3	5	5	5	4	5
412	412	1	1	1	6	3	4	4	5	4	5	5	5
413	413	1	1	1	5	2	3	4	4	3	4	5	4
414	414	1	1	1	6	5	7	3	5	7	5	4	7
415	415	.	1	1	.	3	4	4	2	.	2	.	6
416	416	1	1	1	6	5	7	4	4	6	4	4	7
417	417	1	1	1	5	5	.	.	.	7	4	.	4
418	418	1	1	1	6	5	6	4	4	5	.	5	4
419	419	1	1	1	4	2	3	3	3	3	5	5	.
420	420	1	.	1	6	4	5	3	5	5	4	2	6
421	421	1	1	1	5	4	6	4	3	6	4	5	5
422	422	1	1	.	.	2	3	.	3	3	5	5	3
423	423	1	1	1	6	6	.	.	5	.	.	.	.
424	424	1	1	1	4	5	7	4	4	6	6	6	4
425	425	1	1	1	5	3	3	3	.	3	4	4	3
426	426	1	1	1	6	5	.	2	2	6	.	3	7
427	427	1	1	1	6	3	4	4	5	4	3	3	6

Data View　Variable View

SPSS Processor is ready

Start　Eudora　Eudora　Microsoft Word　Santa Fe Grill data...　9:13 AM

the variable names assigned to each data field (i.e., "id" is the label for the questionnaire number, "x_s1" represents the first screening question, x1 is the first question on the survey after the three screening questions, etc.). The numbers in the columns are the coded values that were entered. The dots indicate missing responses. While the process is somewhat tedious, the analyst can view the actual entered data for accuracy and can tell where any errors occurred.

Data Tabulation

Tabulation The simple process of counting the number of observations (cases) that are classified into certain categories.

One-way tabulation Categorization of single variables existing in a study.

Cross-tabulation Simultaneously treating two or more variables in the study; categorizing the number of respondents who have answered two or more questions consecutively.

Tabulation is counting the number of responses in categories. Two common forms of tabulation are used in marketing research projects: one-way tabulation and cross-tabulations. A **one-way tabulation** looks at single variables in the study. In most cases, a one-way tabulation shows the number of respondents who gave each possible answer to each question on the questionnaire. The number of one-way tabulations is determined by the number of variables measured in the study.

Cross-tabulation simultaneously compares two or more nominal variables in the study. Cross-tabulations categorize the number of responses to two or more questions, thus showing the relationship between those two variables. For example, a cross-tabulation could show the number of male and female respondents who spent more than $7.00 eating at McDonald's versus those who spent less. We show you how to use software to develop cross-tabulations in the next chapter.

One-Way Tabulation

One-way tabulations serve several purposes. First, they can be used to determine the amount of nonresponse to individual questions. Based on the coding scheme used for missing data, one-way tabulations identify the number of respondents who did not answer various questions on the questionnaire. Second, one-way tabulations can be used to locate simple blunders in data entry.

If a specific range of codes has been established for a given response to a question, say 1 through 5, a one-way tabulation can illustrate if an inaccurate code was entered, say, a 7 or 8. It does this by providing a list of all responses to the particular question. In addition, means, standard deviations, and related descriptive statistics often are determined from a one-way tabulation. Finally, one-way tabulations are also used to communicate the results of the research project. One-way tabulations can profile sample respondents, identify characteristics that distinguish between groups (for example, heavy users versus light users), and show the percentage of respondents who respond differently to different situations, for instance, the percentage of people who purchase fast food from drive-thru windows versus those who use dine-in facilities.

The most basic way to illustrate a one-way tabulation is to construct a one-way frequency table. A one-way frequency table shows the number of respondents who answered each possible response to a question given the available alternatives. An example of a one-way frequency table is shown in Exhibit 11.6, which shows which Mexican restaurants the respondents dined at in the last 30 days. The information indicates that 99 individuals (20.1 percent) ate at Superior Grill in the last 30 days, 74 (15.0 percent) ate at Mamacita's, 110 (22.3 percent) ate at Ninfa's, and so on. Typically, a computer printout will be prepared with one-way frequency tables for each question on the survey. In

Exhibit 11.6   Example of One-Way Frequency Distribution

File   Edit   View   Insert   Format   Analyze   Graphs   Utilities   Window   Help

Restaurant

		Frequency	Percent	Valid Percent	Cumulative Percent
Valid	Superior Grill	99	20.1	20.1	20.1
	Mamacitas	74	15.0	15.0	35.1
	Ninfa's	110	22.3	22.3	57.4
	Moe's southwestern Grill	47	9.5	9.5	66.9
	Santa Fe Grill	38	7.7	7.7	74.6
	Jose's	36	7.3	7.3	81.9
	Papacita's	32	6.5	6.5	88.4
	Other	24	4.9	4.9	93.3
	None	23	4.7	4.7	98.0
	Don't Remember	10	2.0	2.0	100.0
	Total	493	100.0	100.0	

addition to listing the number of responses, one-way frequency tables also identify missing data and show valid percentages and summary statistics. In reviewing the output, look for the following:

1. *Indications of missing data.* One-way frequency tables show the number of missing responses for each question. As shown in Exhibit 11.7, a total of 27 respondents, or 6.3 percent of the sample, did not respond to how frequently they patronized the Santa Fe Grill. It is important to recognize the actual number of missing responses when estimating percentages from a one-way frequency table. In order to establish valid percentages, missing responses must be removed from the calculation.

2. *Determining valid percentages.* To determine valid percentages one must remove incomplete surveys or particular questions. For example, the one-way frequency table in Exhibit 11.7 actually constructs valid percentages (the third column). While the total number of responses for this particular question was 427, only 400 are used to develop the valid percentage of response across categories because the 27 missing responses were removed from the calculations.

3. *Summary statistics.* Finally, one-way frequency tables illustrate a variety of summary statistics. In Exhibit 11.7 the summary statistics for question X25 are the mean, median, mode, and standard deviation. These statistics help the researcher

| Exhibit 11.7 | One-Way Frequency Table Illustrating Missing Data |

Output1 - SPSS Viewer

File Edit View Insert Format Analyze Graphs Utilities Window Help

Frequencies

Statistics

X25 -- Frequency of Patronizing Santa Fe Grill

N	Valid	400
	Missing	27
Mean		3.27
Median		3.00
Mode		3
Std. Deviation		1.302

X25 -- Frequency of Patronizing Santa Fe Grill

		Frequency	Percent	Valid Percent	Cumulative Percent
Valid	1 Very Infrequently	49	11.5	12.3	12.3
	2 Somewhat Infrequently	62	14.5	15.5	27.8
	3 Occasionally	111	26.0	27.8	55.5
	4 Somewhat Frequently	88	20.6	22.0	77.5
	5 Very Frequently	90	21.1	22.5	100.0
	Total	400	93.7	100.0	
Missing	System	27	6.3		
Total		427	100.0		

better understand the average responses. For example, the mean of 3.27 indicates that many respondents are occasional patrons of the Santa Fe Grill. Note that variable X25 ranges from one to five, with larger numbers indicating higher patronage frequency.

Descriptive Statistics

Descriptive statistics are used to summarize and describe the data obtained from a sample of respondents. Two types of measures are often used to describe data. One of those is measures of central tendency and the other is measures of dispersion. Both are described in detail in the next chapter. For now we refer you to Exhibit 11.8, which provides an overview of the major types of descriptive statistics used by marketing researchers.

Exhibit 11.8	Overview of Descriptive Statistics

To clarify descriptive statistics, we use a simple data set to illustrate each of the major ones. Assume that data has been collected from 10 students about satisfaction with their Apple iPod. Satisfaction is measured on a 7-point scale with the end points labeled "Highly Satisfied = 7" and "Not Satisfied at All = 1." The results of this survey are shown below by respondent.

Respondent	Satisfaction Rating
1	7
2	5
3	6
4	4
5	6
6	5
7	7
8	5
9	4
10	5

Descriptive Statistics

Frequency = Number of times a number (response) is in the data set

To compute it, count how many times the number is in the data set. For example, the number 7 is in the data set twice.

Frequency distribution = Summary of how many times each possible response to a question appears in the data set

To develop a frequency distribution, count how many times each number appears in the data set and make a table that shows the results. For example, create a chart like the one shown below:

Satisfaction Rating	Count
7	2
6	2
5	4
4	2
3	0
2	0
1	0
Total	10

Percentage distribution = Result of converting a frequency distribution into percentages

To develop a percentage distribution, divide each frequency count for each rating by the total count.

Satisfaction Rating	Count	Percentage
7	2	20%
6	2	20
5	4	40
4	2	20
3	0	0
2	0	0
1	0	0
Total	10	100%

Exhibit 11.8	*continued*

Cumulative percentage distribution = Each individual percentage added to the previous to get a total

To develop a cumulative percentage distribution, arrange the percentages in descending order and sum the percentages one at a time and show the result.

Satisfaction Rating	Count	Percentage	Cumulative Percentage	
7	2	20%	20	
6	2	20	40	
5	4	40	80	← median
4	2	20	100%	
3	0	0		
2	0	0		
1	0	0		
Total	10	100%		

Mean = Arithmetic average of all the raw responses

To calculate the mean, add up all the values of a distribution of responses and divide the total by the number of valid responses.

The mean is: $(7 + 5 + 6 + 4 + 6 + 5 + 7 + 5 + 4 + 5) = 54 / 10 = 5.4$

Median = Descriptive statistic that splits the data into a hierarchical pattern where half the data is above the median value and half is below

To determine the median, look at the cumulative percentage distribution and find either where the cumulative percentage is equal to 50 percent or where it includes 50 percent. The median is marked in the table above.

Mode = Most frequently occurring response to a given set of questions

To determine the mode, find the number which has the largest frequency (count). In the responses above, the number 5 has the largest count and is the mode.

Range = Statistic that represents the spread of the data and is the distance between the largest and the smallest values of a frequency distribution

To calculate the range, subtract the lowest rating point from the highest rating point and the difference is the range. For the above data, the maximum number is 7 and the minimum number is 4 so the range is $7 - 4 = 3$.

Standard deviation = Measure of the average dispersion of the values in a set of responses about their mean. (It provides an indication of how similar or dissimilar the numbers are in the set of responses.)

To calculate the standard deviation, subtract the mean from the square of each number and sum them. Then divide that sum by the total number of responses minus one, and then take the square root of the result.

Graphical Illustration of Data

The next logical step following development of frequency tables is to translate them into graphical illustrations. Graphical illustrations can be very powerful for communicating key research results generated from preliminary data analysis. We discuss graphical illustration of data using bar charts, pie charts, and similar techniques in Chapter 14.

MARKETING RESEARCH IN ACTION
Deli Depot

In this chapter we have shown you simple approaches to examine data. In later chapters, we show you more advanced statistical techniques to analyze data. The most important consideration in deciding how to analyze data is to enable businesses to use data to make better decisions. To help students more easily understand the best ways to examine data, we have prepared several databases that can be applied to various research problems. This case is about Deli Depot, a sandwich restaurant. The database is available at **www.mhhe.com/ hairessentials1e**.

Deli Depot sells cold and hot sandwiches, soup and chili, yogurt, and pies and cookies. The restaurant is positioned in the fast-food market to compete directly with Subway and similar sandwich restaurants. Its competitive advantages include special sauces on sandwiches, supplementary menu items like soup and pies, and quick delivery within specified zones. As part of their marketing research class, students conducted a survey for the owner of a local restaurant near their campus.

The students obtained permission to conduct interviews with customers inside the restaurant. Information was collected for 17 questions. Customers were first asked their perceptions of the restaurant on six factors (variables X1–X6) and then asked to rank the same six factors in terms of their importance in selecting a restaurant where they wanted to eat (variables X12–X17). Finally, respondents were asked how satisfied they were with the restaurant, how likely they were to recommend it to a friend, how often they eat there, and how far they drove to eat a meal at Deli Depot. Interviewers recorded the sex of the respondents without asking it. The variables, sample questions, and their coding are shown below.

Performance Perceptions Variables

The performance perceptions were measured as follows.

Listed below is a set of characteristics that could be used to describe Deli Depot. Using a scale from 1 to 10, with 10 being "Strongly Agree" and 1 being "Strongly Disagree," to what extent do you agree or disagree that Deli Depot has:

    X1—Friendly Employees
    X2—Competitive Prices
    X3—Competent Employees
    X4—Excellent Food Quality
    X5—Wide Variety of Food
    X6—Fast Service

If a respondent chose a 10 on Friendly Employees, this would indicate strong agreement that Deli Depot has friendly employees. On the other hand, if a respondent chose a 1 for Fast Service, this would indicate strong disagreement and the perception that Deli Depot offers very slow service.

Classification Variables

Data for the classification variables was asked at the end of the survey, but in the database it is recorded as variables X7–X11. Responses were coded as follows:

X7—Gender (1 = Male; 0 = Female)

X8—Recommend to Friend (7 = Definitely Recommend; 1 = Definitely Not Recommend)

X9—Satisfaction Level (7 = Highly Satisfied; 1 = Not Very Satisfied)

X10—Usage Level (1 = Heavy User—eats at Deli Depot 2 or more times each week; 0 = Light User—eats at Deli Depot fewer than 2 times a week)

X11—Market Area (1 = Came from within 1 mile; 2 = Came from 1–3 miles; 3 = Came from more than 3 miles)

Selection Factor Rankings

Data for the selection factors were collected as follows.

Listed below is a set of attributes (reasons) many people use when selecting a fast-food restaurant to eat at. Regarding your visits to fast-food restaurants in the last 30 days, please rank each attribute from 1 to 6, with 6 being the most important reason for selecting the fast-food restaurant and 1 being the least important reason. There can be no ties, so make sure you rank each attribute with a different number.

X12—Friendly Employees

X13—Competitive Prices

X14—Competent Employees

X15—Excellent Food Quality

X16—Wide Variety of Food

X17—Fast Service

The questionnaire for the Deli Depot survey is shown in Exhibit 11.9.

Hands-On Exercise

1. How would you improve the Deli Depot survey and questionnaire?
2. What are the competitive advantages and disadvantages of Deli Depot over Subway?

Exhibit 11.9 Deli Depot Questionnaire

Screening and Rapport Questions

Hello. My name is _____ and I work for Decision Analyst, a market research firm in Dallas, Texas. We are talking to people today/tonight about eating out habits.

1. How often do you eat out?"   __ Often   __ Occasionally   __ Seldom
2. "Did you just eat at Deli Depot?"   __ Yes   __ No
3. "Have you completed a restaurant
   questionnaire on Deli Depot before?"   __ Yes   __ No

If respondent answers "Often" or "Occasionally" to the first question, "Yes" to the second question, and "No" to the third question, then say:

We would like you to answer a few questions about your experience today/tonight at Deli Depot, and we hope you will be willing to give us your opinions. The survey will only take a few minutes and it will be very helpful to management in better serving its customers. We will pay you $5.00 for completing the questionnaire.

If the person says yes, give them a clipboard with the questionnaire on it, briefly explain the questionnaire, and show them where to complete the survey.

DINING OUT SURVEY

Please read all questions carefully. If you do not understand a question, ask the interviewer to help you.

Section 1: Perceptions Measures

Listed below is a set of characteristics that could be used to describe Deli Depot. Using a scale from 1 to 10, with 10 being "Strongly Agree" and 1 being "Strongly Disagree", to what extent do you agree or disagree that Deli Depot has: Circle the correct response.

1. Friendly Employees

   Strongly Disagree — Strongly Agree

   1 2 3 4 5 6 7 8 9 10

2. Competitive Prices

   Strongly Disagree — Strongly Agree

   1 2 3 4 5 6 7 8 9 10

3. Competent Employees

   Strongly Disagree — Strongly Agree

   1 2 3 4 5 6 7 8 9 10

4. Excellent Food Quality

   Strongly Disagree — Strongly Agree

   1 2 3 4 5 6 7 8 9 10

5. Wide Variety of Food

   Strongly Disagree — Agree Strongly

   1 2 3 4 5 6 7 8 9 10

6. Fast Service

   Strongly Disagree — Strongly Agree

   1 2 3 4 5 6 7 8 9 10

Section 2: Classification Variables

Circle the response that describes you.

7. Your Gender   1 Male
                       0 Female

Exhibit 11.9 *continued*

8. How likely are you to recommend Deli Depot
to a friend?

	Definitely	Definitely
	Not Recommend	Recommend
	1 2 3 4 5 6 7	

9. How satisfied are you with Deli Depot?

	Not Very	Highly
	Satisfied	Satisfied
	1 2 3 4 5 6 7	

10. How often do you patronize Deli Depot?

1 = eat at Deli Depot 2 or more times each week.

0 = eat at Deli Depot fewer than 2 times each week.

11. How far did you drive to get to Deli Depot?

1 = came from within one mile

2 = 1–3 miles

3 = came from more than 3 miles

Section 3: Selection Factors

Listed below is a set of attributes (reasons) many people use when selecting a fast-food restaurant to eat at. Regarding your visits to fast-food restaurants in the last 30 days, please rank each attribute from 1 to 6, with 6 being the most important reason for selecting the restaurant and 1 being the least important reason. There can be no ties so make sure you rank each attribute with a different number.

Attribute	Ranking
12. Friendly Employees	
13. Competitive Prices	
14. Competent Employees	
15. Excellent Food Quality	
16. Wide Variety of Food	
17. Fast Service	

Thank you very much for your help. Please give your questionnaire to the interviewer and you will be given your $5.00.

Summary

Describe the process for data preparation and analysis.

The value of marketing research is its ability to provide accurate decision-making information to the user. To accomplish this, the data must be converted into usable information or knowledge. After collecting data through the appropriate method, the task becomes one of ensuring that the data provides meaning and value. Data preparation is the first part of the process of transforming data into useful knowledge. This process involves several steps: (1) data validation, (2) editing and coding, (3) data entry, (4) error detection, and (5) data tabulation. Data analysis follows data preparation and facilitates proper interpretation of the findings.

Discuss validation, editing, and coding of survey data.

Data validation attempts to determine whether surveys, interviews, or observations were conducted correctly and are free from fraud. In recontacting selected respondents, the researcher asks whether the interview (1) was falsified, (2) was conducted with a qualified respondent, (3) took place in the proper procedural setting, (4) was completed correctly and accurately, and (5) was accomplished in a courteous manner. The editing process involves scanning of interviews or questionnaire responses to determine whether the proper questions were asked, the answers were recorded according to the instructions given, and the screening questions were executed prop-

erly, as well as whether open-ended questions were recorded accurately. Once edited, the questionnaires are coded by assigning numerical values to all responses. Coding is the process of providing numeric labels to the data so they can be entered into a computer for subsequent statistical analysis.

Explain data entry procedures as well as how to detect errors.

There are several methods for entering coded data into a computer. First is the PC keyboard. Data also can be entered through terminals having touch-screen capabilities, or through the use of a handheld electronic pointer or light pen. Finally, data can be entered through a scanner using optical character recognition. Data entry errors can be detected through the use of error edit routines in the data entry software. Another approach is to visually scan the actual data after it has been entered.

Describe data tabulation and analysis approaches.

Two common forms of data tabulation are used in marketing research. A one-way tabulation indicates the number of respondents who gave each possible answer to each question on a questionnaire. Cross-tabulation provides categorization of respondents by treating two or more variables simultaneously. Categorization is based on the number of respondents who have responded to two or more consecutive questions.

Key Terms and Concepts

Review Questions

1. Briefly describe the process of data validation. Specifically, discuss the issues of fraud, screening, procedure, completeness, and courtesy.
2. What are the differences between data validation, data editing, and data coding?
3. Explain the differences between developing codes for open-ended questions and for closed-ended questions.
4. Briefly describe the process of data entry. What changes in technology have simplified this procedure?
5. What is the purpose of a simple one-way tabulation? How does this relate to a one-way frequency table?

Discussion Questions

1. Explain the importance of following the sequence for data preparation and analysis described in Exhibit 11.1.

2. Identify four problems a researcher might find while screening questionnaires and preparing data for analysis.

3. How can data tabulation help researchers better understand and report findings?

4. **SPSS EXERCISE.** Using SPSS and the Deli Depot database, develop frequencies, means, modes, and medians for all the relevant variables on the questionnaire. A description of the Deli Depot case and questionnaire is contained in the *Marketing Research in Action* section of this chapter.

Basic Data Analysis for Quantitative Research

Chapter 12

Learning Objectives   After reading this chapter, you will be able to:

1. Explain measures of central tendency and dispersion.
2. Describe how to test hypotheses using univariate and bivariate statistics.
3. Apply and interpret analysis of variance (ANOVA).
4. Utilize perceptual mapping to present research findings.

Data Analysis Facilitates Smarter Decisions

In his book *Thriving on Chaos,* Tom Peters says, "We are drowning in information and starved for knowledge." Indeed, the amount of information available for business decision making has grown tremendously over the last decade. But until recently, much of that information just disappeared. It either was not used or was discarded because collecting, storing, extracting, and interpreting it was too expensive. Now, decreases in the cost of data collection and storage, development of faster data processors and user–friendly client–server interfaces, and improvements in data analysis and interpretation made possible through data mining enable businesses to convert what had been a "waste by-product" into a new resource to improve business and marketing decisions. The data may come from secondary sources or surveys of customers or be internally generated by enterprise or CRM software, such as SAP. To convert this information into knowledge so it can be useful for decision making, the data must be organized, categorized, analyzed, and shared among company employees.

Data analysis facilitates the discovery of interesting patterns in databases that are difficult to identify and have potential for improving decision making and creating knowledge. Data analysis methods are widely used today for commercial purposes. Fair Isaac & Co. (**www.fairisaac.com**) is an $800 million business built around the commercial use of multivariate statistical techniques. The firm developed a complex analytical model that can accurately predict who will pay bills on time, who will pay late, who will not pay at all, who will file for bankruptcy, and so on. Its models are useful for both the consumer and business-to-business markets. Similarly, the IRS uses data analysis to identify which returns to audit. State Farm uses multivariate statistics to decide whom to sell insurance to, and Progressive Insurance combines multivariate methods with global positioning technology to identify where and how fast you drive so that they can raise your auto insurance premiums if you drive in a hazardous manner.

To make accurate business decisions in today's increasingly complex environment, intricate relationships with many intervening variables must be examined. Sophisticated statistical methods, such as data mining, are powerful analytical techniques used by marketing researchers to examine and better understand these relationships.

Value of Statistical Analysis

Once the data have been collected and prepared for analysis, several statistical procedures can help to better understand the responses. It is difficult to understand the entire set of responses because there are too many numbers to look at. Consequently, almost all data needs summary statistics to describe the information it contains. Basic statistics and descriptive analysis achieve this purpose.

We describe some of the statistics common to almost all research projects in this chapter. First we explain measures of central tendency and dispersion. Next, we discuss the Chi-square statistic to examine cross tabulations, and then the t-statistic for testing differences in means. Finally, the chapter closes with an introduction to analysis of variance, a powerful technique for detecting differences between three or more sample means.

Measures of Central Tendency

Frequency distributions can be useful for examining the different values for a variable. Frequency distribution tables are easy to read and provide a great deal of basic information. There are times, however, when the amount of detail is too great. In such situations the researcher needs a way to summarize and condense all the information in order to get at the underlying meaning. Researchers use descriptive statistics to accomplish this task. The mean, median, and mode are measures of central tendency. These measures locate the center of the distribution. For this reason, the mean, median, and mode are sometimes also called measures of location.

We use variable X25—Frequency of Patronage from the Santa Fe Grill database to illustrate the measures of central tendency (Exhibit 12.1). Looking first at the frequency distribution, note that 400 respondents indicated how frequently they patronize the Santa Fe Grill using a 5-point scale, with 1 = Very Infrequently, 2 = Somewhat Infrequently, 3 = Occasionally, 4 = Somewhat Frequently, and 5 = Very Frequently. The total sample was 427, but 27 respondents did not answer this question and therefore are considered missing data. The numbers in the Percent column are calculated using the total sample size of 427, while the numbers in the Valid % and Cumulative % columns are calculated using the total sample size minus the number of missing responses to this question (427 − 27 = 400).

Mean The arithmetic average of the sample; all values of a distribution of responses are summed and divided by the number of valid responses.

Mean The **mean** is the average value within the distribution and is the most commonly used measure of central tendency. The mean tells us, for example, the average number of cups of coffee the typical student drinks during finals to stay awake. The mean can be calculated when the data scale is either interval or ratio. Generally, the data will show some degree of central tendency, with most of the responses distributed close to the mean.

The mean is a very robust measure of central tendency. It is fairly insensitive to data values being added or deleted. The mean can be subject to distortion, however, if extreme values are included in the distribution. For example, suppose you ask four students how many cups of coffee they drink in a single day. Respondent answers are as follows: Respondent A = 1 cup; Respondent B = 10 cups; Respondent C = 5 cups; and Respondent D = 6 cups. Let's also assume that we know that respondents A and B are males and respondents B and C are females and we want to compare consumption of coffee between males and females. Looking at the males first (Respondents A and B), we calculate the mean number of cups to be 5.5 (1 + 10 = 11/2 = 5.5). Similarly, looking at the females next (Respondents C and D), we calculate the mean number of cups to be 5.5 (5 + 6 = 11/2 = 5.5). If we look only at the mean number of cups of coffee consumed by males and females, we would

Exhibit 12.1 Output for Mean, Median, and Mode for X25—Frequency of Patronage

Output1 - SPSS Viewer

File Edit View Insert Format Analyze Graphs Utilities Window Help

➡ **Frequencies**

Statistics

X25 -- Frequency of Patronizing Santa Fe Grill

N	Valid	400
	Missing	27
Mean		3.27
Median		3.00
Mode		3
Std. Deviation		1.302

X25 -- Frequency of Patronizing Santa Fe Grill

		Frequency	Percent	Valid Percent	Cumulative Percent
Valid	Very Infrequently	49	11.5	12.3	12.3
	Somewhat Infrequently	62	14.5	15.5	27.8
	Occasionally	111	26.0	27.8	55.5
	Somewhat Frequently	88	20.6	22.0	77.5
	Very Frequently	90	21.1	22.5	100.0
	Total	400	93.7	100.0	
Missing	System	27	6.3		
Total		427	100.0		

conclude there are no differences in the two groups. If we consider the underlying distribution, however, we must conclude there are some differences and the mean in fact distorts our understanding of coffee consumption patterns of males and females.

Mode The most common value in the set of responses to a question; that is, the response most often given to a question.

Mode The **mode** is the value that appears in the distribution most often. For example, the average number of cups of coffee students drink per day during finals may be 5 (the mean), while the number of cups of coffee that most students drink is only 3 (the mode). The mode is the value that represents the highest peak in the distribution's graph. The mode is especially useful as a measure for data that have been somehow grouped into categories. The mode of the data distribution in Exhibit 12.1 is "Occasionally" because when you look in the Frequency column you will see the largest number of responses is 111 for the "Occasionally" label, which has a value of 3.

Median The **median** is the middle value of the distribution when the distribution is ordered in either an ascending or a descending sequence. For example, if you interviewed a sample of students to determine their coffee-drinking patterns during finals, you might find that the median number of cups of coffee consumed is 4. The number of cups of coffee consumed above and below this number would be the same (the median number is the exact middle of the distribution). If the number of data observations is even, the median is generally considered to be the average of the two middle values. If there is an odd number of observations, the median is the middle value. The median is especially useful as a measure of central tendency for ordinal data and for data that is skewed to either the right or left. For example, income data is skewed to the right because there is no upper limit on income.

Each measure of central tendency describes a distribution in its own manner, and each measure has its own strengths and weaknesses. For nominal data, the mode is the best measure. For ordinal data, the median is generally best. For interval or ratio data, the mean is appropriate, except when there are extreme values within the interval or ratio data. In this case, the median and the mode are likely to provide more information about the central tendency of the distribution.

SPSS Applications—Measures of Central Tendency

You can use the Santa Fe Grill database with the SPSS software to calculate measures of central tendency. The SPSS "click-through" sequence is ANALYZE → DESCRIPTIVE STATISTICS → FREQUENCIES. Let's use X25—Frequency of Patronage of Santa Fe Grill as a variable to examine. Click on X25 to highlight it and then on the arrow box for the Variables box to use in your analysis. Next, open the Statistics box and click on Mean, Median, and Mode, and then Continue and OK. The dialog boxes for this sequence are shown in Exhibit 12.2.

Let's look back at the output for the measures of central tendency shown in Exhibit 12.1. In the Statistics table we see the mean is 3.27, the median is 3.00, the mode is 3, and there are 27 observations with missing data. Recall that this variable is measured on a 5-point scale, with lower numbers indicating lower frequency of patronage and larger numbers indicating higher frequency. The three measures of central tendency can all be different within the same distribution, as described above in the coffee-drinking example. But it also is possible that all three measures can be the same. In our example, the median and the mode are the same, but the mean is different.

Measures of Dispersion

Measures of central tendency often do not tell the whole story about a distribution of responses. For example, if data have been collected about consumers' attitudes toward a new brand of a product, you could calculate the mean, median, and mode of the distribution of answers. However, you might also want to know if most of the respondents had similar opinions. One way to answer this question is to examine the measures of dispersion associated with the distribution of responses to your questions. Measures of dispersion describe how close to the mean or other measure of central tendency the rest of the values in the distribution fall. Two measures of dispersion that describe the variability in a distribution of numbers are the *range* and the *standard deviation*.

Range The **range** defines the spread of the data. It is the distance between the smallest and largest values of the variable. Another way to think about it is that the range identifies the endpoints of the distribution of values. For variable X25—Frequency of Patronizing the

Exhibit 12.2 Dialog Boxes for Calculating the Mean, Median, and Mode

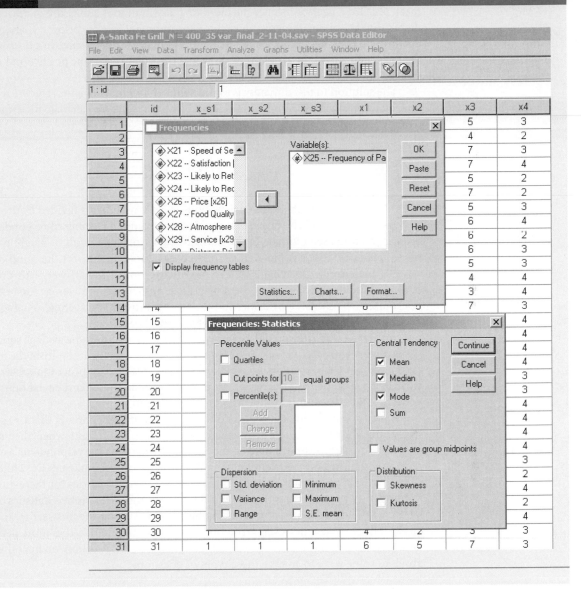

Santa Fe Grill, the range is the difference between the response category 3 (largest value) and response category 1 (smallest value); that is, the range is 2. In this example, since we defined a narrow range of response categories in our survey, the range doesn't tell us much. However, many questions have a much wider range. For example, if we asked how often in a month respondents rent DVDs, or how much they would pay to buy a DVD player that also records songs, the range would be quite informative. In this case, the respondents, not the researchers, would be defining the range by their answers. For this reason, the range is more often used to describe the variability of open-ended questions such as our DVD example. For variable X25—Frequency of Patronizing the Santa Fe Grill, the range is calculated as the distance between the largest and smallest values in the set of responses and equals 2 ($3 - 1 = 2$).

Standard deviation The average distance of the distribution values from the mean.

Standard Deviation The **standard deviation** describes the average distance of the distribution values from the mean. The difference between a particular response and the distribution mean is called a deviation. Since the mean of a distribution is a measure of central tendency, there should be about as many values above the mean as there are below it (particularly if the distribution is symmetrical). Consequently, if we subtracted each value in a distribution from the mean and added them up, the result would be close to zero (the positive and negative results would cancel each other out).

The solution to this difficulty is to square the individual deviations before we add them up (squaring a negative number produces a positive result). To calculate the estimated standard deviation, we use the formula below.

$$\text{Standard deviation (s)} = \sqrt{\frac{\sum_{i=1}^{n} (x_i - \bar{x})^2}{n - 1}}$$

Once the sum of the squared deviations is determined, it is divided by the number of respondents minus 1. The number 1 is subtracted from the number of respondents to help produce an unbiased estimate of the standard deviation. The result of dividing the sum of the squared deviations is the average squared deviation. To convert the result to the same units of measure as the mean, we take the square root of the answer. This produces the estimated standard deviation of the distribution. Sometimes the average squared deviation is also used as a measure of dispersion for a distribution. The average squared deviation, called the **variance,** is used in a number of statistical processes.

Variance The average squared deviation about the mean of a distribution of values.

Since the estimated standard deviation is the square root of the average squared deviations, it represents the average distance of the values in a distribution from the mean. If the estimated standard deviation is large, the responses in a distribution of numbers do not fall very close to the mean of the distribution. If the estimated standard deviation is small, you know that the distribution values are close to the mean.

Another way to think about the estimated standard deviation is that its size tells you something about the level of agreement among the respondents when they answered a particular question. For example, in the Santa Fe Grill database, respondents were asked to rate the restaurant on the friendliness and knowledge of its employees (X12 and X19). We will use the SPSS program later to examine the standard deviations for these questions.

Together with the measures of central tendency, these descriptive statistics can reveal a lot about the distribution of a set of numbers representing the answers to an item on a questionnaire. Often, however, marketing researchers are interested in more detailed questions that involve more than one variable at a time. The next section, on hypothesis testing, provides some ways to analyze those types of questions.

SPSS Applications—Measures of Dispersion

We will use the Santa Fe Grill database with the SPSS software to calculate measures of dispersion, just as we did with the measures of central tendency. Note that to calculate the measures of dispersion we will be using the database with a sample size of 400, so we have eliminated all respondents with missing data. The SPSS click-through sequence is ANALYZE → DESCRIPTIVE STATISTICS → FREQUENCIES. Let's use X22—Satisfaction as a variable to examine. Click on X22 to highlight it and then on the arrow box to move X22 to the Variables box. Next open the Statistics box, go to the Dispersion box in the lower-left-hand corner, and click on Standard deviation, Variance, Range, Minimum and Maximum, and then Continue.

Exhibit 12.3	Output for Measures of Dispersion

Output3 - SPSS Viewer

File Edit View Insert Format Analyze Graphs Utilities Window Help

➡ **Frequencies**

Statistics

X22 -- Satisfaction

N	Valid	400
	Missing	0
Mean		4.64
Median		4.50
Mode		4
Std. Deviation		.955
Variance		.911
Range		3
Minimum		3
Maximum		6

Exhibit 12.3 shows the output for the measures of dispersion for variable X22. First, the highest response on the 7-point scale is 6 (maximum) and the lowest response is 3 (minimum). The range is 3 ($6 - 3 = 3$), the standard deviation is .955, and the variance is .911. A standard deviation of .955 on a 7-point scale tells us the responses are dispersed fairly closely around the mean of 4.64.

Analyzing Relationships of Sample Data

Researchers often wish to test hypotheses about proposed relationships in the sample data. In this section we will discuss several methods used to test hypotheses. We first introduce Chi-square analysis, a statistic used with nominal and ordinal data. We then discuss the *t* distribution and describe its function for testing hypotheses using interval and ordinal data. Before discussing these methods of testing hypotheses, we review some basic statistical terminology.

Sample Statistics and Population Parameters

The purpose of inferential statistics is to make a determination about a population on the basis of a sample from that population. As we explained in Chapter 7, a sample is a subset of the population. For example, if we wanted to determine the average number of cups of coffee consumed per day by students during finals at your university, we would not interview all the students. This would be costly, take a long time, and might be impossible since we may not be able to find them all or some would decline to participate. Instead, if there are 16,000 students at your university, we may decide that a sample of 200 females and 200 males is sufficiently large to provide accurate information about the coffee-drinking habits of all 16,000 students.

You may recall that sample statistics are measures obtained directly from the sample or calculated from the data in the sample. A population parameter is a variable or some sort of measured characteristic of the entire population. Sample statistics are useful in making inferences regarding the population's parameters. Generally, the actual population parameters are unknown since the cost to perform a true census of almost any population is prohibitive.

A frequency distribution displaying the data obtained from the sample is commonly used to summarize the results of the data collection process. When a frequency distribution displays a variable in terms of percentages, then this distribution represents proportions within a population. For example, a frequency distribution showing that 40 percent of the people patronize Burger King indicates the percentage of the population that meets the criterion (eating at Burger King). The proportion may be expressed as a percentage, a decimal value, or a fraction.

Univariate Statistical Tests

Marketing researchers often form hypotheses regarding population characteristics based on sample data. The process typically begins by calculating frequency distributions and averages, and then moves on to actually test the hypotheses. When the hypothesis testing involves examining one variable at a time, it is referred to as a univariate statistical test. When the hypothesis testing involves two variables it is called a bivariate statistical test. We first discuss univariate statistical tests.

Suppose a marketing researcher has agreed to help the Santa Fe Grill owners determine whether customers think their menu prices are reasonable. Respondents have answered this question using a 7-point scale where 1 = "Strongly Disagree" and 7 = "Strongly Agree." The scale is assumed to be an interval scale, and previous research using this measure has shown the responses to be approximately normally distributed.

Researchers must perform a couple of tasks before attempting to answer the question posed above. First, the null and alternative hypotheses must be developed. Then the level of significance for rejecting the null hypothesis and accepting the alternative hypothesis must be selected. At that point, the researcher can conduct the statistical test and determine the answer to the research question.

In this example, the owners believe that customers will perceive the prices of food at the Santa Fe Grill to be about average. If the owners are correct, the mean response to this question will be around 4 (halfway between 1 and 7 on the response scale). The null hypothesis is that the mean of the X16—Reasonable Prices will not be significantly different from 4. Recall the null hypothesis asserts the status quo: any difference from what is thought to be true is due to random sampling. The alternative hypothesis is that the mean of the answers to X16—Reasonable Prices will not be 4. If the alternative hypothesis is true, then there is in fact a true difference between the sample mean we find and the mean the owners expected to find (4).

Assume also that the owners want to be 95 percent certain the mean is not 4. Therefore, the significance level will be set at .05. Using this significance level means that if the survey of Santa Fe Grill customers is conducted many times, the probability of incorrectly rejecting the null hypothesis when it is true would happen less than 5 times out of 100 (.05).

SPSS Application—Univariate Hypothesis Test

Using the SPSS software, you can test the responses in the Santa Fe Grill database to find the answer to the research question posed above. The click-through sequence is: ANALYZE → COMPARE MEANS → ONE-SAMPLE *T*-TEST. When you get to the dialog box, click on

X16—Reasonable Prices to highlight it. Then click on the arrow to move X16 into the Test Variables box. In the box labeled Test Value, enter the number 4. This is the number you want to compare the respondents' answers against. Click on the Options box and enter 95 in the confidence interval box. This is the same as setting the significance level at .05. Then, click on the Continue button and OK to execute the program.

The SPSS output is shown in Exhibit 12.4. The top table is labeled One-Sample Statistics and shows the mean, standard deviation, and standard error for X16—Reasonable Prices (a mean of 4.34 and standard deviation of 1.228). The One-Sample Test table below in the exhibit shows the results of the *t*-test for the null hypothesis that the average response to X16 is 4 (Test Value = 4). The *t*-test statistic is 5.537, and the significance level is .000. This means that the null hypothesis can be rejected and the alternative hypothesis accepted with a high level of confidence from a statistical perspective.

From a practical standpoint, in terms of the Santa Fe Grill, the results of the univariate hypothesis test indicate respondents perceived that menu prices were somewhat reasonable. The mean of 4.34 is somewhat higher than the mid-point of 4 on the 7-point scale (7 = Strongly Agree prices are reasonable). Thus, the Santa Fe Grill owners can conclude that their prices are not perceived as unreasonable. But on the other hand, there is a lot of room to improve between the mean of 4.34 on the 7-point scale and the highest value of 7. This is definitely an area that the owners need to examine.

Bivariate Statistical Tests

In many instances marketing researchers test hypotheses that compare the characteristics of two groups or two variables. For example, the marketing researcher may be interested in

Exhibit 12.4   Univariate Hypothesis Test Using X16—Reasonable Prices

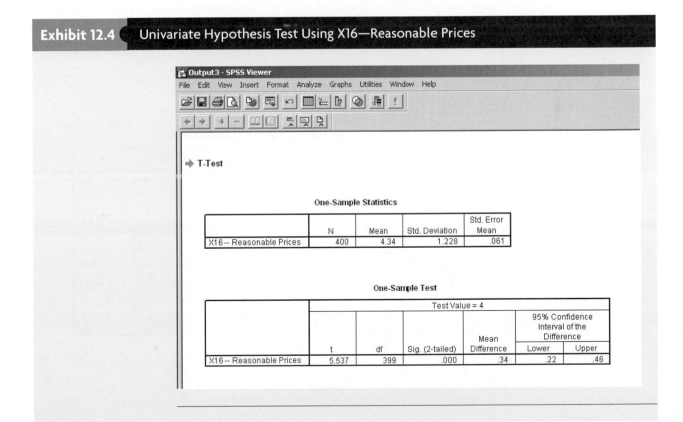

T-Test

One-Sample Statistics

	N	Mean	Std. Deviation	Std. Error Mean
X16 -- Reasonable Prices	400	4.34	1.228	.061

One-Sample Test

	Test Value = 4					
					95% Confidence Interval of the Difference	
	t	df	Sig. (2-tailed)	Mean Difference	Lower	Upper
X16 -- Reasonable Prices	5.537	399	.000	.34	.22	.46

determining whether there is a difference in the importance of a DVD player between older and younger new car purchasers. In this situation, bivariate (two variable) analysis is appropriate. In the following section, we first explain the concept of cross-tabulation, which examines two variables. We then describe three types of bivariate hypothesis tests: Chi-square, which is used with nominal data, and the *t*-test (to compare two means) and analysis of variance (compares three or more means), both of which are used with either interval or ratio data.

Cross-Tabulation

In Chapter 11 we introduced one-way frequency tables to report the findings for a single variable. The next logical step in data analysis is to perform cross-tabulation using two variables. Cross-tabulation is useful for examining relationships and reporting the findings for two variables. The purpose of cross-tabulation is to determine if differences exist between subgroups of the total sample. In fact, cross-tabulation is the primary form of data analysis in some marketing research projects. To use cross-tabulation you must understand how to develop a cross-tabulation table and how to interpret the outcome.

Exhibit 12.5 shows a cross-tabulation between gender and recall of Santa Fe Grill ads. The cross-tabulation shows frequencies and percentages, with percentages existing for both rows and columns. One way to interpret this table, for example, would be to look at those

Exhibit 12.5	Example of a Cross-Tabulation: Gender by Ad Recall

Output4 - SPSS Viewer

File Edit View Insert Format Analyze Graphs Utilities Window Help

Crosstabs

X31 -- Ad Recall * X32 -- Gender Crosstabulation

			X32 -- Gender		Total
			Males	Females	
X31 -- Ad Recall	Do Not Recall Ads	Count	158	103	261
		% within X31 -- Ad Recall	60.5%	39.5%	100.0%
		% within X32 -- Gender	66.9%	62.8%	65.3%
		% of Total	39.5%	25.8%	65.3%
	Recall Ads	Count	78	61	139
		% within X31 -- Ad Recall	56.1%	43.9%	100.0%
		% within X32 -- Gender	33.1%	37.2%	34.8%
		% of Total	19.5%	15.3%	34.8%
Total		Count	236	164	400
		% within X31 -- Ad Recall	59.0%	41.0%	100.0%
		% within X32 -- Gender	100.0%	100.0%	100.0%
		% of Total	59.0%	41.0%	100.0%

individuals who do not recall ads for Santa Fe Grill. These individuals represent 65.3 percent of the sample, with 39.5 percent being male and 25.8 percent female. Thus, our preliminary interpretation suggests that males are less likely to recall Santa Fe Grill ads than females.

You must consider several issues in developing and interpreting cross-tabulation tables. Looking at Exhibit 12.5, note that we calculated percentages for each cell of the cross-tabulation table. The top number within each cell represents the absolute frequency of responses for each variable or question (for example, 158 male respondents do not recall ads). Below the absolute frequency is the row percentage per cell. For example, the 158 male respondents who do not recall Santa Fe ads represent 60.5 percent of the total in the "do not recall" category (261). The cell also shows the total percentage of respondents within cells based on the total sample. So, for example, with a total sample of 400, 39.5 percent of the sample is males who do not recall ads and 19.5 percent are males who do recall ads.

When constructing a cross-tabulation table, the researcher selects the variables to use when examining relationships. Selection of variables should be based on the objectives of the research project. Paired variable relationships (for example, sex of respondent and ad recall) are selected on the basis of whether they answer the research questions in the research project.

Demographic variables or lifestyle/psychographic characteristics are typically the starting point in developing cross-tabulations. These variables are usually the columns of the cross-tabulation table, and the rows are variables like purchase intention, usage, or actual sales data. Cross-tabulation tables show percentage calculations based on column variable totals. Thus, the researcher can make comparisons of behaviors and intentions for different categories of predictor variables such as income, sex, and marital status.

Cross-tabulation provides the research analyst with a powerful tool to summarize survey data. It is easy to understand and interpret and can provide a description of both total and subgroup data. Yet the simplicity of this technique can create problems. It is easy to produce an endless variety of cross-tabulation tables. In developing these tables, the analyst must always keep in mind both the project objectives and specific research questions of the study.

Chi-Square Analysis

Marketing researchers often analyze survey data using one-way frequency counts and cross-tabulations. One purpose of cross-tabulations is to study relationships among variables. The research question is "Do the numbers of responses that fall into different categories differ from what is expected if there is no relationship between the variables?" The null hypothesis is always that the two variables are not related. Thus, the null hypothesis in our example would be that the percentage of men and women customers who recall Santa Fe Grill ads is the same. The alternative hypothesis is that the two variables are related, or that men and women differ in their recall of Santa Fe Grill ads. This hypothesis can be answered using Chi-square analysis. Below are some other examples of research questions that could be examined using Chi-square statistical tests:

- Is usage of the Internet (low, moderate, and high) related to sex of respondent?
- Does frequency of patronage (infrequent, moderately frequent, and very frequent) differ between males and females?
- Do part-time and full-time workers differ in terms of how often they are absent from work (seldom, occasionally, frequently)?
- Do college students and high school students differ in their preference for Coke versus Pepsi?

Chi-square (X^2) **analysis** enables researchers to test for statistical significance between the frequency distributions of two (or more) nominally scaled variables in a cross-tabulation table to determine if there is any association between the variables. Categorical data from questions about sex, education, or other nominal variables can be tested with this statistic. Chi-square analysis compares the observed frequencies (counts) of the responses with the expected frequencies. The Chi-square statistic tests whether or not the observed data are distributed the way we would expect them to be, given the assumption that the variables are not related. The expected cell count is a theoretical value, while the observed cell count is the actual cell count based on your study. For example, to test whether women recall Santa Fe Grill ads better than men, we would compare the observed recall frequency for each sex with the frequency we would expect to find if there is no difference between women's and men's ad recall. The Chi-square statistic answers questions about relationships between nominally scaled data that cannot be analyzed with other types of statistical analysis, such as ANOVA or t-tests.

Calculating the X^2 Value

To help you to better understand the Chi-square statistic, we will show you how to calculate it. The formula is shown below:

$$\text{Chi-square formula} \qquad x^2 = \sum_{i-1}^{n} \frac{(\text{Observed}_i - \text{Expected}_i)^2}{\text{Expected}_i}$$

where

$$\text{Observed}_i = \text{Observed frequency in cell } i$$
$$\text{Expected}_i = \text{Expected frequency in cell } i$$
$$n = \text{Number of cells}$$

When you apply the above formula to the Santa Fe Grill data shown in Exhibit 12.6, you get the following:

Calculation of Chi-square value:

$$\frac{(88 - 103)^2}{103} + \frac{(95 - 75)^2}{75} + \frac{(58 - 57.8)^2}{57.8} + \frac{(40 - 40.2)^2}{40.2} + \frac{(90 - 70.2)^2}{75} + \frac{(29 - 48.8)^2}{48.8} =$$
$$\text{Chi-square value} = 22.6$$

As the above equation indicates, we subtract the expected frequency from the observed frequency and then square it to eliminate any negative values before we use the results in further calculations. After squaring, we divide the resulting value by the expected frequency to take into consideration cell size differences. Then each of these calculations, which we performed for each cell of the table, is summed over all cells to arrive at the final Chi-square value. The Chi-square value tells you how far the observed frequencies are from the expected frequencies. Conceptually, the larger the Chi-square is, the more likely it is that the two variables are related. This is because Chi-square is larger whenever the number actually observed in a cell is more different than what we expected to find, given the assumption that the two variables are not related. The computed Chi-square statistic is compared to a table of Chi-square values to determine if the differences are statistically significant. If the calculated Chi-square is larger than the Chi-square reported in standard statistical tables, then the two variables are related for a given level of significance, typically .05.

Some marketing researchers call Chi-square a "goodness-of-fit" test. That is, the test evaluates how closely the actual frequencies "fit" the expected frequencies. When the differences between observed and expected frequencies are large, you have a poor fit and you reject your null hypothesis. When the differences are small, you have a good fit and you would accept that null hypothesis that there is no relationship between the two variables.

One word of caution is necessary in using Chi-square. The Chi-square results will be distorted if more than 20 percent of the cells have an expected count of less than 5, or if any cell has an expected count of less than 1. In such cases, you should not use this test. SPSS will tell you if these conditions have been violated. One solution to small counts in individual cells is to collapse them into fewer cells to get larger counts.

SPSS Application—Chi-Square

Based on their conversations with customers, the owners of the Santa Fe Grill believe that male customers come to the restaurant from farther away than do female customers. The Chi-square statistic can be used to determine if this is true. The null hypothesis is that the same proportion of male and female customers make up each of the response categories for X30—Distance Driven. The alternative hypothesis is that these proportions are different by sex.

To conduct this analysis, the click-through sequence is ANALYZE → DESCRIPTIVE STATISTICS → CROSSTABS. Click on X30—Distance Traveled for the Row variable and on X32—Gender for the Column variable. Click on the Statistics button and the Chi-square box, and then Continue. Next, click on the Cells button and on Expected frequencies (Observed frequencies is usually already checked). Then, click Continue and OK to execute the program.

The SPSS results are shown in Exhibit 12.6. The top table shows the actual number of responses (count) for males and females for each of the categories of X30—Distance Driven. Also in this table you will see the expected frequencies, or the number that we expect to find in the cell if the null hypothesis of no difference is true. For example, 88 males drove a distance of less than 1 mile (108 were "expected" in this cell) while 95 females drove from this same distance (we expected to find 75).

The expected frequencies (count) are calculated on the basis of the proportion of the sample represented by a particular group. For example, the total sample of Santa Fe Grill customers is 400 and 236 are males and 164 are females. This means 59 percent of the sample is male and 41 percent is female. When we look in the Total column for the distance driven category labeled "Less than 1 mile" we see that there are a total of 183 male and female respondents. To calculate the expected frequencies, you multiply the proportion a particular group represents times the total number in that group. For example, with males you calculate 59 percent of 183 and the expected frequency is 107.397. Similarly, females are 41 percent of the sample so the expected number of females = 75.03 (.41 × 183). The other expected frequencies are calculated in the same way.

Look again at the observed frequencies. Note that a higher proportion than expected of male customers of Santa Fe Grill drive farther to get to Santa Fe Grill. That is, we would expect only 70.2 men to drive to the Santa Fe Grill from more than 3 miles, but actually 90 men drove from this far away. Similarly, there are fewer female customers than expected who drive from more than three miles away (expected = 48.8 and actual only 29).

Information in the Chi-Square Tests table shows the results for this test. The Pearson Chi-Square value is 22.616 and it is significant at the .000 level. Since this level of significance is much less than our standard criterion of .05, we can reject the null hypothesis with a high degree of confidence. The interpretation of this finding suggests that there is a high probability that male customers drive from farther away to get to the Santa Fe Grill. There also is a tendency for females to drive shorter distances to get to the restaurant.

Exhibit 12.6 SPSS Chi-Square Crosstab Example

Crosstabs

x30 -- Distance Driven * X32 -- Gender Crosstabulation

			X32 -- Gender Males	X32 -- Gender Females	Total
x30 -- Distance Driven	Less than 1 mile	Count	88	95	183
		Expected Count	108.0	75.0	183.0
		% within X32 -- Gender	37.3%	57.9%	45.8%
	1 -- 3 miles	Count	58	40	98
		Expected Count	57.8	40.2	98.0
		% within X32 -- Gender	24.6%	24.4%	24.5%
	More than 3 miles	Count	90	29	119
		Expected Count	70.2	48.8	119.0
		% within X32 -- Gender	38.1%	17.7%	29.8%
Total		Count	236	164	400
		Expected Count	236.0	164.0	400.0
		% within X32 -- Gender	100.0%	100.0%	100.0%

Chi-Square Tests

	Value	df	Asymp. Sig. (2-sided)
Pearson Chi-Square	22.616[a]	2	.000
Likelihood Ratio	23.368	2	.000
Linear-by-Linear Association	22.343	1	.000
N of Valid Cases	400		

a. 0 cells (.0%) have expected count less than 5. The minimum expected count is 40.18.

Comparing Means: Independent versus Related Samples

In addition to examining frequencies, marketing researchers often want to compare the means of two groups. There are two possible situations when researchers compare means. The first is when the means are from independent samples, and the second is when the samples are related. An example of an independent sample comparison would be the results of interviews with male and female coffee drinkers. The researcher may want to compare the average number of cups of coffee consumed per day by male students with the average number of cups of coffee consumed by female students. An example of the second situation, related samples, is when the researcher compares the average number of cups of coffee consumed per day by male students with the average number of soft drinks consumed per day by the same sample of male students.

In a related sample situation, the marketing researcher must take special care in analyzing the information. Although the questions are independent, the respondents are the same.

This is called a paired sample. When testing for differences in related samples the researcher must use what is called a paired samples *t*-test. The formula to compute the *t* value for paired samples is not presented here. Students are referred to more advanced texts for the actual calculation of the *t* value for related samples. The SPSS package contains options for both the related-samples and the independent samples situations.

Using the *t*-Test to Compare Two Means

Just as with the univariate *t*-test, the bivariate *t*-test requires interval or ratio data. Also, the *t*-test is especially useful when the sample size is small ($n < 30$) and when the population standard deviation is unknown. Unlike the univariate test, however, we assume that the samples are drawn from populations with normal distributions and that the variances of the populations are equal.

t-test A hypothesis test that utilizes the *t* distribution; used when the sample size is smaller than 30 and the standard deviation is unknown.

Essentially, the **t-test** for differences between group means can be conceptualized as the difference between the means divided by the variability of the means. The *t* value is a ratio of the difference between the two sample means and the standard error. The *t*-test provides a mathematical way of determining if the difference between the two sample means occurred by chance. The formula for calculating the *t* value is:

$$Z = \frac{\overline{X}_1 - \overline{X}_2}{S\overline{x}_1 - \overline{x}_2}$$

where

$$\overline{x}_1 \quad = \text{mean of sample 1}$$
$$\overline{x}_2 \quad = \text{mean of sample 2}$$
$$S\overline{x}_1 - \overline{x}_2 = \text{standard error of the difference between the two means}$$

SPSS Application—Independent Samples *t*-Test

To illustrate the use of a *t*-test for the difference between two group means, we turn to the Santa Fe Grill database. Santa Fe Grill owners want to find out if there are differences in the level of satisfaction between male and female customers. To do that we can use the SPSS "Compare Means" program.

The SPSS click-through sequence is ANALYZE → COMPARE MEANS → INDEPENDENT-SAMPLES *t*-TEST. When you get to this dialog box click variable X22—Satisfaction into the Test Variables box and variable X32—Gender into the Grouping Variable box. For variable X32 you must define the range in the Define Groups box. Enter a 0 for Group 1 and a 1 for Group 2 (males were coded 0 in the database and females were coded 1) and then click Continue. For the Options we will use the defaults, so just click OK to execute the program.

Results are shown in Exhibit 12.7. The top table shows the Group Statistics. Note that 236 male customers and 164 female customers are in the data set. Also, the mean satisfaction level for males is a bit higher at 4.83, compared with 4.38 for the female customers. The standard deviation for females is somewhat smaller (.874) than for the males (.966).

To find out if the two means are significantly different, we look at the information in the Independent Samples Test table. We calculate the statistical significance of the difference in two means differently if the variances of the two means are equal versus unequal. The Levene's test for equality of variances is reported on the left side of the table. In this case the test shows the two variances are equal (Sig. value of .059), but almost significantly

| Exhibit 12.7 | Comparing Two Means with the Independent-Samples *t*-Test |

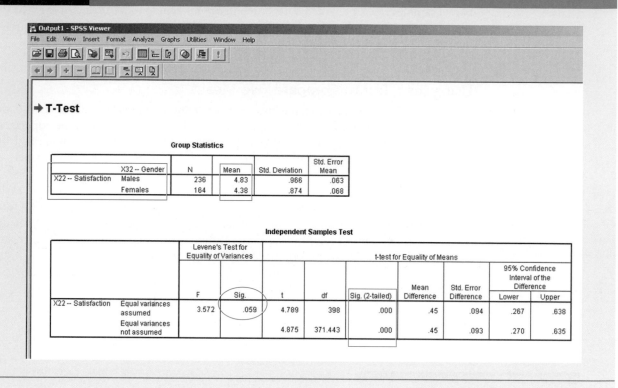

different. In all cases where this value is < .05 you would use the "Equal variances not assumed" test. In the column labeled Sig. (2-tailed), you will note that the two means are significantly different (< .000), whether we assume equal or unequal variances. Thus, there is no support for the null hypothesis that the two means are equal, and we conclude that male customers are significantly more satisfied than female customers. There is other information in this table, but we do not need to concern ourselves with it at this time.

SPSS Application—Paired Samples *t*-Test

Sometimes marketing researchers want to test for differences in two means for variables in the same sample. For example, the owners of the Santa Fe Grill noticed that the taste of their food is rated 5.31 while the food temperature is rated only 4.57. Since the two food variables are likely to be related, they want to know if the ratings for taste really are significantly higher (more favorable) than for temperature. To examine this, we use the paired samples test for the difference in two means. This test examines whether two means from two different questions using the same scaling and answered by the same respondents are significantly different. The null hypothesis is the mean ratings for the two food variables (X18 and X20) are equal.

To test this hypothesis we use the SPSS paired-samples *t*-test. The click-through sequence is ANALYZE → COMPARE MEANS → PAIRED-SAMPLES *t*-TEST. When you get to this dialog box, highlight both X18—Food Taste and X20—Food Temperature and then click on the arrow button to move them into the Paired Variables box. For the Options we will use the defaults, so just click OK to execute the program.

Results are shown in Exhibit 12.8. The top table shows the Paired Samples Statistics. The mean for food taste is 5.31 and for food temperature is 4.57. The *t* value for this comparison is 17.649 (see Paired Samples Test table) and it is significant at the .000 level. Thus, we can reject the null hypothesis that the two means are equal and conclude that Santa Fe Grill customers have more favorable perceptions of food taste than food temperature.

Analysis of Variance (ANOVA)

Analysis of variance (ANOVA)
A statistical technique that determines whether three or more means are statistically different from each other.

Researchers use **analysis of variance (ANOVA)** to determine the statistical difference between three or more means. For example, if a researcher finds that the average number of cups of coffee consumed per day by freshman during finals is 3.7, while the average number of cups of coffee consumed per day by seniors and graduate students is 4.3 cups and 5.1 cups, respectively, are these observed differences statistically significant?

The technique is really quite straightforward. In this section we describe a one-way ANOVA. The term "one-way" is used because there we are using only one independent variable in our analysis. In ANOVA, researchers can examine the effects of multiple

Exhibit 12.8   Paired Samples *t*-Test

T-Test

Paired Samples Statistics

		Mean	N	Std. Deviation	Std. Error Mean
Pair 1	X18 -- Excellent Food Taste	5.31	400	1.088	.054
	X20 -- Proper Food Temperature	4.57	400	1.104	.055

Paired Samples Test

		Paired Differences							
					95% Confidence Interval of the Difference				
		Mean	Std. Deviation	Std. Error Mean	Lower	Upper	t	df	Sig. (2-tailed)
Pair 1	X18 -- Excellent Food Taste - X20 -- Proper Food Temperature	.74	.841	.042	.66	.83	17.649	399	.000

independent variables simultaneously, which enables analysts to estimate both the individual and joint effects of several independent variables on the dependent variable.

An example of an ANOVA problem may be to compare light, medium, and heavy drinkers of Starbucks coffee on their attitude toward a particular Starbucks advertising campaign. In this instance there is one independent variable—consumption of Starbucks coffee—but it is divided into three different levels. Our earlier *t* statistics won't work here because we have more than two groups to compare.

ANOVA requires that the dependent variable, in this case the attitude toward the Starbucks advertising campaign, be metric. That is, the dependent variable must be either interval or ratio scaled. A second data requirement is that the independent variable, in this case the coffee consumption variable, be categorical.

The null hypothesis for ANOVA always states that there is no difference between the dependent variable groups—in this situation, the ad campaign attitudes of the groups of Starbucks coffee drinkers. In specific terminology, the null hypothesis would be:

$$\mu1 = \mu2 = \mu3$$

ANOVA examines the variance within a set of data. Recall from the earlier discussion of measures of dispersion that the variance of a variable is equal to the average squared deviation from the mean of the variable. The logic of ANOVA is that if we calculate the variance between the groups and compare it to the variance within the groups, we can make a determination as to whether the group means (attitudes toward the advertising campaign) are significantly different.[1] When within-group variance is high, it swamps any between-group differences we see unless those differences are large.

Determining Statistical Significance in ANOVA

F-test The test used to statistically evaluate the differences between the group means in ANOVA.

In ANOVA, researchers use the ***F*-test** to evaluate the differences between group means for statistical significance. For example, suppose the heavy users of Starbucks coffee rate the advertising campaign 4.4 on a five-point scale, with 5 = "Very favorable." The medium users of Starbucks coffee rate the campaign 3.9, and the light users of Starbucks coffee rate the campaign 2.5. The *F*-test in ANOVA will tell us if these observed differences are statistically significant.

The *total variance* in a set of responses to a question is made up of between-group and within-group variance. The *between-group variance* measures how much the sample means of the groups differ from one another. In contrast, the *within-group variance* measures how much the observations within each group differ from one another. The *F* distribution is the ratio of these two components of total variance and can be calculated as follows:

$$F \text{ ratio} = \frac{\text{Variance between groups}}{\text{Variance within groups}}$$

The larger the difference in the variance between groups, the larger the *F*-ratio. Since the total variance in a data set is divisible into between- and within-group components, if there is more variance explained or accounted for by considering differences between groups than there is within groups, then the independent variable probably has a significant impact on the dependent variable. Larger *F* ratios imply significant differences between the groups. Thus, the larger the *F* ratio, the more likely it is that the null hypothesis will be rejected.

ANOVA, however, is able to tell the researcher only that statistical differences exist between at least one pair of the group means. The technique cannot identify which pairs of means are significantly different from each other. In our example of Starbucks coffee drinkers' attitudes toward the advertising campaign, we can conclude that differences in attitudes toward the advertising campaign exist among light, medium, and heavy coffee drinkers, but we would not be able to determine if the differences are between light and medium, or between light and heavy, or between medium and heavy, and so on. We are able to say only that there are significant differences somewhere among the groups. Thus, the marketing researcher still must determine where the mean differences lie. Follow-up "post-hoc" tests will identify the pairs of groups that have significantly different mean responses.

There are several **follow-up tests** available in statistical software packages such as SPSS and SAS. All of these methods involve multiple comparisons, or simultaneous assessment of confidence interval estimates of differences between the means. All means are compared two at a time. The differences between the techniques lie in their ability to control the error rate. We shall briefly describe one follow-up test, the Scheffé procedure. Relative to other follow-up tests, the Scheffé procedure is a more conservative method for detection of significant differences between group means.

The Scheffé follow-up test essentially establishes simultaneous confidence intervals, which hold the entire experiment's error rate to a specified α level. The test exposes differences between all pairs of means to a high and low confidence interval range. If the difference between each pair of means falls outside the range of the confidence interval, then we reject the null hypothesis and conclude that the pairs of means falling outside the range are statistically different. The Scheffé test might show that one, two, or all three pairs of means in our Starbucks example are different. The Scheffé test is equivalent to simultaneous two-tailed hypothesis tests. Because the technique holds the experimental error rate to α, the confidence intervals tend to be wider than in the other methods, but the researcher has more assurance that true mean differences exist. Recall that the Scheffé test is very conservative so you may wish to look at one of the other tests available in your statistical software.

Follow-up test A test that flags the means that are statistically different from each other; follow-up tests are performed after an ANOVA determines there are differences between means.

n-Way ANOVA

Discussion of ANOVA to this point has been devoted to one-way ANOVA in which there is only one independent variable. In the examples, the usage category (consumption of Starbucks coffee) was the independent variable. It is not at all uncommon, however, for the researcher to be interested in several independent variables simultaneously. In such cases an *n-way ANOVA* would be used.

Often researchers are interested in the region of the country where a product is sold as well as consumption patterns. Using multiple independent factors creates the possibility of an interaction effect. That is, the multiple independent factors can act together to affect group means. For example, heavy consumers of Starbucks coffee in the Northeast may have different attitudes about advertising campaigns than heavy consumers of Starbucks coffee in the West, and there may be still further differences between the various coffee-consumption-level groups, as shown earlier.

Another situation that may require *n*-way ANOVA is the use of experimental designs, where the researcher uses different levels of a stimulus (for example, different prices or ads) and then measures responses to those stimuli. For example, a marketer may be interested in finding out whether consumers prefer a humorous ad to a serious one and whether that preference varies across gender. Each type of ad could be shown to different groups of customers (both male and female). Then, questions about their preferences for the ad and the product it advertises could be asked. The primary difference between the groups would be the difference in ad execution (humorous or nonhumorous) and customer gender. An *n*-way ANOVA could be used to find out whether the ad execution differences helped cause differences in ad and product preferences, as well as what effects might be attributable to customer gender.

From a conceptual standpoint, *n*-way ANOVA is similar to one-way ANOVA, but the mathematics is more complex. However, statistical packages such as SPSS will conveniently perform *n*-way ANOVA.

SPSS Application—ANOVA

To help you understand how ANOVA is used to answer research questions, we refer to the Santa Fe Grill database to answer a typical question. The owners want to know first whether customers who come to the restaurant from greater distances differ from customers who live nearby in their willingness to recommend the restaurant to a friend. Second, they also want to know whether that difference in willingness to recommend, if any, is influenced by the sex of the customers. The database variables are X24—Likely to Recommend, measured on a 7-point scale, with 1 = "Definitely Will Not Recommend" and 7 = "Definitely Recommend"; X30—Distance Driven, where 1 = "Less than 1 mile," 2 = " 1–3 miles," and 3 = "More than 3 miles"; and X32—Gender, where 0 = male and 1 = female.

On the basis of informal comments from customers, the owners think customers who come from more than 3 miles will be more likely to recommend the restaurant. Moreover, they believe female customers will be more likely to recommend the restaurant than males. The null hypotheses were that there would be no difference between the mean ratings for X24—Likely to Recommend for customers who traveled different distances to come to the restaurant (X30) and between females and males (X32).

The purpose of the ANOVA analysis is to see if the differences that do exist are statistically significant. To examine the differences, an *F* ratio is used. The bigger the *F* ratio, the bigger the difference among the means of the various groups with respect to their likelihood of recommending the restaurant.

SPSS can help you conduct the statistical analysis to test the null hypotheses. The best way to analyze the Santa Fe Grill data to answer the owners' questions is to use a factorial model. A factorial model is a type of ANOVA in which the individual effects of each independent variable on the dependent variable are considered separately and then the combined effects (an interaction) of the independent variables on the dependent variable are analyzed. The click-through sequence is ANALYZE → GENERAL LINEAR MODEL → UNIVARIATE. Highlight the dependent variable X24—Likely to Recommend by clicking on it and move it to the Dependent Variable box. Next, highlight X30—Distance Driven and X32—Gender, and move them to the Fixed Factors box. Click OK, since we don't need to specify any other options for this test.

The SPSS output for ANOVA is shown in Exhibit 12.9. The Tests of Between-Subjects Effects table shows that the *F* ratio for X30—Distance Driven is 80.452, which is statistically significant at the .000 level. This means that customers who come from different distances to eat at the restaurant vary in their likelihood of recommending the restaurant. The *F* ratio for X32—Gender is 49.421, which also is statistically significant at the .000 level. This means the sex of customers influences their likelihood of recommending the restaurant.

We now know that both X30—Distance Driven and X32—Gender influence likelihood of recommending the Santa Fe Grill. But we do not know how. To answer this question we must look at the means for these two variables. To get the means, we follow the same steps as we did to run the ANOVA, but this time we click on the Options box on

Exhibit 12.9   ANOVA for X24—Likely to Recommend, X30—Distance Driven, and X32—Gender

Output5 - SPSS Viewer

File   Edit   View   Insert   Format   Analyze   Graphs   Utilities   Window   Help

➡ **Univariate Analysis of Variance**

Between-Subjects Factors

		Value Label	N
x30 -- Distance Driven	1	Less than 1 mile	119
	2	1 -- 3 miles	98
	3	More than 3 miles	183
X32 -- Gender	0	Males	236
	1	Females	164

Tests of Between-Subjects Effects

Dependent Variable: X24 -- Likely to Recommend

Source	Type III Sum of Squares	df	Mean Square	F	Sig.
Corrected Model	149.397[a]	5	29.879	60.100	.000
Intercept	4018.202	1	4018.202	8082.330	.000
X30	79.995	2	39.997	80.452	.000
X32	24.570	1	24.570	49.421	.000
X30 * X32	.454	2	.227	.456	.634
Error	195.881	394	.497		
Total	5127.000	400			
Corrected Total	345.278	399			

a. R Squared = .433 (Adjusted R Squared = .425)

the right side of the SPSS screen (after you click on Univariate) to get the dialog box shown in Exhibit 12.10. When you get this box look in the Estimated Marginal Means box and highlight (OVERALL) as well as X30, X32, and X30* X32 and move them all into the "Display Means for" box. Next place a check in "Compare main effects," and then click Continue and finally OK. We show the results in Exhibit 12.11.

Look at the numbers in the top of Exhibit 12.11 and you will see that the average likelihood of recommending the Santa Fe Grill to a friend increases as the distance driven by the respondent decreases. In short, customers who come from within 1 mile of the

---

Exhibit 12.10 Dialog Box for ANOVA Means

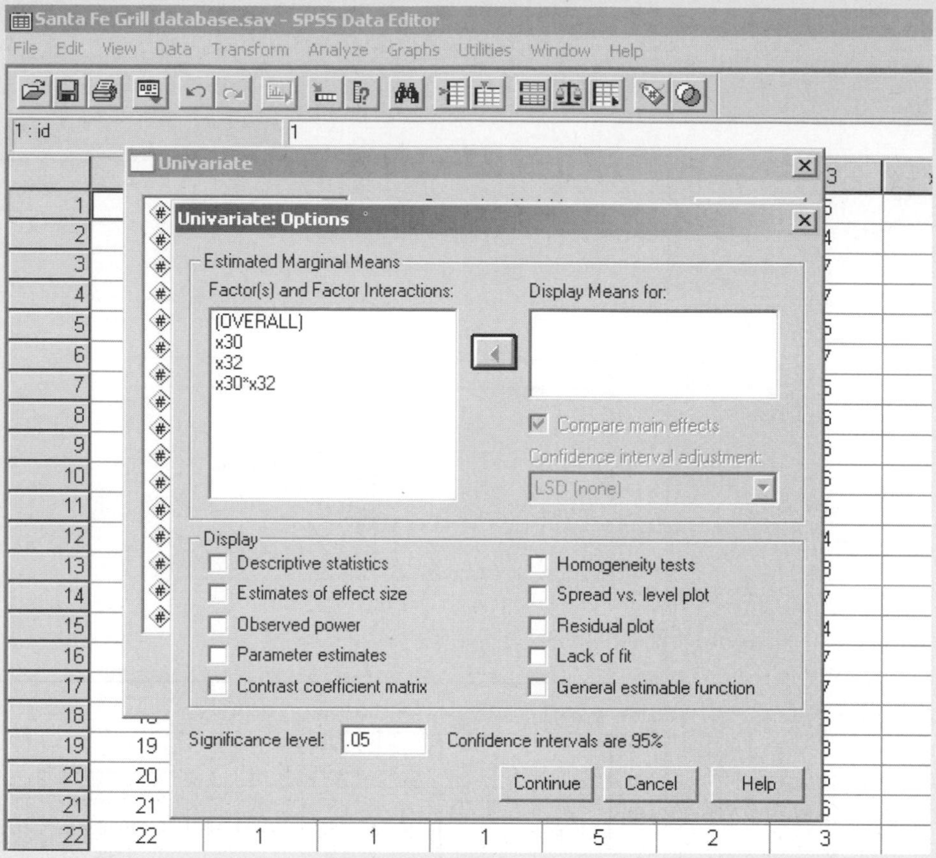

Santa Fe Grill show an average likelihood to recommend of 4.017, compared with a 3.576 and 2.905 average likelihood for customers who come from 1–3 and more than 3 miles away, respectively.

The Santa Fe Grill owners were also interested in whether there is a difference in the likelihood of males versus females recommending the Santa Fe Grill. The F ratio for gender is again quite large (49.421; see Exhibit 12.9) and statistically significant (.000). Looking at the means of the customer groups based on gender (see Exhibit 12.11), we see that indeed males are more likely to recommend the Santa Fe Grill (mean = 3.773) as compared to females (mean = 3.226). The null hypothesis is rejected, and we conclude there is a difference in the average likelihood of male and female customers to recommend the Santa Fe Grill.

The interaction between distance traveled and gender has an F ratio of .456, with a probability level of .634, meaning that the difference in the likelihood of recommendation when both independent variables are considered together is not statistically significant. This means there is no interaction between distance driven, gender, and likelihood of recommending the Santa Fe Grill.

Exhibit 12.11	Comparison of Likely to Recommend for Male and Female Customers Who Drove Different Distances to Dine at the Santa Fe Grill

Dependent Variable: X24—Likely to Recommend by Distance Driven

X30—Distance Driven	Mean
Less than 1 mile	4.017
1–3 miles	3.576
More than 3 miles	2.905

Pairwise Comparisons
Dependent Variable: X24—Likely to Recommend

(I) X30—Distance Driven	(J) X30—Distance Driven	Mean Difference (I-J)	Sig.
Less than 1 mile	1–3 miles	.441	.000
	More than 3 miles	−1.112	.000
1–3 miles	Less than 1 mile	.441	.000
	More than 3 miles	−.671	.000
More than 3 miles	Less than 1 mile	1.112	.000
	1–3 miles	−.671	.000

Dependent Variable: X24—Likely to Recommend by Gender

X32—Gender	Mean
Males	3.773
Females	3.226

Pairwise Comparisons
Dependent Variable: X24—Likely to Recommend

(I) X32—Gender	(J) X32—Gender	Mean Difference (I-J)	Sig.
Males	Females	.547	.000
Females	Males	−.547	.000

Continuing Case: The Santa Fe Grill

With the survey completed, edited, and entered into a digital file, researchers will now make decisions regarding the best way to analyze the data to understand the interviewed individuals. Then, researchers and decision makers will determine how the information can be used to improve the restaurant's operations. The data analysis should be connected directly to the research objectives. The researcher and the owners have been brainstorming about how to best analyze the data to better understand the situation.

1. Draw several conceptual models to represent relationships that could be tested with the customer survey.
2. Which statistical techniques would be appropriate to test the proposed relationships?
3. Give examples of relationships that could be tested with Chi-square and with ANOVA.

Perceptual Mapping

Perceptual mapping A process that is used to develop maps showing the perceptions of respondents. The maps are visual representations of respondents' perceptions of a company, product, service, brand, or any other object in two dimensions.

Perceptual mapping is a process that is used to develop maps that show the perceptions of respondents. The maps are visual representations of respondents' perceptions of a company, product, service, brand, or any other object in two dimensions. A perceptual map typically has a vertical and a horizontal axis that are labeled with descriptive adjectives. Possible adjectives for our restaurant example might be food temperature and/or freshness, speed of service, good value for the money, and so on.

Several different approaches can be used to develop perceptual maps. These include rankings, medians, and mean ratings. To illustrate perceptual mapping, data from an example involving ratings of fast-food restaurants are shown in Exhibit 12.12. Researchers gave customers a set of six fast-food restaurants and asked them to express how they perceive each restaurant. The perceptions of the respondents are then plotted on a two-dimensional map using two of the adjectives, freshness of food and food temperature. Inspection of the map, shown in Exhibit 12.13, illustrates that customers perceive Wendy's and Back Yard Burgers as quite similar to each other, as are McDonald's and Burger King. Customers perceive Arby's and Hardee's as somewhat similar, but do not view these restaurants as favorably as the others. However, Back Yard Burgers and McDonald's were perceived as very dissimilar.

Perceptual Mapping Applications in Marketing Research

While our fast-food example illustrates how perceptual mapping groups pairs of restaurants together based on perceived ratings, perceptual mapping has many other important applications in marketing research. Other applications include:

- *New-product development.* Perceptual mapping can identify gaps in perceptions and thereby help to position new products.
- *Image measurement.* Perceptual mapping can be used to identify the image of the company to help to position one company relative to the competition.
- *Advertising.* Perceptual mapping can assess advertising effectiveness in positioning the brand.
- *Distribution.* Perceptual mapping could be used to assess similarities of brands and channel outlets.

Exhibit 12.12	Ratings of Six Fast-Food Restaurants	
	Food Freshness	**Food Temperature**
McDonald's	1.8	3.7
Burger King	2.0	3.5
Wendy's	4.0	4.5
Back Yard Burger	4.5	4.8
Arby's	4.0	2.5
Hardee's	3.5	1.8

Key: Food temperature, 1 = Warm, 5 = Hot; Food freshness, 1 = Low, 5 = High.

Exhibit 12.13   Perceptual Map of Six Fast-Food Restaurants

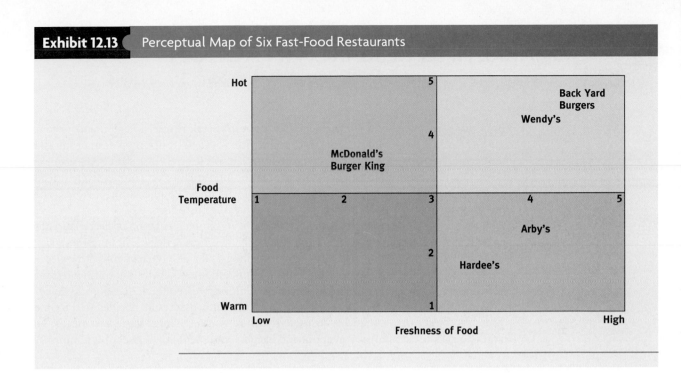

MARKETING RESEARCH IN ACTION
Examining Restaurant Image Positions—Remington's Steak House

About three years ago, John Smith opened Remington's Steak House, a retail theme restaurant located in a large Midwestern city. Smith's vision was to position his restaurant as a unique, theme-oriented specialty restaurant. The plan was for the restaurant to have an excellent reputation for offering a wide assortment of high-quality yet competitively priced entrees and services, and knowledgeable employees who understand customers' needs. The overriding goal was to place heavy emphasis on satisfying customers.

Smith used this vision to guide the development and implementation of his restaurant's positioning and marketing strategies. Although Smith knew how to deliver dining experiences, he did not know much about developing, implementing, and assessing marketing strategies.

Recently, Smith began asking himself some fundamental questions about his restaurant's operations and the future of his business. Smith expressed these questions to an account representative at a local marketing research firm and, as a result, decided to do some research to better understand his customers' attitudes and feelings. More specifically, he wanted to gain some information about and insights into the following set of questions:

1. What are the major factors customers use when selecting a restaurant to dine at, and what is the relative importance of each of these factors?
2. What image do customers have of Remington's and its two major competitors?
3. Is Remington's providing quality and satisfaction to its customers?
4. Do any of Remington's current marketing strategies need to be changed, and if so in what ways?

To address Smith's questions, the account representative recommended completing an image survey using an Internet panel approach. Initial contact was made with potential respondents using a random digit dialing telephone survey to screen for individuals who were patrons of Remington's as well as customers of competitors' restaurants (including their main competitors, Outback Steakhouse and Longhorn Steak House) within the market area. Respondents must also have a minimum annual household income of $20,000, and be familiar enough with one of the three restaurant competitors to accurately rate them. If an individual was qualified for the study based on the screening questions, they were directed to a Web site where they completed the survey.

Because this was the first time Smith had conducted any marketing research, the consultant suggested an exploratory approach and recommended a small sample size of 200. She said that if the results of the initial 200 surveys were helpful, the sample size could be increased so that the findings would be more precise. The questionnaire included questions about the importance of various reasons for choosing a restaurant, perceptions of the images of the three restaurant competitors on the same factors, and selected classification information on the respondents. When the researcher reached the quota of 200 usable completed questionnaires, the sample included 86 respondents who were most familiar with Outback, 65 who were most familiar with Longhorn, and 49 who were most familiar with Remington's. This last criterion was used to determine which of Remington's restaurant competitors a respondent evaluated. A database for the questions in this case is available in SPSS format at **www.mhhe.com/hairessentials1e**. The name of the database is Remingtons MRIA_essn.sav. A copy of the questionnaire is shown in Exhibit 12.14.

Exhibit 12.14   The Remington's Steakhouse Questionnaire

Screening and Rapport Questions

Hello. My name is _____ and I work for DSS Research. We are talking to individuals today/tonight about dining out habits.

1. "Do you regularly dine at casual dining restaurants?"   _____ Yes   _____ No
2. "Have you eaten at other casual restaurants in the last six months?"   _____ Yes   _____ No
3. "Is your gross annual household income $20,000 or more?"   _____ Yes   _____ No
4. There are three casual steakhouse restaurants in you neighborhood—Outback, Longhorn, and Remington's. Which of these restaurants are you most familiar with?
   a. Outback _____
   b. Longhorn _____
   c. Remington's _____
   d. None _____

If respondent answers "Yes" to the first three questions, and is familiar with one of the three restaurants, then say:

We would like you to answer a few questions about your recent dining experiences at Outback/Longhorn/Remington's restaurant. The survey will only take a few minutes and it will be very helpful in better serving restaurant customers in this area.

If the person says yes, give them instructions on how to access the Web site and complete the survey.

DINING OUT SURVEY

Please read all questions carefully. In the first section a number of reasons are listed that people use in selecting a particular restaurant to dine at. Using a scale from 1 to 7, with 7 being "Very Important" and 1 being "Not Important at All," please indicate the extent to which a particular selection reason is important or unimportant. Circle only one number for each selection reason.

Section 1: Importance Ratings

How important is/are _____ in selecting a particular restaurant to dine at?

1. Large Portions

   Not Important At All   Very Important
   1 2 3 4 5 6 7

2. Competent Employees

   Not Important At All   Very Important
   1 2 3 4 5 6 7

3. Food Quality

   Not Important At All   Very Important
   1 2 3 4 5 6 7

4. Speed of Service

   Not Important At All   Very Important
   1 2 3 4 5 6 7

5. Atmosphere

   Not Important At All   Very Important
   1 2 3 4 5 6 7

6. Reasonable Prices

   Not Important At All   Very Important
   1 2 3 4 5 6 7

continued

Exhibit 12.14   The Remington's Steakhouse Questionnaire, *continued*

Section 2: Perceptions Measures

Listed below is a set of characteristics that could be used to describe [Outback/Longhorn/Remington's]. Using a scale from 1 to 7, with 7 being "Strongly Agree" and 1 being "Strongly Disagree", to what extent do you agree or disagree that [Remington's—Outback—Longhorn's]: (a particular restaurant's name appeared on the screen based on the familiarity question in the telephone screener)

7. has large portions

Strongly Disagree   Strongly Agree
1 2 3 4 5 6 7

8. has competent employees

Strongly Disagree   Strongly Agree
1 2 3 4 5 6 7

9. has excellent food quality

Strongly Disagree   Strongly Agree
1 2 3 4 5 6 7

10. has quick service

Strongly Disagree   Strongly Agree
1 2 3 4 5 6 7

11. has a good atmosphere

Strongly Disagree   Strongly Agree
1 2 3 4 5 6 7

12. reasonable prices

Strongly Disagree   Strongly Agree
1 2 3 4 5 6 7

Section 3: Relationship Measures

Please indicate your view on each of the following questions:

13. How satisfied are you with _____ ?

Not Satisfied At All   Very Satisfied
1 2 3 4 5 6 7

14. How likely are you to return to _____ in the future?

Definitely Will Not Return   Definitely Will Return
1 2 3 4 5 6 7

15. How likely are you to recommend _____ to a friend?

Definitely Will Not Recommend   Definitely Will Recommend
1 2 3 4 5 6 7

16. Frequency of Patronage
How often do you eat at _____ ?

1 = Occasionally (Less than once a month)
2 = Frequently (1–3 times a month)
3 = Very Frequently (4 or more times a month)

Section 4: Classification Questions

Please circle the number that classifies you best.

17. Number of Children at Home

1   None
2   1–2
3   More than 2 children at home

Exhibit 12.14 *continued*

18. Do your recall seeing any advertisements in the last 60 days for Outback/Longhorn/ Remington's?

    0 No
    1 Yes

19. Your Gender

    0 Male
    1 Female

20. Your Age in Years

    1 18–25
    2 26–34
    3 35–49
    4 50–59
    5 60 and Older

21. Your Annual Gross Household Income

    1 $20,000–$35,000
    2 $35,001–$50,000
    3 $50,001–$75,000
    4 $75,001–$100,000
    5 More than $100,000

22. Competitors: Most familiar with _____?

    1 Outback
    2 Longhorn
    3 Remington's

Thank you very much for your help. Click on the submit button to exit the survey.

Researchers focused their initial analysis of the data on the importance ratings for the restaurant selection factors. The importance ratings are variables X1–X6 in the Remington's database. Exhibit 12.15 shows that food quality and speed of service are the two most important factors. To create this exhibit, the click-through sequence is ANALYZE → DESCRIPTIVE

Exhibit 12.15 Average Importance Ratings for Restaurant Selection Factors

Output1 - SPSS Viewer

File Edit View Insert Format Analyze Graphs Utilities Window Help

➡ **Frequencies**

Statistics

		X1 -- Large Portions	X2 -- Competent Employees	X3 -- Food Quality	X4 -- Speed of Service	X5 -- Atmosphere	X6 -- Reasonable Prices
N	Valid	200	200	200	200	200	200
	Missing	0	0	0	0	0	0
Mean		4.95	3.12	6.09	5.99	4.74	5.39

STATISTICS → FREQUENCIES. Highlight variables X1–X6 and move them to the "Variable(s)" box. Then go to the "Statistics" box and check "Mean," and then click "Continue," and OK. The least important factor is competent employees (mean = 3.12). This does not mean employees are not important. It simply means they are less important compared to the other factors included in the survey. In sum, respondents wanted good food, fast service, and reasonable prices.

The next task was to examine the perceptions of the three restaurant competitors. Using the restaurant image factors, the consultant conducted an ANOVA to see if there were any differences in the perceptions of the three restaurants (Exhibits 12.16 and 12.17). To create these exhibits, the click-through sequence is ANALYZE → COMPARE MEANS → ONE-WAY ANOVA. Highlight variables X1–X6 and move them to the "Dependent List" box, and then highlight variable X22 and move it to the "Factor" box. Next go to the "Options" box, check "Descriptives," and then click "Continue," and OK.

We show the results in Exhibits 12.16 and 12.17. We provide an overview of the findings from Exhibits 12.15–12.17 in Exhibit 12.18.

The findings of the survey were quite revealing. On the most important factor (food quality), Remington's rated the highest (mean = 6.86; see Exhibit 12.16), but Outback was

Exhibit 12.16   One-Way ANOVA for Three Restaurant Competitors

Descriptives

		N	Mean	Std. Deviation	Std. Error	95% Confidence Interval for Mean Lower Bound	Upper Bound	Minimum	Maximum
X7 -- Large Portions	1	86	3.57	.805	.087	3.40	3.74	2	4
	2	65	2.77	.880	.109	2.55	2.99	1	4
	3	49	3.39	.862	.123	3.14	3.64	1	4
	Total	200	3.27	.910	.064	3.14	3.39	1	4
X8 -- Competent Employees	1	86	5.15	.623	.067	5.02	5.28	4	6
	2	65	3.25	.919	.114	3.02	3.47	2	5
	3	49	2.49	.617	.088	2.31	2.67	2	4
	Total	200	3.88	1.355	.096	3.69	4.07	2	6
X9 -- Food Quality	1	86	6.42	.659	.071	6.28	6.56	5	7
	2	65	5.12	.839	.104	4.92	5.33	4	7
	3	49	6.86	.354	.051	6.76	6.96	6	7
	Total	200	6.11	.969	.069	5.97	6.24	4	7
X10 -- Speed of Service	1	86	4.35	.943	.102	4.15	4.55	3	6
	2	65	3.02	.857	.106	2.80	3.23	2	5
	3	49	2.27	.670	.096	2.07	2.46	1	3
	Total	200	3.41	1.216	.086	3.24	3.57	1	6
X11 -- Atmosphere	1	86	6.09	.890	.096	5.90	6.28	4	7
	2	65	4.35	.799	.099	4.16	4.55	3	6
	3	49	6.59	.537	.077	6.44	6.75	5	7
	Total	200	5.65	1.210	.086	5.48	5.82	3	7
X12 -- Reasonable Prices	1	86	5.50	.763	.082	5.34	5.66	4	6
	2	65	5.00	.810	.100	4.80	5.20	4	6
	3	49	5.49	.767	.110	5.27	5.71	4	6
	Total	200	5.34	.810	.057	5.22	5.45	4	6

Exhibit 12.17   One-Way ANOVA of Differences in Restaurant Perceptions

Output1 - SPSS Viewer

File   Edit   View   Insert   Format   Analyze   Graphs   Utilities   Window   Help

→ Oneway

ANOVA

		Sum of Squares	df	Mean Square	F	Sig.
X7 -- Large Portions	Between Groups	24.702	2	12.351	17.349	.000
	Within Groups	140.253	197	.712		
	Total	164.955	199			
X8 -- Competent Employees	Between Groups	259.779	2	129.889	242.908	.000
	Within Groups	105.341	197	.535		
	Total	365.120	199			
X9 -- Food Quality	Between Groups	98.849	2	49.425	110.712	.000
	Within Groups	07.946	197	.446		
	Total	186.795	199			
X10 -- Speed of Service	Between Groups	150.124	2	75.062	102.639	.000
	Within Groups	144.071	197	.731		
	Total	294.195	199			
X11 -- Atmosphere	Between Groups	169.546	2	84.773	136.939	.000
	Within Groups	121.954	197	.619		
	Total	291.500	199			
X12 -- Reasonable Prices	Between Groups	10.810	2	5.405	8.892	.000
	Within Groups	119.745	197	.608		
	Total	130.555	199			

Exhibit 12.18   Summary of ANOVA Findings from Exhibits 12.15   12.17

		Competitor Means			
Attributes	Rankings[a]	Outback	Longhorn	Remington's	Sig.
X7—Large Portions	4	3.57	2.77	3.39	.000
X8—Competent Employees	6	5.15	3.25	2.49	.000
X9—Food Quality	1	6.42	5.12	6.86	.000
X10—Speed of Service	2	4.35	3.02	2.27	.000
X11—Atmosphere	5	6.09	4.35	6.59	.000
X12—Reasonable Prices	3	5.50	5.00	5.49	.000
N = 200 total		86	65	49	.000

[a]Note: Rankings are based on mean importance ratings of attributes.

Exhibit 12.19   Importance-Performance Chart for Remington's Steak House

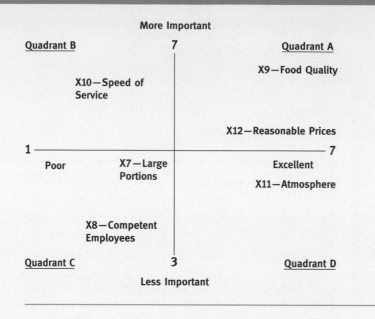

a close second (mean = 6.42). Remington's was also rated the highest on atmosphere (mean = 6.59), but that factor was fifth most important. For speed of service (second most important) and competent employees (least important), Remington's was rated the lowest of the three competitors.

An easy way to convey the results of an image analysis is to prepare an importance performance chart (IPC). An IPC has quadrants (A–D) that are described as follows:

Quadrant A: Modifications are needed.
Quadrant B: Good job—no need to modify.
Quadrant C: Don't worry—low priority.
Quadrant D: Rethink—a possible overkill.

The IPC for Remington's Steak House is shown in Exhibit 12.19. The chart shows that in terms of food quality and prices, Remington's is doing well. But there are several areas for improvement, particularly in comparison to the competition.

Hands-On Exercise

1. What are other areas of improvement for Remington's?
2. Run post hoc ANOVA tests between the competitor groups. What additional problems or challenges did this reveal?
3. What new marketing strategies would you suggest?

Summary

Explain measures of central tendency and dispersion.

The mean is the most commonly used measure of central tendency and describes the arithmetic average of the values in a sample of data. The median represents the middle value of an ordered set of values. The mode is the most frequently occurring value in a distribution of values. All these measures describe the center of the distribution of a set of values. The range defines the spread of the data. It is the distance between the smallest and largest values of the distribution. The standard deviation describes the average distance of the distribution values from the mean. A large standard deviation indicates a distribution in which the individual values are spread out and are relatively farther away from the mean.

Describe how to test hypotheses using univariate and bivariate statistics.

Marketing researchers often form hypotheses regarding population characteristics based on sample data. The process typically begins by calculating frequency distributions and averages, and then moves on to actually test the hypotheses. When the hypothesis testing involves examining one variable at a time, researchers use a univariate statistical test. When the hypothesis testing involves two variables, researchers use a bivariate statistical test. The Chi-square statistic permits us to test for statistically significance differences between the frequency distributions of two or more groups. Categorical data from questions about sex, race, profession, and so forth can be examined and tested for statistical differences. In addition to examining frequencies, marketing researchers often want to compare the means of two groups. There are two possible situations when means are compared. In independent samples the respondents come from different populations, so their answers to the survey questions do not affect each other. In related samples, the same respondent answers several questions, so comparing answers to these questions requires the use of a paired-samples *t*-test. Questions about mean differences in independent samples can be answered by using a *t*-test statistic.

Apply and interpret analysis of variance (ANOVA).

Researchers use ANOVA to determine the statistical significance of the difference between two or more means. The ANOVA technique calculates the variance of the values between groups of respondents and compares it with the variance of the responses within the groups. If the between-group variance is significantly greater than the within-group variance as indicated by the *F* ratio, the means are significantly different. The statistical significance between means in ANOVA is detected through the use of a follow-up test. The Scheffé test is one type of follow-up test. The test examines the differences between all possible pairs of sample means against a high and low confidence range. If the difference between a pair of means falls outside the confidence interval, then the means can be considered statistically different.

Utilize perceptual mapping to present research findings.

Perceptual mapping is used to develop maps that show perceptions of respondents visually. These maps are graphic representations that can be produced from the results of several multivariate techniques. The maps provide a visual representation of how companies, products, brands, or other objects are perceived relative to each other on key attributes such as quality of service, food taste, and food preparation.

Key Terms and Concepts

Review Questions

1. Explain the difference between the mean, the median, and the mode.
2. Why and how would you use Chi-square and *t*-tests in hypothesis testing?
3. Why and when would you want to use ANOVA in marketing research?
4. What will ANOVA tests not tell you, and how can you overcome this problem?

Discussion Questions

1. The measures of central tendency discussed in this chapter are designed to reveal information about the center of a distribution of values. Measures of dispersion provide information about the spread of all the values in a distribution around the center values. Assume you were conducting an opinion poll on voters' approval ratings of the job performance of the mayor of the city where you live. Do you think the mayor would be more interested in the central tendency or the dispersion measures associated with the responses to your poll? Why?

2. If you were interested in finding out whether or not young adults (21–34 years old) are more likely to buy products online than older adults (35 or more years old), how would you phrase your null hypothesis? What is the implicit alternative hypothesis accompanying your null hypothesis?

3. The level of significance (alpha) associated with testing a null hypothesis is also referred to as the probability of a Type I error. Alpha is the probability of rejecting the null hypothesis on the basis of your sample data when it is, in fact, true for the population of interest. Because alpha concerns the probability of making a mistake in your analysis, should you always try to set this value as small as possible? Why or why not?

4. Analysis of variance (ANOVA) allows you to test for the statistical difference between two or more means. Typically, there are more than two means tested. If the ANOVA results for a set of data reveal that the four means that were compared are significantly different from each other, how would you find out which individual means were statistically different from each other? What statistical techniques would you apply to answer this question?

5. **EXPERIENCE THE INTERNET.** Nike, Reebok, and Converse are strong competitors in the athletic shoe market. The three use different advertising and marketing strategies to appeal to their target markets. Use one of the search engines on the Internet to identify information on this market. Go to the Web sites for these three companies (www.Nike.com; www.Reebok.com; www.Converse.com). Gather background information on each, including its target market and market share. Design a questionnaire based on this information and survey a sample of students. Prepare a report on the different perceptions of each of these three companies, their shoes, and related aspects. Present the report in class and defend your findings.

6. **SPSS EXERCISE.** Form a team of three to four students in your class. Select one or two local franchises to conduct a survey on, such as Subway or McDonald's. Design a brief survey (10–12 questions) including questions like ratings on quality of food, speed of service, knowledge of employees, attitudes of employees, and price, as well as several demographic variables such as age, address, how often individuals eat there, and day of week and time of day. Obtain permission from the franchises to interview their customers at a convenient time, usually when they are leaving. Assure the franchiser you will not bother customers and that you will provide the franchise with a valuable report on your findings. Develop frequency charts, pie charts, and similar graphic displays of findings, where appropriate. Use statistics to test hypotheses, such as "Perceptions of speed of service differ by time of day or day of week." Prepare a report and present it to your class; particularly point out where statistically significant differences exist and why.

7. **SPSS EXERCISE.** Using SPSS and the Santa Fe Grill database, provide frequencies, means, modes, and medians for the relevant variables on the questionnaire. The questionnaire is shown in Chapter 11. In addition, develop bar charts and pie charts where appropriate for the data you analyzed. Run an ANOVA using the lifestyle and restaurant perceptions variables to identify any group differences that may exist. Be prepared to present a report on your findings.

8. **SPSS EXERCISE.** Review the *Marketing Research in Action* for this chapter. There were three restaurant competitors—Remington's, Outback, and Longhorn. Results for a one-way ANOVA of the restaurant image variables were provided. Now run post hoc ANOVA follow-up tests to see where the group differences are. Make recommendations for new marketing strategies for Remington's compared to the competition.

Examining Relationships in Quantitative Research

Chapter 13

1. Understand and evaluate the types of relationships between variables.
2. Explain the concepts of association and covariation.
3. Discuss the differences between Pearson correlation and Spearman correlation.
4. Explain the concept of statistical significance versus practical significance.
5. Understand when and how to use regression analysis.

Data Mining Helps Rebuild Procter & Gamble as a Global Powerhouse

Procter & Gamble (P&G) is a global player in consumer household products, with 20 world-ranking brands such as Tide, Folgers, Febreze, Mr. Clean, and Pringles. Three billion times a day, P&G products touch the lives of consumers around the world. Yet, several years ago the company saw its status in jeopardy. While many businesses, including P&G, pursue three overall marketing objectives—to get customers, keep customers, and grow customers—P&G realized it had to change its traditional marketing strategies and tactics in order to rebuild its global image and practices. The new approach was based on answering three key questions: (1) Who are the targeted consumers for each brand? (2) What is the company's desired brand equity or positioning? and (3) How should it be achieved?

P&G, a leader in brand management, turned to information technology and customer relationship management to design their new brand building strategy. From internal employee surveys they recognized a need to recommit to a customer-centric approach. For example, employees' attitudes concerning what P&G was doing "right" and "wrong" helped reestablish five fundamental focal points as operating objectives: (1) respecting the consumer as the "boss" and delivering superior consumer value, (2) making clear strategic choices about where to compete and how to win, (3) being a leader in innovation and branding, (4) leveraging P&G's unique, global operating structure, and (5) executing with excellence as well as more rigorous financial and operating discipline.

P&G mines the information in its data warehouse to retool customer models for its global brand and distributor markets. One objective of the brand models is to acquire new customers worldwide for its brands as well as cross-selling the brands to current customers. Another objective is to use product innovation and acquisition to expand the type of products sold worldwide. Statistical models with high predictive capability were modified and validated for each of the brands' market segments. The models considered factors such as household purchasing power, length of residence, family size, age, gender, attitudes toward a brand, media habits, purchase frequencies, and so on. The results suggest P&G

has made progress in its rebuilding efforts. Brand equity in 19 of 20 of their major brands is growing—30 million times a day consumers choose P&G brand products. Internally, employee confidence in P&G is growing—56 percent of all P&G employees believe P&G is moving in the right direction compared to only 26 percent a year ago. To learn more about P&G's turnaround go to www.pg.com.

Examining Relationships between Variables

Relationships between variables can be described in several ways, including presence, direction, strength of association, and type. We will describe each of these concepts in turn.

The first issue is whether two or more variables are related at all. If a systematic relationship exists between two or more variables, then a relationship is present. To measure whether a relationship exists, we rely on the concept of statistical significance. If we test for statistical significance and find that it exists, then we say that a relationship is present. Stated another way, we say that knowledge about the behavior of one variable enables us to make a useful prediction about the behavior of another. For example, if we find a statistically significant relationship between perceptions of the quality of Santa Fe Grill food and overall satisfaction, we would say a relationship is present.

If a relationship is present between two variables, it is important to know the direction. The direction of a relationship can be either positive or negative. Using the Santa Fe Grill example, a positive relationship exists if respondents who rate the quality of the food high are also highly satisfied. Alternatively, a negative relationship exists between two variables if low levels of one variable are associated with high levels of another. For example, as the number of service problems experienced when dining at the Santa Fe Grill increases, satisfaction is likely to decrease. Thus, number of service problems is negatively related to customer satisfaction.

An understanding of the strength of association also is important. Researchers generally categorize the strength of association as no relationship, weak relationship, moderate relationship, or strong relationship. If a consistent and systematic relationship is not present, then there is no relationship. A weak association means the variables may have some variance in common, but not much. A moderate or strong association means there is a consistent and systematic relationship, and the relationship is much more evident when it is strong. The strength of association is determined by the size of the correlation coefficient, with larger coefficients indicating a stronger association.

A fourth important concept is the type of relationship. If we say two variables are related, then we pose this question: "What is the nature of the relationship?" How can the link between Y and X best be described? There are a number of different ways in which two variables can share a relationship. Variables Y and X can have a **linear relationship,** which means the strength and nature of the relationship between them remains the same over the range of both variables, and can be best described using a straight line. A second type of relationship between Y and X is a **curvilinear relationship,** which means the strength and/or direction of the relationship changes over the range of both variables. For example, the relationship can be curvilinear if moderate levels of X are strongly related to high levels of Y, whereas both low and high levels of X are only slightly related. For example, if moderate levels of fear appeal in an advertisement are strongly related to positive attitudes toward the ad, whereas both low and high levels of fear appeal are only slightly related, then the relationship between strength of fear appeal and attitude toward the ad would be curvilinear.

Linear relationship A relationship between two variables whereby the strength and nature of the relationship remains the same over the range of both variables.

Curvilinear relationship A relationship between two variables whereby the strength and/or direction of their relationship changes over the range of both variables.

A linear relationship is much simpler to work with than a curvilinear relationship. If we know the value of variable X, then we can apply the formula for a straight line ($Y = a + bX$) to determine the value of Y. But when two variables have a curvilinear relationship, the formula that best describes the linkage is more complex. Therefore, most marketing researchers work with relationships they believe are linear.

Marketers are often interested in describing the relationship between variables they think influence purchases of their product(s). There are four questions to ask about a possible relationship between two variables. First, "Is there a relationship between the two variables of interest?" If there is a relationship, "How strong is that relationship?" "What is the direction of the relationship?" and "Is the relationship linear or nonlinear?" Once these questions have been answered, the researcher can interpret results, make conclusions, and recommend managerial actions.

Covariation and Variable Relationships

Covariation The amount of change in one variable that is consistently related to the change in another variable of interest.

Scatter diagram A graphic plot of the relative position of two variables using a horizontal and a vertical axis to represent the values of the respective variables.

Since we are interested in finding out whether two variables describing our customers are related, the concept of covariation is a very useful idea. **Covariation** is defined as the amount of change in one variable that is consistently related to a change in another variable. For example, if we know that DVD purchases are related to age, then we want to know the extent to which younger persons purchase more DVDs. Another way of stating the concept of covariation is that it is the degree of association between two variables. If two variables are found to change together on a reliable or consistent basis, then we can use that information to make predictions that will improve decision making about advertising and marketing strategies.

One way of visually describing the covariation between two variables is with the use of a **scatter diagram.** A scatter diagram plots the relative position of two variables using horizontal and vertical axes to represent the variable values. Exhibits 13.1 through 13.4 show some examples of possible relationships between two variables that might show up on a scatter diagram. In Exhibit 13.1, the best way to describe the visual impression left by the

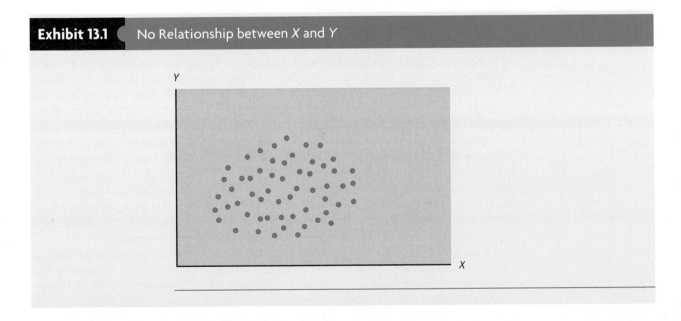

Exhibit 13.1   No Relationship between X and Y

Exhibit 13.2   Positive Relationship between *X* and *Y*

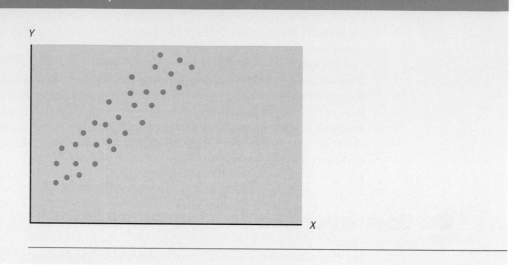

dots representing the values of each variable is probably a circle. That is, there is no particular pattern to the collection of dots. Thus, if you take two or three sample values of variable *Y* from the scatter diagram and look at the values for *X*, there is no predictable pattern to the values for *X*. Knowing the values of *Y* or *X* would not tell you very much (maybe nothing at all) about the possible values of the other variable. Exhibit 13.1 suggests there is no systematic relationship between *Y* and *X* and that there is very little or no covariation shared by the two variables. If we measured the amount of covariation shared by these two variables, which you will learn how to do in the next section, it would be very close to zero.

In Exhibit 13.2, the two variables present a very different picture from that of Exhibit 13.1. There is a distinct pattern to the dots. As the values of *Y* increase, so do the values of *X*. This pattern can be described as a straight line or an ellipse (a circle that has been stretched out from both sides). We could also describe this relationship as positive, because increases in the value of *Y* are associated with increases in the value of *X*. That is, if we know the relationship between *Y* and *X* is a linear, positive relationship, we would know the values of *Y* and *X* change in the same direction. As the values of *Y* increase, so do the values of *X*. Similarly, if the values of *Y* decrease, the values of *X* should decrease as well. If we try to measure the amount of covariation shown by the values of *Y* and *X*, it would be relatively high. Thus, changes in the value of *Y* are systematically related to changes in the value of *X*.

Exhibit 13.3 shows the same type of pattern between the values of *Y* and *X*, but the direction of the relationship is the opposite of Exhibit 13.2. There is a linear pattern, but now increases in the value of *Y* are associated with decreases in the values of *X*. This type of relationship is known as a negative relationship. The amount of covariation shared between the two variables is still high, because *Y* and *X* still change together, though in a direction opposite from that shown in Exhibit 13.2. The concept of covariation refers to the strength of the relationship between two variables, not the direction of the relationship between two variables.

Finally, Exhibit 13.4 shows a more complicated relationship between the values of *Y* and *X*. This pattern of dots can be described as curvilinear. That is, the relationship between the values of *Y* and the values of *X* is different for different values of the variables. Part of the relationship is positive (increases in the small values of *Y* are associated with

Exhibit 13.3	Negative Relationship between *X* and *Y*

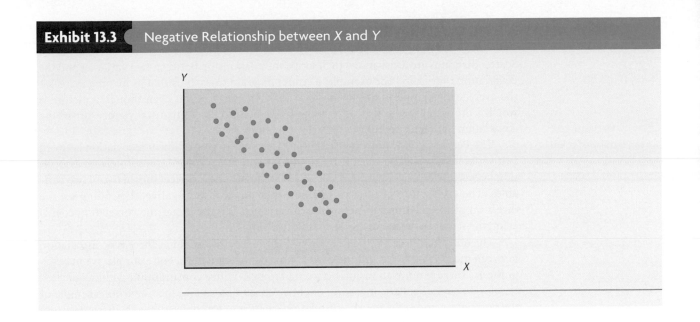

increases in the small values of *X*), but then the relationship becomes negative (increases in the larger values of *Y* are now associated with decreases in the larger values of *X*).

This pattern of dots cannot be described as a linear relationship. Many of the statistics marketing researchers use to describe association assume the two variables have a linear relationship. These statistics do not perform well when used to describe a curvilinear relationship. In Exhibit 13.4, we can still say the relationship is strong, or that the covariation exhibited by the two variables is strong. But now we cannot talk very easily about the direction (positive or negative) of the relationship, because the direction changes. To make matters more difficult, many statistical methods of describing relationships between variables cannot be applied to situations where you suspect the relationship is curvilinear.

Exhibit 13.4	Curvilinear Relationship between *X* and *Y*

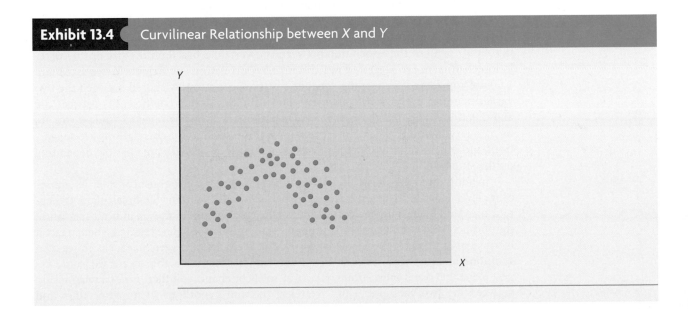

◼︎ Correlation Analysis

Scatter diagrams are a visual way to describe the relationship between two variables and the covariation they share. For example, a scatter diagram can tell us that as income increases the average consumption of Starbucks coffee increases too. But even though a picture is worth a thousand words, it is often more convenient to use a quantitative measure of the covariation between two items.

The **Pearson correlation coefficient** measures the degree of linear association between two variables. It varies between −1.00 and 1.00, with 0 representing absolutely no association between two variables, and −1.00 or 1.00 representing a perfect link between two variables. The correlation coefficient can be either positive or negative, depending on the direction of the relationship between two variables. But the larger the correlation coefficient, the stronger the association between two variables.

Pearson correlation coefficient A statistical measure of the strength of a linear relationship between two metric variables.

The null hypothesis for the Pearson correlation coefficient states there is no association between the two variables and the correlation coefficient is zero. For example, we may hypothesize there is no relationship between Starbucks coffee consumption and income levels. If a researcher collects measures of coffee consumption and income from a sample of the population and estimates the correlation coefficient for that sample, the basic question is "What is the probability of getting a correlation coefficient of this size in my sample if the correlation coefficient in the population is actually zero?" That is, if you calculate a large correlation coefficient between the two variables in your sample, and your sample was properly selected from the population of interest, then the chances the population correlation coefficient is really zero are relatively small. Therefore, if the correlation coefficient is statistically significant, the null hypothesis is rejected, and you can conclude with some confidence the two variables you are examining do share some association in the population. In short, Starbucks coffee consumption is related to income.

Earlier in the chapter we stated that the first question of interest was "Does a relationship between Y and X exist?" This question is equivalent to asking whether a correlation coefficient is statistically significant. If this is the case, then you can move on to the second and third questions: "If there is a relationship between Y and X, how strong is the relationship?" and "What is the best way to describe that relationship?"

The size of the correlation coefficient can be used to quantitatively describe the strength of the association between two variables. Some rules of thumb for characterizing the strength of the association between two variables based on the size of the correlation coefficient are suggested in Exhibit 13.5. Correlation coefficients between .81 and 1.00 are considered very strong. That is, covariance is strongly shared between the two variables under study. At the other extreme, if the correlation coefficient is between .00 and .20, there is a good chance the null hypothesis will not be rejected (unless you are using a large sample). These interpretations of the strength of correlations are suggestions and other ranges and descriptions of relationship strength are possible depending on the situation.

In addition to the size of the correlation coefficient, we also must consider its significance level. How do we do this? Most statistical software, including SPSS, calculates the significance level for a computed correlation coefficient. The SPSS software indicates statistical significance, which is the probability that the null hypothesis will be rejected when in fact it is true. For example, if the calculated correlation coefficient between Starbucks coffee consumption and income is .61 with a statistical significance of .05, this means we would expect to get that result only 5 times out of 100 solely by chance—if there is not a relationship between the two variables. Thus, we reject the null hypothesis of no association and

Exhibit 13.5	Rules of Thumb about the Strength of Correlation Coefficients

Range of Coefficient	Description of Strength
±.81 to ±1.00	Very strong
±.61 to ±.80	Strong
±.41 to ±.60	Moderate
±.21 to ±.40	Weak
±.00 to ±.20	Weak to No Relationship

conclude that Starbucks coffee consumption and income are related. In the SPSS output, statistical significance is identified as the "Sig." value.

Pearson Correlation Coefficient

In calculating the Pearson correlation coefficient, we are making several assumptions. First, we assume the two variables have been measured using interval- or ratio-scaled measures. If this is not the case, there are other types of correlation coefficients that can be computed which match the type of data on hand. A second assumption is the relationship we are trying to measure is linear. That is, a straight line describes the relationship between the variables of interest.

Use of the Pearson correlation coefficient also assumes the variables you want to analyze have a normally distributed population. The assumption of normal distributions for the variables under study is a common requirement for many statistical techniques. But determining whether it holds for the sample data you are working with is sometimes difficult and research analysts too often take the assumption of normality for granted.

SPSS Application—Pearson Correlation

We use the Santa Fe Grill database to examine the Pearson correlation. The owners anticipate that the relationship between satisfaction with the restaurant and likelihood to recommend the restaurant would be significant and positive. Looking at the database variables you note that information was collected on Likely to Recommend (variable X24) and Satisfaction (variable X22).

With SPSS it is easy to compute a Pearson correlation between these two variables and test this assumption. The SPSS click-through sequence is ANALYZE → CORRELATE → BIVARIATE, which leads to a dialog box where you select the variables. Transfer variables X22 and X24 into the Variables box. Note that we will use all three default options—Pearson correlation, two-tailed test of significance, and flag significant correlations. Next go to the Options box, and after it opens click on Means and Standard Deviations and then Continue. Finally, click on OK at the top right of the dialog box SPSS to calculate the Pearson correlation.

The Pearson correlation results are shown in Exhibit 13.6. As you can see in the Correlations table, the correlation between variable X24—Likely to Recommend and X22—Satisfaction is .672, and the statistical significance of this correlation is .000. Thus, we have confirmed our hypothesis that satisfaction is positively related to "likely to recommend."

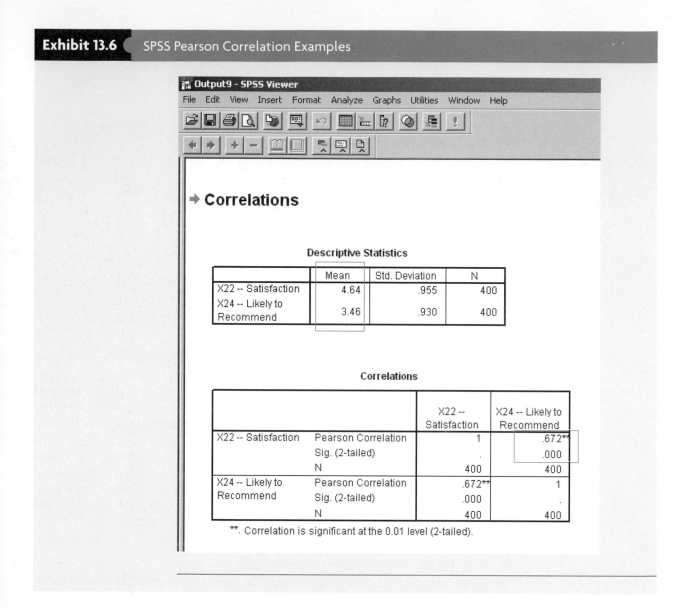

Exhibit 13.6 SPSS Pearson Correlation Examples

When we examine the means of the two variables, we see that satisfaction (4.64) is somewhat higher than likely to recommend (3.46) but we know the pattern of the responses to these questions is similar. That is, there is covariation between the responses to the two variables: as one goes up, so does the other (and as one goes down, so does the other). In short, more satisfied respondents are more likely to recommend Santa Fe Grill. The descriptive results (the means) give us information that adds to our understanding of the two variables. There is room for improvement in both satisfaction and intentions to recommend because these variables are measured on a 7-point scale and both means are near the mid-point of the scale.

Substantive Significance of the Correlation Coefficient

When the correlation coefficient is strong and significant, you can be confident the two variables are associated in a linear fashion. In our Santa Fe Grill example, we can be reasonably confident that likelihood of recommending the restaurant is in fact related to satisfaction.

When the correlation coefficient is weak, two possibilities must be considered: (1) there is no consistent, systematic relationship between the two variables; or (2) the association exists, but it is not linear, and other types of relationships must be investigated further.

When you square the correlation coefficient, you arrive at the **coefficient of determination,** or r^2. This number ranges from .00 to 1.0 and shows the proportion of variation explained or accounted for in one variable by another. In our Santa Fe Grill example, the correlation coefficient was .672. Thus, the $r^2 = .452$, meaning that approximately 45.2 percent of the variation in likelihood to recommend is associated with satisfaction. The larger the size of the coefficient of determination, the stronger the linear relationship between the two variables being examined. In our example, we have accounted for almost one-half of the variation in likelihood of recommending Santa Fe Grill by relating it to satisfaction.

There is a difference between statistical significance and substantive significance. Thus, you need to understand *substantive significance.* In other words, do the numbers you calculate provide useful information for management? Since the statistical significance calculation for correlation coefficients depends partly on sample size, it is possible to find statistically significant correlation coefficients that are too small to be of much practical use to management. This is because large samples result in more confidence a relationship exists, even if it is weak. For example, if we had correlated satisfaction with the likelihood of recommending the Santa Fe Grill to others, and the correlation coefficient was .20 (significant at the .05 level) the coefficient of determination would be .04. Can we conclude the results are meaningful? It is unlikely they are since the amount of shared variance is only 4 percent. Always look at both types of significance (statistical and substantive) before you develop conclusions.

Influence of Measurement Scales on Correlation Analysis

Sometimes research questions can be measured only with ordinal or nominal scales. What options are available when ordinal scales are used to collect data, or when the data simply cannot be measured with an interval scale or better? The **Spearman rank order correlation coefficient** is the recommended statistic to use when two variables have been measured using ordinal scales. If either one of the variables is represented by rank order data, the best approach is to use the Spearman rank order correlation coefficient, rather than the Pearson correlation.

SPSS Application—Spearman Rank Order Correlation

The Santa Fe Grill customer survey collected data that ranked four restaurant selection factors. These data are represented by variables X26 to X29. Management is interested in knowing whether "Food Quality" is a more important selection factor than "Service." Since these variables are ordinal, the Pearson correlation is not appropriate. The Spearman correlation is the appropriate coefficient to calculate. Variables X27—Food Quality and X29—Service are the variables we will use.

The SPSS click-through sequence is ANALYZE → CORRELATE → BIVARIATE, which leads to a dialog box where you select the variables. Transfer variables X27 and X29 into the Variables box. You will note the Pearson correlation is the default along with the two-tailed test of significance, and flag significant correlations. "Uncheck" the Pearson correlation and click on Spearman. Then click on OK at the top right of the dialog box to execute the program.

The SPSS results for the Spearman correlation are shown in Exhibit 13.7. As you can see in the Correlations table, the correlation between variable X27—Food Quality and X29—Service is −130, and the significance value is .01 (see footnote to Correlations table).

Coefficient of determination (r^2) A number measuring the proportion of variation in one variable accounted for by another. The r^2 measure can be thought of as a percentage and varies from 0.0 to 1.00.

Spearman rank order correlation coefficient A statistical measure of the linear association between two variables where both have been measured using ordinal (rank order) scales.

| Exhibit 13.7 | SPSS Spearman Rank Order Correlation |

Output6 - SPSS Viewer

File   Edit   View   Insert   Format   Analyze   Graphs   Utilities   Window   Help

➡ **Nonparametric Correlations**

Correlations

			X27 -- Food Quality	X29 -- Service
Spearman's rho	X27 -- Food Quality	Correlation Coefficient	1.000	-.130**
		Sig. (2-tailed)	.	.009
		N	400	400
	X29 -- Service	Correlation Coefficient	-.130**	1.000
		Sig. (2-tailed)	.009	.
		N	400	400

**. Correlation is significant at the .01 level (2-tailed).

Thus, we have confirmed there is a statistically significant relationship between the two restaurant selection factors, although it is very small. The negative correlation indicates that a customer who ranks food quality high in importance tends to rank service significantly lower in importance.

SPSS Application—Calculating Median Rankings

To better understand the Spearman correlation findings, we need to calculate the median rankings of the four selection factors. To do this, the SPSS click-through sequence is ANALYZE → DESCRIPTIVE STATISTICS → FREQUENCIES. Click on variables X26–X29 to highlight them and then on the arrow box for the Variables box to use them in your analysis. We use all four selection factors because this will enable us to examine the overall relative rankings of all the restaurant selection factors. Next, open the Statistics box and click on median and then Continue. For the Charts and Format options we will use the defaults, so click on OK to execute the program.

The SPSS results for median rankings are shown in the Statistics table in Exhibit 13.8. Recall that medians are descriptive data and can only be used to describe respondents. The variable with the lowest median is ranked the highest and is the most important, and the variable with the highest median is the least important, since the four selection factors were ranked from 1 to 4, with 1 = most important, and 4 = least important. Food quality is ranked as the most important (median = 1.0) while atmosphere and service are the least important. Our Spearman rank correlation compared food quality (median = 1) with service (median = 3.0), so food quality is significantly more important in restaurant selection than service.

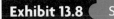 **Exhibit 13.8**   SPSS Median Example for Restaurant Selection Factors

Output13 - SPSS Viewer

File   Edit   View   Insert   Format   Analyze   Graphs   Utilities   Window   Help

Frequencies

Statistics

		X26 -- Price	X27 -- Food Quality	X28 -- Atmosphere	X29 -- Service
N	Valid	400	400	400	400
	Missing	0	0	0	0
Median		2.00	1.00	3.00	3.00

What Is Regression Analysis?

Correlation can determine if a relationship exists between two variables. The correlation coefficient also tells you the overall strength of the association and the direction of the relationship between the variables. However, managers sometimes still need to know how to describe the relationship between variables in greater detail. For example, a marketing manager may want to predict future sales or how a price increase will affect the profits or market share of the company. There are a number of ways to make such predictions: (1) extrapolation from past behavior of the variable; (2) simple guesses; or (3) use of a regression equation that uses information about related variables to assist in the prediction. Extrapolation and guesses (educated or otherwise) usually assume that past conditions and behaviors will continue into the future. They do not examine the influences behind the behavior of interest. Consequently, when sales levels, profits, or other variables of interest to a manager differ from those in the past, extrapolation and guessing do not explain why.

Bivariate regression analysis is a statistical technique that uses information about the relationship between an independent or predictor variable and a dependent variable to make predictions. Values of the independent variable are selected, and the behavior of the dependent variable is observed using the formula for a straight line. For example, if you wanted to find the current level of your company's sales volume, you would apply the following straight-line formula:

Sales volume (Y) = $0 + (Price per unit = b) $\times$ (Number of units sold = X)

Bivariate regression analysis
A statistical technique that analyzes the linear relationship between two variables by estimating coefficients for an equation for a straight line. One variable is designated as a dependent variable and the other is called an independent or predictor variable.

You would not expect any sales volume if no units are sold. Thus, the constant or *x*-intercept is $0. Price per unit (*b*) determines the amount that sales volume (*Y*) increases with each unit sold (*X*). In this example, the relationship between sales volume and number of units sold is linear.

Once a regression equation has been developed to predict values of *Y*, we want to find out how good that prediction is. A place to begin is to compare the values predicted by our regression model with the actual values we collected in our sample. By comparing this actual value (Y_i) with our predicted value (*Y*), we can tell how well our model predicts the actual value of our dependent variable.

A couple of points should be made about the assumptions behind regression analysis. First, as with correlation, regression analysis assumes a linear relationship is a good description of the relationship between two variables. If the scatter diagram showing the positions of the values of both variables looks like the scatter plots in Exhibits 13.2 or 13.3, this assumption is a good one. If the plot looks like Exhibits 13.1 or 13.4, however, then regression analysis is not a good choice. Second, even though the terminology of regression analysis commonly uses the labels *dependent* and *independent* for the variables, these labels do not mean we can say one variable *causes* the behavior of the other. Regression analysis uses knowledge about the level and type of association between two variables to make predictions. Statements about the ability of one variable to cause changes in another must be based on conceptual logic or preexisting knowledge rather than on statistical calculations alone.

Finally, the use of a simple regression model assumes (1) the variables of interest are measured on interval or ratio scales (except in the case of dummy variables, which are discussed on our Web site—**www.mhhe.com/hairessentials1e**); (2) the variables come from a normal population; and (3) the error terms associated with making predictions are normally and independently distributed.

Fundamentals of Regression Analysis

A fundamental basis of regression analysis is the assumption of a straight line relationship between the independent and dependent variables. This relationship is illustrated in Exhibit 13.9. The general formula for a straight line is:

$$Y = a + bX + e_i$$

where

Y = the dependent variable
a = the intercept (point where the straight line intersects the *y*-axis when $X = 0$)
b = the slope (the change in *Y* for every 1 unit change in *X*)
X = the independent variable used to predict *Y*
e_i = the error for the prediction

In regression analysis, we examine the relationship between the independent variable *X* and the dependent variable *Y*. To do so, we use the actual values of *X* and *Y* in our data set and the computed values of *a* and *b*. The calculations are based on the least squares procedure. The *least squares procedure* determines the best-fitting line by minimizing the vertical distances of all the data points from the line, as shown in Exhibit 13.10. The best-fitting line is the regression line. Any point that does not fall on the line is the result of **unexplained variance,** or the variance in *Y* that is not explained by *X*. This unexplained variance is called *error* and is represented by the vertical distance between the estimated straight regression line and the actual data points. The distances of all the points not on the line are squared and added together to determine the *sum of the squared errors,* which is a measure of total error in the regression.

Unexplained variance Is the amount of variation in the dependent variable that cannot be accounted for by the combination of independent variables.

Exhibit 13.9   The Straight Line Relationship in Regression

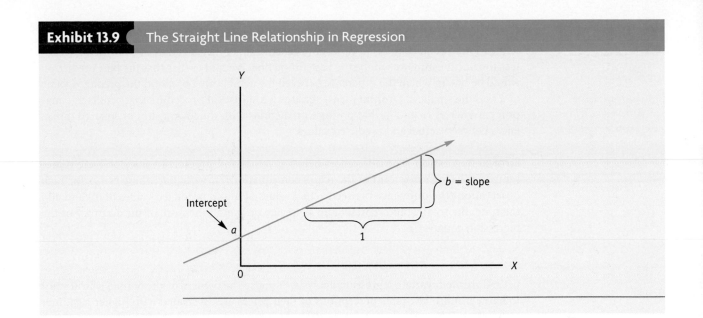

In the case of bivariate regression analysis, we are looking at one independent variable and one dependent variable. However, managers frequently want to look at the combined influence of several independent variables on one dependent variable. For example, are DVD purchases related only to age, or are they also related to income, ethnicity, gender, geographic location, and education level? Similarly, in the Santa Fe Grill database, we might ask whether customer satisfaction is related only to perceptions of the restaurant's food taste (X18), or is satisfaction also related to perceptions of friendly employees (X12), reasonable prices (X16), and speed of service (X21)? Multiple regression is the appropriate technique to measure these multivariate relationships. We discuss bivariate or simple regression analysis before moving on to multiple regression analysis.

Exhibit 13.10   Fitting the Regression Line Using the "Least Squares" Procedure

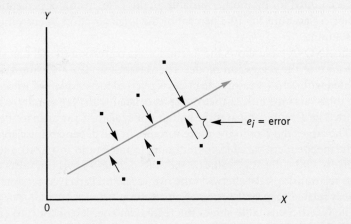

Developing and Estimating the Regression Coefficients

Regression uses an estimation procedure called ordinary least squares (OLS) that guarantees the line it estimates will be the best-fitting line. We said earlier that the best prediction would be one in which the difference between the actual value of Y and the predicted value of Y was the smallest. **Ordinary least squares** is a statistical procedure that results in equation parameters (a and b) that produce predictions with the lowest sum of squared differences between actual and predicted values.

Error in Regression The differences between actual and predicted values of Y are represented by e_i (the error term of the regression equation). If we square these errors for each observation (the difference between actual values of Y and predicted values of Y) and add them up, the total would represent an aggregate or overall measure of the accuracy of the regression equation.

SPSS Application—Bivariate Regression

Let's illustrate bivariate regression analysis. Suppose the owners of the Santa Fe Grill want to know if more favorable perceptions of their prices are associated with higher customer satisfaction. The obvious answer would be "of course they would be." But how much improvement would be expected in customer satisfaction if the owners improved the perceptions of prices? Bivariate regression provides information to answer this question.

In the Santa Fe Grill database X22 is a measure of customer satisfaction, with 1 = Not Satisfied at All and 7 = Highly Satisfied. Variable X16 is a measure of respondents' perceptions of the reasonableness of the restaurant's prices (1 = Strongly Disagree, 7 = Strongly Agree). The null hypothesis is there is no relationship between X22—Satisfaction and X16—Reasonable Prices.

The SPSS click-through sequence is ANALYZE → REGRESSION → LINEAR. Click on X22—Satisfaction and move it to the Dependent Variable box. Click on X16—Reasonable Prices and move it to the Independent Variables box. We use the defaults for the other options, so click OK to run the bivariate regression.

Exhibit 13.11 contains the results of the bivariate regression analysis. The table labeled Model Summary has three types of "R's" in it. The R on the far left is the correlation coefficient (.321). The R-square is .103; you get this value by squaring the correlation coefficient (.321) for this regression. The R-square shows the percentage of variation in one variable that is accounted for by another variable. In this case, customer perceptions of the Santa Fe Grill's prices account for 10.3 percent of the total variation in customer satisfaction with the restaurant.

The ANOVA table shows the F ratio for the regression model that shows the statistical significance of the regression model. The variance in X22—Customer Satisfaction that is associated with X16—Reasonable Prices is referred to as *explained variance*. The remainder of the total variance in X22 that is not associated with X16 is referred to as *unexplained variance*. The F ratio compares the amount of explained variance to the unexplained variance. The larger the F ratio the more variance in the dependent variable that is associated with the independent variable. In our example, the F ratio = 45.810, and the statistical significance is .000—the "Sig." value on the SPSS output—so we can reject the null hypothesis that no relationship exists between the two variables. Perceived reasonableness of prices is positively related to overall customer satisfaction.

The Coefficients table shows the regression coefficient for X16 (reasonable prices). The column labeled Unstandardized Coefficients indicates the unstandardized regression coefficient (b) for X16 is .250. The column labeled Sig. shows the statistical significance of

Exhibit 13.11   SPSS Results for Bivariate Regression

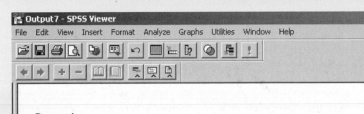

Regression

Model Summary

Model	R	R Square	Adjusted R Square	Std. Error of the Estimate
1	.321[a]	.103	.101	.905

a Predictors: (Constant), X16 -- Reasonable Prices

ANOVA[b]

Model		Sum of Squares	df	Mean Square	F	Sig.
1	Regression	37.530	1	37.530	45.810	.000[a]
	Residual	326.060	398	.819		
	Total	363.590	399			

a. Predictors: (Constant), X16 -- Reasonable Prices

b. Dependent Variable: X22 -- Satisfaction

Coefficients[a]

Model		Unstandardized Coefficients		Standardized Coefficients	t	Sig.
		B	Std. Error	Beta		
1	(Constant)	3.561	.166		21.400	.000
	X16 -- Reasonable Prices	.250	.037	.321	6.768	.000

a. Dependent Variable: X22 -- Satisfaction

the regression coefficient for X16, as measured by the *t*-test. The *t*-test examines the question of whether the regression coefficient is different enough from zero to be statistically significant. The *t* statistic is calculated by dividing the regression coefficient by its standard error (labeled Std. Error in the Coefficients table). If you divide .250 by .037, you will get a *t* value of 6.768, which is significant at the .000 level.

The Coefficients table also shows the result for the Constant component in the regression equation. This item is a term in the equation for a straight line we discussed earlier. It is the *X*-intercept, or the value of *Y* when *X* is 0. If the independent variable takes on a value of 0, the dependent measure (X22) would have a value of 3.561. Combining the results of the "Coefficients" table into a regression equation, we have:

Predicted value of X22 = 3.561 + .250 · (value of X16) + .905 (avg. error in prediction)

The relationship between customer satisfaction and reasonable prices is positive but weak. The regression coefficient for X16 is interpreted as "For every unit that X16 (the rating of reasonable prices) increases, X22 (satisfaction) will increase by .250 units." Recall that the Santa Fe Grill owners asked: "If the prices in our restaurant are perceived as being reasonable, will this be associated with improved customer satisfaction?" The answer is yes, but in a small way, because the model was significant at the .000 level, but the R-square was only .103.

Significance

Once the statistical significance of the regression coefficients is determined, we have answered the first question about our relationship: "Is there a relationship between our dependent and the independent variable?" In this case, the answer is yes. But recall our discussion of statistical versus substantive significance. The logic of that discussion also applies when we evaluate whether regression coefficients are meaningful. A second question to ask is: "How strong is that relationship?" The output of regression analysis includes the coefficient of determination, or r^2—which describes the amount of variation in the dependent variable associated with the variation in the independent variable. The regression r^2 also tells you what percentage of the total variation in your dependent variable you can explain by using the independent variable. The r^2 measure varies between .00 and 1.00 and is calculated by dividing the amount of variation you have been able to explain with your regression equation by the total variation in the dependent variable. In the previous Santa Fe Grill example that examined the relationship between reasonable prices and satisfaction, the r^2 was .107. That means 10.7 percent of the variation in customer satisfaction is associated with the variation in respondents' perceptions of the reasonableness of prices.

When examining the substantive significance of a regression equation, you should look at the size of the r^2 for the regression equation and the size of the regression coefficient. The regression coefficient may be statistically significant, but still relatively small, meaning that your dependent measure won't change very much for a given unit change in the independent measure. In our Santa Fe Grill example, the unstandardized regression coefficient was .254, which is not a very strong relationship. When regression coefficients are significant but small, we say a relationship is present in our population, but that it is weak. In this case, Santa Fe Grill owners need to consider additional independent variables that will help them to better understand and predict customer satisfaction.

Multiple Regression Analysis

Multiple regression analysis A statistical technique which analyzes the linear relationship between a dependent variable and multiple independent variables by estimating coefficients for the equation for a straight line.

In most problems faced by managers, there are several independent variables that need to be examined for their influence on a dependent variable. **Multiple regression analysis** is the appropriate technique to use for these situations. The technique is an extension of bivariate regression. Multiple independent variables are entered into the regression equation, and for each variable a separate regression coefficient is calculated that describes its relationship with the dependent variable. The coefficients enable the marketing researcher to examine the relative influence of each independent variable on the dependent variable. For example, Santa Fe Grill owners want to examine not only reasonable prices, but also customer perceptions of employees, atmosphere, and service. This gives them a more accurate picture of what to consider when developing marketing strategies.

The relationship between each independent variable and the dependent measure is still linear. Now, however, with the addition of multiple independent variables we have to think of multiple independent variables instead of just a single one. The easiest way to analyze the relationships is to examine the regression coefficient for each independent variable, which represents the average amount of change expected in Y given a unit change in the value of the independent variable you are examining.

With the addition of more than one independent variable, we have some new issues to consider. One is the possibility that each independent variable is measured using a different scale. To solve this problem, we calculate the *standardized regression coefficient*. It is called a **beta coefficient,** and it shows the change in the dependent variable for each unit change in the independent variable. Standardization removes the effects of using different scales of measurement. For example, years of age and annual income are measured on different scales. Beta coefficients will range from .00 to 1.00, and can be either positive or negative. A *positive beta* means that as the size of an independent variable increases, then the size of the dependent variable increases. A *negative beta* means that as the size of the independent variable increases, then the size of the dependent variable gets smaller.

Statistical Significance

After the regression coefficients have been estimated, you must examine the statistical significance of each coefficient. This is done in the same manner as with bivariate regression. Each regression coefficient is divided by its standard error to produce a t statistic, which is compared against the critical value to determine whether the null hypothesis can be rejected. The basic question is still the same: "What is the probability we would get a coefficient of this size if the real regression coefficient in the population were zero?" You should examine the t-test statistics for each regression coefficient. Many times not all the independent variables in a regression equation will be statistically significant. If a regression coefficient is not statistically significant, that means the independent variable does not have a relationship with the dependent variable and the slope describing that relationship is relatively flat: the value of the dependent variable does not change at all as the value of the statistically insignificant independent variable changes.

When using multiple regression analysis, it is important to examine the overall statistical significance of the regression model. The amount of variation in the dependent variable you have been able to explain with the independent measures is compared with the total variation in the dependent measure. This comparison results in a statistic called a **model F statistic** which is compared against a critical value to determine whether or not to reject the null hypothesis. If the F statistic is statistically significant, it means the chances of the regression model for your sample producing a large r^2 when the population r^2 is actually 0 are acceptably small.

Substantive Significance

Once we have estimated the regression equation, we need to assess the strength of the association. The multiple r^2 or multiple coefficient of determination describes the strength of the relationship between all the independent variables in our equation and the dependent variable. The larger the r^2 measure, the more of the behavior of the dependent measure is associated with the independent measures we are using to predict it. Higher values for r^2 mean stronger relationships between the group of independent variables and the dependent measure.

To summarize, the elements of a multiple regression model to examine in determining its significance include the r^2; the model F statistic; the individual regression coefficients for each independent variable; their associated t statistics; and the individual beta coefficients. The appropriate procedure to follow in evaluating the results of a regression analysis is:

Beta coefficient An estimated regression coefficient that has been recalculated to have a mean of 0 and a standard deviation of 1. Such a change enables independent variables with different units of measurement to be directly compared on their association with the dependent variable.

Model F statistic A statistic that compares the amount of variation in the dependent measure "explained" or associated with the independent variables to the "unexplained" or error variance. A larger F statistic indicates that the regression model has more explained variance than error variance.

(1) assess the statistical significance of the overall regression model using the F statistic and its associated probability; (2) evaluate the obtained r^2 to see how large it is; (3) examine the individual regression coefficients and their t statistics to see which are statistically significant; and (4) look at the beta coefficients to assess relative influence. Taken together, these elements give you a comprehensive picture of the answers to our three basic questions about the relationships between your dependent and independent variables.

SPSS Application—Multiple Regression

Regression can be used to examine the relationship between a single metric dependent variable and one or more metric independent variables. If you examine the Santa Fe Grill database you will note that the first 21 variables are metric independent variables. They are lifestyle variables and perceptions of the restaurant, measured using a 7-point rating scale with 7 representing the high end of the scale and 1 the low end. Variables X22, X23, and X24 are metric dependent variables measured on a seven-point rating scale. Variable X25—Frequency of Patronage, X30—Distance Driven, X31—Ad Recall, and X32—Gender are nonmetric. Variables X26 to X29 also are nonmetric variables because they are ranking data and thus cannot be used in regression.

A simple problem to examine with multiple regression is the relationship between perceptions of the food in the restaurant and overall customer satisfaction. In this case, the single metric dependent variable is X22—Satisfaction, and the independent variables would be X15—Fresh Food, X18—Food Taste, and X20—Food Temperature. The null hypothesis would be that there is no relationship between the three food variables and X22. The alternative hypothesis would be that X15, X18, and X20 are significantly related to X22—Customer Satisfaction.

The SPSS click-through sequence to examine this relationship is ANALYZE → REGRESSION → LINEAR. Highlight X22 and move it to the Dependent Variables box. Highlight X15, X18, and X20 and move them to the Independent Variables box. We will use the defaults for the other options so click OK to run the multiple regression.

The SPSS output for the multiple regression is shown in Exhibit 13.12. The Model Summary table shows that the R-square for this model is .381. This means that 38.1 percent of the variation in satisfaction (dependent variable) can be explained by the three independent variables. The regression model results in the ANOVA table indicate that the R-square for the overall model is significantly different from zero (F ratio = 81.231; probability level ("Sig.") = .000). This probability level means there are .000 chances that the regression model results come from a population where the R-square actually is zero. That is, there are no chances out of 1,000 that the actual correlation coefficient is zero.

To determine if one or more of the food independent variables are significant predictors of satisfaction we examine the information provided in the Coefficients table. Looking at the Standardized Coefficients Beta column reveals that X15—Fresh Food has a beta coefficient of .523 which is significant (.000). Similarly, X18—Food Taste and X20—Food Temperature have beta coefficients of −0.268 and 0.375, respectively (Sig. level of .000). This means we can reject the null hypothesis that the three food variables are not related to X22—Customer Satisfaction. Thus, this regression analysis tells us that customer perceptions of food in the Santa Fe Grill are a good predictor of the level of satisfaction with the restaurant.

A word of caution is needed at this point regarding the Beta coefficients. Recall that the size of the individual coefficients shows how strongly each independent variable is related to the dependent variable. The signs (negative or positive) also are important. A positive sign indicates a positive relationship (higher independent variable values are associated with higher dependent variable values). A negative sign indicates a negative relationship.

Exhibit 13.12   SPSS Multiple Regression Example

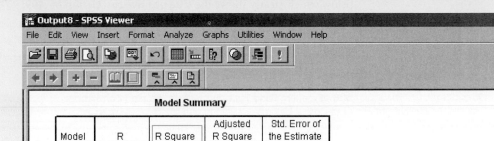

Model Summary

Model	R	R Square	Adjusted R Square	Std. Error of the Estimate
1	.617[a]	.381	.376	.754

a. Predictors: (Constant), X20 -- Proper Food Temperature, X15 -- Fresh Food, X18 -- Excellent Food Taste

ANOVA[b]

Model		Sum of Squares	df	Mean Square	F	Sig.
1	Regression	138.511	3	46.170	81.231	.000[a]
	Residual	225.079	396	.568		
	Total	363.590	399			

a. Predictors: (Constant), X20 -- Proper Food Temperature, X15 -- Fresh Food, X18 -- Excellent Food Taste

b. Dependent Variable: X22 -- Satisfaction

Coefficients[a]

Model		Unstandardized Coefficients		Standardized Coefficients		
		B	Std. Error	Beta	t	Sig.
1	(Constant)	2.007	.199		10.094	.000
	X15 -- Fresh Food	.418	.053	.523	7.889	.000
	X18 -- Excellent Food Taste	-.235	.062	-.268	-3.812	.000
	X20 -- Proper Food Temperature	.324	.050	.375	6.527	.000

a. Dependent Variable: X22 -- Satisfaction

Multicollinearity A situation in which several independent variables are highly correlated with each other. This characteristic can result in difficulty in estimating separate or independent regression coefficients for the correlated variables.

The negative sign of X18–Food Taste suggests, therefore, that less favorable perceptions of food taste are associated with higher levels of satisfaction. This result is clearly not logical and points out one of the weaknesses of multiple regression. When the independent variables are highly correlated with each other, the signs of the beta coefficients may be reversed in a regression model, which happened in this case. Highly correlated independent variables are described as exhibiting **multicollinearity.**

Because multicollinearity can create problems in using regression, analysts must always examine the logic of the signs for the regression betas when independent variables are highly correlated. If an expected relationship is the opposite of what is anticipated, one must look at a simple bivariate correlation of the two variables. This can be seen in the table below which clearly shows the true positive correlation of .409.

Correlations		X22—Satisfaction
X18—Excellent Food Taste	Pearson Correlation	.409[*]
	Sig. (2-tailed)	.000
	N	.400

[*]Correlation is significant at the 0.01 level (2-tailed).

The topics of multicollinearity and using nonmetric dummy variables in regression are beyond the scope of this book. To help you understand these topics we have placed material about them on our Web site at www.mhhe.com/hairessentials1e.

Examination of the SPSS tables reveals that there is a lot of information provided that we did not discuss. Experts in statistics may use this information, but managers typically do not. One of the challenges for you will be to learn which information is most important to analyze and present in a report.

MARKETING RESEARCH IN ACTION
The Role of Employees in Developing a Customer Satisfaction Program

The plant manager of QualKote Manufacturing is interested in the impact his year-long effort to implement a quality improvement program is having on the satisfaction of his customers. The plant foreman, assembly-line workers, and engineering staff have closely examined their operations to determine which activities have the most impact on product quality and reliability. Together, the managers and employees have worked to better understand how each particular job affects the final delivered quality of the product as the customer perceives it.

To answer his questions about customer satisfaction, the plant manager conducted an internal survey of plant workers and managers using a 7-point scale (endpoints are 1 = Strongly Disagree and 7 = Strongly Agree). His plans are to get opinions from within the company first and then do a customer survey on similar topics. He has collected completed surveys from 57 employees. The following are examples of the topics that were covered in the questionnaire:

- Data from a variety of external sources such as customers, competitors, and suppliers is used in the strategic planning process. Independent variable A10.
- Customers are involved in the product quality planning process. Independent variable A12.
- Customer requirements and expectations of the company's products are used in developing strategic plans and goals. Independent variable A17.
- There is a systematic process to translate customer requirements into new/improved products. Independent variable A23.
- There is a systematic process to accurately determine customers' requirements and expectations. Independent variable A31.
- The company's product quality program has improved the level of customer satisfaction. Dependent variable A36.
- The company's product quality program has improved the likelihood that customers will recommend us. Dependent variable A37.
- Gender of the employee responding: Male = 1; Female = 0. Classification variable A40.

A multiple regression was run using SPSS with responses of the 57 employees as input to the model. The output is shown in Exhibits 13.13 and 13.14. There is a database of QualKote employee responses to these questions available in SPSS format at **www.mhhe.com/hairessentials1e**. The database is labeled Qualkote MRIA_essn.sav.

Results indicate a statistically significant relationship between the metric dependent variable (A36—Satisfaction) and at least some of the five metric independent variables. The r^2 for the relationship is 67.0 and it is statistically significant at the .000 level. This suggests that when employees have more favorable perceptions about some aspects of the implementation of the quality improvement program, they also believe the program has improved customer satisfaction.

Exhibit 13.13   Descriptive Statistics

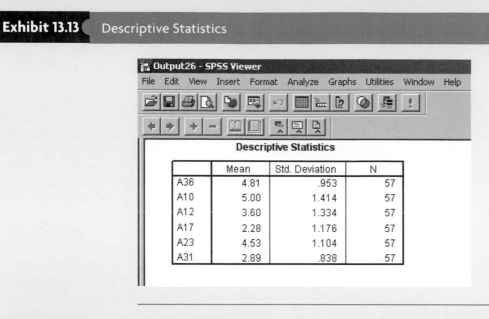

Descriptive Statistics

	Mean	Std. Deviation	N
A36	4.81	.953	57
A10	5.00	1.414	57
A12	3.60	1.334	57
A17	2.28	1.176	57
A23	4.53	1.104	57
A31	2.89	.838	57

Exhibit 13.14   Multiple Regression of Qualkote Satisfaction Variables

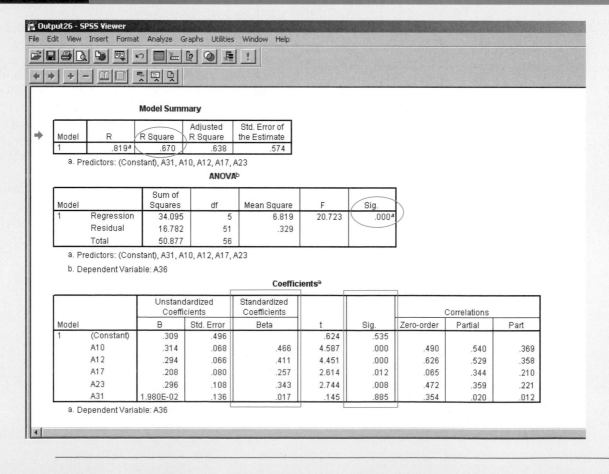

Model Summary

Model	R	R Square	Adjusted R Square	Std. Error of the Estimate
1	.819[a]	.670	.638	.574

a. Predictors: (Constant), A31, A10, A12, A17, A23

ANOVA[b]

Model		Sum of Squares	df	Mean Square	F	Sig.
1	Regression	34.095	5	6.819	20.723	.000[a]
	Residual	16.782	51	.329		
	Total	50.877	56			

a. Predictors: (Constant), A31, A10, A12, A17, A23

b. Dependent Variable: A36

Coefficients[a]

Model		Unstandardized Coefficients B	Unstandardized Coefficients Std. Error	Standardized Coefficients Beta	t	Sig.	Correlations Zero-order	Correlations Partial	Correlations Part
1	(Constant)	.309	.496		.624	.535			
	A10	.314	.068	.466	4.587	.000	.490	.540	.369
	A12	.294	.066	.411	4.451	.000	.626	.529	.358
	A17	.208	.080	.257	2.614	.012	.065	.344	.210
	A23	.296	.108	.343	2.744	.008	.472	.359	.221
	A31	1.980E-02	.136	.017	.145	.885	.354	.020	.012

a. Dependent Variable: A36

Hands-On Exercise

1. Will the results of this regression model be useful to the QualKote Plant manager? If yes, how?
2. Which independent variables are helpful in predicting A36—Customer Satisfaction?
3. How would the manager interpret the mean values for the variables reported in Exhibit 13.13?
4. What other regression models might be examined with the questions from this survey?

Summary

Understand and evaluate the types of relationships between variables.

Relationships between variables can be described in several ways, including presence, direction, strength of association, and type. Presence tells us whether a consistent and systematic relationship exists. Direction tells us whether the relationship is positive or negative. Strength of association tells us whether we have a weak or strong relationship, and the type of relationship is usually described as either linear or nonlinear.

Two variables may share a linear relationship, in which changes in one variable are accompanied by some change (not necessarily the same amount of change) in the other variable. As long as the amount of change stays constant over the range of both variables, the relationship is termed linear. Relationships between two variables that change in strength and/or direction as the values of the variables change are referred to as curvilinear.

Explain the concepts of association and covariation.

The terms covariation and association refer to the attempt to quantify the strength of the relationship between two variables. Covariation is the amount of change in one variable of interest that is consistently related to change in another variable under study. The degree of association is a numerical measure of the strength of the relationship between two variables. Both these terms refer to linear relationships.

Discuss the differences between Pearson correlation and Spearman correlation.

Pearson correlation coefficients are a measure of linear association between two variables of interest. The Pearson correlation coefficient is used when both variables are measured on an interval or ratio scale. When one or more variables of interest are measured on an ordinal scale, the Spearman rank order correlation coefficient should be used.

Explain the concept of statistical significance versus practical significance.

Because some of the procedures involved in determining the statistical significance of a statistical test include consideration of the sample size, it is possible to have a very low degree of association between two variables show up as statistically significant (i.e., the population parameter is not equal to zero). However, by considering the absolute strength of the relationship in addition to its statistical significance, the researcher is better able to draw the appropriate conclusion about the data and the population from which they were selected.

Understand when and how to use regression analysis.

Regression analysis is useful in answering questions about the strength of a linear relationship between a dependent variable and one or more independent variables. The results of a regression analysis indicate the amount of change in the dependent variable that is associated with a one-unit change in the independent variables. In addition, the accuracy of the regression equation can be evaluated by comparing the predicted values of the dependent variable to the actual values of the dependent variable drawn from the sample.

Key Terms and Concepts

Beta coefficient 297

Bivariate regression analysis 291

Coefficient of determination (r^2) 289

Covariation 283

Curvilinear relationship 282

Linear relationship 282

Model F statistic 297

Multicollinearity 299

Multiple regression analysis 296

Ordinary least squares 294

Pearson correlation coefficient 286

Scatter diagram 283

Spearman rank order correlation coefficient 289

Unexplained variance 292

Review Questions

1. Explain the difference between testing for significant differences and testing for association.
2. Explain the difference between association and causation.
3. What is covariation? How does it differ from correlation?
4. What are the differences between univariate and bivariate statistical techniques?
5. What is regression analysis? When would you use it?
6. What is the difference between simple regression and multiple regression?

Discussion Questions

1. Regression and correlation analysis both describe the strength of linear relationships between variables. Consider the concepts of education and income. Many people would say these two variables are related in a linear fashion. As education increases, income usually increases (although not necessarily at the same rate). Can you think of two variables that are related in such a way that their relationship changes over their range of possible values (i.e., in a curvilinear fashion)? How would you analyze the relationship between two such variables?
2. Is it possible to conduct a regression analysis on two variables and obtain a significant regression equation (significant F ratio), but still have a low r^2? What does the r^2 statistic measure? How can you have a low r^2 yet still get a statistically significant F ratio for the overall regression equation?
3. The ordinary least squares (OLS) procedure commonly used in regression produces a line of "best fit" for the data to which it is applied. How would you define best fit in regression analysis? What is there about the procedure that guarantees a best fit to the

data? What assumptions about the use of a regression technique are necessary to produce this result?
4. When multiple independent variables are used to predict a dependent variable in multiple regression, multicollinearity among the independent variables is often a concern. What is the main problem caused by high multicollinearity among the independent variables in a multiple regression equation? Can you still achieve a high r^2 for your regression equation if multicollinearity is present in your data?
5. **EXPERIENCE THE INTERNET.** Choose a retailer that students are likely to patronize that sells in both catalogs and on the Internet (for example, Victoria's Secret). Prepare a questionnaire that compares the experience of shopping from the catalog with shopping online. Then ask a sample of students to visit the Web site, look at the catalogs you have brought to class, and then complete the questionnaire. Enter the data into a software package and assess your findings statistically. Prepare a report that compares catalog and online shopping. Be able to defend your conclusions.

6. **SPSS EXERCISE.** Choose one or two other students from your class and form a team. Identify the different retailers from your community where DVD players, TVs, and other electronics products are sold. Team members should divide up, visit all the different stores, and describe the products and brands that are sold in each. Also observe the layout in the store, the store personnel, and the type of advertising the store uses. In other words, familiarize yourself with each retailer's marketing mix. Use your knowledge of the marketing mix to design a questionnaire. Interview approximately 100 people who are familiar with all the retailers you selected and collect their responses. Analyze the responses using a statistical software package such as SPSS. Prepare a report of your findings, including whether the perceptions of each of the stores are similar or different, and particularly whether the differences are statistically or substantively different. Present your findings in class and be prepared to defend your conclusions and your use of statistical techniques.

7. **SPSS EXERCISE.** Santa Fe Grill owners believe one of their competitive advantages is that the restaurant is a fun place to eat. Use the Santa Fe Grill database and run a bivariate correlation analysis between X13—Fun Place to Eat and X22—Satisfaction to test this hypothesis. Could this hypothesis be further examined with multiple regression?

Reporting and Presenting Results

Chapter 14

1. Understand the objectives of a research report.
2. Describe the format of a marketing research report.
3. Discuss several techniques for graphically displaying research results.
4. Clarify problems encountered in preparing reports.
5. Understand the importance of presentations in marketing research.

It Takes More than Numbers to Communicate

Visual display of data is not easy and even research experts do not always do it well. After all, the kinds of people who are good at statistics are not necessarily the ones that are good at visual presentation. Nevertheless, the ability to present data visually in a way that is illuminating is important in writing research reports.

The person most known for his expertise in presenting visual data is Professor Edward Tufte. The author of several books on the topic, including *The Display of Quantitative Information,* Professor Tufte hails from the field of political science but his advice applies to any field. Business graphics have the same goals as any other graphics: to convey information, to summarize reasoning, and to solve problems. Tufte explains the importance of visual displays of data: "Good design is clear thinking made visible, and bad design is stupidity made visible. . . . So when you see a display filled with chart junk, there's a deeper corruption: they don't know what they're talking about."[1]

Tufte has implicated poor presentation of statistics and information in the *Challenger* disaster. A NASA PowerPoint slide show buried statistics revealing that rubber O ring seals in the boosters tended to leak at low temperatures. The failure of an O-ring ultimately resulted in the death of seven astronauts. Of course, poor graphic presentations rarely have such tragic and dramatic consequences. However, business opportunities are missed, time is wasted, and audiences are bored.

The *New York Times* calls Tufte the Leonardo da Vinci of data presentation. But Professor Tufte emphasizes that presenting statistics well is not about creating slick graphics. "The task is not to have 'high-impact' presentations, or 'point, click, wow,' or 'power pitches.' The point is to explain something. . . . The right metaphor for presentations is not power or PowerPoint, and it's not television or theater. It's teaching."[2]

Value of Communicating Research Findings

No matter how well research projects are designed and implemented, if the results cannot be effectively communicated to the client, the project is not a success. An effective marketing research report is one way to ensure that the rewards for the time, effort, and money that went into the research project will be completely realized. The purpose of this chapter is to introduce you to the style and format of the marketing research report. We show how the marketing research report is designed and explain the objectives of each section. We then discuss industry best practices regarding effective presentation of research reports.

Marketing Research Reports

A professional marketing research report has four objectives: (1) to effectively communicate the findings of the marketing research project, (2) to provide interpretations of those findings in the form of sound and logical recommendations, (3) to establish the credibility of the research project, and (4) to serve as a future reference document for strategic or tactical decisions.

The first objective of the research report is to effectively *communicate* the findings of the marketing research project. Since a major purpose of the research project is to obtain information to answer questions about a specific business problem, the report must explain both how the information was obtained and what relevance it has to the research questions. A detailed description of the following topics should be communicated to the client:

1. The research objectives.
2. The research questions.
3. Literature review and relevant secondary data.
4. A description of the research methods.
5. Findings displayed in tables, graphs, or charts.
6. Interpretation and summary of the findings.
7. Conclusions and recommendations.

In Chapter 10, we explained how to write a qualitative research report. Quantitative reports include the same general information as do qualitative reports. But some of the issues faced in developing a research report are different. The objectives and questions in qualitative research tend to be broader, more general, and more open-ended than in quantitative research. The literature review and relevant secondary data may be integrated in the analysis of findings in qualitative data analysis, rather than being presented separately from other findings. The description of research methods in both qualitative and quantitative research helps to develop credibility for both kinds of research projects, but different kinds of evidence are offered in developing credibility in quantitative and qualitative analyses. Data display is important in both methods. Qualitative researchers rarely present statistics, but statistics are the bread and butter of a quantitative presentation. Writing conclusions and recommendations is the final step in both qualitative and quantitative reports.

Too often quantitative researchers are so concerned about doing statistical analyses they forget to provide a clear, logical *interpretation* of their results, the second objective of research reports. Researchers must recognize clients are seldom knowledgeable about sampling methods and statistics. Thus, researchers must present technical or complex information in a manner that is understandable to all parties. Many words used to teach research to students are not necessary in a marketing research report. For example, the word "hypothesis" seldom appears in a marketing research report. When Crosstabs, ANOVAs, *t*-tests, correlation, and regression are used, they are presented with simplicity and clarity. The name of the analysis technique may not even be used in the presentation and discussion of results. Most market researchers do not even include information about statistical significance in their reports, although we recommend that you do so.

In writing a report, researchers must cross the gap from doing and understanding statistics to communicating findings in a way that is completely understandable to nontechnical readers. Most researchers are comfortable with statistics, computer outputs, questionnaires, and other project-related material. In presenting results to the client, researchers should keep the original research objectives in mind. The task is to focus on the objectives and communicate how each part of the project is related to the completion of an objective.

For example, Exhibit 14.1 illustrates a research objective that focused on identifying senior Internet adoption and use segments. While a great deal of numerical data was necessary

---

Exhibit 14.1   Example of Concise Presentation of Findings from Senior Internet Adoption Study

	Senior Internet Adoption Segments	
	Light Use	**Heavy Use**
Self Adoption 20%	**Demographics** High income and education, more male **Self-Directed Values** Low curiosity and proactive coping **Technology Attitudes/Behavior** Low technology discomfort Medium technology optimism, innovativeness **12%**	**Demographics** High income and education, younger, more male **Self-Directed Values** High curiosity and proactive coping **Technology Attitudes/Behavior** Earliest adoption Low technology discomfort High technology optimism, innovativeness **8%**
Helped Adoption 21%	**Demographics** Medium education and income, more female **Self-Directed Values** Medium curiosity and proactive coping **Technology Attitudes/Behavior** Latest adoption High technology discomfort Medium technology optimism, innovativeness **13%**	**Demographics** Medium income and education, more female **Self-Directed Values** High curiosity and proactive coping **Technology Attitudes/Behavior** High technology discomfort High technology optimism, innovativeness **8%**
Non Adopters 59%	**Demographics** Low income, and education, more female, older **Self-Directed Values** Low curiosity and high proactive coping **Technology Attitudes/Behavior** High technology discomfort, low technology optimism, and low innovativeness	

to prepare the chart, the data have been reduced to a format that is compact and easy to understand. In this chapter, we show you how to use graphics to summarize the statistical analyses covered in our text. The PowerPoint slide in Exhibit 14.1 summarizes a number of statistical analyses that show predictors of senior Internet adoption (self-adoption, helped adoption, or nonadoption) and resulting usage behavior (heavy and light usage). The slide also shows that a segment of highly motivated senior adopters were nevertheless high in technology discomfort and thus waited longer to adopt. But eventually they got help to adopt and became heavy users (see the quadrant that shows heavy users by helped adoption). Researchers are always looking for ways to summarize information in a meaningful and compact way. They must be careful, however, that results are still easy to interpret and provide text (even in a PowerPoint slide show) to help readers focus on important points. In this chapter, we provide suggestions on how to present various kinds of analysis. But there are always multiple ways to present the same data, and researchers must use their creativity and continually think about if and how their presentation makes the points they want to make.

In addition to presenting and interpreting results in an easy-to-understand fashion, a third objective of the research report is to establish **credibility** for the research methods, findings, and conclusions. This can be accomplished only if the report is accurate, believable, and professionally organized. These three dimensions cannot be treated separately, for they collectively operate to build credibility in the research document. For the report to be accurate, all of the input must be accurate. No degree of carelessness in handling data, reporting statistics, or incorrect interpretation can be tolerated. Errors in mathematical calculations, grammatical errors, and incorrect terminology diminish the credibility of the entire report.

Clear and logical thinking, precise expression, and accurate presentation create **believability.** When the underlying logic is fuzzy or the presentation imprecise, readers may have difficulty understanding what they read. If readers do not understand what they read, they may not believe what they read. It is important to note that whenever findings are surprising, or are different from what the client expects, research analysts can expect to be questioned. The methodology will be scrutinized to find an explanation for the surprising findings. Sampling method, question wording, and nonresponse error are some of the most common ways of explaining away surprising findings. Researchers must anticipate these questions and have clear explanations for all findings.

Finally, the credibility of the research report is affected by the quality and organization of the document itself. The report must be clearly developed and professionally organized. The overall look of the report must not only clearly communicate results, but also convey the professionalism of the research effort. Also, the document must reflect the preferences and technical sophistication of the reader. Reports are written to reflect three levels of readers: (1) readers who will read only the executive summary, (2) readers who will read the executive summary and look at the body of findings more closely, and (3) readers with some technical expertise, who may read the entire report and look to the appendix for more detailed information.

It is helpful to prepare an outline of all major points, with supporting details in their proper position and sequence. The report should have sections that address each of the research objectives. Use short, concise sentences and paragraphs. Always select wording consistent with the background and knowledge of readers. Rewrite the report several times. This will force you to remove clutter and critically evaluate the document for improvements.

The fourth and final objective of the research report is to be a future reference. Most marketing research studies cover a variety of different objectives and seek to answer several research questions. This is accomplished in the report using both statistical and narrative formats. To retain all of this information is virtually impossible for the client. As a result, the research report becomes a reference document that is reviewed over an extended period.

Credibility The accuracy, believability, and professional organization of a research report.

Believability The quality of a report that is based on clear and logical thinking, precise expression, and accurate presentation.

Many marketing research reports become a part of a larger project conducted in various stages over time. It is not uncommon for one marketing research report to serve as a baseline for additional studies. Also, many reports are used for comparison purposes. For example, they are used to compare promotional changes, image building tactics, or even strengths and weaknesses of the firm.

Format of the Marketing Research Report

Every marketing research report is unique in that it is based on the needs of the client, the research purpose, and the study objectives. Yet all reports contain some common elements. Although the terminology may differ among industries, the basic format discussed in this section will help researchers plan and prepare reports for various clients. The elements common to all marketing research reports are the following:

1. Title page
2. Table of contents
3. Executive summary
    a. Research objectives
    b. Concise statement of method
    c. Summary of key findings
    d. Conclusions and recommendations
4. Introduction
5. Research method and procedures
6. Data analysis and findings
7. Conclusions and recommendations
8. Limitations
9. Appendices

Title Page

The title page indicates the subject of the report and the name of the recipient, along with his or her position and organization. Any numbers or phrases to designate a particular department or division also should be included. Most important, the title page must contain the name, position, employing organization, address, and telephone number of the person (or persons) submitting the report and the date the report is submitted.

Table of Contents

The table of contents lists the topics of the report in sequential order. Usually, the contents page will highlight each topical area, the subdivisions within each area, and corresponding page numbers. It is also common to include tables and figures and the pages where they can be found.

Executive Summary

Executive summary The part of a marketing research report that presents the major points; it must be complete enough to provide a true representation of the document but in summary form.

The **executive summary** is the most important part of the report. Many consider the executive summary to be the soul of the report, insofar as many executives read only the report summary. The executive summary presents the major points of the report. It must be complete enough to provide a true representation of the entire document but in summary form. Make sure your executive summary can stand alone. The rest of your report supports the key findings included in the summary, but the overview provided by the executive summary

---

Exhibit 14.2 Research Objectives

Research Objectives

- Measure and model the impact of Apex advertising on employees.
  - Measure employees perceptions of effectiveness, organizational accuracy, promise exaggeration, and value-congruence of Apex ads.
  - Measure outcome variables after viewing Apex ads: pride, trust, organizational identification, organizational commitment, customer focus.
- Measure the effect of preexisting employee organizational identification and customer focus on response to Apex ads.

---

must nevertheless seem complete. While the executive summary comes near the front of the report, it should actually be written last. Until all the analyses are done, researchers cannot determine which findings are most important.

The executive summary has several purposes: (1) to convey how and why the research was undertaken, (2) to summarize the key findings, and (3) to suggest future actions. In other words, the executive summary must contain the research objectives, a concise statement of method, a summary of the findings, and specific conclusions and recommendations.

Research objectives should be as precise as possible, but not longer than approximately one page. The research purpose along with the questions or hypotheses that guided the project should also be stated in this section. Exhibit 14.2 shows a PowerPoint slide that summarizes research objectives for a project in which employees' reactions to their company's consumer ads was measured. After explaining the research purpose and objectives, a brief description of the sampling method, the research design, and any procedural aspects is given in one or two paragraphs. Following this is a statement of key findings.

Exhibit 14.3 shows a slide that summarizes a few of the key findings from a research project. The findings presented in the summary must agree with those found in the findings

---

Exhibit 14.3 Selected Key Findings from a Research Project

Key Findings

- Apex employees identify strongly with Apex, averaging 6.3 on a 7-point scale across all Organizational Identity items.
- Perceived advertising effectiveness with consumers has strong effects on all outcome variables. Employees thus care about the effectiveness of advertising. In particular, effectiveness is very strongly associated with employee pride.
- The perception that ads portray the organization accurately has moderate to strong effects on all outcome variables. Employees thus desire for Apex to be portrayed in ads consistent with how they see their company.

section of the full report. Only key findings that relate to the research objectives should be included.

Finally, the summary contains a brief statement of conclusions and recommendations. The conclusion section of the report summarizes your findings. Conclusions concisely explain research findings and the meaning that can be attached to the findings. Recommendations, in contrast, are for appropriate future actions. Recommendations focus on specific marketing tactics or strategies the client can use to gain a competitive advantage. Conclusions and recommendations typically are stated in one to two paragraphs.

Introduction

The *introduction* contains background information necessary for a complete understanding of the report. Definition of terms, relevant background information, and the study's scope and emphasis are communicated in the introduction. The introduction also lists specific research objectives and questions the study was designed to answer, as well as hypotheses, length of the study, and any research-related problems. Usually hypotheses are not stated formally. They are stated in everyday language. For example, a research team can summarize their hypotheses about the variables they believe will affect senior Internet adoption as follows: "We expected the following factors to be positively related to senior adoption: income, education, curiosity, and technology optimism." Upon reading the introduction, the client should know exactly what the report is about, why the research was conducted, and what relationships exist between the current study and past or future research endeavors.

Research Methods and Procedures

The objective of the *methods-and-procedures section* is to communicate how the research was conducted. Issues addressed in this section include the following:

1. The research design used: exploratory, descriptive, and/or causal.
2. Types of secondary data included in the study, if any.
3. If primary data were collected, what procedure was used (observation, questionnaire) and what administration procedures were employed (personal, mail, telephone, Internet).
4. Sample and sampling processes used. The following issues are usually addressed:
   a. How was the sample population defined and profiled?
   b. Sampling units used (for example, businesses, households, individuals).
   c. The sampling list (if any) used in the study.
   d. How was the sample size determined?
   e. Was a probability or nonprobability sampling plan employed?

Many times when writing the methods-and-procedures section, the writer gets bogged down in presenting too much detail. If on completion of this section, the reader can say what was done, how it was done, and why it was done, the objective of the writer has been fulfilled. A slide summarizing the methodology used in the senior adoption of the Internet study appears in Exhibit 14.4.

Data Analysis and Findings

The *body* of the marketing research report consists of the study's findings. Data analysis requirements differ for each project, so the presentation of findings will be somewhat different for each project. No matter how complicated the statistical analysis, the challenge for researchers is to summarize and present the analysis in a way that makes it easy to understand for nonspecialists. Findings should always include a detailed presentation with supporting

Exhibit 14.4   Slide Summarizing Research Methodology

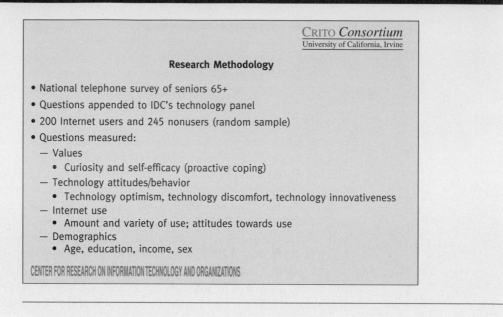

CRITO *Consortium*
University of California, Irvine

Research Methodology

- National telephone survey of seniors 65+
- Questions appended to IDC's technology panel
- 200 Internet users and 245 nonusers (random sample)
- Questions measured:
  — Values
    - Curiosity and self-efficacy (proactive coping)
  — Technology attitudes/behavior
    - Technology optimism, technology discomfort, technology innovativeness
  — Internet use
    - Amount and variety of use; attitudes towards use
  — Demographics
    - Age, education, income, sex

CENTER FOR RESEARCH ON INFORMATION TECHNOLOGY AND ORGANIZATIONS

tables, figures, and graphs. All results must be logically arranged to correspond with each research objective or research question listed in the report. This portion of the report is not simply an undifferentiated dump of the findings. When reporting results, no writer should claim the results are "obvious," or "self-evident." Rather, report writers both present and interpret their results. The researcher must decide how to group the findings into sections that facilitate understanding. Best practices suggest that tables, figures, and graphs be used when results are presented. Graphs and tables should provide a simple summation of the data in a clear, concise, and nontechnical manner.

When writing the report, the information must be explained in the body of the report in a straightforward fashion without technical output and language. Technical information which most readers will have trouble understanding is best suited for the appendix section of the report. Below are several strategies for presenting analyses using graphs and tables. There is probably no one best way to present a particular analysis. Instead there often are several effective ways to portray a particular finding or set of findings. We discuss some specific methods to illustrate frequencies, crosstabs, *t*-tests, ANOVAs, correlations, and regressions. With some patience, you can master the simpler presentation techniques in this chapter. If you become comfortable working with the chart editor in SPSS, you will find there are many more options we have not covered. Once you have mastered the basic techniques, you can teach yourself more by experimenting with the chart editor in SPSS. In addition, you can convert your SPSS data into an Excel spreadsheet and use the graphing functions from Excel to present your findings.

Reporting Frequencies   Frequencies can be reported in tables, bar charts, or pie charts. For example, Exhibit 14.5 contains a table illustrating the results for the research question, "How often do you patronize the Santa Fe Grill?" This table illustrates the data output in a simple and concise manner, enabling the reader to easily view how often respondents eat at the Santa Fe Grill. Notice that all digits past the decimal point have been removed. This is common practice in reporting percentages in marketing research. The extra digits create clutter without

Exhibit 14.5   Findings Illustrating Simple Readable Results of Frequencies

How often do you patronize the Santa Fe Grill?

	Frequency	Percent	Cumulative Percent
Very Infrequently	49	12%	12%
Somewhat Infrequently	62	16	28
Occasionally	111	28	56
Somewhat Frequently	88	22	78
Very Frequently	90	23	100*
Total	400	100*	

* Does not exactly add to 100% due to rounding.

providing very much information. Moreover, because most research involves sampling error, carrying percentages out past the decimal point is misleading. Researchers usually cannot estimate the results with the degree of precision the extra decimal points imply.

Using Bar Charts to Display Frequencies   Exhibit 14.6 shows the simplest type of bar chart that can be made in SPSS. While you will see more options on the screen in the chart editor interface in SPSS Version 14.0 (which was used to make the charts in this chapter), most of

Exhibit 14.6   A Simple Bar Chart

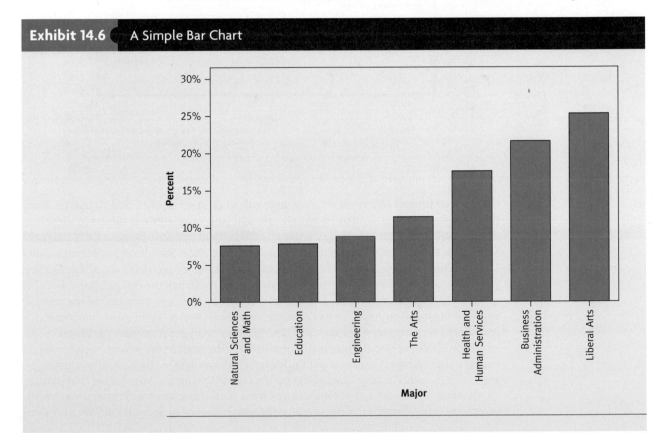

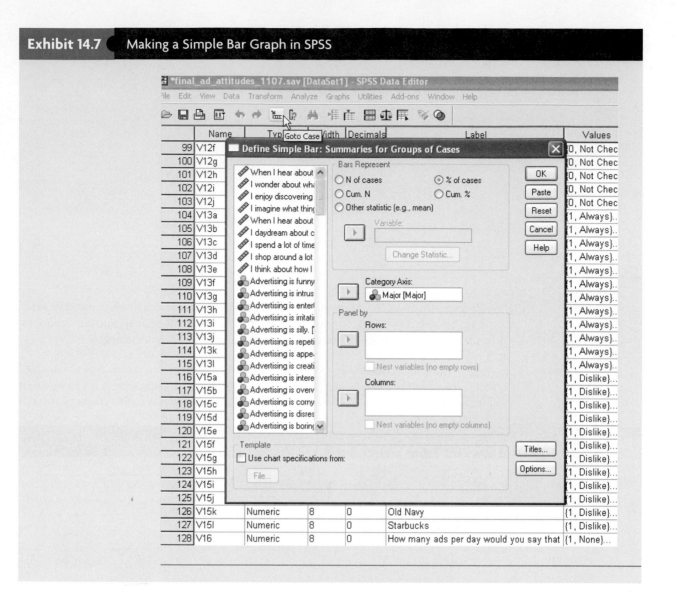

Exhibit 14.7 Making a Simple Bar Graph in SPSS

the same command sequences we show here will work in versions 12 and 13 chart editors. If your version of SPSS is 12 or 13, you will see that your chart editor is similar to the one in version 14, but that the interface occasionally offers fewer options. To make a bar chart, the SPSS click-through sequence is GRAPH → BAR. Leave the default on Simple and under "Data in chart are," you also use the default of "Summaries for groups of cases." On the next screen (shown in Exhibit 14.7), you will usually want to change the default choice from "N of cases" to "% of cases." On the left side of your screen highlight the name of the variable you want in your bar graph (in this case, the variable is "Major") and move it across to the space that says Category Axis, and click OK. SPSS will then generate your bar graph.

To make changes to the graph, you double-click the chart in the output, which will take you to a chart editor. There you will find several options for the chart. Double-clicking on any of the elements in your chart brings up the relevant menu for customizing that particular element. For example, double-clicking on the bars in the chart will bring up a Properties menu with several tabs. To produce the graph shown in Exhibit 14.6 we chose the

Categories tab on the Properties menu. On the categories menu, we selected the "sort by" option and then "statistic/ascending." This option arranges the graph by lowest percent to highest percent, which makes the graph easier for readers to understand.

By experimenting with various tabs on the Properties menu, students will find they can change the color, font, and font size on the graph. It is often desirable to enlarge the font if the graph will be exported to either Word or PowerPoint. The orientation of the bar labels can be changed as well. If you click on the bar labels while in the chart editor, the Properties menu will appear, and one of the tabs will be Labels and Ticks. Using this menu, the orientation of labels can be chosen: vertical, horizontal, or staggered. You should experiment with options until everything on your graph is clear and readable. Then, you can right-click on your finished chart, choose the "copy chart" option, and cut and paste the result to a Word or PowerPoint document. The finished result is shown in Exhibit 14.6.

Portraying Frequencies Using Pie Charts Pie Charts are particularly good at portraying the relative proportion of response to a question. The process for creating a pie chart is similar to that used for creating the bar chart. From the SPSS menu, choose GRAPH → PIE. A menu will appear with three radio buttons. The default choice "Summaries for groups of cases" is the correct option for a simple pie chart. Click Define and a new menu will appear. On this menu, although "N of cases" is the default option, in most cases you will be more interested in reporting percentages, so click the button next to "% of cases." Move the variable name from the variable list (in this case V16, which is labeled "How many ads per day do you pay attention to?") into the blank next to Define Slices by. Then click OK. SPSS will now create your chart in an output file.

As with the bar chart, when you double-click on the pie chart in the output file, you will open the chart editor in SPSS. From the toolbar in the editor, you can choose Elements → Show Data Labels and the percentages will be displayed on the pie chart for each slice. However, you want to remove any extra digits after the decimal place from the percentages displayed in your chart. You can double-click on the percentages box, which will give you a Properties menu. Choose the Number Format tab and next to decimal places, enter 0 (see Exhibit 14.8). Note that if you don't click in the right place, the Properties menu may not show the appropriate tab. If you don't see the tab you want on the Properties menu, try double-clicking the relevant part of the chart that you want to change again.

If you spend some time investigating the Options and Properties menus, you will see that you can make fonts bigger, change the font style, and alter the color and appearance of the slices in the pie. When you are done, you can right-click on the chart and copy and paste it to Word or PowerPoint.

Reporting Means of Thematically Related Variables Researchers may want to report the means of several thematically related variables in the same chart or table. This can be accomplished with either a bar chart or a table. A table may be preferred when a researcher feels that the entire question needs to be portrayed in order to fully understand the findings. Exhibit 14.9 shows a table that was constructed in PowerPoint using the table function. The results of the table are based on SPSS output, using the command sequence Analyze → Descriptive Statistics → Frequencies. A menu will appear, and then you click the Statistics button near the bottom of that menu. Then choose Mean and Standard Deviation. Click OK, and the results will be generated by SPSS.

Note that the items in the table have been ordered from the highest to the lowest average. Sorting responses in this manner often facilitates reader understanding. There are two other important elements of the table to note: (1) the maximum value of 7 is clearly

Exhibit 14.8   Changing the Properties of a Pie Chart in the SPSS Chart Editor

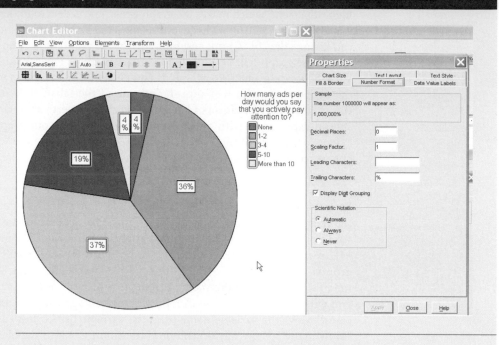

Exhibit 14.9   A Table Summarizing Means of Thematically Related Items

College Students' Attitudes towards Advertising

Item	Number of Responses	Average 7 = Strongly Agree	Standard Deviation
Ads can be a good way to learn about products.	312	5.2	1.5
The purpose of marketing is to attract customers by learning what they want.	308	5.2	1.5
Advertising is an interesting business.	308	5.2	1.5
Advertising sometimes encourages me to seek out more information about products I am interested in.	312	5.0	1.5
I think it would be fun to work for an advertising agency.	306	4.5	1.9
Overall, I am satisfied with advertising.	308	4.3	1.3
Advertising is usually designed to sell things that people don't really need.	310	4.3	1.8
Advertising appeals to the selfishness in human beings.	303	3.6	1.8
If there was less advertising, the world would be a better place.	304	3.4	1.7
I try to avoid advertising whenever possible.	304	3.3	1.7
Advertising is bad for society.	310	2.6	1.5

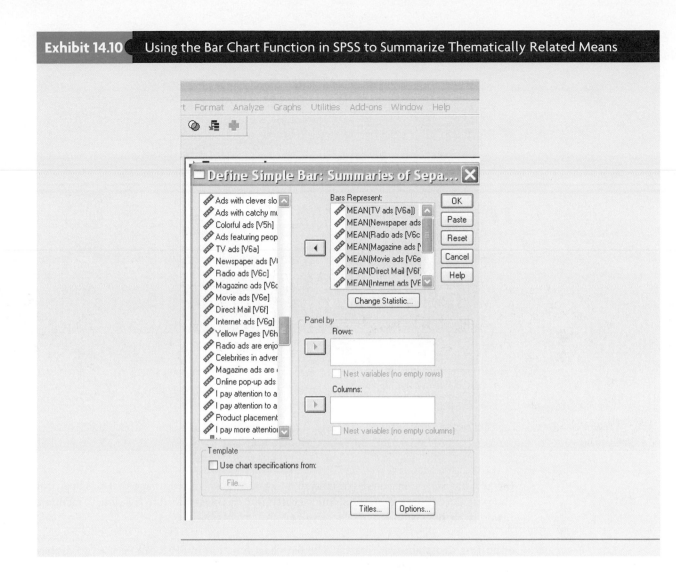

indicated so that readers can easily compare the mean to the maximum possible score, and (2) the mean and standard deviations are shown with only one digit past the decimal. While percentages should have no decimals past the decimal point, means should generally display one digit past the decimal point.

It is also possible to portray thematically related means on a bar chart in SPSS. In order to do so, you begin as you did when portraying one variable by choosing Graphs → Bar from the toolbar and leaving the default bar chart type Simple selected. However, you will change the default at the bottom of the menu from "Summaries of groups of cases" to "Summaries of separate variables." Then click Define. From there, move the variables you want in the graph from the variable list on the left into the window labeled Bars Represent (see Exhibit 14.10). The default is Mean so you will not have to change any options. Once you click OK, the bar graph will be created. When you double-click on the bar chart in the output, this will take you to the chart editor. As we explained earlier in the chapter, you can double-click elements within the chart and change the properties and

Exhibit 14.11   A Bar Chart Displaying Multiple Thematically Related Means

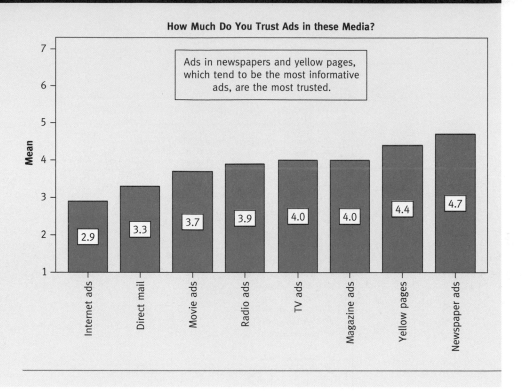

the appearance of the bar chart. Exhibit 14.11 shows a finished image that has been cut and pasted to a PowerPoint slide. An interpretation has been added to the slide to facilitate reader comprehension.

Reporting Crosstabs (Bar Charts) The bar chart function in SPSS can be used to display Crosstabs. Once again, you can start with Graphs → Bar → Summaries for groups of cases. From there, choose Cluster rather than the default option Simple and click Define. Under Bars Represent, choose "% of cases." Your independent or causing variable should be entered in the Category Axis blank. In this case, sex is the independent variable. The variable you are explaining, in this case, liking of the Carl Jr.'s Paris Hilton ad, is entered in the Define Clusters blank (see Exhibit 14.12). Then click OK, and the Crosstab bar chart will be created. As with the other charts, you can double-click on the graph to bring up the chart editor.

Because this particular Crosstab crosses only two categories by two categories, we excluded the bars representing "don't like" from the graph. This is because in a 2 × 2, once you know the values for one category, the other category is completely defined (the two categories must add to 100%). Removing a category is straightforward. You can double-click on any of the bars in the graph. This will bring up the Properties menu. One of the tabs will be Categories. You will see the categories displayed on the menu. If you click on the category you want to exclude (in this case Don't Like,) and then click the red X button next to the box labeled Order, the label will be moved to the box below under Excluded. Click Apply and your Crosstab will now display only one category of the outcome variable, in

Exhibit 14.12   Using the SPSS Bar Chart Function to Portray Crosstabs

this case, the percentage of respondents within each sex who liked the Carl's Jr. Paris Hilton ad. The resulting graph is displayed in Exhibit 14.13.

Reporting *t*-tests and ANOVAs (Bar Charts) Exhibit 14.14 shows a table created in PowerPoint that pictures the results of four different *t*-tests that are thematically related. Each *t*-test compares outcome measures for two groups: employees with low and high identification with their company. The average for each group of employees for each variable appears in the cells, along with the number of employees in each group. Again, significant *p* values are indicated.

Both *t*-tests and ANOVAs can be displayed on bar charts created in SPSS. Our example will focus on using the bar charts for an ANOVA, but the command sequence within SPSS is the same. Start with Graphs → Bar → Simple. Leave the box chosen next to "Summaries are groups of cases," and click Define. On the next screen (pictured in Exhibit 14.15), under Bars Represent, choose Other and enter the outcome variable (in this case, "Liking for Touching/Emotional ads) into the blank under Variable. For Category Axis, enter the

Exhibit 14.13   Bar Chart Portraying a Crosstab

Percentage of Men and Women Who Like Paris Hilton's Carl's Junior Ad

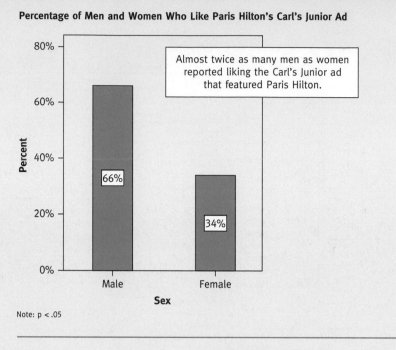

> Almost twice as many men as women reported liking the Carl's Junior ad that featured Paris Hilton.

Note: p < .05

Exhibit 14.14   A Table Showing *t*-Tests

Preexisting Organizational Identification Affected All Ad Evaluations

Constructs	Less Identified Employees	More Identified Employees	Standard Deviation
Organizational Accuracy (max=35)	21.6 (n=341)	24.0* (n=209)	Lo=6.1 Hi=7.0
Promise Exaggeration (max=21)	9.2 (n=351)	8.1* (n=207)	Lo=8.1 Hi=8.8
Value Congruence (max=21)	12.6 (n=345)	14.5* (n=208)	Lo=3.8 Hi=4.1
Ad Effectiveness (max=28)	19.2 (n=355)	20.2* (n=218)	Lo=5.7 Hi=6.1

Employees more strongly identified with Apex rated the ads as more accurate in presenting the organization, less exaggerated, more consistent with their values, and believed the ads to be more effective. Despite the fact that on average more strongly identified individuals were more predisposed to see the ads positively, they as well varied more in their responses than did the less identified employees.

All differences significant at *p < .05

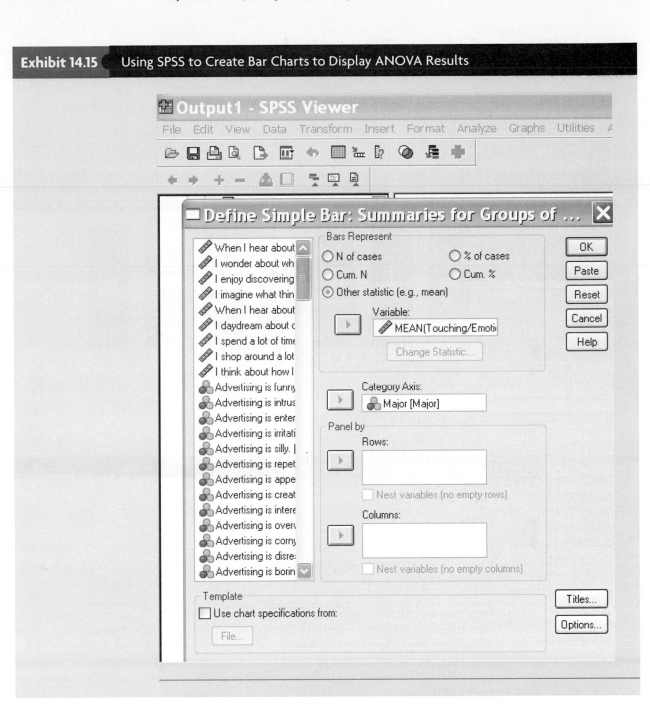

independent variable (in this case Major). Then click OK and the graph will be produced. Using Options we added a title and a footnote to the graph. Click on the *y*-axis, which shows the scale that we used in the survey, and you get the Properties menu along with a tab labeled Scale. In that menu, we changed the minimum to 1 and the maximum to 7 (the endpoints in the actual scale). SPSS will often change the scale points represented to maximize the space in the chart, but the resulting default chart may distort your findings. In many cases, you will want to change the axis to show the actual endpoints of your

Exhibit 14.16   Bar Chart Portraying ANOVA Results

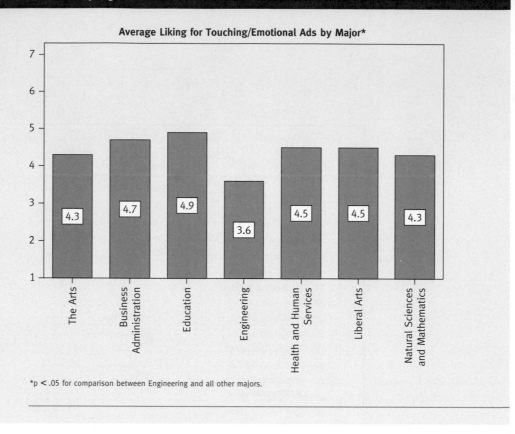

Average Liking for Touching/Emotional Ads by Major*

*p < .05 for comparison between Engineering and all other majors.

scale. A footnote shows an ANOVA analysis performed separately using Scheffe's post hoc test to examine the significance of categorical differences. The final graph is displayed in Exhibit 14.16.

Reporting Correlation and Regression   Correlations may be included in a report to illustrate relationships between several variables that are later used in a regression or to show the relationship of several variables to an outcome variable of interest. Exhibit 14.17 is a table showing the correlation of several variables with overall satisfaction for a retailer named Primal Elements. To facilitate comparison of the sizes of the correlations, they are arranged from strongest to mildest. Note that the negative correlation is sorted by its strength because the negative value indicates the direction of the relationship only. The significance levels are once again indicated with a star. The sample size is included on the graph in the footnote if the sample size used in the correlation analysis is different from the overall sample size reported in the methodology section of the report. The interpretation of the table is not included in the exhibit, but accompanying text would explain the strong role of perceptions of store atmosphere in satisfaction and may focus as well on the milder effects of other variables.

Recall that regression is a multivariate technique that estimates the impact of multiple explanatory or independent variables on one dependent variable. One of the simplest

Exhibit 14.17   Correlations of Item Ratings with Overall Satisfaction with Primal Elements

Item	Correlation
Store atmosphere	.59*
How intimidating the store is	−.30*
Expense of products	−.25*
Interior appearance of store	−.25*
Quantity of information workers provide about products	.21*
Exterior appearance of store	.16

*p < .05, N = 94. Correlations vary in strength from −1 to +1 with 0 meaning "no relationship."

ways to present regression findings is to create a diagram in Word or in PowerPoint that pictures the predictor and the outcome variables with arrows showing the relationships between the variables (see Exhibit 14.18). These diagrams were referred to as conceptual models in Chapter 3. The title of the analysis clearly describes the picture. The standardized Betas are

Exhibit 14.18   Displaying Regression Findings

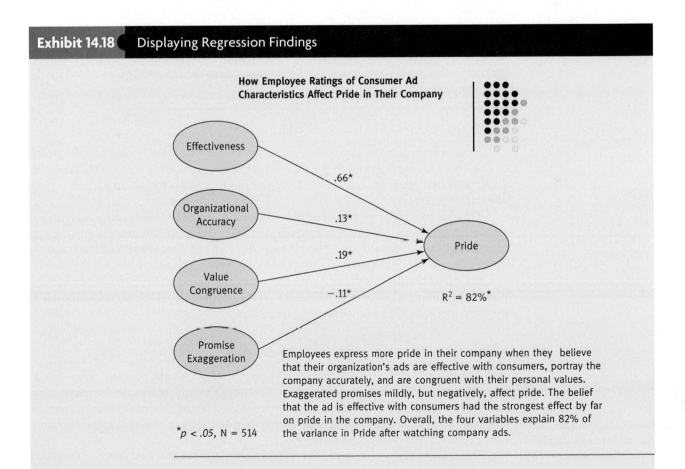

How Employee Ratings of Consumer Ad Characteristics Affect Pride in Their Company

Effectiveness —— .66* ——> Pride

Organizational Accuracy —— .13* ——> Pride

Value Congruence —— .19* ——> Pride

Promise Exaggeration —— −.11* ——> Pride

$R^2 = 82\%$*

Employees express more pride in their company when they believe that their organization's ads are effective with consumers, portray the company accurately, and are congruent with their personal values. Exaggerated promises mildly, but negatively, affect pride. The belief that the ad is effective with consumers had the strongest effect by far on pride in the company. Overall, the four variables explain 82% of the variance in Pride after watching company ads.

*p < .05, N = 514

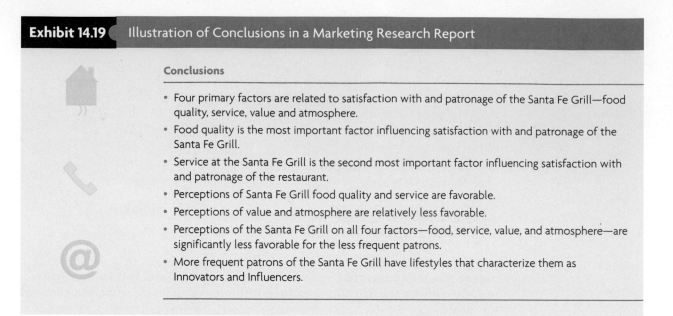

Exhibit 14.19 Illustration of Conclusions in a Marketing Research Report

Conclusions

- Four primary factors are related to satisfaction with and patronage of the Santa Fe Grill—food quality, service, value and atmosphere.
- Food quality is the most important factor influencing satisfaction with and patronage of the Santa Fe Grill.
- Service at the Santa Fe Grill is the second most important factor influencing satisfaction with and patronage of the restaurant.
- Perceptions of Santa Fe Grill food quality and service are favorable.
- Perceptions of value and atmosphere are relatively less favorable.
- Perceptions of the Santa Fe Grill on all four factors—food, service, value, and atmosphere—are significantly less favorable for the less frequent patrons.
- More frequent patrons of the Santa Fe Grill have lifestyles that characterize them as Innovators and Influencers.

portrayed above the appropriate arrow because the Beta shows the strength of the relationship between the independent and dependent variables. As in the other pictured analyses, a star may be used to indicate statistical significance. The R^2 appears in the diagram and is briefly explained in the accompanying text. The text summarizes the information provided by the regression analysis in the picture.

Conclusions and Recommendations

Conclusions and recommendations are derived specifically from the findings. As illustrated in Exhibit 14.19, conclusions are descriptive statements generalizing the results, not necessarily the numbers generated by statistical analysis. Each conclusion directly references research objectives.

Recommendations are generated by critical thinking. The task is one where the researcher must critically evaluate each conclusion and develop specific areas of applications for strategic or tactical actions. Recommendations must address how the client can solve the problem at hand through the creation of a competitive advantage.

Exhibit 14.20 outlines the recommendations that correspond to the conclusions displayed in Exhibit 14.19. You will notice each recommendation, unlike the conclusions, is in the form of a clear action statement.

Limitations

Researchers always strive to develop and implement a flawless study for the client. But all research has limitations. Researchers must note the limitations of a project, and speculate intelligently about if and how the limitations may have affected their conclusions. Common **limitations** associated with marketing research include sampling bias, financial constraints, time pressures, and measurement error.

Every study has limitations and the researcher has to make the client aware of them. Researchers should not be embarrassed by limitations but rather admit openly that they exist.

Limitations Any shortcomings of the research effort; they are communicated in the research report.

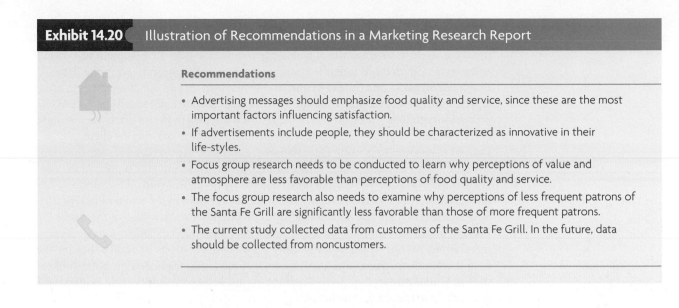

Exhibit 14.20 Illustration of Recommendations in a Marketing Research Report

Recommendations

- Advertising messages should emphasize food quality and service, since these are the most important factors influencing satisfaction.
- If advertisements include people, they should be characterized as innovative in their life-styles.
- Focus group research needs to be conducted to learn why perceptions of value and atmosphere are less favorable than perceptions of food quality and service.
- The focus group research also needs to examine why perceptions of less frequent patrons of the Santa Fe Grill are significantly less favorable than those of more frequent patrons.
- The current study collected data from customers of the Santa Fe Grill. In the future, data should be collected from noncustomers.

However, limitations should not be stated in a way that undermines the credibility of the entire project. Researchers cover limitations, but do so in a way that develops reasonable confidence in the conclusions made in the report. Treatment of limitations in the research report usually involves a discussion of results and accuracy. For example, researchers should tell clients about the generalizability of the results beyond the sample used in the study. Any weaknesses in specific scales should be addressed, along with other potential sources of nonsampling error. If limitations are not stated and are later discovered by the client, mistrust and skepticism toward the entire report may result. When properly reported, limitations rarely diminish the credibility of the report but instead improve client perceptions of the quality of the project.

Appendices

Appendix A section following the main body of the report; used to house complex, detailed, or technical information.

An **appendix,** many times referred to as a "technical appendix," contains complex, detailed, or technical information not necessary for the formal report. Common items contained in appendices include the questionnaire or data collection instrument used for the research project, interviewer forms, statistical calculations, and detailed sampling maps. Researchers know the appendix is rarely read in the same context as the report itself. In fact, most appendices are treated as points of reference in the report. That is, information in the appendix is cited in the report to guide the reader to further technical or statistical detail.

◼ Common Problems in Preparing the Marketing Research Report

Industry best practices suggest five problem areas that may arise in writing a marketing research report:

1. **Lack of data interpretation.** In some instances, researchers get so involved in constructing results tables that they fail to provide proper interpretation of the data in the tables. The researcher always provides unbiased interpretation of any findings.

2. **Unnecessary use of complex statistics.** To impress clients, many researchers unnecessarily use sophisticated multivariate statistical techniques. In many research reports, the most sophisticated statistical technique required will be a Chi-square test. Avoid using statistical methods unless they are essential to derive meaning from the data.

3. **Emphasis on packaging instead of quality.** Many researchers go out of their way to make reports look classy or flamboyant using sophisticated computer-generated graphics. While professional graphic representation of the results is essential in the report, never lose sight of the primary purpose—to provide valid and credible information to the client.

4. **Lack of relevance.** Reporting data, statistics, and information that are not consistent with the study's objectives can be a major problem when writing the report. Always develop the report with the research objectives clearly in focus. Avoid adding unnecessary information just to make the report longer. Always remain in the realm of practicality. Suggest ideas that are relevant, doable, and consistent with the results of the study.

5. **Placing too much emphasis on a few statistics.** Never base all conclusions or recommendations on one or a few statistically significant questions or results, but on the weight of evidence from your literature review, secondary data, and the pattern of results in your entire report. Always attempt to find substantial supporting evidence for any recommendation or conclusion.

The final research document is the end product of the researcher. Individual credibility can be enhanced or damaged by the report, and credibility is what helps a researcher gain repeat business and referrals from clients. The quality, dedication, and honesty one places into the report have the potential to generate future business, career promotions, and salary raises.

The Critical Nature of Presentations

Presentation of marketing research results can be as important as, if not more important than, the results of the research itself. This is true for several reasons. First, any research, no matter how well done or how important, cannot be properly acted upon if the results are not effectively communicated to those who will use the information in making decisions. Managers need accurate information if they are going to make good decisions, and if they do not understand the marketing research findings, they may well make poor decisions that lead to difficulty not only for the organization but also for individuals in the organization affected by those decisions. Second, the report or presentation is often the only part of the marketing research project that will be seen by those commissioning the report. Senior managers often do not have the time to review all aspects of a research project, so they rely on the researcher to carry out the research properly and then present the findings clearly and concisely. Third, the content and presentation form of the research are closely intertwined. Poorly organized presentations presented in an unclear, lengthy, difficult-to-access format often lead audiences to discount the content.

Guidelines for Preparing the Visual Presentation

The visual presentation is a separate but equal component of the marketing research report. The visual presentation has one primary goal: to provide a visual summary of the marketing research report, designed in a manner that will complement and enhance oral communication of the written marketing research report.

In many cases, Microsoft PowerPoint is the preferred method of preparing the visual marketing research presentation. Given the versatility of PowerPoint, the visual presentation may employ graphics as simple as those in this chapter. But these presentations may also employ a full multimedia array of techniques, including sound, animation, color graphics, and video. Regardless of the complexity in the presentation, industry practices suggest the following guidelines:

1. Begin with a slide showing the title of the presentation and the individual(s) doing the presentation. In addition, the client and the marketing research firm should be identified.
2. A sequence of slides should be developed indicating the objectives of the research and the specific research questions to be addressed, followed by the research methodology employed and a description of the sample surveyed.
3. Additional slides should be developed that highlight the research findings or particular results of the study which the researcher deems important for communication purposes.
4. Finally, the presentation should conclude with recommendations, conclusions, and research implications as they pertain to the study at hand.

MARKETING RESEARCH IN ACTION
Who Are the Early Adopters of Technology?

The latest DVD recorders do a lot more than just record material on DVDs. The latest models let you play and record VHS video, while others include hard drives and programming guides with TiVo-like functionality. Stand-alone DVD recorders use the same drive technology as PCs, only they provide a home theater platform. The DVD discs take up less physical space than bulky VHS tapes, plus they have menus that let you easily jump to a specific point within a recording. Moreover, the quality is much better than a VCR, with the ability to record up to 700 horizontal lines of resolution compared to only 250 with a VCR.

The DVD market is large and rapidly getting much larger. No longer limited to home entertainment playback boxes, it is being combined with increasing numbers of consumer electronics products: computers, portable devices, appliances, and industrial systems.

DVDs hit the market in the late 1990s and enjoyed very fast growth. Indeed, the DVD market experienced the most rapid rise of any consumer electronics technology ever introduced. The total market for all types of DVD systems (players, recorders, set-tops, PCs) is expected to exceed 500 million units by 2008.

DVD player/recorders have caught the imagination and interest of consumers. DVD set-top box players boomed in sales due not only to their functionality, but also to their rapidly falling prices. The average selling price fell from about $500 in 1998 to $130 in major retail outlets in early 2006, with some units selling for as low as $40. The six most popular brands of DVD recorders are Apex DRX-9000, Panasonic DMR-E60, Philips DVDR80, Pioneer DVR-810H-S, Sharp DV-RW2U, and Sony RDR-GX7. *PC World* recently evaluated these six brands and rated the Sony RDR-GX7 as the best.

Two of the biggest challenges for electronics marketers are (1) the successful introduction of new technology-based product innovations into consumer markets and (2) stimulating the diffusion of those innovations to profitable penetration levels. To meet these challenges, researchers must gain clearer insights into the key factors consumers use in deciding whether to adopt technology innovations in consumer electronics.

Researchers recently completed a study to investigate opinions of potential purchasers of DVDs. The study compares the innovator and early adopter segments with regard to product usage, DVD purchase likelihood, demographics, and related issues. The primary questions addressed were "Are there attitudinal and behavioral differences between consumers who are innovators versus those who are early adopters?" and "Can these differences be systematically associated with purchase likelihood of DVDs?"

Using an Internet panel, data was collected from a sample of 200 individuals. The sample frame was consumers with annual household incomes $20,000 or more and ages 18 to 35 years. Data was collected over a two-week period. Participants had to be living in North America because the market study was limited to this geographic area. The questionnaire included questions about innovativeness, lifestyle, product, and brand image. Some of the questions employed interval level measures while others were nominal and ordinal. There is a database for the questions which is available in SPSS format at **www.mhhe.com/ hairessential1e**. The database is labeled DVD Survey MRIA.sav. A copy of the questionnaire is provided in Exhibit 14.21.

To begin the analysis, researchers classified respondents as innovators or early adopters. The Innovativeness scale consisted of five variables: X3, X4, X5, X6, and X9. Cluster

Exhibit 14.21 Questionnaire for Electronics Products Opinion Survey

This is a project being conducted by a marketing research class at The University of Oklahoma. The purpose of this project is to better understand the attitudes and opinions of consumers toward electronics products. The questionnaire will take only a few minutes to complete, and all responses will remain strictly confidential. Thank you for your help on this project.

I. Attitudes

The following questions relate to your attitudes about shopping for electronics products. On a scale of 1 to 7, with 7 being Strongly Agree and 1 being Strongly Disagree, please circle the number that best expresses the your degree of agreement with each of the following statements.

	Strongly Disagree						Strongly Agree
1. The Internet is a good place to get lower prices.	1	2	3	4	5	6	7
2. I don't shop for specials.	1	2	3	4	5	6	7
3. People come to me for advice.	1	2	3	4	5	6	7
4. I often try new brands before my friends and neighbors.	1	2	3	4	5	6	7
5. I would like to take a trip around the world.	1	2	3	4	5	6	7
6. My friends and neighbors come to me for advice and consultation.	1	2	3	4	5	6	7
7. Coupons are a good way to save money.	1	2	3	4	5	6	7
8. I seldom look for the lowest price when I shop.	1	2	3	4	5	6	7
9. I like to try new and different things.	1	2	3	4	5	6	7

10. To what extent do you believe you need a DVD player? Please indicate on the scale provided below:

Product I Definitely Do Not Need					Product I Definitely Need	
1	2	3	4	5	6	7

11. How likely are you to purchase a DVD player? Please indicate whether you are moderately likely or highly likely to purchase a DVD player. (Note: respondents who were not likely to purchase a DVD player were screened out of the survey.)

6 = Moderately Likely
7 = Highly Likely

II. Classification Information

Please tell us a little about yourself. We use the data for classification purposes only.

12. What is the highest level of education you have attained? (Check only ONE.)
a. __ High school graduate
b. __ College graduate

continued

| Exhibit 14.21 | Questionnaire for Electronics Products Opinion Survey, *continued* |

13. Electronics Products Ownership. Please indicate the level of electronics products ownership that best describes you.
a. __ Own few electronics products
b. __ Own a moderate amount of electronics products
c. __ Own many electronics products

14. Please check the category that best indicates your total annual household income before taxes. (Check ONE only.)
1. __ $20,000–$35,000
2. __ $35,001–$50,000
3. __ $50,001–$75,000
4. __ $75,001–$100,000
5. __ More than $100,000

THANK YOU FOR SHARING YOUR OPINIONS WITH OUR MARKETING RESEARCH CLASS.

---

analysis was utilized to identify respondents who rated themselves higher (more innovative) on these five scales. The analysis produced 137 Innovators and 63 Early Adopters. This categorical variable (X14) was then used to learn more about the respondents. The initial variables we examine here are X10—DVD Product Perceptions, X11—Purchase Likelihood, and X16—Price Consciousness. The results are shown in Exhibit 14.22.

All of the comparisons are significantly different. Looking first at variable X10, the mean value for innovators is larger than for early adopters (5.45 vs. 3.17). This indicates that innovators believe they need a DVD player much more than do early adopters. A similar finding is true for variable X11—Purchase Likelihood (coded 1 = highly likely and 0 = moderately likely). The higher mean value for innovators (.83 vs. .10) indicates they are much more likely to purchase a DVD player. Finally, looking at X16—Price Conscious we see that innovators are less price conscious than are early adopters (.39 vs. .59; coded 1 = more price conscious and 0 = less price conscious).

| Exhibit 14.22 | Comparison of Innovators and Adopters |

	Group	N	Mean	Sig.
X10—DVD Product Perceptions	**0 = Early Adopters**	63	3.17	
	1 = Innovators	137	5.45	
	Total	200	4.74	.000
X11—Purchase Likelihood	**0 = Early Adopters**	63	.10	
	1 = Innovators	137	.83	
	Total	200	.60	.000
X16—Price Conscious	**0 = Early Adopters**	63	.59	
	1 = Innovators	137	.39	
	Total	200	.46	.011

This study suggests that DVDs have left the innovation stage of the diffusion process and are making inroads into the early adopter phase. But DVD manufacturers and retail marketers alike must continue to develop strategies that attract more potential early adopters as well as create awareness and desire among the early majority.

Hands-On Exercise

1. What other issues can be examined with this survey?
2. What problems do you see with the questionnaire?
3. What are the important topics to include in a presentation of the findings?

Summary

Understand the objectives of a research report.

The key objective of a marketing research report is to provide the client with a clear, concise interpretation of the research project. The research report is a culmination of the entire study and therefore must communicate the systematic manner in which the study was designed and implemented. Secondary objectives of the report are to provide accurate, credible, easy-to-understand information to the client. The end result of the report is its ability to act as a reference document to guide future research and serve as an information source.

Describe the format of a marketing research report.

The research report generally includes the following: a title page; a table of contents; and an executive summary, which includes a statement of the research objectives, a detailed statement of the research method and procedures, a brief statement of findings, and conclusions and recommendations. Following the executive summary are the introduction to the report, a description of the methodology employed, and a discussion of data analysis techniques and findings. The final elements are conclusions and recommendations and a description of limitations. An appendix may include technical explanations or documentation.

Discuss several techniques for graphically displaying research results.

A vast array of graphic techniques is available to display research results. A variety of bar charts can be used to display analyses from simple frequencies to Crosstabs, t-tests, and ANOVA. Pie charts can be used to display the results of frequencies. Tables are especially helpful for portraying related results, including means, t-tests, and correlations. Diagrams with arrows showing relationships between variables are often used to portray regression results.

Clarify problems encountered in preparing reports.

Problem areas that may arise in the preparation of the research report are (1) lack of data interpretation, (2) unnecessary use of multivariate statistics, (3) emphasis on packaging rather than quality, (4) lack of relevance, and (5) placing too much emphasis on a few statistical outcomes.

Understand the importance of presentations in marketing research.

Presentations are important because research results must be effectively communicated to those seeking to use the information in decision making. The report or presentation may be the only part of the research project that will be seen by those commissioning the report. The content of the research and the presentation form of the research are closely intertwined.

Key Terms and Concepts

Appendix 327

Believability 310

Credibility 310

Executive summary 311

Limitations 326

Review Questions

1. What are the primary objectives of the marketing research report? Briefly discuss the objectives and why they are so important.
2. In the context of the marketing research report, what is the primary goal of the executive summary?
3. What is the primary purpose of the research methods and procedures section of a marketing research report?
4. Why are conclusions and recommendations included in a marketing research report?
5. What are the common problems associated with the marketing research report?
6. Why is it important to explain limitations in your marketing research report?

Discussion Questions

1. **EXPERIENCE THE INTERNET.** Go to the following Web site: **www.microsoft.com/Education/Tutorials.aspx**. Complete the Tutorials dialog box by typing in higher education in the Grade Level box, technology in the Learning Area box, and PowerPoint in the Product box. After selecting and completing the tutorial, provide written comments on the benefits you received by taking this tutorial.
2. Select the Santa Fe Grill data or one of the other databases provided with this text (see Deli Depot; Remington's; Qualkote; or DVD Survey on the Web site), analyze the data using the appropriate statistical techniques, prepare a PowerPoint presentation of your findings, and present it to your research class.
   a. Select an appropriate variable from the data set and prepare a simple bar chart of the findings in SPSS.
   b. Select an appropriate variable from the data set and prepare a simple pie chart of the findings in SPSS.
   c. Select a group of thematically related items that are on metric scales. Present the results in a table and also in a bar chart using SPSS.
   d. Find two categorical items that are appropriate for a Crosstab and present your results in a bar chart made with SPSS.
   e. Find a categorical independent variable and a metric dependent variable. Present the results in a bar chart made with SPSS.
   f. Choose an outcome variable that can be explained by two or more independent variables. Run a regression and then develop a diagram (using PowerPoint or Word) that displays your findings.
3. There are several Powerpoint presentations for the Santa Fe Grill restaurant study on the book's Web site at **www.mhhe.com/hairessentials1e**. The presentations demonstrate how findings of a statistical analysis of data from a survey can be reported. Review the presentations and select the one you believe most effectively communicates the findings. Justify your choice.

A

Abstraction Collapsing some categories or themes into a larger category or higher order conceptual construct.

Acquiescence Error A specific type of response bias that can occur when the respondent perceives what answer would be the most desirable to the sponsor.

Active Data Data acquired by a business when customers interact with the business's Web site.

Administrative Error Bias that can stem from data processing mistakes, interviewer distortion of the respondents' answers, or systemic inaccuracies created by using a faulty sampling design.

Affect Global Approach The theoretical approach of viewing the structure of a person's attitude as nothing more than the overall (global) expression of his or her favorable or unfavorable feeling toward a given object or behavior.

Affective Component That part of an attitude which represents the person's feelings toward the given object, idea, or set of information.

Alpha Factor The desired or acceptable amount of difference between the expected and the actual population parameter values; also referred to as the *tolerance level of error* (α).

Alternative Hypothesis A statement that is the opposite of the null hypothesis, where the difference in reality is not simply due to random error.

Ambiguity Contamination of internal validity measures due to unclear determination of cause–effect relationships between investigated constructs.

Analysis of Variance (ANOVA) A statistical technique that determines whether two or more means are statistically different from each other.

Appendix A section at the end of the final research report used to house complex, detailed, or technical information.

Appropriateness of Descriptors The extent to which the scale point elements match the data being sought.

Archives Secondary sources of recorded past behaviors and trends.

Area Sampling A form of cluster sampling where clusters are formed by geographic designations such as cities, subdivisions, and blocks. Any geographic unit with boundaries can be used, with one-step or two-step approaches.

Assignment The scaling property that allows the researcher to employ any type of descriptor to identify each object (or response) within a set; this property is also known as *description* or *category*.

Assignment Property The employment of unique descriptors to identify each object in a set.

Attitude-toward-behavior Model A multiplicative-additive model approach that attempts to capture a person's attitude toward a behavior rather than to the object itself; where the attitude is a separate, indirectly derived composite measure of a person's combined thoughts and feelings for or against carrying out a specific action or behavior.

Attitude-toward-object Model A multiplicative-additive model approach that attempts to capture a person's attitude about a specific object; where the attitude is a separate indirectly derived composite measure of a person's combined thoughts and feelings for or against a given object.

Attribute-importance Estimate The importance of an attribute of an object as estimated by conjoint analysis. It is calculated by subtracting the minimum part-worth estimate from the maximum part-worth estimate.

Auspices Error A type of response bias that occurs when the response is dictated by the image or opinion of the sponsor rather than the actual question.

Automatic Replenishment System (ARS) A continuous, automated inventory control system designed to analyze inventory levels, merchandise order lead times, and forecasted sales.

Availability of Information The degree to which the information has already been collected and assembled in some type of recognizable format.

Axial Coding Specifying the conditions, context, or variables that lead to a particular category or construct, and the outcomes from the construct.

B

Bad Questions Any question or directive that obscures, prevents, or distorts the fundamental communications between respondent and researcher.

Balancing Positive/Negative Scale Descriptors The researcher's decision to maintain objectivity in a scale that is designed to capture both positive and negative state-of-mind data from respondents; the same number of relative magnitudes of positive and negative scale descriptors are used to make up the set of scale points.

Bar Code A pattern of varied-width electronic-sensitive bars and spaces that represents a unique code of numbers and letters.

Behavior Intention Scale A special type of rating scale designed to capture the likelihood that people will demonstrate some type of predictable behavior toward purchasing an object or service.

Believability The quality achieved by building a final report that is based on clear, logical thinking, precise expression, and accurate presentation.

Benefit and Lifestyle Studies Studies conducted to examine similarities and differences in needs; used to identify two or more segments within a market for the purpose of identifying customers for the product category of interest to a particular company.

Beta Coefficient An estimated regression coefficient that has been recalculated to have a mean of 0 and a standard deviation of 1. This statistic enables the independent variables with different units of measurement to be directly compared on their association with the dependent variable.

Bias A particular tendency or inclination that skews results, thereby preventing accurate consideration of a research question.

Bivariate Regression Analysis A statistical technique that analyzes the linear relationship between two variables by estimating coefficients for an equation for a straight line. One variable is designated as a dependent variable, and the other as an independent (or predictor) variable.

Boolean Operators Key words that form a logic string to sort through huge numbers of sites on the World Wide Web.

Brand Awareness The percentage of respondents having heard of a designated brand; brand awareness can be either unaided or aided.

Business Ethics The moral principles and standards that guide behavior in the world of business.

Business Intelligence A procedure for collecting daily operational information pertinent to the company and the markets it serves.

C

Call Record Sheet A recording document that gathers basic summary information about an interviewer's performance efficiency (e.g., number of contact attempts, number of completed interviews, length of time of interview).

Cardinal Numbers Any set of consecutive whole integers.

Case Studies An exploratory research technique that intensively investigates one or several existing situations which are similar to the current problem/opportunity situation.

Categorization Placing portions of transcripts into similar groups based on their context.

Causal Research Research that focuses on collecting data structures and information that will allow the decision maker or researcher to model cause–effect relationships between two or more variables under investigation.

Census A study that includes data about or from every member of a target population. Sampling is often used because it is impossible or unreasonable to conduct a census.

Central Limit Theorem (CLT) The theoretical backbone of sampling theory. It states that the sampling distribution of the sample mean ($\bar{x}$) or the sample proportion ($\bar{p}$) value derived from a simple random sample drawn from the target population will be approximately normally distributed provided that the associated sample size is sufficiently large (e.g., when n is greater than or equal to 30). In turn, the sample mean value ($\bar{x}$) of that random sample with an estimated sampling error (S_g) (estimated standard error) fluctuates around the true population mean value (μ) with a standard error of σ/n and has a sampling distribution that is approximately a standardized normal distribution, regardless of the shape of the probability frequency distribution curve of the overall target population.

Cheating The deliberate falsification of respondents' answers on a survey instrument.

Chi-square (X^2) Statistic The standardized measurement of the observed difference squared between two frequency distributions that allows for the investigation of statistical significance in analyzing frequency distribution of data.

Claris Home Page A specific software program that can be used to create Web pages that can integrate both text and graphics with other types of computer files.

Classification (or prediction) Matrix The classification matrix in discriminant analysis that contains the number of correctly classified and misclassified cases.

Cluster Analysis A multivariate interdependence technique whose primary objective is to classify objects into relatively homogeneous groups based on the set of variables considered.

Clusters The mutually exclusive and collectively exhaustive subpopulation groupings that are then randomly sampled.

Cluster Sampling A method of probability sampling where the sampling units are selected in groups (or clusters) rather than individually. Once the cluster has been identified, the elements to be sampled are drawn by simple random sampling or all of the units may be included in the sample.

Code of Ethics A set of guidelines that states the standards and operating procedures for ethical decisions and practices by researchers.

Codes Labels or numbers that are used to track categories in a qualitative study.

Code Sheet A sheet of paper that lists the different themes or categories for a particular study.

Coding The activities of grouping and assigning values to various responses from a survey instrument.

Coefficient Alpha See Cronbach's Alpha.

Coefficient of Determination (r^2) A statistical value (or number) that measures the proportion of variation in one variable accounted for by another variable; the r^2 measure can be thought of as a percentage and varies from .00 to 1.00.

Cognitive Component That part of an attitude which represents the person's beliefs, perceptions, preferences, experiences, and knowledge about a given object, idea, or set of information.

Commercial/Syndicated Data Data that have been compiled and displayed according to some standardized procedure.

Company Ethics Program The framework through which a firm establishes internal codes of ethical behavior to serve as guidelines for doing business.

Comparative Rating Scale A scale format that requires a judgment comparing one object, person, or concept against another on the scale.

Comparative Scale Scale used when the scaling objective is to have a respondent express an attitude, feeling, or behavior about an object (or person, or phenomenon) or its attributes on the basis of some other object (or person, or phenomenon) or its attributes.

Comparison The process of developing and refining theory and constructs by analyzing the differences and similarities in passages, themes, or types of participants.

Competitive Intelligence Analysis Specific procedures for collecting daily operational information pertaining to the competitive companies and markets they serve.

Completely Automated Telephone Survey (CATS) A survey administered by a computer with no human interviewer. The computer dials a telephone number and the respondent listens to the electronic voice, responding by pushing keys on the Touch-Tone telephone keypad.

Completeness The depth and breadth of the data.

Completion Deadline Date Part of the information included in a cover letter that directly communicates to a prospective respondent the date by which his or her completed questionnaire must be returned to the researcher.

Complexity of the Information One of the two fundamental dimensions used to determine the level of information being supplied by the information research process; it relates to the degree to which the information is easily understood and applied to the problem or opportunity under investigation.

Computer-administered Survey A survey design that incorporates the use of a computer to ask questions and record responses.

Computer-assisted Personal Interviewing An interview in which the interviewer reads respondents the questions from a computer screen and directly keys in the response.

Computer-assisted Self-interviewing An interview in which respondents are directed to a computer where they read questions from the computer screen and directly enter their responses.

Computer-assisted Telephone Interview (CATI) The computer controls and expedites the interviewing process.

Computer-assisted Telephone Survey A survey that uses a fully automated system in which the respondent listens to an electronic voice and responds by pushing keys on a Touch-Tone telephone keypad.

Computer Disks by Mail A survey procedure in which computer disks are mailed to respondents; the respondents complete the survey on their own computer and return the disk to the researcher via the mail.

Computer-generated Fax Survey A survey procedure in which a computer is used to send a survey to potential respondents via fax; the respondent completes the survey and returns it via fax or mail.

Computerized Secondary Data Sources Data sources designed by specific companies that integrate both internal and external data with online information sources.

Conative Component That part of an attitude which refers to the person's behavioral response or specific action/reaction toward the given object, idea, or set of information; it tends to be the observable outcome driven by the interaction of a person's cognitive and affective components toward the object or behavior.

Concept and Product Testing Information for decisions on product improvements and new product introductions.

Conceptualization Development of a model that shows variables and hypothesized or proposed relationships between variables.

Confidence Interval A statistical range of values within which the true value of the target population parameter of interest is expected to fall based on a specified confidence level.

Confidence Levels Theoretical levels of assurance of the probability that a particular confidence interval will accurately include or measure the true population

parameter value. In information research, the three most widely used levels are 90 percent, 95 percent, and 99 percent.

Confidentiality to Client The agreement between a researcher and the client that all activities performed in the process of conducting marketing research will remain private and the property of the client, unless otherwise specified by both parties.

Confidentiality to Respondent The expressed assurance to the prospective respondent that his or her name, while known to the researcher, will not be divulged to a third party, especially the sponsoring client.

Confirmation/Invitation Letter A specific follow-up document sent to prospective focus group participants to encourage and reinforce their willingness and commitment to participate in the group session.

Conformance to Standards The researcher's ability to be accurate, timely, mistake free, and void of unanticipated delays.

Conjoint Analysis A multivariate technique that estimates the utility of the levels of various attributes or features of an object, as well as the relative importance of the attributes themselves.

Connectors Logic phrases and symbols that allow search terms to be linked together in a Boolean logic format.

Connect Time The length of time, frequently measured in minutes and seconds, that a user is logged on to an electronic service or database. The amount of connect time is generally used to bill the user for services.

Consent Forms Formal signed statements of agreement by the participants approving the taping

or recording of the information provided in group discussions and releasing that data to the moderator, researcher, or sponsoring client.

Constant Sums Eating Scale A scale format that requires the respondents to allocate a given number of points, usually 100, among several attributes or features based on their importance to the individual; this format requires a person to value each separate feature relative to all the other listed features.

Construct A hypothetical variable made up of a set of component responses or behaviors that are thought to be related.

Construct Development An integrative process of activities undertaken by researchers to enhance understanding of what specific data should be collected for solving defined research problems.

Construct Development Error A type of nonsampling (systematic) error that is created when the researcher is not careful in fully identifying the concepts and constructs to be included in the study.

Constructs Hypothetical variables composed of a set of component responses or behaviors that are thought to be related.

Construct Validity The degree to which researchers measure what they intended to measure, and to which the proper identification of the independent and dependent variables were included in the investigation.

Consumer Panels Large samples of households that provide certain types of data for an extended period of time.

Content Analysis The technique used to study written or taped materials by breaking the data into meaningful aggregate units or categories using a predetermined set of rules.

Content Validity That property of a test which indicates that the entire domain of the subject or construct of interest was properly sampled. That is, the identified factors are truly components of the construct of interest.

Control Group That portion of the sample which is not subjected to the treatment.

Controlled Test Markets Test markets performed by an outside research firm that guarantees distribution of the test product through prespecified outlets in selected cities.

Control Variables Extraneous variables that the researcher is able to account for according to their systematic variation (or impact) on the functional relationship between the independent and dependent variables included in the experiment.

Convenience Sampling A method of nonprobability sampling where the samples are drawn on the basis of the convenience of the researcher or interviewer; also referred to as *accidental sampling*. Convenience sampling is often used in the early stages of research because it allows a large number of respondents to be interviewed in a short period of time.

Convergent Validity The degree to which different measures of the same construct are highly correlated.

Cost Analysis An analysis of alternative logistic system designs that a firm can use for achieving its performance objective at the lowest total cost.

Covariation The amount of change in one variable that is consistently related to the change in another variable of interest.

Cover Letter A separate letter that either accompanies a self-administered questionnaire or is mailed prior to an initial interviewer contact call and whose main purpose is to secure a respondent's willingness to participate in the research project; sometimes referred to as a *letter of introduction*.

Cover Letter Guidelines A specific set of factors that should be included in a cover letter for the purpose of increasing a prospective respondent's willingness to participate in the study.

Credibility The quality that comes about by developing a final report that is accurate, believable, and professionally organized.

Critical Questions Questions used by a moderator to direct the group to the critical issues underlying the topics of interest.

Critical Tolerance Level of Error The observed difference between a sample statistic value and the corresponding true or hypothesized population parameter.

Critical z Value The book z value and the amount of acceptable variability between the observed sample data results and the prescribed hypothesized true population values measured in standardized degrees of standard errors for given confidence levels.

Cronbach's Alpha A widely used measurement of the internal consistency of a multi-item scale in which the average of all possible split-half coefficients is taken.

Cross-researcher Reliability The degree of similarity in the coding of the same data by different researchers.

Cross-tabulation The process of simultaneously treating (or counting) two or more variables in the study. This process categorizes the number of respondents who have responded to two or more questions consecutively.

Curbstoning Cheating or falsification of data during the collection process that occurs when interviewers fill in all or part of a survey themselves.

Curvilinear Relationship An association between two variables whereby the strength and/or direction of their relationship changes over the range of both variables.

Customer-centric Approach Use of granular data to anticipate and fulfill customers' desires.

Customer Interaction The relationship between the enterprise and the customer.

Customer Knowledge The collection of customer interaction information used to create customer profiles that can be used to tailor interactions, segment customers, and build strong customer relationships.

Customer Knowledge Information Information volunteered by customers that might be outside the marketing function of an organization.

Customer Relationship Management (CRM) Management of customer relationships based on the integration of customer information throughout the business enterprise in order to achieve maximum customer satisfaction and retention.

Customer Satisfaction Studies Studies designed to assess both the strengths and weaknesses customers perceive in a firm's marketing mix.

Customer-volunteered Information Data provided by the customer without solicitation.

Cycle Time The time that elapses between taking a product or service from initial consumer contact to final delivery.

D

Data Facts relating to any issue or subject.

Data Analysis Error A "family" of nonsampling errors that are created when the researcher subjects the data to inappropriate analysis procedures.

Database A collection of secondary information indicating what customers are purchasing, how often they purchase, and how much they purchase.

Database Technology The means by which data are transformed into information.

Data Coding Errors The incorrect assignment of computer codes to the responses.

Data Editing Errors Inaccuracies due to careless verifying procedures of data to computer data files.

Data Enhancement The process of weaving data into current internal data for the purpose of gaining a more valuable categorization of customers relative to their true value to the company.

Data Entry The direct inputting of the coded data into some specified software package that will ultimately allow the research analyst to manipulate and transform the data into data structures.

Data Entry Errors The incorrect assignment of computer codes to their predesignated location on the computer data file.

Data Field A basic characteristic about a customer that is filled in on a database.

Data Interaction Matrix A procedure used to itemize the type and amount of data required by each functional area of the company regardless of the cost of data collection.

Data Mining The process of finding hidden patterns and relationships among variables/characteristics contained in data stored in the data warehouse.

Data Processing Error A specific type of nonsampling error that can occur when researchers are not accurate or complete in transferring data from respondents to computer files.

Data Reduction The categorization and coding of data that is part of the theory development process in qualitative data analysis.

Data Silo Collection of data by one area of a business that is not shared with other areas.

Data Validation A specific control process that the researcher undertakes to ensure that his or her representatives collected the data as required. The process is normally one of recontacting about 20 percent of the selected respondent group to determine that they did participate in the study.

Data Warehouse A central repository for all significant pieces of information that an organization collects.

Debriefing Analysis The technique of comparing notes, thoughts, and feelings about a focus group discussion between the moderator, researcher, and sponsoring client immediately following the group interview.

Decision Opportunity The presence of a situation in which market performance can be significantly improved by undertaking new activities.

Defined Target Population A specified group of people or objects for which questions can be asked or observations made to develop the required data structures and information; also referred to as the *working population*. A precise definition of the target population is essential when undertaking a research project.

Degree of Manipulation The extent to which data and results have been interpreted and applied to a specific situation.

Deliberate Falsification When the respondent and/or interviewer intentionally gives wrong answers or deliberately cheats on a survey.

Demand Characteristics Contamination to construct validity measures created by test subjects trying to guess the true purpose behind the experiment and therefore give socially acceptable responses or behaviors.

Demographic Characteristics Physical and factual attributes of people, organizations, or objects.

Deontologists Individuals who emphasize good intentions and the rights of the people involved in an action; they are much less concerned with the results from any ethical decision.

Dependence Techniques Appropriate multivariate procedures when one or more of the variables can be identified as dependent variables and the remaining as independent variables.

Dependent Variable A singular observable attribute that is the measured outcome derived from manipulating the independent variable(s).

Depth The overall number of key data fields or variables that will make up the data records.

Description The process of discovering patterns, associations, and relationships among key customer characteristics.

Descriptive Questionnaire Design A questionnaire design that allows the researcher to collect raw data that can be turned into facts about a person or object. The questions and scales primarily involve the collecting of state-of-being and state-of-behavior data.

Descriptive Research Research that uses a set of scientific methods and procedures to collect data that are used to identify, determine, and describe the existing characteristics of a target population or market structure.

Diffusion of Treatment Contamination to construct validity measures due to test subjects discussing the treatment and measurement activities with individuals yet to receive the treatment.

Direct Cognitive Structural Analysis A data analysis procedure in which respondents are simply asked to determine the extent to which an attribute is part of the construct's structural makeup and its importance to construct.

Direct (positive) Directional Hypothesis A statement about the perceived relationship between two questions, dimensions, or subgroups of attributes that suggests that as one factor moves in one direction, the other factor moves in the same direction.

Directed Data Comprehensive data about customers collected through the use of computers.

Direct Mail Survey A questionnaire distributed to and returned from respondents via the postal service.

Directness of Observation The degree to which the researcher or trained observer actually observes the behavior/event as it occurs; also termed *direct observation*.

Direct Self-administered Questionnaire A survey instrument designed to have the respondent serve as both an interviewer and a respondent during the question-and-answer encounter.

Discretion of Primary Descriptors The carefulness that a researcher must use in selecting the actual words used to distinguish the relative magnitudes associated with each of the primary descriptors in a scale design.

Discriminant Analysis A multivariate technique for analyzing marketing research data when the dependent variable is categorical and the independent variables are interval.

Discriminant Function The linear combination of independent variables developed by discriminant analysis which will best discriminate between the categories of the dependent variable.

Discriminant Function Coefficient The multipliers of variables in the discriminant function when the variables are in the original units of measurement.

Discriminant Score In discriminant analysis, this represents the score of each respondent on the discriminant function.

Discriminant Validity The degree to which measures of different constructs are uncorrelated.

Discriminatory Power The scale's ability to significantly differentiate between the categorical scale responses (or points).

Disguised Sponsorship When the true identity of the person or company for which the research is being conducted is not divulged to the prospective respondent.

Diversity of Respondents The degree to which the respondents in the study share some similarities.

Domain of Observables The set of observable manifestations of a variable that is not itself directly observable. A domain represents an identifiable set of components that indirectly make up the construct of interest.

Drop-off Survey A questionnaire that is left with the respondent to be completed at a later time. The questionnaire may be picked up by the researcher or returned via some other mode.

Dummy Variables Artificial variables introduced into a regression equation to represent the categories of a nominally scaled variable (such as sex or marital status). There will be one dummy variable for each of the nominal categories of the independent variable, and the values will typically be 0 and 1, depending on whether the variable value is present or absent for a particular respondent (e.g., male or female).

E

Editing The process in which the interviews or survey instruments are checked for mistakes that may have occurred by either the interviewer or the respondent during data collection activities.

Electronic Database A high-speed, computer-assisted information source or library.

Electronic Data Interchange (EDI) A specific system designed to speed the flow of information as well as products from producer to distributor to retailer.

Electronic Test Markets Test procedures that integrate the use of selected panels of consumers who use a special identification card in recording their product purchasing data.

Element The name given to the object about which information is sought. Elements must be unique, countable, and, when added together, make up the whole of the target population.

E-mail Survey A survey in which electronic mail is used to deliver a questionnaire to respondents and receive their responses.

Emic Validity An attribute of qualitative research that affirms that key members within a culture or subculture agree with the findings of a research report.

Empirical Testing The actual collection of data in the real world using research instruments and then subjecting that data to rigorous analysis to either support or refute a hypothesis.

Ending Questions Questions used by a focus group moderator to bring closure to a particular topic discussion; encourages summary-type comments.

Enterprise The total business unit, including all facets of the business as well as suppliers and retailers.

Environmental Information Secondary information pertaining to a firm's suppliers and/or distributors.

Equivalent Form A method of assessing the reliability associated with a scale measurement; the researcher creates two basically similar yet different scale measurements for the given construct and administers both forms to either the same sample of respondents or two samples of respondents from the same target population.

Error The difference between the true score on a research instrument and the actual observed score.

Estimated Sample Standard Deviation A quantitative index of the dispersion of the distribution of drawn sampling units' actual data around the sample's arithmetic average measure of central tendency;

this sample statistical value specifies the degree of variation in the data responses in a way that allows the researcher to translate the variations into normal curve interpretations.

Estimated Sample Variance The square of the estimated sample standard deviation.

Estimated Standard Error of the Sample Statistic A statistical measurement of the sampling error that can be expected to exist between the drawn sample's statistical values and the actual values of all the sampling units' distributions of those concerned statistics. These indexes are referred to as *general precision.*

Estimates Sample data facts that are transformed through interpretation procedures to represent inferences about the larger target population.

Ethical Dilemmas Specific situations in which the researcher, decision maker, or respondent must choose between appropriate and inappropriate behavior.

Ethics The field of study that tries to determine what behaviors are considered to be appropriate under certain circumstances by established codes of behavior set forth by society.

Ethnography A form of qualitative data collection that records behavior in natural settings to understand how social and cultural influences affect individuals' behaviors and experiences.

Evaluation Apprehension Contamination to construct validity measures caused by test subjects being fearful that their actions or responses will become known to others.

Executive Interview A person-administered interview of a business executive. Frequently, these inter-

views will take place in the executive's office.

Executive Summary The part of the final research report that illustrates the major points of the report in a manner complete enough to provide a true representation of the entire document.

Expected Completion Rate (ECR) The percentage of prospective respondents who are expected to participate and complete the survey; also referred to as the *anticipated response rate.*

Experience Surveys An informal gathering of opinions and insights from people who are considered to be knowledgeable on the issues surrounding the defined research problem.

Experimental Design Reliability The degree to which the research design and its procedures can be replicated and achieve similar conclusions about hypothesized relationships.

Experimental Research An empirical investigation that tests for hypothesized relationships between dependent variables and manipulated independent variables.

Expert Systems Advanced computer-based systems that function in the same manner as a human expert, advising the analyst on how to solve a problem.

Exploratory Research Research designed to collect and interpret either secondary or primary data in an unstructured format using sometimes an informal set of procedures.

External Secondary Data Data collected by outside agencies such as the federal, state, or local government; trade associations; or periodicals.

External Validity The extent to which the measured data results of a study based on a sample can be expected to hold in the entire defined target population. In addition, it is the extent that a causal relationship found in a study can be expected to be true for the entire defined target population.

Extraneous Variables All variables other than the independent variables that affect the responses of the test subjects. If left uncontrolled, these variables can have a confounding impact on the dependent variable measures that could weaken or invalidate the results of an experiment.

Extremity Error A type of response bias when the clarity of extreme scale points and ambiguity of midrange options encourage extreme responses.

F

Factor Analysis A class of statistical procedures primarily used for data reduction and summarization.

Factor Loadings Simple correlations between the variables and the factors.

Factor Scores Composite scores estimated for each respondent on the derived factors.

Facts Pieces of information that are observable and verifiable through a number of external sources.

Faulty Recall The inability of a person to accurately remember the specifics about the behavior under investigation.

Fax Survey A questionnaire distributed to the sample via fax machines.

Field Experiments Causal research designs that manipulate the independent variables in order to measure the dependent variable in a natural test setting.

Finite Correction Factor (fcf) An adjustment factor to the sample size that is made in those situations where the drawn sample is expected to equal 5 percent or more of the defined target population. The fcf is equal to the overall square root of $N - n/N - 1$.

Focus Group Facility A professional facility that offers a set of specially designed rooms for conducting focus group interviews; each room contains a large table and comfortable chairs for up to 13 people, with a relaxed atmosphere, built-in audio equipment, and normally a one-way mirror for disguised observing by the sponsoring client or researcher.

Focus Group Incentives Specified investment programs to compensate focus group participants for their expenses associated with demonstrating a willingness to be a group member.

Focus Group Moderator A special person who is well trained in interpersonal communications; listening, observation, and interpretive skills; and professional mannerisms and personality. His or her role in a session is to draw from the participants the best and most innovative ideas about an assigned topic or question.

Focus Group Research A formalized qualitative data collection method for which data are collected from a small group of people who interactively and spontaneously discuss one particular topic or concept.

Follow-up Test A statistical test that flags the means that are statistically different from each other; follow-up tests are performed after an ANOVA determines there are differences between means.

Forced-choice Scale Measurements Symmetrical scale measurement designs that do not have a logical "neutral" scale descriptor to divide the positive and negative domains of response descriptors.

Formal Rating Procedures The use of structured survey instruments or questionnaires to gather information on environmental occurrences.

Formative Composite Scale Scale used when each of the individual scale items measures some part of the whole construct, object, or phenomenon.

F-ratio The statistical ratio of between-group mean squared variance to within-group mean squared variance; the F value is used as an indicator of the statistical difference between group means in an ANOVA.

Free-choice Scale Measurements Symmetrical scale measurement designs that are divided into positive and negative domains of scale-point descriptors by a logical center "neutral" response.

Frequency Distributions A summary of how many times each possible response to a scale question/setup was recorded by the total group of respondents.

F-test The test used to statistically evaluate the difference between the group means in ANOVA.

Full-text Option of having the entire document, news story, article, or numerical information available for downloading.

Fully Automated Self-interviewing A procedure in which respondents independently approach a central computer station or kiosk, read the questions, and respond—all without researcher intervention.

Fully Automated Telephone Interviewing A data collection procedure in which the computer calls respondents and asks questions; the respondent records his or her answers by using the keypad of a Touch-Tone telephone.

Fully Automatic Devices High-tech devices that interact with respondents without the presence of a trained interviewer during the question/response encounter.

Functional Relationship An observable and measurable systematic change in one variable as another variable changes.

G

Garbage In, Garbage Out A standard phrase used in marketing research to represent situations where the process of collecting, analyzing, and interpreting data into information contains errors or biases, creating less than accurate information.

Gatekeeper Technology Any device used to help protect one's privacy against intrusive marketing practices such as telemarketing solicitors, unwanted direct marketers, illegal scam artists, and "sugging" (caller ID, voice messengers, answering machines).

Generalizability The extent to which the data are an accurate portrait of the defined target population; the representativeness of information obtained from a small subgroup of members to that of the entire target population from which the subgroup was selected.

Generalizability of Data The degree to which sample data can be used to draw accurate inferences about the defined target population, that is, the extent to which the research can extrapolate results from a sample to the defined target population.

General Precision The amount of general sampling error associated with the given sample of data that was generated through some type of data collection activity; no specific concern for any level of confidence.

Granular Data Highly detailed, highly personalized data specifi-

cally structured around an individual customer.

Graphic Rating Scale Descriptors A scale point format that presents respondents with some type of graphic continuum as the set of possible responses to a given question.

Group Dynamics The degree of spontaneous interaction among group members during a discussion of a topic.

H

Hits The number of documents or other items that meet the search terms in an online search.

Hypertext Markup Language (HTML) The language used to create Web pages for communicating the research results as well as other information on the Internet.

Hypothesis A yet-unproven proposition or possible solution to a decision problem that can be empirically tested using data that are collected through the research process; it is developed in order to explain phenomena or a relationship between two or more constructs or variables.

Hypothesis Guessing Contamination to construct validity measures due to test subjects' believing they know the desired functional relationship prior to the manipulation treatment.

I

Iceberg Principle The general notion indicating that the dangerous part of many marketing decision problems is neither visible nor well understood by marketing managers.

Importance-performance Analysis A research and data analysis procedure used to evaluate a firm's and its competitors' strengths and

weaknesses, as well as future actions that seek to identify key attributes that drive purchase behavior within a given industry.

Inadequate Preoperationalization of Variables Contamination to construct validity measures due to inadequate understanding of the complete makeup of the independent and dependent variables included in the experimental design.

Inappropriate Analysis Bias A type of data analysis error that creates the wrong data structure results and can lead to misinterpretation errors.

Independent Variable An attribute of an object whose measurement values are directly manipulated by the researcher, also referred to as a *predictor* or *treatment variable*. This type of variable is assumed to be a causal factor in a functional relationship with a dependent variable.

In-depth Interview A formalized, structured process of a subject's being asked a set of semistructured, probing questions by a well-trained interviewer usually in a face-to-face setting.

Informational Data Data collected through On-Line Analytical Processing (OLAP) software for analysis purposes as a decision-making tool for marketing programs.

Information Objectives The clearly stated reasons why data must be collected; they serve as the guidelines for determining the data requirements.

Information Requirements The identified factors, dimensions, and attributes within a stated information objective for which data must be collected.

Information Research Process The 10 systematic task steps involved in the four phases of gathering, analyzing, interpreting, and transforming data and results into information for use by decision makers.

Information Research Questions Specific statements that address the problem areas the research study will attempt to investigate.

In-home Interview A person-administered interview that takes place in the respondent's home.

Instrumentation Contamination to internal validity measures from changes in measurement processes, observation techniques, and/or measuring instruments.

Integration The process of moving from the identification of themes and categories to the development of theory.

Intention to Purchase A person's planned future action to buy a product or service.

Interdependence Techniques Multivariate statistical procedures in which the whole set of interdependent relationships is examined.

Internal Consistency Reliability The extent to which the items of a scale represent the same domain of content and are highly correlated both with each other and summated scale scores. It represents the degree to which the components are related to the same overall construct domain.

Internal Quality Movement One of the underlying factors for which many organizations are restructuring away from old traditional functional control/power systems of operating to new cross-functional structures where team building, decision teams, and sharing of information and responsibility are the important factors, not control and power.

Internal Secondary Data Facts that have been collected by the individual company for accounting and marketing activity purposes.

Internal Validity The certainty with which a researcher can state that the observed effect was caused by a specific treatment; exists when the research design accurately identifies causal relationships.

Internet A network of computers and technology linking computers into an information superhighway.

Internet Survey The method of using the Internet to ask survey questions and record responses of respondents.

Interpersonal Communication Skills The interviewer's abilities to articulate the questions in a direct and clear manner so that the subject understands what she or he is responding to.

Interpretive Bias Error that occurs when the wrong inference about the real world or defined target population is made by the researcher or decision maker due to some type of extraneous factor.

Interpretive Skills The interviewer's capabilities of accurately understanding and recording the subject's responses to questions.

Interval Scales Any question/scale format that activates not only the assignment and order scaling properties but also the distance property; all scale responses have a recognized absolute difference between each of the other scale points (responses).

Interviewer Error A type of nonsampling error that is created in situations where the interviewer distorts information, in a systematic way, from respondents during or after the interviewer/respondent encounter.

Interviewer Instructions The vehicle for training the interviewer on how to select prospective respondents, screen them for eligibility, and conduct the actual interview.

Interviewer/Mechanical Devices The combination of highly skilled people who are aided by high-technology devices during the questioning/responding encounters with respondents.

Introductory Questions Questions used by a focus group moderator to introduce the general topic of discussion and opportunities of reflecting their past experiences.

Inverse (negative or indirect) Directional Hypothesis A statement about the perceived relationship between two questions, dimensions, or subgroupings of attributes that suggests that as one factor moves in one direction, the other factor moves in an opposite fashion.

Iteration Working through the data several times in order to modify early ideas and to be informed by subsequent analyses.

J

Judgment Sampling A nonprobability sampling design that selects participants for a sample based on an experienced individual's belief that the participants will meet the requirements of the research study.

Junk Mail A categorical descriptor that prospective respondents attach to surveys that are administered through the direct mail delivery system or an unwanted telephone interview that is viewed as being nothing more than a telemarketing gimmick to sell them something they do not want or need.

L

Laboratory Experiments Experiments conducted in an artificial setting.

Lead Country Test Markets Field test markets that are conducted in specific foreign countries.

Leading Question A question that tends to purposely elicit a particular answer.

Library A large group of related information.

Lifetime Value Models Procedures developed using historical data, as well as actual purchase behavior, not probability estimates, to predict consumer behavior.

Likert Scale A special rating scale format that asks respondents to indicate the extent to which they agree or disagree with a series of mental belief or behavioral belief statements about a given object; it is a cognitive-based scale measurement.

Limitations A section of the final research report in which all extraneous events that place certain restrictions on the report are fully communicated.

Linear Relationship An association between two variables whereby the strength and nature of the relationship remains the same over the range of both variables.

Literature Review A comprehensive examination of available information that is related to your research topic.

Lottery Approach A unique incentive system that pools together either individual small cash incentives into a significantly larger dollar amount or a substantial nonmonetary gift and then holds a drawing to determine the winner or small set of winners. The drawing procedure is designed so that all respondents who complete and return their survey have an equal chance of receiving the larger reward.

M

Mail Panel Survey A representative sample of individual respondents who have agreed in advance to participate in a mail survey.

Mall-intercept Interview An interview technique in which mall patrons are stopped and asked for feedback. The interview may take place in the mall's common areas or in the research firm's offices at the mall.

Managerial Function Software System A computer-based procedure that includes forecasting, brand management, and promotional budget capabilities.

Marketing The process of planning and executing pricing, promotion, product, and distribution of products, services, and ideas in order to create exchanges that satisfy both the firm and its customers.

Marketing Knowledge A characteristic that complements a researcher's technical competency.

Marketing Research The function that links an organization to its market through the gathering of information. The information allows for the identification and definition of market-driven opportunities and problems. The information allows for the generation, refinement, and evaluation of marketing actions.

Market Intelligence The use of real-time customer information (customer knowledge) to achieve a competitive advantage.

Market Performance Symptoms Conditions that signal the presence of a decision problem and/or opportunity.

Maturation Contamination to internal validity measures due to changes in the dependent variable based on the natural function of time and not attributed to any specific event.

Mean The arithmetic average of all the responses; all values of a distribution of responses are summed and divided by the number of valid responses.

Measurement Rules for assigning numbers to objects so that these numbers represent quantities of attributes.

Measurement/Design Error A "family" of nonsampling errors that result from inappropriate designs in the constructs, scale measurements, or survey measurements used to execute the asking and recording of people's responses to a study's questions.

Measures of Central Tendency The basic sample statistics that could be generated through analyzing the collected data; they are the mode, the median, and the mean.

Measures of Dispersion The sample statistics that describe how all the data are actually dispersed around a given measure of central tendency; they are the frequency distribution, the range, and the estimated sample standard deviation.

Mechanical Devices High-technology instruments that can artificially observe and record either current behavioral actions or physical phenomena as they occur.

Mechanical/Electronic Observation Some type of mechanical or electronic device is used to capture human behavior, events, or marketing phenomena.

Median The sample statistic that splits the data into a hierarchical pattern where half the data is above the median statistic value and half is below.

Media Panels Selected households that are primarily used in measuring media viewing habits as opposed to product/brand consumption patterns.

Member Checking Asking key informants to read the researcher's report to verify that the analysis is accurate.

Memoing Writing down thoughts as soon as possible after each interview, focus group, or site visit.

Method Bias The error source that results from selecting an inappropriate method to investigate the research question.

Misinterpretation Error An inaccurate transformation of data structures and analysis results into usable bits of information for the decision maker.

Mode The most frequently mentioned (or occurring) raw response in the set of responses to a given question/setup.

Model *F* Statistic A statistic which compares the amount of variation in the dependent measure "explained" or associated with the independent variables to the "unexplained" or error variance. A larger *F*-statistic value indicates that the regression model has more explained variance than error variance.

Moderator's Guide A detailed document that outlines the topics, questions, and subquestions that serve as the basis for generating the spontaneous interactive dialogue among the focus group participants.

Modified Likert Scale Any version of the agreement/disagreement-based scale measurement that is not the original five-point "strongly agree" to "strongly disagree" scale.

Monetary Compensation An individual cash incentive used by the researcher to increase the likelihood of a prospective respondent's willingness to participate in the survey.

Monomethod Bias A particular type of error source that is created when only a single method is used to collect data about the research question.

Moral Philosophy A person's basic orientation toward problem solving. Within the ethical decision-making process, philosophical thinking will come from teleology, deontology, and/or relativity orientations.

Mortality Contamination to internal validity measures due to changing the composition of the test subjects in the experiment.

Multicollinearity A situation in which several independent variables are highly correlated with each other. This characteristic can result in difficulty in estimating separate or independent regression coefficients for the correlated variables.

Multiple-item Scale Designs Method used when the researcher has to measure several items (or attributes) simultaneously in order to measure the complete object or construct of interest.

Multiple Regression Analysis A statistical technique which analyzes the linear relationships between a dependent variable and multiple independent variables by estimating coefficients for the equation for a straight line.

Multivariate Analysis (Techniques) A group of statistical techniques used when there are two or more measurements on each element and the variables are analyzed simultaneously.

Mystery Shopper Studies Studies in which trained, professional shoppers visit stores, financial institutions, or companies and "shop" for various products and assess service quality factors or levels.

N

Negative Case Analysis Deliberately looking for cases and instances that contradict the ideas and theories that researchers have been developing.

Negative Relationship An association between two variables in which one increases while the other decreases.

Netnography A research technique that draws on ethnography but uses "found data" on the Internet that is produced by virtual communities.

Nominal Scales Question/scale structures that ask the respondent to provide only a descriptor as the response; the response does not contain any level of intensity.

Nomological Validity The extent to which one particular construct theoretically networks with other established constructs which are related yet different.

Nonapplicable Response Descriptor The alternative response attached to even-point (or forced-choice) scale designs that allows respondents not to directly respond to a given scale dimension or attribute if they feel uncomfortable about expressing thoughts or feelings about a given object because they lack knowledge or experience.

Noncomparative Scale Scale used when the scaling objective is to have a respondent express an attitude, emotion, action, or intention about one specific object (person, phenomenon) or its attributes.

Nondirectional Hypothesis A statement regarding the existing relationship between two questions, dimensions, or subgroupings of attributes as being significantly different but lacking an expression of direction.

Nonequivalent Control Group A quasi-experimental design that combines the static group comparison and one-group, pretest-posttest preexperimental designs.

Nonmonetary Compensation Any type of individual incentive excluding direct cash (e.g., a free T-shirt) used by the researcher to encourage a prospective respondent's participation.

Nonparticipant Observation An ethnographic research technique that involves extended contact with a natural setting, but without participation by the researcher.

Nonprobability Sampling Sampling designs in which the probability of selection of each sampling unit is not known. The selection of sampling units is based on the judgment or knowledge of the researcher and may or may not be representative of the target population.

Nonresponse Error An error that occurs when the portion of the defined target population not represented or underrepresented in the response pool is systematically and significantly different from those that did respond.

Nonsampling Error A type of bias that occurs in a research study regardless of whether a sample or census is used.

North American Industry Classification System (NAICS) Codes numerical industrial listings designed to promote uniformity in data reporting procedures for the U.S. government.

Not at Home A specific type of nonresponse bias that occurs when a reasonable attempt to initially reach a prospective respondent fails to produce an interviewer/respondent encounter.

Null Hypothesis A statement of the perceived existing relationship between two questions, dimensions, or subgroupings of attributes as being not significantly different; it asserts the status quo condition, and any change from what has been thought to be true is due to random sampling error.

O

Object Any tangible item in a person's environment that can be clearly and easily identified through the senses.

Objectivity The degree to which a researcher uses scientific procedures to collect, analyze, and create nonbiased information.

Observation The systematic process of witnessing and recording the behavioral patterns of objects, people, and occurrences without directly questioning or communicating with them.

Observing Mechanism How the behaviors or events will be observed; *human observation* is when the observer is either a person hired and trained by the researcher or the researcher himself; *mechanical observation* refers to the use of a technology-based device to do the observing rather than a human observer.

Odd or Even Number of Scale Points When collecting either state-of-mind or state-of-intention data, the researcher must decide whether the positive and negative scale points need to be separated by a neutral scale descriptor; even-point scales (known as *forced-choice scales*) do not require a neutral response, but odd-point scales (known as *free-choice scales*) must offer a neutral scale response.

One-group, Pretest-posttest A pre-experimental design where first a pretreatment measure of the dependent variable is taken (O_1), then the test subjects are exposed to the independent treatment (X), then a posttreatment measure of the dependent variable is taken (O_2).

One-shot Study A single group of test subjects is exposed to the independent variable treatment (X), and then a single measurement on the dependent variable is taken (O_1).

One-way Tabulation The categorization of single variables existing in the study.

Online Services Providers of access to electronic databases and other services in real time.

Opening Questions Questions used by a focus group moderator to break the ice among focus group participants; identify common group member traits; and create a comfort zone for establishing group dynamics and interactive discussions.

Operational Data Data collected through online transaction processing (OLTP) and used for the daily operations of the business.

Opportunity Assessment The collection of information on product-markets for the purpose of forecasting how they will change in the future. This type of assessment focuses on gathering information relevant to macroenvironments.

Optical Scanner An electronic device that optically reads bar codes; this scanner captures and translates unique bar code numbers into product information.

Ordinally Interval Scales Ordinal questions or scale formats that the researcher artificially redefines as being interval by activating an assumed distance scaling property into the design structure;

this hybrid-type scale format incorporates both primary ordinal scale descriptors and a secondary set of cardinal numbers used to redefine the original primary descriptors.

Ordinal Scales A question/scale format that activates both the assignment and order scaling properties; the respondent is asked to express relative magnitudes between the responses to a question.

Ordinary Least Squares A statistical procedure that estimates regression equation coefficients which produce the lowest sum of squared differences between the actual and predicted values of the dependent variable.

Overall Incidence Rate (OIR) The percentage of the defined target population elements who actually qualify for inclusion into the survey.

Overall Reputation The primary dimension of perceived quality outcomes. Quality of the end product can be gauged in direct proportion to the level of expertise, trust, believability, and contribution the research brings to the client.

Overregistration When a sampling frame contains all of the eligible sampling units of the defined target population plus additional ones.

P

Parameter The true value of a variable.

Participant Observation An ethnographic research technique that involves extended observation of behavior in natural settings in order to fully experience cultural or subcultural contexts.

Part-worth Estimates Estimates of the utility survey that respon-

dents place on each individual level of a particular attribute or feature.

Passive Data Data supplied to a business when a consumer visits the company's Web site.

Pearson Correlation Coefficient A statistical measure of the strength and direction of a linear relationship between two metric variables.

Peer Review A process in which external qualitative methodology or topic area specialists are asked to review the research analysis.

Perceptual Map A graphic representation of respondents' beliefs about the relationship between objects with respect to two or more dimensions (usually attributes or features of the objects).

Performance Rating Scale Descriptors A scale that uses an evaluative scale point format that allows the respondents to express some type of postdecision evaluative judgment about an object.

Person-administered Survey A survey in which an individual interviewer asks questions and records responses.

Phantom Respondents A type of data falsification that occurs when the researcher takes an actual respondent's data and duplicates it to represent a second (nonexisting) set of responses.

Physical Audits (or Traces) Tangible evidence (or artifacts) of some past event or recorded behavior.

Plus-one Dialing The method of generating telephone numbers to be called by choosing numbers randomly from a telephone directory and adding one digit.

Population The identifiable total set of elements of interest being investigated by a researcher.

Population Mean Value The actual calculated arithmetic aver-

age parameter value based on interval or ratio data of the defined target population elements (or sampling units).

Population Proportion Value The actual calculated percentage parameter value of the characteristic of concern held by the target population elements (or sampling units).

Population Size The determined total number of elements that represent the target population.

Population Specification Error An incorrect definition of the true target population to the research question.

Population Standard Deviation A quantitative index of the dispersion of the distribution of population elements' actual data around the arithmetic average measure of central tendency.

Population Variance The square of the population standard deviation.

Positioning The desired perception that a company wants to be associated with its target markets relative to its products or brand offerings.

Positive Relationship An association between two variables in which they increase or decrease together.

Posttest-only, Control Group A true experimental design where the test subjects are randomly assigned to either the experimental or control group; the experimental group is then exposed to the independent treatment after which both groups receive a posttreatment measure of the dependent variable.

PowerPoint A specific software package used to develop slides for electronic presentation of the research results.

Precise Precision The amount of measured sampling error

associated with the sample's data at a specified level of confidence.

Precision The degree of exactness of the data in relation to some other possible response of the target population.

Predictions Population estimates that are carried into a future time frame; they are derived from either facts or sample data estimates.

Predictive Bias A specific type of data analysis error that occurs when the wrong statistical facts and estimates invalidate the researcher's ability to predict and test relationships between important factors.

Predictive Questionnaire Design A design that allows the researcher to collect data that can be used in predicting changes in attitudes and behaviors as well as testing hypothesized relationships. The question/scales primarily involve the collecting of state-of-mind and state-of-intention data.

Predictive Validity The extent to which a scale can accurately predict some event external to the scale itself.

Pre-experimental Designs A family of designs (one-shot study, one-group pretest-posttest, static group comparison) that are crude experiments that are characterized by the absence of randomization of test subjects; they tend not to meet internal validity criteria due to a lack of equivalent group comparisons.

Pretesting The conducting of a simulated administering of a designed survey (or questionnaire) to a small, representative group of respondents.

Pretest-posttest, Control Group A true experimental design where the test subjects are randomly assigned to either the experimental or the control group and each group re-

ceives a pretreatment measure of the dependent variable. Then the independent treatment is exposed to the experimental group, after which both groups receive a posttreatment measure of the dependent variable.

Primary Data Data structures of variables that have been specifically collected and assembled for the current research problem or opportunity situation; they represent "firsthand" structures.

Primary Information Firsthand facts or estimates that are derived through a formalized research process for a specific current problem situation.

Probability Distribution of the Population The relative frequencies of a population's parameter characteristic emulating a normal bell-shaped pattern.

Probability Sampling Sampling designs in which each sampling unit in the sampling frame (operational population) has a known, nonzero probability of being selected for the sample.

Problem Definition A statement that seeks to determine precisely what problem management wishes to solve and the type of information necessary to solve it.

Project Costs The price requirements of doing marketing research.

Projective Techniques A family of qualitative data collection methods where subjects are asked to project themselves into specified buying situations and then asked questions about those situations.

Propensity Scoring Weighting underrepresented respondents more heavily in results.

Purchase Intercept Interview An interview similar to a mall intercept except that the respondent is stopped at the point of purchase

and asked a set of predetermined questions.

Q

Qualitative Research Selective types of research methods used in exploratory research designs where the main objective is to gain a variety of preliminary insights to discover and identify decision problems and opportunities.

Quality of the Information One of the two fundamental dimensions that is used to determine the level of information being provided by the research process; it refers to the degree to which the information can be depended on as being accurate and reliable.

Quantitative Research Data collection methods that emphasize using formalized, standard, structured questioning practices where the response options have been predetermined by the researcher and administered to significantly large numbers of respondents.

Quasi-experimental Designs Designs in which the researcher can control some variables in the study but cannot establish equal experimental and control groups based on randomization of the test subjects.

Query Part of an MDSS that enables the user to retrieve information from the system without having to have special software requirements.

Questionnaire A set of questions and scales designed to generate enough data for accomplishing the information requirements that underlie the research objectives.

Questionnaire Development Process A specific yet integrative series of logical activities that are undertaken to design a systematic survey instrument for the purpose of collecting primary data from sets of people (respondents).

Questionnaire Format/Layout The integrative combination of sets of question/scale measurements into a systematic structured instrument.

Question/Setup Element The question and/or directive that is asked of the respondent for which the respondent is to supply a response; it is one of the three elements that make up any scale measurement.

Quota Sampling The selection of participants based on specific quotas regarding characteristics such as age, race, gender, income, or specific behaviors. Quotas are usually determined by specific research objectives.

Quota Sheets A simple tracking form that enhances the interviewer's ability to collect data from the right type of respondents; the form helps ensure that representation standards are met.

R

Random-digit Dialing A random selection of area code, exchange, and suffix numbers.

Random Error An error that occurs as the result of chance events affecting the observed score.

Randomization The procedure whereby many subjects are assigned to different experimental treatment conditions, resulting in each group's averaging out any systematic effect on the investigated functional relationship between the independent and dependent variables.

Random Sampling Error The statistically measured difference between the actual sampled results and the estimated true population results.

Ranges Statistics that represent the grouping of data responses into mutually exclusive subgroups with each having distinct identifiable lower and upper boundary designation values in a set of responses.

Rank-order Rating Scale A scale point format that allows respondents to compare their responses to each other by indicating their first preference, then their second preference, then their third preference, etc., until all the desired responses are placed in some type of rank order, either highest to lowest or lowest to highest.

Rating Cards Cards used in personal interviews that represent a reproduction of the set of actual scale points and descriptions used to respond to a specific question/setup in the survey. These cards serve as a tool to help the interviewer and respondent speed up the data collection process.

Ratio Scales Question/scale formats that simultaneously activate all four scaling properties; they are the most sophisticated scale in the sense that absolute differences can be identified not only between each scale point but also between individuals' responses. Ratio scales request that respondents give a specific singular numerical value as their response to the question.

Reachable Rate (RR) The percentage of active addresses on a mailing list or other defined population frame.

Reader-sorter An electronic mechanism located at the point-of-purchase (POP) that resembles a miniature automated bank teller machine. This device enables consumers to pay for transactions with credit cards, ATM cards, or debit cards.

Real-time Transactional Data Data collected at the point of sale.

Recursive A relationship in which a variable can both cause and be caused by the same variable.

Reflective Composite Scale Scale used when a researcher measures an individual subcomponent (dimension) of a construct, object, or phenomenon.

Refusal A particular type of nonresponse bias that is caused when a prospective respondent declines the role of a respondent, or simply is unwilling to participate in the question/answer exchange.

Relational Database System A database in table format of rows and columns, with tables (not data fields) being linked together depending on the output requirements.

Relationship Marketing A management philosophy that focuses on treating each customer as uniquely different with the overall goal of building a long-term, interactive relationship and loyalty with each customer.

Relationships Associations between two or more variables.

Relativists Individuals who let present practice set the standard for ethical behavior.

Reliability The extent to which the measurements taken with a particular instrument are repeatable.

Reliability of Data Data structures that are consistent across observations or interviews.

Reliability of the Scale The extent to which the designed scale can reproduce the same measurement results in repeated trials.

Reliability of Service The researcher's ability to be consistent and responsive to the needs of the client.

Reputation of the Firm The culmination of a research firm's ability to meet standards, reliability of service, marketing knowledge, and technical competency for purposes of providing quality outcomes.

Research Instrument A microscope, radiation meter, ruler, questionnaire, scale, or other device designed for a specific measurement purpose.

Research Objectives Statements that the research project will attempt to achieve. They provide the guidelines for establishing a research agenda of activities necessary to implement the research process.

Research Proposal A specific document that serves as a written contract between the decision maker and researcher.

Respondent Characteristics The attributes that make up the respondents being included in the survey; three important characteristics are diversity, incidence, and participation.

Respondent Error The type of nonsampling errors that can occur when selected prospective respondents cannot be initially reached to participate in the survey process, do not cooperate, or demonstrate an unwillingness to participate in the survey.

Respondent Participation The overall degree to which the selected people have the ability and the willingness to participate as well as the knowledge of the topics being researched.

Response Error The tendency to answer a question in a particular and unique systematic way. Respondents may consciously or unconsciously distort their answers and true thoughts.

Response Rate The percentage of usable responses out of the total number of responses.

Retailing Research Research investigations that focus on topics such as trade area analysis, store image/perception, in-store traffic patterns, and location analysis.

S

Sample A randomly selected group of people or objects from the overall membership pool of a target population.

Sample Design Error A family of nonsampling errors that occur when sampling plans are not appropriately developed and/or the sampling process is improperly executed by the researcher.

Sample Mean Value The actual calculated arithmetic average value based on interval or ratio data of the drawn sampling units.

Sample Percentage Value The actual calculated percentage value of the characteristic of concern held by the drawn sampling units.

Sample Selection Error A specific type of sample design bias that occurs when an inappropriate sample is drawn from the defined target population because of incomplete or faulty sampling procedures or because the correct procedures have not been carried out.

Sample Size The determined total number of sampling units needed to be representative of the defined target population; that is, the number of elements (people or objects) that have to be included in a drawn sample to ensure appropriate representation of the defined target population.

Sample Statistic The value of a variable that is estimated from a sample.

Sampling The process of selecting a relatively small number of elements from a larger defined group of elements so that the information gathered from the smaller group allows one to make judgments about that larger group of elements.

Sampling Distribution The frequency distribution of a specific sample statistic value that would be found by taking repeated random samples of the same size.

Sampling Error Any type of bias in a survey study that is attributable to mistakes made in either the selection process of prospective sampling units or determining the size of a sample required to ensure its representativeness of the larger defined target population.

Sampling Frame A list of all eligible sampling units for a given study.

Sampling Frame Error An error that occurs when a sample is drawn from an incomplete list of potential or prospective respondents.

Sampling Gap The representation difference between the population elements and sampling units in the sample frame.

Sampling Plan The blueprint or framework used to ensure that the data collected are, in fact, representative of a larger defined target population structure.

Sampling Units Those elements that are available for selection during the sampling process.

Satisfaction of Experience A person's evaluative judgment about his or her postpurchase consumption experience of a specified object.

Scale Dimensions and Attributes Element The components of the object, construct, or concept that is being measured; it identifies what should be measured and is one of the three elements of a scale measurement.

Scale Measurement The process of assigning a set of descriptors to represent the range of possible responses that an individual gives in answering a question about a particular object, construct, or factor under investigation.

Scale Points The set of assigned descriptors that designate the degrees of intensity to the responses concerning the investigated characteristics of an object, construct, or factor; it is one of the three elements that make up scale measurements.

Scale Reliability The extent to which a scale can produce the same measurement results in repeated trials.

Scanner-based Panel A group of participating households which have an unique bar-coded card as an identification characteristic for inclusion in the research study.

Scatter Diagram A graphic plot of the relative position of two variables using a horizontal and a vertical axis to represent the values of the respective variables.

Scientific Method The systematic and objective process used to develop reliable and valid firsthand information by using the information research process.

Scoring Models Procedures that attempt to rank customer segments by their potential profitability to the company.

Screening Forms A set of preliminary questions that are used to determine the eligibility of a prospective respondent for inclusion in the survey.

Screening Question/Scales Specific questions or scales that are used to qualify prospective respondents for a survey or eliminate unqualified respondents from answering question/scales in a study.

Search A computer-assisted scan of the electronic databases.

Search Engine An electronic procedure that allows the researcher to enter keywords as search criteria for locating and gathering secondary information off the Internet.

Search Words The terms that the computer looks for in electronic databases.

Secondary Data Historical data structures of variables that have been previously collected and assembled for some research problem or opportunity situation other than the current situation.

Secondary Information Information (facts or estimates) that has already been collected, assembled, and interpreted at least once for some other specific situation.

Selection Bias Contamination of internal validity measures created by inappropriate selection and/or assignment processes of test subjects to experimental treatment groups.

Selective Coding Building a storyline around one core category or theme; the other categories will be related to or subsumed to this central overarching category.

Selective Perception Bias A type of error that occurs in situations where the researcher or decision maker uses only a selected portion of the survey results to paint a tainted picture of reality.

Self-administered Survey A survey in which respondents read the survey questions and record their responses without the assistance of an interviewer.

Semantic Differential Scale A special type of symmetrical rating scale that uses sets of bipolar adjectives and/or adverbs to describe some type of positive and negative poles of an assumed continuum; it is used to capture respondents' cognitive and affective components of specified factors and create perceptual image profiles relating to a given object or behavior.

Semistructured Question A question that directs the respondent toward a specified topic area, but the responses to the question are unbounded; the interviewer is not looking for any preconceived right answer.

Sentence Completion Test A projective technique where subjects are given a set of incomplete sentences and asked to complete them in their own words.

Separate Sample, Pretest-posttest A quasi-experimental design where two different groups of test subjects are drawn for which neither group is directly exposed to the independent treatment variable. One group receives the pretest measure of the dependent variable; then after the insignificant independent treatment occurs, the second group of test subjects receives a posttest measure of the dependent variable.

Sequential Database System A sorting procedure that displays data in a very simple pattern, usually where the data are organized by a simple path, linkage, or network.

Service Sensitivity Analysis A procedure that helps an organization in designing a basic customer service program by evaluating cost-to-service trade-offs.

Silo Data in one functional area of a business not shared with other areas of the business.

Similarity Judgments A direct approach to gathering perceptual data for multidimensional scaling; where the respondents use a Likert scale to rate all possible pairs of brands in terms of their similarity.

Simple Random Sampling (SRS) A method of probability sampling in which every sampling unit has an equal, nonzero chance of being selected. Results generated by using simple random sampling can be projected to the target population with a prespecified margin of error.

Simulated Test Markets Quasi-test market experiments where the test subjects are preselected, then interviewed and observed on their purchases and attitudes toward the test products; also referred to as *laboratory tests* or *test market simulations.*

Single-item Scale Descriptors A scale used when the data requirements focus on collecting data about only one attribute of the object or construct being investigated.

Situational Characteristics Factors of reality such as budgets, time, and data quality that affect the researcher's ability to collect accurate primary data in a timely fashion.

Situation Analysis An informal process of analyzing the past, present, and future situations facing an organization in order to identify decision problems and opportunities.

Skip Interval A selection tool used to identify the position of the sampling units to be drawn into a systematic random sample design. The interval is determined by dividing the number of potential sampling units in the defined target population by the number of units desired in the sample.

Skip Questions/Scales Questions designed to set the conditions a respondent must meet in order to be able to respond to additional questions on a survey; also referred to as *conditional* or *branching questions.*

Snowball Sampling A nonprobability sampling method that involves the practice of identifying a set of initial prospective respondents who can, in turn, help in identifying additional people to be included in the study.

Social Desirability A type of response bias that occurs when the respondent assumes what answer is socially acceptable or respectable.

Solomon Four Group A true experimental design that combines the pretest-posttest, control group and posttest only, control group designs and provides both "direct" and "reactive" effects of testing.

Spearman Rank Order Correlation Coefficient A statistical measure of the linear association between two variables where both have been measured using ordinal (rank-order) scale instruments.

Split-half Test A technique used to evaluate the internal consistency reliability of scale measurements that have multiple attribute components.

Standard Deviation The measure of the average dispersion of the values in a set of responses about their mean.

Standard Error of the Population Parameter A statistical measure used in probability sampling that gives an indication of how far the sample result lies from the actual population measure we are trying to estimate.

Standard Industrial Classification (SIC) Codes The numerical scheme of industrial listings designed to promote uniformity in data reporting procedures for the U.S. government.

Staple Scales Considered a modified version of the semantic differential scale; they symmetrically center the scale point domain within a set of plus (+) and minus (−) descriptors.

State-of-behavior Data Responses that represent an individual's or organization's current observable actions or reactions or recorded past actions/reactions.

State-of-being Data Responses that are pertinent to the physical and/or demographic or socioeconomic characteristics of individuals, objects, or organizations.

State-of-intention Data Responses that represent an individual's or organization's expressed plans of future actions/reactions.

State-of-mind Data Responses that represent the mental attributes or emotional feelings of individuals which are not directly observable or available through some type of external source.

Static Group Comparisons A pre-experimental design of two groups of test subjects; one is the experimental group (EG) and is exposed to the independent treatment; the second group is the control group (CG) and is not given the treatment; the dependent variable is measured in both groups after the treatment.

Statistical Conclusion Validity The ability of the researcher to make reasonable statements about covariation between constructs of interest and the strength of that covariation.

Statistical Regression Contamination to internal validity measures created when experimental groups are selected on the basis of their extreme responses or scores.

Statistical Software System A computer-based system that has capabilities of analyzing large volumes of data and computing basic types of statistical procedures, such as means, standard deviations, frequency distributions, and percentages.

Store Audits Formal examinations and verifications of how much of a particular product or brand has been sold at the retail level.

Strata The subgroupings that are derived through stratified random sampling procedures.

Stratified Random Sampling (STRS) A method of probability sampling in which the population is divided into different subgroups (called strata) and samples are selected from each stratum.

Structured Questions Questions that require the respondent to make a choice among a limited number of prelisted responses or scale points; they require less thought and effort on the part of the respondent; also referred to as *closed-ended questions*.

Subjective Information Information that is based on the decision maker's or researcher's past experiences, assumptions, feelings, or interpretations without any systematic assembly of facts or estimates.

Subject's Awareness The degree to which subjects consciously know their behavior is being observed; *disguised observation* is when the subject is completely unaware that he or she is being observed, and *undisguised observation* is when the person is aware that he or she is being observed.

Supervisor Instructions A form that serves as a blueprint for training people on how to execute the interviewing process in a standardized fashion; it outlines the process by which to conduct a study that uses personal and telephone interviewers.

Survey Instrument Design Error A "family" of design or format errors that produce a questionnaire that does not accurately collect the appropriate data; these nonsampling errors severely limit the generalizability, reliability, and validity of the collected data.

Survey Instrument Error A type of error that occurs when the survey instrument induces some type of systematic bias in the response.

Survey Research Methods Research design procedures for collecting large amounts of data using interviews or questionnaires.

Symptoms Conditions that signal the presence of a decision problem or opportunity; they tend to be observable and measurable results of problems or opportunities.

Syndicated (or Commercial) Data Data and information that have been compiled according to some standardized procedure which provides customized data for companies such as market share, ad effectiveness, and sales tracking.

Systematic Error The type of error that results from poor instrument design and/or instrument construction causing scores or readings on an instrument to be biased in a consistent manner; creates some form of systematic variation in the data that is not a natural occurrence or fluctuation on the part of the surveyed respondents.

Systematic Random-digit Dialing The technique of randomly dialing telephone numbers, but only numbers that meet specific criteria.

Systematic Random Sampling (SYMRS) A method of probability sampling that is similar to simple random sampling but requires that the defined target population be naturally ordered in some way.

T

Table of Random Numbers A table of numbers that have been randomly generated.

Tabulation The simple procedure of counting the number of observations, or data items, that are classified into certain categories.

Target Market Analysis Information for identifying those people (or companies) that an organization wishes to serve.

Target Population A specified group of people or objects for which questions can be asked or observations made to develop required data structures and information.

Task Characteristics The requirements placed on the respondents in their process of providing answers to questions asked.

Task Difficulty How hard the respondent needs to work to respond, and the level of preparation required to create an environment for the respondent.

Technical Competency The degree to which the researcher possesses the necessary functional requirements to conduct the research project.

Teleologists Individuals who follow a philosophy that considers activities to be ethical if they produce desired results.

Telephone-administered Survey A survey in which individuals working out of their homes or from a central location use the telephone medium to ask participants questions and record the responses.

Telephone Interview A question-and-answer exchange that is conducted via telephone technology.

Test Marketing A controlled field experiment conducted for gaining information on specified market performance indicators or factors.

Test-retest A procedure used to assess the reliability of a scale measurement; it involves repeating the administration of the scale measurement to either the sample set of sampled respondents at two different times or two different samples of respondents from the same defined target population under as nearly the same conditions as possible.

Test-retest Reliability The method of accumulating evidence of reliability by using multiple administrations of an instrument to the same sample. If those administrations are consistent, then evidence of test-retest reliability exists.

Theory A large body of interconnected propositions about how some portion of a certain phenomenon operates.

Thick Description An ethnographic research report that contextualizes behavior within a culture or subculture.

Topic Sensitivity The degree to which a specific question or investigated issue leads the respondent to give a socially acceptable response.

Topographically Integrated Geographic Encoding and Referencing (TIGER) System The U.S. government's new system that provides the researcher with the ability to prepare detailed maps of a variety of areas within the United States.

Touchpoint Specific customer information gathered and shared by all individuals in an enterprise.

Traditional Test Markets Test markets that use experimental design procedures to test a product and/or a product's marketing mix variables through existing distribution channels; also referred to as *standard test markets.*

Trained Interviewers Highly trained people, with excellent communication and listening skills, who ask research participants specific questions and accurately record their responses.

Trained Observers Highly skilled people who use their various sensory devices to observe and record either a person's current behaviors or physical phenomena as they take place.

Transactional Data Secondary information derived from transactions by consumers at the retail level.

Transition Questions Questions used by a moderator to direct a focus group's discussion toward the main topic of interest.

Triangulation Addressing the topic analysis from multiple perspectives, including using multiple methods of data collection and analysis, multiple data sets, multiple researchers, multiple time periods, and different kinds of relevant research informants.

Trilogy Approach The theoretical approach of viewing a person's attitude toward an object as consisting of three distinct components: cognitive, affective, and conative.

True Experimental Designs Designs that ensure equivalence between the experimental and control groups of subjects by random assignment of subjects to the groups ("pretest-posttest, with control group," "posttest-only, with control group," Solomon Four Group).

t-test (also referred to as *t* statistic) A hypothesis test procedure that uses the *t*-distribution: *t*-tests are used when the sample size of subjects is small (generally less than 30) and the standard deviation is unknown.

Type I Error The error made by rejecting the null hypothesis when it is true; represents the probability of alpha error.

Type II Error The error of failing to reject the null hypothesis when the alternative hypothesis is true; represents the probability of beta error.

U

Underregistration When eligible sampling units are left out of the sampling frame.

Undisguised Sponsorship When the true identity of the person or company for which the research is being conducted is directly revealed to the prospective respondent.

Unexplained Variance In multivariate methods, it is the amount of variation in the dependent construct that cannot be accounted for by the combination of independent variables.

Unstructured Questions - Question/scale formats that require respondents to reply in their own words; this format requires more thinking and effort on the part of respondents in order to express their answers; also called *open-ended questions.*

V

Validity The degree to which a research instrument serves the purpose for which it was constructed; it also relates to the extent to which the conclusions drawn from an experiment are true.

Validity of Data The degree to which data actually do represent what was to be measured.

Variability A measure of how data are dispersed; the greater the dissimilarity or "spread" in data, the larger the variability.

Variable Any observable, measurable element (or attribute) of an event.

Variance The average squared deviations about a mean of a distribution of values.

Verbatims Quotes from research participants that are used in research reports.

W

Web-based TV Test Markets Use of broadband interactive TV (iTV) and advances in interactive multimedia communication technologies to conduct field experiments. Preselected respondents are shown various stimuli and asked questions online through their iTV.

Web Home Page The guide to a Web site; generally the home page is the first Web page accessed at the Web site.

Web Page A source of secondary information that is likely to be linked to other complementary pages; includes text, graphics, and even audio.

Web Site An electronic location on the World Wide Web.

Width The total number of records contained in the database.

Wireless Phone Survey The method of conducting a marketing survey in which the data are collected on standard wireless phones.

Word Association Test A projective technique in which the subject is presented with a list of words or short phrases, one at a time, and asked to respond with the first thoughts (word) that comes to mind.

World Wide Web (WWW) A graphical interface system that allows for text linkage between different locations on the Internet.

Wrong Mailing Address A type of nonresponse bias that can occur when the prospective respondent's mailing address is outdated or no longer active.

Wrong Telephone Number A type of nonresponse bias that can occur when the prospective respondent's telephone number either is no longer in service or is incorrect on the sample list.

Z

ZMET (Zaltman Metaphor Elicitation Technique) A visual research technique used in on-depth interviewing that encourages research participants to share emotional and subconscious reactions to a particular topic.

z-test (also referred to as z statistic) A hypothesis test procedure that uses the z distribution; z-tests are used when the sample size is larger than 30 subjects and the standard deviation is unknown.

Endnotes

CHAPTER 1

1. American Marketing Association, *Official Definition of Marketing Research*, www. marketingpower.com, accessed October 2006.
2. Michael R. Solomon, *Consumer Behavior*, 6th ed. (Upper Saddle River, NJ: Pearson/Prentice Hall, 2004), pp. 242–45.
3. "Value Added Research," *Marketing Research*, Fall 1997.
4. "Survey of Top Marketing Research Firms," *Advertising Age*, June 27, 1997.
5. "Fostering Professionalism," *Marketing Research*, Spring 1997.
6. "Market Research Society Code of Conduct," www.mrs.org.uk/ code.htm, accessed October 29, 2006.

CHAPTER 2

1. R. K. Wade, "The When/What Research Decision Guide," *Marketing Research: A Magazine and Application* 5, no. 3 (Summer 1993), pp. 24–27; and W. D. Perreault, "The Shifting Paradigm in Marketing Research," *Journal of the Academy of Marketing Science* 20, no. 4 (Fall 1992), p. 369.

CHAPTER 3

1. Jakob Nielsen, "Usability 101: Intro to Usability," 2001, http:// www.useit.com/alertbox/ 20010805.html; also see Jakob Nielsen, "Quantitative Studies: How Many Users to Test," 2005, http://www.useit.com/alertbox/ 20050815.html; also see Jakob

Nielsen, "Putting A/B Testing methods in Its Place, 2005, http://www.useit.com/alerbox/ 20050214.html; also see Jakob Nielsen, "Risks of Quantitative Studies," 2004, http://www.useit. com/alertbox/20040301.html; also see Jakob Nielsen (2001), "First Rule of Usability? Don't Listen to Users," 2001, http:// www.useit.com/alertbox/ 20010805.html; accessed August 26, 2006.
2. Sally Barr Ebest, Gerald J. Alred, Charles T. Brusaw, and Walter E. Oliu, *Writing from A to Z: An Easy-to-Use Reference Handbook*, 4th Ed. (Boston: McGraw-Hill, 2002), pp. 36–37.
3. Ibid., pp. 44–46 and 54–56.
4. Mary C. Gilly and Mary Wolfinbarger, "Advertising's Internal Audience," *Journal of Marketing* 62 (January 1998), pp. 69–88.
5. Mary Wolfinbarger and Mary C. Gilly, "eTailQ: Dimensionalizing, Measuring and Predicting etail Quality," *Journal of Retailing* 79 (2003), pp. 183–198.

CHAPTER 4

1. Stacey Bell, "Launching Profits with Customer Loyalty," *Customer Relationship Management*, April 2000, p. 58.
2. "Secondary Research," *Marketing Research Magazine*, Fall 1997.
3. William Pride and O. C. Ferrell, *Marketing*, 11th ed. (Boston: Houghton Mifflin, 2006).
4. *Sourcebook of Demographics and Buying Power for Every Zip Code in the U.S.A.*, 2006.

5. *The Wall Street Journal Index*, www.wallstreetjournal.com, accessed September 2006.
6. NPD Group, www.npdgroup. com, accessed September 2006.
7. AC Nielsen Media Research, www. nielsenmedia.com, accessed September 2006.
8. Arbitron, www.arbitron.com, accessed September 2006.

CHAPTER 5

1. Clotaire Rapaille, *The Culture Code: An Ingenious Way to Understand Why People around the World Buy and Live as They Do* (New York: Broadway Books, 2006), pp. 1–11.
2. Yvonne Lincoln and Egon G. Guba, "Introduction: Entering the Field of Qualitative Research," in *Handbook of Qualitative Research*, ed. Norman Denzin and Yvonna Lincoln (Thousand Oaks, CA: Sage, 1994), pp. 1–17.
3. Gerald Zaltman, *How Customers Think: Essential Insights into the Mind of the Market*, (Boston: Harvard Business School, 2003).
4. Melanie Wallendorf and Eric J. Arnould, "We Gather Together: The Consumption Rituals of Thanksgiving Day," *Journal of Consumer Research* 19, no. 1 (1991), pp. 13–31.
5. Dennis W. Rook, "The Ritual Dimension of Consumer Behavior," *Journal of Consumer Research* 12, no. 3 (1985), pp. 251–264.
6. Alfred E. Goldman and Susan Schwartz McDonald, *The Group Depth Interview: Principles and*

Practice (Englewood Cliffs, NJ: Prentice Hall, 1987), p. 161.

7. Mary Modahl, *Now or Never: How Companies Must Change Today to Win the Battle for Internet Consumers* (New York: HarperCollins, 2000).

8. Power Decisions Group, "Market Research Tools: Qualitative Depth Interviews," 2006, http://www.powerdecisions.com/qualitative-depth-interviews.cfm, accessed July 17, 2006.

9. Harris Interactive, "Online Qualitative Research," 2006, http://www.harrisinteractive.com/services/qualitative.asp, accessed July 17, 2006.

10. Zaltman, *How Customers Think: Essential Insights into the Mind of the Market.*

11. Ibid.

12. Robert M. Schindler, "The Real Lesson of New Coke: The Value of Focus Groups for Predicting the Effects of Social Influence," *Marketing Research: A Magazine of Management & Applications,* December 1992, pp. 22–27.

13. Clifford Geertz, *Interpretation of Cultures* (New York: Basic Books, 2000).

14. Richard L. Celsi, Randall L. Rose, and Thomas W. Leigh, "An Exploration of High-Risk Leisure Consumption through Skydiving," *Journal of Consumer Research* 20, no. 1 (1993), pp. 1–23.

15. Jennifer McFarland, "Margaret Mead Meets Consumer Fieldwork: The Consumer Anthropologist" *Harvard Management Update,* Sept. 24, 2001, http://hbswk.hbs.edu/archive/2514.html, accessed July 18, 2006.

16. Robert V. Kozinets, "The Field behind the Screen: Using Netnography for Marketing Research in Online Communities," *Journal of Marketing Research* 39 (February 2002), p. 69.

17. Ibid., pp. 61–72.

18. Arch G. Woodside and Elizabeth J. Wilson, "Case Study Research Methods for Theory Building," *Journal of Business and Industrial Marketing* 18, no. 6/7 (2003), pp. 493–508.

19. Gerald Zaltman, "Rethinking Market Research: Putting People Back In," *Journal of Marketing Research* 34, no. 4 (1997), pp. 424–37.

20. Emily Eakin, "Penetrating the Mind by Metaphor," *New York Times,* February 23, 2002, p. B11; also see Zaltman, *How Customers Think: Essential Insights into the Mind of the Market.*

21. Eakin, "Penetrating the Mind by Metaphor."

CHAPTER 6

1. Terry L. Childers and Steven J. Skinner, "Toward a Conceptualization of Mail Survey Response Behavior," *Psychology and Marketing* 13 (March 1996), pp. 185–225.

2. Kathy E. Green, "Sociodemographic Factors and Mail Survey Response Rates," *Psychology and Marketing* 13 (March 1996), pp. 171–74.

3. M. G. Dalecki, T. W. Ilvento, and D. E. Moore, "The Effect of Multi-Wave Mailings on the External Validity of Mail Surveys," *Journal of Community Development Society* 19 (1988), pp. 51–70.

4. "Mobile Memoir: The Power of the Thumb," Mobile Memoir LLC 2004, April 2004, www.kinesissurvey.com/phonesolutions.html, accessed August 11, 2006.

5. Leslie Townsend, "The Status of Wireless Survey Solutions: The Emerging Power of the Thumb," *Journal of Interactive Advertising* Fall 2005, http://jiad.org/vol6/no1/townsend/index.htm, accessed August 2006.

6. "Mobile Memoir: The Power of the Thumb."

7. Townsend, "The Status of Wireless Survey Solutions."

8. "Hanging Up the Old Phone," *USA Today,* September 11, 2006, p. 1A.

9. Townsend, "The Status of Wireless Survey Solutions."

10. Kevin B. Wright, "Research Internet-Based Populations: Advantages and Disadvantages of Online Survey Research, Online Questionnaire Authoring Software Packages, and Web Survey Services," *Journal of Computer-Mediated Communication* 10, (2005), article 11, http://jcmc.indiana.edu/vol10/issue3/wright.html, accessed August 11, 2006.

11. Maryann Jones Thompson, "Market Researchers Embrace the Web," *The Industry Standard,* January 26, 1999, http://www.thestandard.com/article/0,1902,3274,00.html, accessed September 17, 2006.

CHAPTER 7

1. www.ssisamples.com. Actual prices of lists will vary according to the number and complexity of characteristics needed to define the target population.

2. www.clickz.com/stats, accessed June 2006.

CHAPTER 8

1. K. C. Schneider, "Uninformed Response Rate in Survey Research," *Journal of Business Research,* April 1985 pp. 153–62; also see Del I. Hawkins and K. A. Coney, "Uninformed Response Error in Survey Research," *Journal of Marketing Research* 18 (August 1981), pp. 370–74.

2. Roobina Ohanian, "Construction and Validation of a Scale to Measure Celebrity Endorsers' Perceived Expertise, Trustworthiness, and Attractiveness," *Journal of Advertising* 19, no. 3

(1990), pp. 39–52: and Robert T. W. Wu and Susan M. Petroshius, "The Halo Effect in Store Image Management," *Journal of Academy of Marketing Science* 15 (1987), pp. 44–51.

3. Rajendar K. Garg, "The Influence of Positive and Negative Wording and Issues Involvement on Response to Likert Scales in Marketing Research," *Journal of the Marketing Research Society* 38, no. 3 (July 1996), pp. 235–46.

4. See www.burke.com, and Amanda Prus and D. Randall Brandt, "Understanding Your Customers—What You Can Learn from a Customer Loyalty Index," *Marketing Tools*, July/August 1995, pp. 10–14.

CHAPTER 10

1. Barney G. Glaser and Anselm Strauss, *The Discovery of Grounded Theory: Strategies for Qualitative Research* (Chicago, IL: Aldine Publishing, 1967); also see Anselm Strauss and Juliet M. Corbin, *Basics of Qualitative Research: Grounded Theory Procedures and Techniques* (Newbury Park, CA: Sage, 1990).

2. Alfred E. Goldman and Susan Schwartz McDonald, *The Group Depth Interview: Principles and Practice* (Englewood Cliffs, NJ: Prentice Hall, 1987), p. 161.

3. Matthew B. Miles and A. Michael Huberman, *Qualitative Data Analysis: An Expanded Sourcebook* (Thousand Oaks, CA: Sage, 1994).

4. Clifford Geertz, *Interpretation of Cultures* (New York: Basic Books, 2000); also see Eric J. Arnould and Craig J. Thompson, "Consumer Culture Theory (CCT): Twenty Years of Research," *Journal of Consumer Research* 31, no. 2 (2005), pp. 868–82.

5. Matthew B. Miles and A. Michael Huberman, *Qualitative Data Analysis: An Expanded Source-book* (Thousand Oaks, CA: Sage, 1994).

6. Susan Spiggle, "Analysis and Interpretation of Qualitative Data in Consumer Research," *Journal of Consumer Research* 21, no. 3 (1994), pp. 491–503.

7. Mary Wolfinbarger and Mary Gilly, "Shopping Online for Freedom, Control and Fun," *California Management Review* 43, no. 2 (Winter 2001), pp. 34–55.

8. Spiggle, "Analysis and Interpretation of Qualitative Data in Consumer Research"; also see Miles and Huberman, *Qualitative Data Analysis.*

9. Mary Wolfinbarger, Mary Gilly, and Hope Schau, "A Portrait of Venturesomeness in a Later Adopting Segment," working paper, 2006.

10. Spiggle, "Analysis and Interpretation of Qualitative Data in Consumer Research"; also see Miles and Huberman, *Qualitative Data Analysis.*

11. Mary C. Gilly, and Mary Wolfinbarger, "Advertising's Internal Audience," *Journal of Marketing,* 62 (January 1998), pp. 69–88.

12. Wolfinbarger and Gilly, "Shopping Online for Freedom, Control and Fun."

13. Richard L. Celsi, Randall L. Rose, and Thomas W. Leigh, "An Exploration of High-Risk Leisure Consumption through Skydiving," *Journal of Consumer Research* 20, no. 1 (1993), pp. 1–23.

14. Robin A. Coulter, Linda L. Price, and Lawrence Feick, "Rethinking the Origins of Involvement and Brand Commitment: Insights from Postsocialist Central Europe," *Journal of Consumer Research* 31, no. 2 (2003), pp. 151–69.

15. Spiggle, "Analysis and Interpretation of Qualitative Data in Consumer Research"; also see Strauss and Corbin, *Basics of Qualitative Research: Grounded Theory Procedures and Techniques.*

16. Hope Jensen Schau and Mary C. Gilly, "We Are What We Post? Self-Presentation in Personal Web Space," *Journal of Consumer Research* 30, no. 3 (2003), pp. 385–404; Albert M. Muniz and Hope Jensen Schau, "Religiosity in the Abandoned Apple Newton Brand Community," *Journal of Consumer Research* 31, no. 4 (2005), pp. 737–747; Wolfinbarger, Gilly, and Schau, "A Portrait of Venturesomeness in a Later Adopting Segment"; Lisa Penaloza, "Atravesando Fronteras/Border Crossings: A Critical Ethnographic Exploration of the Consumer Acculturation of Mexican Immigrants," *Journal of Consumer Research* 21, no. 1 (1993), pp. 32–54.

17. Strauss and Corbin, *Basics of Qualitative Research: Grounded Theory Procedures and Techniques.*

18. Goldman and McDonald, *The Group Depth Interview: Principles and Practice;* also see Miles and Huberman, *Qualitative Data Analysis: An Expanded Sourcebook.*

19. Miles and Huberman, *Qualitative Data Analysis: An Expanded Sourcebook.*

20. Goldman and McDonald, *The Group Depth Interview: Principles and Practice.*

21. Barney G. Glaser and Anselm L. Srauss, *The Discovery of Grounded Theory: Strategies for Qualitative Research* (Hawthorne, New York: Aldine de Gruyter, 1967); also see Strauss and Corbin, *Basics of Qualitative Research: Grounded Theory Procedures and Techniques.*

22. Yvonne S. Lincoln and Egon G. Guba, *Naturalistic Inquiry* (Beverly Hills, CA: Sage, 1985), p. 290.

23. Caroline Stenbecka, "Qualitative Research Requires Quality Concepts of its Own," *Management*

Decision 39, no. 7 (2001), pp. 551–55.

24. Glaser and Strauss, *The Discovery of Grounded Theory: Strategies for Qualitative Research;* also see Strauss and Corbin, *Basics of Qualitative Research: Grounded Theory Procedures and Techniques.*

25. Goldman and McDonald, *The Group Depth Interview: Principles and Practice.*

26. Ibid., p. 147.

27. Ibid., p. 175.

28. Rebekah Nathan, *My Freshman Year: What a Professor Learned by Becoming a Student* (Ithaca, New York: Cornell University Press, 2005).

CHAPTER 11

1. Barry Deville, "The Data Assembly Challenge," *Marketing Research Magazine,* Fall/Winter 1995, p. 4.

CHAPTER 12

1. For a more detailed discussion of Analysis of Variance (ANOVA), see Gudmund R. Iversen and Helmut Norpoth, *Analysis of Variance* (Newbury Park, CA: Sage, 1987); and John A. Ingram and Joseph G. Monks, *Statistics for Business and Economics* (San Diego, CA: Harcourt Brace Jovanovich, 1989).

CHAPTER 14

1. David Corcoran, "Talking Numbers with Edward R. Tufte; Campaigning for the Charts That Teach," *New York Times,* February 6, 2000, www.NYTimes.com, accessed on September 18, 2006.

2. Ibid.

Name Index

Subject Index